Global Good Samaritans

Global Good Samaritans
Human Rights as Foreign Policy

Alison Brysk

OXFORD
UNIVERSITY PRESS

2009

OXFORD
UNIVERSITY PRESS

Oxford University Press, Inc., publishes works that further
Oxford University's objective of excellence in research, scholarship, and education.

Oxford   New York
Auckland   Cape Town   Dar es Salaam   Hong Kong   Karachi
Kuala Lumpur   Madrid   Melbourne   Mexico City   Nairobi
New Delhi   Shanghai   Taipei   Toronto

With offices in
Argentina   Austria   Brazil   Chile   Czech Republic   France   Greece
Guatemala   Hungary   Italy   Japan   Poland   Portugal   Singapore
South Korea   Switzerland   Thailand   Turkey   Ukraine   Vietnam

Published by Oxford University Press, Inc.
198 Madison Avenue, New York, New York 10016

www.oup.com

Oxford is a registered trademark of Oxford University Press

Library of Congress Cataloging-in-Publication Data
Brysk, Alison, 1960–
Global good Samaritans : human rights as foreign policy / Alison Brysk.
    p.   cm.
Includes bibliographical references and index.
ISBN 978-0-19-538157-3; 978-0-19-538158-0 (pbk.)
1. International relations—Moral and ethical aspects.   2. Human rights.   I. Title.
JZ1306.B79 2009
172'.4—dc22   2008029807

9 8 7 6 5 4 3 2 1
Printed in the United States of America
on acid-free paper

The Kindness of Strangers

Over water, more than lust, we thirst
To tell our stories: I was beaten, I traveled, my mother—
We are all the same.

I come bearing questions—strange carried
Through tumbled cities, thickets of
Meaning/rice/soup/coffee.

The legend tucked, like a slip of prayer,
between my withered roots;
The dozen Just in every generation.

I trumpet a many-splendored legion—
Samaritans slouching towards the line of scrimmage
On the muddy, bloody playing fields of hope.

—Capetown, October 30, 2006

Acknowledgments

This project has been an experience as well as a study of many forms of generosity. Five years of research on five continents has renewed my faith in humanity, and taught me many important lessons far beyond the scholarly endeavor. Hundreds of strangers have shared with me their time, resources, work, wisdom, and comforts—and some strangers have become friends. I am profoundly grateful, and can only hope this contribution justifies in some small measure their efforts, despite its inevitable shortcomings (for which I bear sole responsibility).

Every phase of this research benefited from generous and timely financial support. In the summer of 2003, I traveled to Costa Rica with the support of the University of California's Latin American Studies program, under a U.S. Department of Education grant. The following year, I participated in a UCI Study Abroad program at Lund University, and received supplementary funding for summer research from my university's Center for Global Peace and Conflict Studies. My 2005 multisited summer trip to Canada was underwritten by the Canadian Consulate's Canadian Studies program. The research in Japan, the Netherlands, and South Africa was all completed during a 2006 sabbatical, generously funded by the Abe Foundation/SSRC Fellowship in Global Issues (which also provided support during my stay in Japan via CGP, the Center for Global Partnership). In 2007, I was honored to receive a Fulbright Fellowship at the Centre for International Governance Innovation (Waterloo), which enabled me to return to Canada to complete the research on that country as well as the chapter on intergovernmental networks.

I was also fortunate in receiving early and sustained academic feedback, which contributed immeasurably to the development of the project. The research on Costa Rica was presented at the 2004 Latin American Studies Association conference, whereas preliminary findings on Sweden and Costa Rica were discussed at the University of Ottawa in 2005. The Canada research was refined further in a 2006 presentation at the John F. Kennedy Institute at the Free University of Berlin, as well as the 2007 International Studies Association, and a 2007 roundtable at CIGI. South African colleagues at UNISA (National University of South Africa) helped to develop that portion at a presentation concluding my 2006 stay in that country. The Japan chapter was presented at an Abe Fellowship Retreat in January 2007, and ably commented upon by Hiroshi Fukurai. Later on, colleagues in each country provided detailed and constructive comments on chapter drafts from afar, especially Peter Baehr on the Netherlands, Rhoda Howard and Don Hubert on Canada, Paul Graham and Patrick Bond on South Africa, and Magnus Jerneck on Sweden.

Versions of two chapters have been previously published in revised form. A prior discussion of chapter 2 was published in Germany as "Making Values Make Sense: The Social Construction of Human Rights Foreign Policy," *Journal for Human Rights* [Zeitschrift für Menschenrechte] 2 (2007). Chapter 5 appeared as "Global Good Samaritans?: Costa Rica's Human Rights Foreign Policy," in *Global Governance* 11, no. 3 (Summer 2005). My thanks to those journals for permitting revised use of this material.

During the design and academic development of the project, Gershon Shafir, Richard Falk, Jack Donnelly, Sanjeev Khagram, and Wayne Sandholtz offered extraordinary inspiration, analysis, and advice. To implement that vision, I was privileged to receive extensive and extremely able research assistance from graduate students who participated in preparing the introductory comparative data and the intergovernmental networks profiles (Brodie Ross, CIGI), refining the research on Costa Rica (Madeline Baer, UCI), completing the data on Sweden (Ted Svensson, University of Warwick), and updating the chapter on Sweden and overall references (Daniel Wehrenfennig, UCI). Upon completion, I have been blessed to find a home for the manuscript with Angela Chnapko of Oxford University Press, whose professionalism and editorial support are unparalleled.

Within each country I visited, my research was supported by a dense network of colleagues, contacts, institutional and residential hosts. Space and memory force me to compress the thanks that properly accrue to dozens of people in each site to a few key individuals who played extensive academic roles. Every one of the dozens of people I interviewed contributed valuable understanding, and a number of them went beyond the norm as they rearranged their schedules, invited me to their homes, drove me to my next appointment, or gave me their last supply of imported cold medicine. Beyond my official "informants," I extend my gratitude to enablers like professor/innkeeper Randolph von Breyman in San José, Willie and Pieter of Ellensgate—who supplied my every need in Pretoria.

In Costa Rica, I received networking support and advice from the University of Costa Rica Political Science Department. This was followed by extremely helpful pre-, post-, and onsite research assistance from UCR Master's student Patricia Guevara. During my stay, professor/diplomat/party leader Luis Guillermo Solís very graciously oriented me and arranged critical connections for interviews.

In Sweden, colleagues at the University of Lund kindly referred me to interviews, sources, and literature. Professor Magnus Jerneck played an extraordinary role. Master's student Ted Svensson moved from logistics to translation to conducting independent interviews after my departure, with great aplomb.

Prior to my first trip to Canada, I was privileged to meet former foreign minister Lloyd Axworthy in an academic setting. *Global Good Samaritans* achieved critical mass in 2005 when this historic figure opened his heart and his Rolodex to a younger colleague's vision. During my 2007 stay in Canada, I was hosted by Waterloo's Centre for International Governance Innovation, which provided very generous research support and facilities as well as a national network. From many valued colleagues there, I must single out postdoctoral fellow Andrew Thompson of CIGI for his outstanding contributions as a collaborator, host, and friend. Canadian scholars Claude Denis and Rhoda Howard have supported the project and its author in ways too numerous to name, but deeply appreciated.

I am grateful to my institutional home in Japan, United Nations University, and Vice-Rector Ramesh Thakur for hosting me. Professor Kenhide Mushakoji was a very supportive colleague and source of alternative perspectives. Most of all, my stay in Japan was facilitated in every way by my former student Isao Takada (Claremont Graduate University), who cared for me from the moment I stepped off the plane—providing everything from interviews and translation to a foster family in the wilderness of Tokyo.

In the Netherlands, I was a visiting scholar at the Van Vollenhoven Institute of Leiden University. My academic and personal affiliations in Holland were fostered by friend and Leiden colleague Willem Assies. Among the new friends I discovered in Amsterdam, the late Frank Buijs (Free University of Amsterdam) was extraordinarily kind and resourceful, during what turned out to be the last summer of his life.

Professor Gay Seidman (University of Wisconsin) provided helpful guidance and referrals before my trip to South Africa. Once I arrived there, Garth LePere (Institute for Global Dialogue) and Adam Habib (Social and Human Science Research Council) were astoundingly generous with contacts and referrals, their own publications, and their time. On another note, Professors Josie Van Wyck of UNISA and Janis van der Westhuizen of Stellenbosch University each quickly moved from colleagues to boon companions.

First, last, and always, my friends and family have sustained me to this season. My parents and grandparents raised me to ask Hillel's question: *if I am only for myself, what am I?* In one sense, this project is a search for exemplars of that spirit. My daughters Miriam and Ana each accompanied me on some of the journeys of this book, and waited patiently through my absences. With typical esprit, Ana expressed one of the core findings as a youthful observer: "there are no small countries, only small governments." Their father, Mark Freeman, also supported my solo journeys and vision and cared ably for the home team, even when we no longer shared a destination. From my family of friends, I learn and relearn the larger lesson of hope—another world is possible. Thank you so much, my band of angels: Carol, Claude, Gershon, Robert, Teivo. Hobbes and Gandhi were both right; life *is* nasty and short—and compassion *can* change the world, and our hearts.

Contents

Global Good Samaritans

THE PARABLE OF THE GOOD SAMARITAN

—Luke 10:25–37 (New International Version)

On one occasion an expert in the law stood up to test Jesus. "Teacher," he asked, "what must I do to inherit eternal life?"

"What is written in the Law?" he replied. "How do you read it?"

He answered: "'Love the Lord your God with all your heart and with all your soul and with all your strength and with all your mind'; and, 'Love your neighbor as yourself.'"

"You have answered correctly," Jesus replied. "Do this and you will live."

But he wanted to justify himself, so he asked Jesus, "And who is my neighbor?"

In reply Jesus said: "A man was going down from Jerusalem to Jericho, when he fell into the hands of robbers. They stripped him of his clothes, beat him and went away, leaving him half dead. A priest happened to be going down the same road, and when he saw the man, he passed by on the other side. So too, a Levite, when he came to the place and saw him, passed by on the other side. But a Samaritan, as he traveled, came where the man was; and when he saw him, he took pity on him. He went to him and bandaged his wounds, pouring on oil and wine. Then he put the man on his own donkey, took him to an inn and took care of him. The next day he took out two silver coins and gave them to the innkeeper. 'Look after him,' he said, 'and when I return, I will reimburse you for any extra expense you may have.' Which of these three do you think was a neighbor to the man who fell into the hands of robbers?"

The expert in the law replied, "The one who had mercy on him."

Jesus told him, "Go and do likewise."

1

Introduction

States as Global Citizens

When and why do some states protect helpless foreigners from the abuses of their own governments, distant wars, and global crises? Dozens of Canadian peacekeepers have died in Afghanistan, defending humanitarian reconstruction in a shattered faraway land with no resources or ties to their own. Each year, Sweden contributes over $3 billion to aid the world's poorest citizens and struggling democracies, asking nothing in return. A generation ago, Costa Rica defied U.S. power to broker a peace accord that ended civil wars in three neighboring countries. Now, that small developing country has joined with principled peers like South Africa to support the United Nations' International Criminal Court, the body established to bring global justice to gross human rights violators—despite U.S. pressure and aid cuts. The Netherlands has led campaigns of condemnation that have shattered the impunity of torturers around the world. Hundreds of thousands of refugees are alive today because they have been sheltered by one of these nations, even at economic, political, and social costs to the host country.

In a relentlessly troubled world, some states are part of the solution. Humanitarian internationalism is more than episodic altruism—it is a pattern of persistent principled politics. Although global Good Samaritans are clearly a minority of states, they add up to more than scattered exceptions, and the small circle of like-minded states can be key initiators or swing votes on important humanitarian developments, from the antiapartheid campaign to the land mines treaty. The struggle for international human rights standards, monitoring, and implementation is often depicted as a problem of increasing the influence of transnational civil society over international institutions—and thus, indirectly affecting state policies (Keck and Sikkink 1998; Risse, Ropp, and Sikkink 1999). However, some states directly support human rights in global institutions and project human rights in their foreign policies. Their influence can be critical for framing and ratifying treaties, creating and staffing multilateral institutions, monitoring and sanctioning offenders, assisting victims, directing resources, implementing peace processes, catalyzing transnational initiatives on emerging issues, and introducing new understandings of rights to the global agenda (Forsythe 2000).

The existence of such states, from diverse origins and along varied pathways, shows that more could follow. Understanding their transformation and challenges can help to expand the vision of political possibility that is the first step in all social change. A rich tradition of foreign policy analysis maps the performance of leading countries as value promoters, often focusing on the potential and shortfalls of the United States (Johansen 1980, Sikkink 2004, Mertus 2004). Such studies often focus on strategic, ideological, and institutional barriers to global good citizenship. But the positive record of a diverse set of small and middle powers suggests that such barriers can be overcome, even during eras of wavering hegemonic promotion.

The metaphor of the "global Good Samaritan" highlights the critical elements of human rights foreign policy. The defining principle of a Good Samaritan is that s/he identifies with the interests of the Other: "Love your neighbor as yourself." Similarly, human rights promoters identify national interest with global interests. The expert in the law seeking guidance in the parable is not born loving his neighbor, but rather aspires to learn from the Good Samaritan, in order to fulfill a set of norms believed to bring both personal salvation and universal benefit. In a similar fashion, most good citizen states seek to support the global system and foster global principles as much as to succor specific victims. The transformative element of the parable is cosmopolitanism: when the teacher pushes the seeker to define the suffering stranger as part of a community of fate ("Who is your neighbor?"). And it is not the hegemonic authority figure of the priest or the Levite bureaucrat who administers aid, but rather a member of the stigmatized Samaritan minority group, who has secured a modicum of resources and fosters diffuse reciprocity (paying the innkeeper to care for the victim with a future promise). This emphasizes the power and responsibility of nondominant members of the system to provide aid, and the promulgation of modeling ("Go forth and do likewise").

At the international level, human rights foreign policy is more than guilt or charity—it is a constructive form of identity politics. Principled foreign policy defies the realist prediction of untrammeled pursuit of national interest, and suggests the utility of constructivist approaches that investigate the role of ideas, identities, and roles as influences on state action. Even in a world of security dilemmas, some societies will come to see the linkage between their long-term interest and the common good—at some times and places, states can overcome their bounded origins as sovereign security managers to act as "global citizens." The activities of global Good Samaritan states help to construct and expand the international human rights regime, the thin layer of international understandings, institutions, and exchanges that seek to protect individual human dignity from abuses of power. As such principled states build global governance, they reshape the meaning of sovereignty to implant a slowly emerging legitimacy norm—universal human rights.

Humanitarian internationalism is an umbrella term for a variety of cooperative, value-oriented foreign policies involving aid, diplomacy, the use of force, and sometimes migration. The values being promoted may be labeled human rights, democratization, building civil society, protection of civilians, peace promotion, global humanism, or human security. These goals will have the meaning and effect of "human rights foreign policy" for this analysis when such policies seek to protect and empower citizens of other countries in order to secure the fundamental rights and core freedoms outlined in the Universal Declaration of Human Rights and the two International Covenants (Civil and Political Rights, as well as Economic, Cultural, and Social Rights). While these widely subscribed standards entail a broad set of interconnected security and social rights, in practice most international and state action concentrates on acute threats to life, liberty, and bodily integrity. Although most countries at most times pursue policies for a mix of reasons, and often reap unintended consequences, an international activity will qualify as a human rights policy when (1) its primary announced goal is humanitarian protection or empowerment and (2) the resources and strategies used correspond to a reasonable outside observer's standard of humanitarian orientation. This study will analyze why and how countries adopt such policies, deferring the question of the ultimate impact and effectiveness of humanitarian policies on human rights conditions to the many able observers who have examined this issue (on impact assessment, see Landman 2006, Cardenas 2007; on contradictory impacts, see Kennedy 2004).

In terms of social science methodology, this is a theory-driven empirical study, using a combination of case comparisons and process tracing within single cases. Although the remainder of this chapter will present some global numerical information to map what the cases chosen for in-depth study represent from the wider universe, those numbers are simply indicators of country characteristics—we will note associations, but will not engage in systematic techniques of quantitative inference. The case comparisons combine several logics. Sweden and the Netherlands are most-likely cases, whereas Costa Rica and South Africa are least-likely cases. In the comparative strategy suggested by John Stuart Mill, Sweden and South Africa are "most different systems" leading to a roughly common outcome of human rights promotion, whereas implicitly Japan is a "most similar" case that departs from the OECD norm, as Canada is implicitly compared to the "most similar" United States—with disparate levels of human rights promotion. Within the single cases, process tracing combines a macro-historical analysis of policy with interview-based discourse analysis (see Landman 2006 for an overview of these methodological strategies).

What kinds of countries are equipped to become humane internationalists? Candidate states are usually globalized, democratic, moderately developed, and secure middle or regional powers. Although this book will argue that many more countries could participate, it is the global middle states that are most likely to promote global democracy. Countries struggling for survival are not in a position to promote principle, and conversely the modal position of dominant powers is to provide only selective collective goods that reinforce their own position. Hegemons are not usually global reformers; they tend to prefer stability and the export of dominant values, rather than transformation and empowerment. As a rising power and emerging sponsor of multilateralism, the United States promoted universal human rights to war-weary Europeans; once the power positions reversed, Europeans invested in international institutions for global governance, whereas the United States now prefers unilateral democracy promotion to more universal human rights (Kagan 2003).

In the case of the United States, this generic preference of the current phase of hegemony is exacerbated by weak globalization, thinly democratic foreign policy making, and ideological exceptionalism (detailed in the concluding chapter). Nevertheless, the proliferation of motivated middle powers provides sufficient scope for global humanitarian efforts, and even the basis for a potential counter-hegemonic movement. And even states less likely to be global good citizens may have moments or issues of humane influence, when strong transnational linkages, normative fit, and openings in foreign policy structures align (see Klotz 1995 on the United States and South Africa).

Thus, we turn to profiling "states most likely to succeed." The discussion and charts that follow simply map relevant characteristics, using available numerical indicators to compare widely diverse places. They are not a correlation, proof, prediction, or regression. The overall purpose is to identify like-minded potential promoters, and to place the focus cases in a broader comparative framework. The case studies are configurative (Eckstein 1975), and the current discussion provides a context for assessing their generalizability.

INPUTS: STATES "MOST LIKELY TO SUCCEED"

Humanitarian promoters are usually open societies in all senses. For Good Samaritan states, *globalization* creates the means and motive for internationalism. Globalization is a combination of economic, political, and cultural integration; each provides a channel for human rights projection, and each dimension of interdependence becomes a national interest that flourishes in a stable and principled global environment (Brysk 2002). Economic globalization is measured by the competitiveness index, which incorporates trade, finance, and other forms of exchange. Cultural integration may be seen in the density of international information exchange.

Domestic *democracy* provides an incentive, model, and rationale for global human rights promotion. The Freedom House democracy score is a quick indicator of the basic form of government and freedoms that is deliberately not fully equivalent to a country's own domestic human rights performance (which I argue below influences, but is not perfectly aligned with, foreign policy promotion). This is supplemented by an indication of how many years a country has been a stable democracy, which allows time for the development of human rights policies. Finally, to assess the depth of democratic performance and access by polities with formal democratic institutions, we consider the level of rights and citizenship enjoyed by a universal historically disadvantaged group that comprises half of the population of all states—women, via the Gender Equity Index.

For aspiring internationalists, a moderate threshold of *development* and a modicum of *security* ensure that state survival and welfare needs are sufficiently satisfied to allow the pursuit of long-term cosmopolitan visions. Development is measured by the World Bank's Human Development Index. Security may be gauged by the absence of a recent interstate war or invasion. Because secure countries may adopt disparate neutralist, pacifist, or sheltered strategies, the size or budget of their militaries is not a good measure.

Another positive factor increasing the probability of internationalism is a *middle power* international niche. Middle (and regional) powers play an international role as system builders, alternatives to hegemony, and carriers of collective interests. Middle power status is quickly assessed by population and GDP (or proportion of regional GDP), although politically relevant middle power self-perceptions may linger for decades or even centuries beyond the country's objective position in the world system. Qualitatively, a middle power is defined as much by its niche, technical capacity, and coalition building as by size, military prowess, or geography (Cooper, Higgott, and Nossal 1993: 7).

Table 1.1 shows the level of input characteristics for all countries. All data is the most recent available. Countries that pass the threshold for potential global good citizenship are highlighted in light gray. This analysis yields dozens of states with the *necessary* conditions for humane internationalism. The specific focus cases profiled below in the case chapters are shown in medium gray. The discussion of country cases will outline additional inputs that comprise *sufficient* conditions for global Good Samaritan policies (such as leadership, civil society, and ideology). The countries highlighted in dark gray are contrast cases that have been internationally active and make some claims to promote humanitarian values, but do not pass the thresholds for democracy or development.

The next step is to screen and assess this global set. The input measures that are most broadly predictive of baseline promoter potential are development and democracy. Although capability, globalization, and security input indicators readily account for variance in output, their impact is not universal, so it will be assessed as it pertains to specific cases and regions. Thus, the country list for output assessment is initially filtered to show states that surpass their regional average on the Human

Table 1.1 Inputs: Humanitarians "Most Likely to Succeed"

Country	Middle Power Population (millions)[1]	GDP (billions)[2]	% of Region GDP	Globalization GPI[3]	# of Internet Users (X1000)[4]	% of pop. with internet	Democracy Freedom Rating[5]	Free for more than 10 years[6]	GEI[7]	Security (Years Since Major Interstate War[8])	Development (HDI[9])
Africa											
Algeria	31.889	$ 90.00	11.4	3.90	30	0.09	5.5	N	48	46	0.728
Angola	12.260	$ 28.61	3.6	2.50	172	1.40	5.5	N	52	61	0.439
Benin	8.000	$ 4.60	0.6	3.37	425	5.31	2.0	Y	41	61	0.428
Botswana	1.825	$ 9.76	1.2	3.79	60	3.29	2.0	Y	66	61	0.570
Burkina Faso	14.320	$ 5.82	0.7	3.07	64	0.45	4.0	N	50	61	0.342
Burundi	8.390	$ 0.77	0.1	2.59	25	0.30	4.5	N	63	61	0.384
Cameroon	18.060	$ 16.27	2.1	3.30	167	0.92	6.0	N	47	61	0.506
Cape Verde	0.423	$ 1.13	0.1		25	5.91	1.0	Y	61	61	0.722
Central African Republic	4.369	$ 1.55	0.2		9	0.21	4.5	N	41	61	0.353
Chad	9.885	$ 4.96	0.6	2.61	35	0.35	6.0	N	41	20	0.368
Congo (DR)	65.751	$ 7.98	1.0		140	0.21	5.5	N	47	61	0.391
Congo (Republic of)	3.800	$ 5.16	0.7		36	0.95	5.5	N	44	61	0.520
Djibouti	0.496	$ 0.70	0.1		9	1.81	5.0	N	48	61	0.494
Eritrea	4.906	$ 1.24	0.2		70	1.43	6.5	N	45	7	0.454
Ethiopia	76.511	$ 13.32	1.7	2.99	113	0.15	5.0	N	51	7	0.371
Gabon	1.454	$ 6.90	0.9		67	4.61	5.0	N	51	61	0.633
Gambia	1.688	$ 0.46	0.1	3.43	49	2.90	4.5	N	50	61	0.473
Ghana	22.931	$ 10.20	1.3		401	1.75	1.5	N	58	61	0.532

Country											
Guinea	9.947	$ 3.80	0.5		46	0.46	5.5	N	52	61	0.445
Guinea-Bissau	1.472	$ 0.29	0.0		26	1.77	4.0	N	49	61	0.349
Kenya	36.913	$ 17.43	2.2	3.57	1055	2.86	3.0	N	60	51	0.491
Lesotho	2.125	$ 1.40	0.2	3.22	43	2.02	2.5	N	62	61	0.494
Liberia	3.195	$ 0.90	0.1		1	0.03	3.5	N		61	
Libya	6.036	$ 34.20	4.3		205	3.40	7.0	N		20	0.798
Madagascar	19.448	$ 5.05	0.6	3.27	90	0.46	3.5	N	62	60	0.509
Malawi	13.603	$ 2.20	0.3	3.07	52	0.38	3.5	Y	60	61	0.400
Mali	11.995	$ 5.84	0.7	3.02	60	0.50	3.5	Y	52	61	0.338
Mauritania	3.270	$ 1.57	0.2	3.17	14	0.43	4.5	N		49	0.486
Mauritius	1.250	$ 7.17	0.9	4.20	180	14.40	1.5	Y	54	61	0.800
Morocco	33.757	$ 58.07	7.3	4.01	4600	13.63	4.5	N	42	49	0.640
Mozambique	20.905	$ 6.32	0.8	2.94	138	0.66	3.5	N	65	61	0.390
Namibia	2.055	$ 5.33	0.7	3.74	75	3.65	2.0	Y	72	61	0.626
Niger	12.894	$ 3.64	0.5		24	0.19	3.0	N	47	61	0.311
Nigeria	135.031	$ 83.36	10.5	3.45	5000	3.70	4.0	N	45	61	0.448
Rwanda	9.907	$ 1.97	0.2		38	0.38	5.5	N	84	61	0.450
Seychelles	0.081	$ 0.71	0.1		20	24.69	3.0	N		61	0.842
Sierra Leone	6.144	$ 1.23	0.2		10	0.16	3.5	N	39	61	0.335
Somalia	9.118	$ 2.48	0.3		90	0.99	7.0	N		61	
South Africa	43.997	$ 201.40	25.4	4.36	5100	11.59	2.0	Y	70	61	0.653
Sudan	39.379	$ 25.50	3.2		2800	7.11	7.0	N		61	0.516
Swaziland	1.113	$ 2.19	0.3		36	3.23	6.0	N	49	61	0.500
Tanzania	39.384	$ 13.13	1.7	3.39	333	0.85	3.5	N	72	61	0.430
Togo	5.701	$ 2.08	0.3		300	5.26	5.5	N	41	61	0.495
Tunisia	10.276	$ 33.29	4.2	4.71	953	9.27	5.5	N	51	46	0.760
Uganda	30.262	$ 8.53	1.1		500	1.65	4.5	N	64	61	0.502

(*Continued*)

Table 1.1 (*Continued*)

Country	Middle Power			Globalization			Democracy			Security (Years Since Major Interstate War[8])	Development (HDI[9])
	Population (millions)[1]	GDP (billions)[2]	% of Region GDP	GPI[3]	# of Internet Users (X1000)[4]	% of pop. with internet	Freedom Rating[5]	Free for more than 10 years[6]	GEI[7]		
Zambia	11.477	$ 5.79	0.7	3.16	231	2.01	3.5	N	58	61	0.407
Zimbabwe	12.311	$ 31.50	4.0	3.01	1000	8.12	6.5	N	56	61	0.491
Regional Average	17.447	$ 16.51	2	3.38	530	3	4.3		54	56	0.503
North America											
Canada	33.390	$ 1,088.00	7.2	5.37	21900	65.59	1.0	Y	75	6[10]	0.950
Mexico	108.700	$ 743.50	4.9	4.18	18622	17.13	2.5	N	61	61	0.821
United States	301.139	$13,210.00	87.8	5.61	205327	68.18	1.0	Y	74	4[10]	0.948
Regional Average	147.743	$5,013.83	33	5.05	81950	50	1.5		70	24	0.906
Latin America											
Antigua and Barbuda	0.069	$ 0.91	0.5		20	28.99	2.0	N		61	0.808
Bahamas	0.305	$ 6.15	3.2		93	30.49	1.0	Y	75	61	0.825
Barbados	0.280	$ 3.14	1.7	4.70	160	57.14	1.0	Y	80	61	0.879
Belize	0.294	$ 1.14	0.6		35	11.90	1.5	N	62	61	0.751
Costa Rica	4.133	$ 21.39	11.3	4.25	1000	24.20	1.0	Y	66	61	0.841
Cuba	11.394	$ 40.00	21.1		190	1.67	7.0	Y	66	61	0.826
Dominica	0.072	$ 0.28	0.1		20	27.78	1.0	Y		61	0.793

Dominican Rep.	9.365	$ 20.55	10.9	3.75	938	10.02	2.0	N	65	61	0.751
El Salvador	6.948	$ 15.16	8.0	4.09	637	9.17	2.5	Y	69	38	0.729
Grenada	0.089	$ 0.45	0.2		19	21.35	1.5	Y		24	0.726
Guatemala	12.728	$ 35.25	18.6	3.91	756	5.94	3.5	N	50	61	0.673
Haiti	8.706	$ 5.90	3.1		500	5.74	4.5	N		61	0.482
Honduras	7.483	$ 8.48	4.5	3.58	223	2.98	3.0	Y	61	38	0.683
Jamaica	2.780	$ 9.23	4.9	4.10	1067	38.38	2.5	Y	61	61	0.724
Nicaragua	5.675	$ 4.87	2.6	3.52	140	2.47	3.0	N	52	61	0.698
Panama	3.242	$ 16.47	8.7	4.18	300	9.25	1.5	Y	69	50	0.809
Regional Average	4.598	$ 11.84	6	4.01	381	18	2.4		65	55	0.750

South America

Argentina	40.301	$ 210.00	12.4	4.01	10000	24.81	2.0	Y	70	25	0.863
Bolivia	9.119	$ 10.33	0.6	3.46	480	5.26	3.0	Y	68	61	0.692
Brazil	190.010	$ 967.00	57.2	4.03	25900	13.63	2.0	N	73	61	0.792
Chile	16.284	$ 111.80	6.6	4.85	6700	41.14	1.0	Y	62	61	0.859
Colombia	44.379	$ 106.80	6.3	4.04	4739	10.68	3.0	N	75	61	0.790
Ecuador	13.755	$ 32.73	1.9	3.67	616	4.48	3.0	N	72	61	0.756
Guyana	0.769	$ 0.84	0.0	3.24	160	20.81	2.5	Y	60	61	0.725
Paraguay	6.669	$ 7.75	0.5	3.33	200	3.00	3.0	N	61	61	0.757
Peru	28.674	$ 77.14	4.6	3.94	4600	16.04	2.5	N	65	61	0.767
Suriname	0.470	$ 1.40	0.1	3.45	30	6.38	2.0	N	66	61	0.759

(*Continued*)

Table 1.1 (*Continued*)

Country	Middle Power			Globalization			Democracy			Security (Years Since Major Interstate War[8])	Development (HDI[9])
	Population (millions)[1]	GDP (billions)[2]	% of Region GDP	GPI[3]	# of Internet Users (X1000)[4]	% of pop. with internet	Freedom Rating[5]	Free for more than 10 years[6]	GEI[7]		
Uruguay	3.460	$ 14.50	0.9	3.96	680	19.65	1.0	Y	68	61	0.851
Venezuela	26.023	$149.90	8.9	3.96	3040	11.68	4.0	Y	67	61	0.784
Regional Average	31.659	$140.85	8	3.81	4762	15	2.4		67	58	0.783
Asia											
Afghanistan	31.889	$ 8.80	0.1		30	0.09	5.0	N		6	
Bangladesh	150.448	$ 69.34	0.6	3.46	300	0.20	4.0	N	52	61	0.530
Bhutan	2.327	$ 0.84	0.0		25	1.07	5.5	N		61	0.538
Brunei	0.374	$ 9.53	0.1		56	14.97	5.5	N		61	0.871
Burma (*Myanmar*)	47.373	$ 9.60	0.1		78	0.16	7.0	N		61	
Cambodia	13.995	$ 6.60	0.1	3.39	41	0.29	5.5	N	61	30	0.583
China	1321.851	$ 2,518.00	22.8	4.24	123000	9.31	6.5	N	61	61	0.786
East Timor	1.084	$ 0.35	0.0		1	0.09	3.5	N		61	
India	1129.866	$ 804.00	7.3	4.44	60000	5.31	2.5	N		8	0.611
Indonesia	234.693	$ 264.70	2.4	4.26	16000	6.82	2.5	N	53	61	0.711
Japan	127.433	$ 4,883.00	44.2	5.60	86300	67.72	1.5	Y	60	6*	0.949
Kazakhstan	15.284	$ 53.60	0.5	4.19	400	2.62	5.5	N	64	61	0.774
Korea (south)	49.044	$ 897.00	8.1	5.13	33900	69.12	1.5	Y	56	4*	0.912
Kyrgyzstan	5.284	$ 2.26	0.0	3.31	280	5.30	4.5	N	57	61	0.705
Laos	6.521	$ 2.77	0.0		25	0.38	6.5	N	53	61	0.553

Malaysia	24.821	$ 132.30	1.2	5.11	11016	44.38	4.0	N	58	61	0.805
Maldives	0.369	$ 0.91	0.0		19	5.15	5.5	N	64	61	0.739
Mongolia	2.591	$ 1.54	0.0	3.60	268	10.34	2.0	Y	66	61	0.691
Nepal	28.901	$ 6.95	0.1	3.26	175	0.61	4.5	N	44	61	0.527
Pakistan	164.741	$ 124.00	1.1	3.66	10500	6.37	5.5	N	42	8	0.539
Philippines	91.077	$ 116.90	1.1	4.00	7820	8.59	3.0	Y	76	61	0.763
Russia	141.377	$ 733.60	6.6	4.08	23700	16.76	5.5	N	71	6*	0.797
Singapore	4.553	$ 122.10	1.1	5.63	2422	53.20	4.5	N		61	0.916
Sri Lanka	20.926	$ 27.40	0.2	3.87	280	1.34	4.0	N	58	61	0.755
Tajikistan	7.076	$ 2.07	0.0	3.50	5	0.07	5.5	N		61	0.652
Thailand	65.068	$ 197.70	1.8	4.58	8420	12.94	5.5	N	73	61	0.784
Uzbekistan	27.780	$ 10.83	0.1		880	3.17	7.0	N		61	0.696
Vietnam	85.262	$ 48.43	0.4	3.89	13100	15.36	6.0	N	66	28	0.709
Regional Average	135.786	$ 394.83	4	4.16	14251	13	4.6		60	47	0.716
Europe											
Albania	3.600	$ 9.30	0.1	3.46	75	2.08	3.0	N	57	61	0.784
Armenia	2.971	$ 6.60	0.0	3.75	150	5.05	4.5	N	58	61	0.768
Austria	8.199	$ 310.10	2.1	5.32	4650	56.71	1.0	Y	72	61	0.944
Belarus	9.724	$ 28.98	0.2	5.27	3394	34.90	6.5	N	66	61	0.794
Belgium	10.392	$ 369.60	2.5		5100	49.08	1.0	Y	74	61	0.945
Bosnia and Herzegovina	4.552	$ 9.22	0.1	3.67	806	17.71	3.0	N		14	0.800
Bulgaria	7.332	$ 28.60	0.2	3.96	2200	30.01	1.5	Y	74	61	0.816
Croatia	4.493	$ 37.42	0.3	4.26	1451	32.29	2.0	N	73	61	0.846
Cyprus	0.788	$ 16.37	0.1	4.36	298	37.82	1.0	Y	65	33	0.903
Czech Republic	10.228	$ 118.80	0.8	4.74	5100	49.86	1.0	Y	69	61	0.855
Denmark	5.468	$ 257.30	1.8	5.70	3763	68.82	1.0	Y	79	61	0.943

(Continued)

13

Table 1.1 (Continued)

Country	Population (millions)[1]	Middle Power GDP (billions)[2]	% of Region GDP	Globalization GPI[3]	# of Internet Users (X1000)[4]	% of pop. with internet	Democracy Freedom Rating[5]	Free for more than 10 years[6]	GEI[7]	Security (Years Since Major Interstate War[8])	Development (HDI[9])
Estonia	1.315	$ 13.89	0.1	5.12	690	52.47	1.0	Y	74	61	0.858
Finland	5.238	$ 199.00	1.4	5.76	3286	62.73	1.0	Y	84	61	0.947
France	63.713	$ 2,149.00	14.6	5.31	29945	47.00	1.0	Y	64	6*	0.942
Germany	82.400	$ 2,872.00	19.6	5.58	50616	61.43	1.0	Y	80	6*	0.932
Greece	10.706	$ 223.80	1.5	4.33	3800	35.49	1.5	Y	67	61	0.921
Hungary	9.956	$ 113.20	0.8	4.52	3050	30.63	1.0	Y	70	51	0.869
Iceland	0.301	$ 13.71	0.1	5.40	258	85.71	1.0	Y	79	61	0.960
Ireland	4.109	$ 204.40	1.4	5.21	2060	50.13	1.0	Y	69	61	0.956
Italy	58.147	$ 1,785.00	12.2	4.46	28870	49.65	1.0	Y	63	6	0.940
Latvia	2.259	$ 16.50	0.1	4.57	1030	45.60	1.0	Y	76	61	0.845
Liechtenstein	0.034	$ 2.49	0.0		20	58.82	1.0	Y		61	
Lithuania	3.575	$ 30.20	0.2	4.53	315	8.81	1.0	Y	77	60	0.857
Luxembourg	0.480	$ 34.53	0.2	5.16	315	65.63	1.0	Y	60	61	0.945
Macedonia	2.055	$ 6.23	0.0	3.86	392	19.08	3.0	N	68	61	0.796
Malta	0.401	$ 5.45	0.0	4.54	127	31.67	1.0	Y	59	61	0.875
Moldova	4.320	$ 2.57	0.0	3.71	406	9.40	3.5	Y	74	61	0.694
Montenegro	0.684	$ 2.27	0.0		50	7.31	3.0	N		61	
Netherlands	16.570	$ 612.70	4.2	5.56	10806	65.21	1.0	Y	77	6*	0.947
Norway	4.627	$ 264.40	1.8	5.42	3140	67.86	1.0	Y	83	61	0.965
Poland	38.518	$ 337.00	2.3	4.30	10600	27.52	1.0	Y	72	6*	0.862
Portugal	10.642	$ 176.80	1.2	4.60	7783	73.13	1.0	Y	73	34	0.904
Romania	22.276	$ 80.11	0.5	4.02	4940	22.18	2.0	Y	71	61	0.805
San Marino	0.029	$ 1.05	0.0		14	48.28	1.0	Y		61	

Serbia	10.150	$ 19.19	0.1	3.69	1400	13.79	2.5	N	70	14	0.856
Slovakia	5.447	$ 47.72	0.3	4.55	2500	45.90	1.0	N	72	61	0.910
Slovenia	2.009	$ 37.92	0.3	4.64	1090	54.26	1.0	Y	77	61	0.938
Spain	40.448	$ 1,048.00	7.1	4.77	19205	47.48	1.0	Y	89	61	0.951
Sweden	9.031	$ 373.20	2.5	5.74	6800	75.30	1.0	Y	67	61	0.947
Switzerland	7.554	$ 386.10	2.6	5.81	5098	67.49	1.0	Y			
Ukraine	46.229	$ 82.36	0.6	3.89	5278	11.42	2.5	N	72	57	0.744
United Kingdom	60.776	$ 2,346.00	16.0	5.54	37600	61.87	1.0	Y	74	4[10]	0.940
Regional Average	14.089	$ 349.50	2	4.71	6392	43	1.6		72	49	0.882

Middle East

Azerbaijan	8.120	$ 14.25	1.0	4.06	678	8.35	5.5	N	62	61	0.736
Bahrain	0.708	$ 12.14	0.8	4.28	152	21.47	5.0	N	46	61	0.859
Egypt	80.335	$ 85.37	5.7	4.07	5000	6.22	5.5	N	45	34	0.702
Georgia	4.646	$ 5.23	0.3	3.73	175	3.77	3.0	N	65	61	0.743
Iran	65.397	$ 193.50	12.9		7500	11.47	6.0	N	54	19	0.746
Iraq	27.499	$ 40.66	2.7		36	0.13	6.0	N		4	
Israel	6.426	$ 140.30	9.4	5.38	3700	57.58	1.5	Y	73	1	0.927
Jordan	6.053	$ 12.52	0.8	5.60	629	10.39	4.5	N	47	6[10]	0.760
Kuwait	2.505	$ 60.72	4.1	4.41	700	27.94	4.0	N	49	16	0.871
Lebanon	3.925	$ 19.89	1.3		700	17.83	4.5	N	48	1	0.774
Oman	3.204	$ 27.25	1.8		245	7.65	5.5	N	43	61	0.810
Qatar	0.907	$ 30.76	2.1	4.55	219	24.15	5.5	N	48	61	0.844

(*Continued*)

Table 1.1 (*Continued*)

Country	Middle Power				Globalization		Democracy			Security (Years Since Major Interstate War[8])	Development (HDI[9])
	Population (millions)[1]	GDP (billions)[2]	% of Region GDP	GPI[3]	# of Internet Users (X1000)[4]	% of pop. with internet	Freedom Rating[5]	Free for more than 10 years[6]	GEI[7]		
Saudi Arabia	27.601	$ 276.90	18.5		3200	11.59	6.5	N	42	61	0.777
Syria	19.314	$ 24.26	1.6		1100	5.70	6.5	N	48	34	0.716
Turkey	71.158	$ 358.50	24.0	4.14	16000	22.49	3.0	N	47	6*	0.757
Turkmenistan	5.097	$ 15.18	1.0		36	0.71	7.0	N		61	0.724
United Arab Emirates	4.444	$ 164.00	11.0	4.66	1397	31.44	5.5	N	48	61	0.839
Yemen	22.230	$ 15.07	1.0		220	0.99	5.0	N	31	61	0.492
Regional Average	19.976	$ 83.14	6	4.49	2316	15	5.0		50	37	0.769
Oceania											
Australia	20.434	$ 644.70	77.9	5.29	14664	71.76	1.0	Y	76	4*	0.957
Fiji	0.918	$ 2.05	0.2		61	6.64	5.0	N	56	61	0.758
Kiribati	0.107	$ 76.40	9.2		2	1.87	1.0	Y		61	
Marshall Islands	0.061	$ 0.14	0.0		2	3.28	1.0	Y		61	
Micronesia	0.107	$ 0.23	0.0		14	13.08	1.0	Y		61	
New Zealand	4.115	$ 98.39	11.9	5.15	3200	77.76	1.0	Y	78	50	0.936
Papua New Guinea	5.795	$ 4.17	0.5		170	2.93	3.0	N		61	0.523
Samoa	0.214	$ 0.40	0.0		6	2.80	2.0	Y	51	61	

Solomon Islands	0.566	$ 0.29	0.0	8	1.41	3.5	Y	50	61	0.788
Tonga	0.116	$ 0.24	0.0	3	2.59	4.0	N		61	0.815
Tuvalu	0.011	$ 0.01	0.0	1.3	11.82	1.0	Y		61	
Vanuatu	0.211	$ 0.34	0.0	7.5	3.55	2.0	Y	56	61	0.670
Regional Average	2.721	$ 68.95	8	1512	17	2.1		61	55	0.778

Light gray = Countries that pass the threshold for potential global good citizenship.
Dark gray = Countries that are internationally active and have made claims to promote humanitarian values, but that do not pass the thresholds for democracy or development.
Medium gray = Specific cases profiled in this volume.

[1] CIA, *The World Factbook 2007*, June 19, 2007, https://www.cia.gov/library/publications/the-world-factbook/fields/2119.html.
[2] CIA, *The World Factbook 2007*, June 19, 2007, https://www.cia.gov/library/publications/the-world-factbook/fields/2195.htmlGDP.
[3] The Global Competitiveness Index is a composite indicator that provides a holistic overview of factors driving productivity and competitiveness including institutions, infrastructure, macroeconomics, health and education, market efficiency, technological readiness, business sophistication, and innovation. A higher score denotes greater competitiveness. World Economic Forum, "Global Competitiveness Index 2006," http://www.weforum.org/pdf/Global_Competitiveness_Reports/gcr2006_rankings.xls.
[4] CIA, *The World Factbook 2007*, June 19, 2007, https://www.cia.gov/library/publications/the-world-factbook/fields/2153.html.
[5] A score of 1–2 shows a free nation, 3–5 are partly free and 6–7 are authoritarian regimes. Freedom House, "Freedom in the World Country Ratings 1972–2007," http://www.freedomhouse.org/uploads/fiw/FIWAllScores.xls.
[6] Ibid. This category was determined by examining the countries' freedom ranking in 1996. Countries rated as free in this year are marked with a "Y" and those that were only partly free or authoritarian are marked with a "N."
[7] Scores are ranked 0–100, with 100 being complete gender equality. Social Watch, "Gender Equity Index 2007: Progress and Regression," http://www.socialwatch.org/en/avancesyRetrocesos/IEG/tablas/GEIvalues2007.htm.
[8] This category spans the time period 1946–2007. All countries are considered to have engaged in interstate conflict during WWII.
[9] The Human Development Index is a composite indicator that includes considerations of life expectancy, education, literacy, and economic variables. A higher score indicates a greater level of development. UNDP, "Human Development Report 2006," http://hdr.undp.org/hdr2006/statistics/.
[10] Countries committing more than 1000 troops to Iraq are considered to have engaged in interstate war in 2003, and countries participating in the multinational force in Afghanistan are credited with engaging in interstate war in 2001. Only major interstate wars were considered in this category. Centre for the Study of Civil War, "Armed Conflicts 1946–2005," http://www.prio.no/cwp/armedconflict/current/Conflict_List_1946-2005.pdf.

Table 1.2 Projection of Internal Human Rights Performance

Candidate Country	Political Terror 2006	International Promotion
Botswana	2	C
Cape Verde	1	D+
Ghana	2/3*	C+
Namibia	2	C+
South Africa	3	B+
Canada	1	A–
Mexico	4/3*	B–
United States	3	B–
Bahamas	2/1*	D
Barbados	2	D+
Belize	2	D+
Costa Rica	1	B+
Dominican Republic	3	D+
Panama	1	C
Argentina	1	B
Brazil	4	B–
Chile	2/1*	B+
Uruguay	1	B
India	3/4*	C+
Japan	1	C+
South Korea	2/1*	C
Philippines	4	C+
Austria	2	B
Belgium	2/1*	B+
Cyprus	2	C+
Denmark	1	A–
Finland	1	A–
France	2	B+
Germany	1	B+
Greece	2/3*	B+
Iceland	1	C+
Ireland	1	B+
Italy	1	B+
Luxembourg	1	B–
Netherlands	1	A–
Norway	1	B+
Portugal	2	B–
Slovenia	1	B–
Spain	2	B+
Sweden	1	A–
Switzerland	1/2*	B
United Kingdom	2	A–
Israel	4	C–
Jordan	3	C+
Australia	1	B+
New Zealand	1	B+

*Indicates a disparity between the Amnesty International score (listed first) and the U.S. State Department ranking of that state that year.

Development Index, and those that qualify as "free" (1–2 on the Freedom House rankings). Certain patterns are immediately apparent, such as the very limited set of states that meet even these minimal criteria in Africa, Asia, Oceania, and the Middle East.

A final factor to consider is the influence of a country's own *human rights record* on its human rights foreign policy. We would generally expect democratic, developed countries to treat their own citizens well (Poe, Tate, and Keith 1999), so the only measure of real interest among our good citizen candidates would be significant deviation from this pattern. The best global measure of domestic respect for human rights is the Political Terror Index, compiled on the basis of Amnesty International and the U.S. State Department annual human rights reports for most major countries from 1976 to 2006; countries are rated from 1 to 5 in ascending order of repression (Gibney, Cornett, and Wood, 2007). A handful of the smallest countries from our list of candidates are not reported in the Political Terror Scale, so they cannot be included in this screen.

As far as the impact of internal human rights conditions on international promotion, we can imagine opposite arguments. In a diffusion argument, a country with stronger internal respect for rights will tend to promote human rights internationally, because it is highly socialized with human rights values, linked to multilateral mechanisms, and fosters an empowered civil society for transnational advocacy. On the other hand, human rights promotion abroad might be adopted to compensate for a lagging record at home—a cheap diplomatic defense against internal scrutiny. If we compare our most likely candidate countries' internal records with a preview of their international promotion performance, we will see that there is no clear overall pattern. Strong internal human rights appears to be neither necessary nor sufficient: Cape Verde and the Bahamas receive the highest ratings domestically and the lowest internationally, whereas Brazil and Mexico are reasonable promoters despite disturbing levels of internal abuse. Japan and the Philippines are both lackadaisical promoters, but sit at opposite ends of the scale of internal conditions. There is a rough overall association between freedom at home and promotion abroad, in that all of the A level promoters, and most of the B+, are ranked as 1 or 2 on the Political Terror Scale.

OUTPUTS: ASSESSING GLOBAL GOOD CITIZENSHIP

Of these candidate promoter states, which ones actually implement a set of measures designed to foster greater respect for human rights in the world? How would we qualify a country as a "global Good Samaritan"? Some countries claim more than they produce, or label self-seeking behavior as humanitarian, in order to gain international reputation. Conversely, principled promoters often under-assess their own efforts, discounting modest gains relative to unfulfilled aspirations. Many states are inconsistent, for

example, supporting norms but failing to provide resources, or impos-
ing selective diplomatic standards on allies and enemies. Although better
policies across more areas have a reinforcing effect—for example, multilateralism feeds into peace promotion—many global Good Samaritans
make positive contributions even though they suffer serious contradictions in at least one major policy area. As policy analysts rather than mor-
alists, we are simply trying to assess an evolving cluster of behaviors and
trends; we are looking for a few "good enough" global Good Samaritans
to highlight sources of leadership and latency in the international human
rights regime.

This study will adopt a multidimensional, benchmark rubric for assessment: a report card approach. This means that we can lay out a variety
of areas that contribute to the international promotion of human rights,
and assess the performance of any state across the spectrum of these areas
over the long run. A "good enough" Good Samaritan will make significant
and sustained efforts across most of these areas, although some variation
is normal. In areas of weaker or wavering performance, reform efforts will
also register as mitigating factors. For example, in the globally underperforming area of refugee policy, Sweden's efforts to buffer the impact of
tightening refugee policies merit a more favorable assessment than the
Netherlands, where reversals were not only more severe but relatively
unchecked. Although there are generalizable indicators in some areas,
there are no universal or quantifiable measures of performance. Furthermore, the importance of each domain of human rights policy varies
according to the state, situation, and international conditions, so performance cannot be averaged or summed across the multiple indicators.
Finally, wherever possible, several indicators will be examined, because
any given measure of international activity may be incomplete, unavail-
able to a particular state, or skewed for historical reasons.

The relevant domains of international human rights policy are multilateral diplomacy, bilateral relations, humanitarian assistance, peace promotion, and refugee reception. When individual country cases are profiled,
we will also discuss some policies specific to particular promoters: on the
positive side, support for transnational global civil society and negatively,
arms exports. In this introduction, a benchmark indicator for each of the
universal domains will be collected to map the potential promoters, high-
lighting the outstanding performance of the global Good Samaritan country cases. A qualitative, comprehensive description of promoters' efforts
within each domain follows in the relevant country chapter.

Multilateralism means founding, funding, and joining international
human rights bodies; drafting, sponsoring, and supporting human rights
treaties and resolutions; as well as promoting the development of international law. One snapshot measure of institutional multilateralism is
financial support for the United Nations' High Commissioner on Human
Rights. An excellent test of commitment to international human rights
law is diplomatic support for the International Criminal Court. Adherence

to the Rome Statute contributes substantively to the most authoritative international human rights body in existence. Moreover, because the United States' perverse opposition to that body extended to a pressure campaign to sign bilateral exceptional immunity agreements, many countries were forced to choose between this principled commitment and a loss of U.S. aid. States that absorbed an economic and bilateral diplomatic loss to defend the ICC can truly be said to have "put their money where their mouth is."

Bilateral human rights policy consists of state-to-state diplomacy, sanctions, mediations, and exchanges involving human rights. By definition, it is more difficult to compare across the board; much diplomacy takes place behind the scenes, and even public bilateral mechanisms, such as economic sanctions, operate differently in different political systems. A country's voting record on U.N. resolutions against a geographically diverse set of pariah states provides a rough indicator of human rights diplomacy. As a parallel, support for the Dalai Lama is one concrete measure of political will to support an oppressed community at the risk of alienating a great power that possesses resources, strategic significance, or cross-cutting forms of diplomatic leverage over most countries in the world. Another way to gauge a state's willingness to trade national interest for adherence to universal standards is extraterritorial prosecution of nationals abroad, in this case, for sexual exploitation of children. Extraterritorial prosecution sacrifices the state's core interest in advocating for its own citizens to protect vulnerable noncitizens, who are generally residents of relatively powerless developing countries, on the basis of a purely humanitarian norm.

Overseas development assistance contributes to human rights when it is sufficient in quantity, not unduly tied to donor interests, directed to grassroots groups and basic human needs, and fosters improvements in the rule of law and the empowerment of marginalized sectors. The Commitment to Development Index is a composite measure of aid quantity and quality that may be helpful in assessing the usefulness of aid, along with related economic measures such as trade and debt policies relevant to developing nations and the global poor. It is listed alongside the total amount of aid provided, as well as the proportion of GDP comprised by foreign aid (keeping in mind the long-standing United Nations target of .7%).

Peace promotion includes peace keeping, weapons control, conflict prevention, and postconflict reconstruction efforts, especially those that focus on the protection of civilians and vulnerable populations. Participation in U.N. peacekeeping missions is one measure of peace promotion, although it is incomplete because not all missions have a human rights focus, some countries specialize in expertise rather than troops, and contemporary humanitarian interventions take place under a variety of international umbrellas. A complementary indicator is financial support for demining, removing the weapon most destructive to civilians and most present in vulnerable areas.

Sheltering refugees is the single most direct and immediate measure states can take to assist the victims of human rights abuse. Yet refugees are needy foreigners, who often hail from hostile zones and incompatible cultures, and have no natural constituency within host nations. The number of refugees admitted is one index of compassion: every refugee admitted is one life saved. But refugee admissions must be considered alongside the host country's size and the level of demand (which is sometimes determined by accidents of geography). Thus, the proportion of asylum seekers admitted rounds out the picture.

As above, the focus cases in table 1.3 are highlighted in medium gray. The letter grades in each area are based on a rough assessment of the country's human rights policies in each area. Other things being equal, the more positive indicators present and the higher the measures, the higher the grade. For example, on multilateralism, a country would receive a C if it merely signed the basic treaties, a B if it also provided financial support to the U.N. Human Rights High Commissioner, or an A if it went beyond these to support the ICC. But the grade is not a mechanical sum, because some indicators overlap (such as the Commitment to Development Index and the proportion of aid in GDP), some are anomalous (a particular country may not support the U.N. High Commission but instead donate generously to other agencies), and they are only spot-checks that must be balanced by an overall assessment of the main thrust of policy. Thus, a country with positive scores on two out of three indicators in an issue area might still earn an A if it is a leader in its region, a very small country with limited capacity to contribute, or contributed very significantly to an especially important area even if not across the board. This overall assessment is based on secondary reading, peer assessments, and the author's contact with countries beyond the focus cases in international forums. Issue areas in which a country does not participate for structural reasons, such as foreign aid not generated by less developed countries, are not included in the assessment nor deducted from the grade. The report card grades have been reviewed by several research assistants involved in the project, to secure some measure of "intercoder validity" by knowledgeable participants, appropriate to the nature of the assessment.

What patterns are apparent from examining these rough measures of human rights foreign policy performance? Out of 50 countries examined (47 qualified and 3 added as potential least likely cases), a majority (29) earned As or Bs. Some notable high performers on these indicators are South Africa, Costa Rica, and Canada. Struggling South Africa has sacrificed over $7 million in U.S. aid to support the ICC, and accepts almost two-thirds of refugees. Costa Rica is virtually the only country on its continent to fund the U.N. High Commission on Human Rights, and accepts the highest number of refugees in all of Latin America. Canada, one-tenth the size of the United States, provides half as much funding for the U.N., accepts half the number of refugees, and donates 10 times as much for demining. Even within Europe, Denmark, Finland, Ireland, the

Netherlands, Norway, and Sweden stand out for high U.N. contributions, development indexes and proportions of aid, demining funds, and moderate numbers of refugees. Returning to the input indicators, a distinguishing factor for high performers among the qualified countries is a strong score on the Gender Equity Index.

On the negative side, we can begin to map Japan's shortfalls: the lowest score in the Commitment to Development Index and one of the lowest proportions of asylum seekers accepted of any of the dozens of developed democratic countries in our sample. Similarly, one of our few Middle Eastern cases (Israel) drops out of the picture with minimal U.N. support, no extraterritorial jurisdiction, and a shockingly low number and proportion of refugees. The United States is also a notable laggard in multilateral, aid, and refugee issues. For example, the multilateral indicators of only five treaties subscribed and a minimal contribution to the U.N. High Commission are the tip of an iceberg that includes failure to subscribe the Convention on the Rights of the Child—shared only by Somalia, underfunding of U.N. bodies—including a cut of contributions when the United States was not elected to the U.N. Human Rights Commission, and opposition to the International Criminal Court–extending to the imposition of bilateral immunity agreements on U.S. aid recipients. We are also forced to scrutinize critically the claims of some regional powers such as India to be alternative sources of value promotion, because in the contemporary period they are simply not active in any major area except peacekeeping, and excel only in a passively humane refugee policy.

When we combine the analysis of human rights foreign policy potential and performance, we see that

- significant numbers of countries are contributing to the international human rights regime, yet
- not all countries equipped to do so are performing at their full capacity (only half a dozen As, and 21 Cs or Ds), and
- a few countries that lack some of the structural inputs nevertheless are strong performers.

We can label these clusters as leaders, laggards, and least likely cases.

This implies that some additional factors must be missing to pull the laggards down, and the least likely cases above their expected level of performance. Although globalized, secure, developed, democratic middle powers have the opportunity to pursue humanitarian internationalism, not all choose to do so. Conversely, occasionally countries that are too small or too poor *do* promote human rights, at least in areas within their powers—but countries that are insufficiently democratic or globalized do not.

The country studies suggest that *norms* and *agency* are necessary to activate promoters' potential, and can occasionally overcome structural gaps. Specifically, some socially relevant leaders and sectors of civil society

Table 1.3 Outputs: A Global Good Samaritan Report Card

	Multilateral				Bilateral			
	HR Treaties Ratified[1]	UNOHCHR Voluntary Funding[2]	ICC - lost aid/refused to sign BIA[3]	Multilateralism Grade	Support for U.N. resolutions against pariah states[4]	Dalai Lama Visit?[5]	Extra-territorial Jurisdiction?[6]	Bilateral Grade
Africa								
Botswana	10	—	—	C	-2	N	N	D
Cape Verde	11	—	—	C	0	N	N	D
Ghana	11	—	—	C	1	N	N	D
Mauritius	9	—	—	D	0	N	N	D
Namibia	13	—	$ 325,000	B	-3	N	N	D
South Africa	11	$ 76,184	$7,658,000	A	-4	Y	N	C
North America								
Canada	14	$ 4,540,608	NO BIA	A	6	Y	Y	A
Mexico	15	$ 120,000	—	B	4	Y	Y	A
United States	5	$10,612,484	—	C	6	Y	Y	A
Latin America								
Antigua and Barbuda	9	—	—	D	-1	N	N	D
Bahamas	5	—	—	D	-1	N	N	D
Barbados	8	—	unknown amount	B	-1	N	N	D
Belize	12	—	—	C	1	N	N	D
Costa Rica	16	$ 10,132	$ 450,000	A	6*	Y	N	B+
Dominica	8	—	—	D	0	N	N	D
Dominican Rep.	10	—	—	C	6	N	N	C
Panama	13	$ 1,000	—	B	4	N	N	C
South America								
Argentina	13	—	—	C	6	Y	N	B
Brazil	12	—	—	C	2	Y	N	C
Chile	10	$ 30,000	—	B+	5	Y	N	B
Uruguay	17	—	$7,950,007	B+	5	N	N	C+
Asia								
India	6	$ 55,000	—	C	-5	N	N	D
Japan	9	$ 326,793	—	C+	6	Y	Y	A
Korea (south)	13	$ 110,000	—	B	5	N	N	C
Philippines	12	$ 22,190	—	C+	-1	N	N	D
Europe								
Austria	14	$ 175,296	—	B-	6	Y	Y	A
Belgium	14	$ 1,385,467	NO BIA	A	6	Y	Y	A
Cyprus	12	—	$ 108,000	B	6	N	Y	B
Denmark	16	$ 3,950,340	NO BIA	A	6	Y	Y	A
Finland	14	$ 2,233,277	NO BIA	A	6	Y	Y	A
France	13	$ 2,143,899	NO BIA	A	6	Y	Y	A

	Aid			Peace				Refugees			
CDI[7]	ODA $ (million)[8]	ODA % of GNI[9]	Aid Grade	Number of Peace-keepers[10]	Number of Mis-sions[11]	Contribution to VTF for Demining	Peace Grade	Refugees Accepted[12]	Proportion of Asylum Seekers Accepted[13]	Refugee Grade	Overall Grade
—	—	—		5	1	—	D	3,109	88%	A	C
—	—	—		0	0	—	D	—	n/a	D	D+
—	—	—		2926	9	—	B	53,537	61%	A	C+
—	—	—		2	1	—	D	—	n/a	D	D
—	—	—		655	4	—	B	5,307	49%	B	C+
—	—	—		1185	3	—	B	29,714	63%	A	B+
5.2	$ 3,756	0.34%	B	131	8	$ 21,061,681	A	147,171	50%	A	A-
—	—	—		0	0	—	D	3,229	41%	B	B-
5.0	$ 27,622	0.22%	B	314	8	$ 2,000,000	A	379,340	33%	C+	B-
—	—	—		0	0	—	D	—	n/a	D	D
—	—	—		0	0	—	D	—	n/a	D	D
—	—	—		0	0	—	D	—	n/a	D	D+
—	—	—		0	0	—	D	624	0%	C	D+
—	—	—		0	0	—	*	11,253	cases pending	B+	B+
—	—	—		0	0	—	D	—	n/a	D	D
—	—	—		4	1	—	D	—	n/a	D	D+
—	—	—		0	0	—	D	1,730	19%	C	C
—	—	—		905	9	—	B	3,074	55%	A	B
—	—	—		1282	7	—	B	3,458	40%	B	B-
—	—	—		520	4	$ 50,000	A	806	72%	B+	B++
—	—	—		2582	10	—	B	121	100%	B+	B
—	—	—		9342	11	—	B	139,283	70%	A	C+
3.1	$ 13,147	0.28%	C	38	1	$15,455,786	C+	1,941	9%	C-	C+
—	—	—		48	5	—	C	69	8%	D	C
—	—	—		627	9	—	B	96	100%	C+	C+
—	$ 1,573	0.23%	C	419	7	$ 1,243,992	A	21,230	43%	B	B
4.9	$ 1,963	0.53%	B	348	4	$ 248,618	B+	15,282	31%	B	B+
—	—	—		2	1	—	D	701	1%	C	C+
6.4	$ 2,109	0.81%	A	126	10	$ 5,750,006	A	44,374	7%	B	A-
5.4	$ 902	0.46%	B	243	7	$ 6,636,398	A	11,809	1%	B-	A-
4.6	$ 10,026	0.47%	B	2074	10	—	B	137,316	22%	B	B+

(*Continued*)

Table 1.3 (*Continued*)

	Multilateral				Bilateral			
	HR Treaties Ratified[1]	UNOHCHR Voluntary Funding[2]	ICC - lost aid/refused to sign BIA[3]	Multilateralism Grade	Support for U.N. resolutions against pariah states[4]	Dalai Lama Visit?[5]	Extra-territorial Jurisdiction?[6]	Bilateral Grade
Germany	15	$ 1,522,727	NO BIA	A	6	Y	Y	A
Greece	13	$ 144,928	NO BIA	B	6	Y	N	B
Iceland	13	—	NO BIA	B	6	N	Y	B
Ireland	15	$ 3,909,953	—	B	6	Y	Y	A
Italy	14	$ 154,214	NO BIA	B	6	Y	Y	A
Luxembourg	14	$ 130,322	NO BIA	B	6	Y	Y	A
Netherlands	14	$ 7,435,897	NO BIA	A	6	Y	Y	A
Norway	15	$ 8,065,996	NO BIA	A	6	Y	Y	A
Portugal	13	$ 80,000	NO BIA	B	6	Y	Y	A
Slovenia	14	$ 30,000	NO BIA	B	6	Y	Y	A
Spain	15	$ 7,413,789	NO BIA	A	6	Y	Y	A
Sweden	16	$ 6,324,239	—	B	6	Y	Y	A
Switzerland	12	$ 2,917,036	—	B	6	Y	Y	A
United Kingdom	15	$ 6,004,559	NO BIA	A	6	Y	Y	A
Middle East								
Israel	10	$ 10,000	—	C	6	Y	N	B
Jordan	7	—	—	D	-1	Y	N	C
Oceania								
Australia	14	$ 484,315	—	B	6	Y	Y	A
Kiribati	4	—	—	D	1	N	N	D
New Zealand	14	$ 1,025,550	—	B+	6	Y	Y	A
Average	12	$ 2,232,694	$3,298,201	B-	4	Y	Y	B-

Dark gray = Countries that are internationally active and have made claims to promote humanitarian values, but that do not pass the thresholds for democracy or development.

[1] This column represents how many of 17 key international human rights treaties the country has signed and ratified as of December 31, 2006. Amnesty International, "Amnesty International Report 2007: Selected International and Regional Human Rights Treaties," http://thereport.amnesty.org/document/2.

[2] Voluntary contributions to OHCHR in 2005. OHCHR, "Annual Report 2005," p. 24, http://www.ohchr.org/english/about/docs/annualreport2005.pdf.

[3] Lost aid as a result of supporting the ICC or refused to sign bilateral immunity agreement for fiscal years 2004, 2005. Coalition for the International Criminal Court, "Countries Opposed to Signing a U.S. Bilateral Immunity Agreement (BIA): U.S. Aid Lost in FY04 and FY05 and Threatened in FY06," http://www.iccnow.org/documents/CountriesOpposedBIA_final_11Dec06_final.pdf.

[4] How many of the U.N. resolutions concerning Belarus, Iran, North Korea, Myanmar, Uzbekistan and the promotion of equitable and mutually respective dialogue on human rights did the country support in line with the U.N. Democracy Caucus? Democracy Coalition Project, "Scorecard: Votes on Selected Human Rights Resolutions in the 61st UNGA 3rd Committee in 2006," http://www.democracycaucus.net/pdf/Scorecard%202006%20Table%20Revised_FINAL.pdf

* Costa Rica's score was taken from 2005, because that country anomalously and strategically abstained in 2006, in order to force the international community to channel resolutions through the new Human Rights Council (unsuccessfully).

[5] The Government of Tibet in Exile, "Countries visited by His Holiness the Dalai Lama," http://www.tibet.com/DL/country.html.

[6] Does the country have extra-territorial jurisdiction to prosecute for sex tourism? (Email from Beyond Borders).

	Aid			Peace				Refugees			
CDI[7]	ODA $ (million)[8]	ODA % of GNI[9]	Aid Grade	Number of Peace-keepers[10]	Number of Mis-sions[11]	Contribution to VTF for Demining	Peace Grade	Refugees Accepted[12]	Proportion of Asylum Seekers Accepted[13]	Refugee Grade	Overall Grade
5.3	$ 10,082	0.36%	B	938	6	$ 2,604,636	A	700,016	17%	B	B+
4.0	$ 384	0.17%	C	225	6	—	B	2,390	1%	B-	B
—	—	—		0	0	—	D	293	0%	C	C+
5.0	$ 719	0.42%	B	201	8	$ 381,295	B+	7,113	10%	B	B+
4.3	$ 5,091	0.29%	B	2588	6	$ 3,560,455	A	20,675	8%	B	B+
—	$ 256	0.84%	A	2	1	$ 128,140	C	1,822	8%	C	B-
6.6	$ 5,115	0.82%	A	203	6	$ 14,852,380	A	118,189	6%	B	A-
6.2	$ 2,786	0.94%	A	82	6	—	C+	43,034	10%	B	B+
4.8	$ 377	0.21%	B	443	2	$ 15,000	B-	363	11%	C	B-
—	—	—		29	3	—	C	251	2%	C	B-
4.8	$ 3,018	0.27%	B	1161	6	$ 2,506,400	A	5,374	11%	B-	B+
6.3	$ 3,362	0.94%	A	177	10	$ 1,314,705	A	74,915	2%	B	A-
5.2	$ 1,767	0.44%	B	38	6	$ 660,000	B	48,030	18%	B	B
5.1	$10,767	0.47%	B	370	7	$ 20,766,118	A	303,181	14%	B	A-
—	—	—		0	0	—	D	609	7%	C	C-
—	—	—		3573	11	—	B	695	55%	B	C+
5.5	$ 1,680	0.25%	B	114	4	$ 1,280,980	A	64,964	17%	B-	B+
—	—	—		0	0	—	D	—	n/a	—	D
6.2	$ 274	0.27%	A	40	4	$ 1,430,630	B	5,307	22%	B	B+
5.2	$ 4,853	0.46%	B	679	4	$ 5,097,361	C+	48,236	29%	C+	C+

[7] The Commitment to Development Index is a composite indicator that measures aid, trade, investment, security, migration, the environment and security. The CDI is measured on a scale of 1–10 with 10 being the highest score. Center for Global Development, "Commitment to Development Index 2006," http://www.cgdev.org/section/initiatives/_active/cdi/data_graphs

[8] OECD Donor Action Committee, "Final ODA Data for 2005," p. 7, http://www.oecd.org/dataoecd/52/18/37790990.pdf.

[9] Ibid.

[10] Number of peacekeepers contributed to current missions as of May 31, 2007. UN Department of Peacekeeping Operations, "Contributors to United Nations Peacekeeping Operations," May 31, 2007, http://www.un.org/Depts/dpko/dpko/contributors/2007/may07_1.pdf.

[11] How many of the 15 current DPKO missions is the country participating in? Stockholm International Peace Research Institute, "Multilateral Peace Mission Database," http://conflict.sipri.org/SIPRI_Internet/.

[12] UNHCR, "UNHCR Statistical Yearbook 2005," http://www.unhcr.org/statistics/STATISTICS/464478a72.html.

[13] Ibid.

Table 1.4 Mapping the Cases

	High Performance	Low Performance
High Inputs	**Leaders:** Sweden	**Laggards:** Japan
Low Inputs	**Least likely cases:** Costa Rica	**LDCs**

must have the ideas of connection to the commonweal and some sense of cosmopolitan identity, and a vocation to reach out to communicate and enact these ideas. Leaders like Olof Palme and Nelson Mandela turn promise into promotion. Their globalist vocation need not reflect any specific culture, religion, or civilization—India under Nehru attempted to foster a Gandhian foreign policy that was based on a non-Western universalism linked to core human rights principles of self-determination and nonviolence (Nayar and Paul 2003). In a parallel vein, it is not just the existence of a human rights–friendly culture or social groups that is important, but a foreign policy structure or process that permits ample participation of civil society in shaping the assessment and projection of national interest. This means that features of democracy beyond regime type—like a parliamentary system, presence of a universalist political party, and a relatively consensual but open foreign policy bureaucracy—increase the opportunities for principled policy by qualified states.

The country cases selected for in-depth study (1) are important constituents of the network of global Good Samaritans, (2) illustrate the patterns of leaders, laggards, and least likely cases, and (3) display a range of sizes, regions, cultures, and levels of development. Japan's 127 million residents contrast with Costa Rica's 4 million, whereas South Africa's staggering unemployment and health crisis differ sharply from Sweden's secure prosperity. The selection of countries from every world region and several cultural clusters allows us to counter simplistic associations between humanitarianism and projection of Northern Protestant cultures (as some authors argue below regarding the historically leading Nordic countries and the Netherlands). Indeed, case analysis shows that Protestant-dominant political cultures pushed to accommodate internal cultural diversity, like the Netherlands and Canada, may be somewhat more internationalist than more homogenous Protestant peers.

Table 1.5 Cases

Country case	Inputs	Outputs	Features
Sweden	Strong	Very good, stable	Nordic middle Power
Netherlands	Strong	Good but wavering	European
Canada	Strong	Solid and steady	North American
Costa Rica	Less likely	Promising	Democratic, least developed country
Japan	Moderate	Disappointing	Non-Western, developed democracy.
South Africa	Least likely	Improving	Non-Western, least developed country

To establish a baseline and map leading states of the international network, first we examine a set of classic promoters: Sweden, the Netherlands, and Canada. Above and beyond its own initiatives, Sweden is also a representative case of the strong Nordic region. Much of Sweden's experience could be generalized to Norway, Denmark, or Finland.[1] Both Sweden and the Netherlands are core members of the EU, but the Netherlands is more fully integrated, as seen by Sweden's persisting use of its national currency (the krone) and occasional cross-cutting coordination with its Nordic subregion.

The Netherlands' culture and position are more illustrative of the European norm. Enmeshed in the core of the world system, the Netherlands contrasts with the sheltered niche of the Nordics and Canada. As the avatar of globalization, Dutch policy displays the linkages and challenges of internationalism as identity.

Canada's position in the Western Hemisphere is important in several respects. Canada is instructive in its departure from its otherwise similar southern neighbor in this area of principled internationalism, which is positioned as a distinguishing feature of national identity. Canada also shows how global and multilateral identities can trump regionalism. Moreover, Canada's subordinate security niche and economic dependency on the United States have not prevented it from pursuing a relatively autonomous humanitarian foreign policy.

Contrasting cases are chosen to show the existence of human rights promotion policies in other regions, at lower levels of economic development, and with different security roles in the international system. Costa Rica is a "least likely case" due to small size, low development, and domination by the regional hegemon. Yet it displays an extraordinarily high level of multilateral diplomacy, peace promotion, and receptivity to refugees, and it acts as a regional leader on human rights issues.

South Africa is notable for its international transformation from human rights pariah to human rights promoter, which precisely parallels its domestic transition to democracy. It is the only potential promoter in Africa, and has emerged as a regional power across various issue areas. With relatively stable structural conditions, a radical change in leadership, ideology, and the role of civil society resulted in a dramatically different foreign policy and investment in the international system.

Japan initially appears as a most likely case: it is the most developed, most democratic, most secure, and most globalized state in the region. However, despite some efforts to reframe aid and promote human security, Japan must register as a laggard in the areas of bilateral relations, peace promotion, most multilateral initiatives, and refugees. These shortfalls are

---

1. For example, in 2007, Norway increased its standing $4 billion annual aid allotment to pledge an additional $1 billion over 10 years for a Clinton Global Initiative special program for maternal and child health in the developing world (Dugger 2007).

clearly traceable to weaknesses of agency, the very factors that permitted South Africa to partially transcend its structural limitations.

The remainder of this book explores why and how states become global Good Samaritans. In the next chapter, I sketch a theoretical argument for the transformation of foreign policy through reconstruction of national identity. The following six chapters provide in-depth case studies of the contrasting experiences of three classic promoters, a laggard, and two least likely cases. After that, we will examine the cumulative impact of networks of global Good Samaritans: interstate organizations catalyzed by promoters as vehicles for humanitarian internationalism. Finally, the conclusion will analyze the lessons learned, and suggest policy guidelines to enhance the strength, numbers, and role of global Good Samaritans in the international human rights regime.

2

Reconstructing the National Interest

Foreign policy is what states make of it.
—Steve Smith 2001

Why do the dozens of Global Good Samaritans sacrifice their national interests to help strangers? The quick answer is—*they don't*. Global good citizen states see the blood, treasure, and political capital they contribute to the international human rights regime as an investment, not a loss. Like other states, global Good Samaritans *are* following their national interest; the difference is that they have a broader, longer-term vision of national interest. Global good citizens have reconstructed their national identity in accordance with universalist norms, roles, and expectations. Thus, they have learned to see themselves as interconnected members of a global community that works best for everyone when human rights are respected. Generations of globalization, democratization, and human rights campaigns have produced a niche, networks, and knowledge that support humanitarian foreign policy.

The study of foreign policy was historically dominated by the assumption that discrete state units strategically calculated their national interest and sought to maximize their relative power in an anarchic international system (Waltz 1979). Each element of this approach was challenged on analytic, normative, and empirical grounds. First, for several generations state power appeared to be increasingly subject to transnational actors and arenas (Keohane and Nye 1971). Second, foreign policy decision makers seemed to be subject to systematic cognitive, bureaucratic, ideological, and cultural influences that distorted or even replaced "national interest" (Jervis 1976, Snyder et al. 2002, Goldstein and Keohane 1993). Finally, the international system was seen to be ordered in some fashion by norms, which did, could, or should inform foreign policy choice (Falk 1977, Wendt 1999). Paraphrasing Alexander Wendt's (1992) constructivist retort to realpolitik's description of an ungovernable international arena—"Anarchy Is What States Make of It"—Steve Smith (2001) applies a similar dialectical sense of agency to statecraft: "foreign policy is what states make of it."

A constructivist theory of foreign policy can help us to understand how cosmopolitan political cultures like human rights make values make sense—and how such cultures are learned. Constructivism analyzes world politics through the constitution and reconstruction of norms—global discourses, rules, institutions, and identities (Onuf 1989). For constructivists, "the identities, interests and behavior of political agents are socially constructed by collective meaning, interpretations and assumptions about the world" (Adler 1997: 324). Constructivist approaches to foreign policy stress that power is always directed and legitimated by social purpose (Ruggie 1983, Risse-Kappen 1994). Values do not stop at the water's edge—and values can reconstitute interests (Finnemore 1996).

For global citizen states, the principled pursuit of human rights is a consciously constructed alternative pathway of enlightened self-interest. Policy makers are neither mechanical Machiavellians nor blind idealists; they seek to rationally maximize values and project identities. Those identities are global, modern, and democratic: their values are cosmopolitan, seeking a liberal, plural but universal, rule-governed world order (Appiah 2006). Instead of asking how they can pursue material interests—"What's in it for us?" (Finnemore and Sikkink 1998: 914)—global good citizens ask, "What can my state do to build a better world, which will be a better world for us in the end?" A growing global culture of humanitarianism tells them what that better world looks like, and instructs democratic members of the community of nations in their responsibility to participate in pathways to progress like foreign aid and international law (Lumsdaine 1993).

Constructivism also draws our attention to the active and political work of putting ideas into practice. New ideas must be mobilized, contested, and institutionalized by empowered political actors. It takes a global village of "moral entrepreneurs," transnational activists and experts, charismatic national leaders, dedicated diplomats, and cosmopolitan civil societies to socialize states. Humanitarian identities shape foreign policies through the same systematic political processes that socialize states' military or economic policies, hidden in the taken-for-granted pursuit of more material constructions of national interest. Norms filter states' perceptions of their interests and needs, construct foreign policy roles and mutual expectations in international society, build constraining institutions that link principles to consequences, and provide domestic political rationales and constituencies for foreign policy makers (Saideman 2002, Kowert 2001).

An emphasis on normative change can be combined with a recognition of rationalist parameters or structural dialectics of foreign policy. Studies by Risse, Ropp, and Sikkink (1999), Daniel Thomas (2001), and Darrell Hawkins (1997) all show the influence of ideas *via material leverage* by strong states' pressure on pariahs, defections in repressive coalitions, and investments in international institutions. For human rights foreign policy promoters, this type of synthetic analysis of normative and material factors can elucidate the rise and some aspects of the behavior of global Good Samaritans. Global good citizens do not arise out of sheer voluntarism. Some structural base of threshold size, stability, development, and democratic regime type precedes the mobilization of cosmopolitan values—and significant decline in these characteristics can endanger traditions of human rights foreign promotion.

Moreover, the interplay of moral and material interests can help to explain the selectivity and targeting of principled foreign policy. As we will see in Canadian trade or Dutch migration, a strong countervailing material concern will tend to swamp the normative agenda—especially in bilateral relations. Norm promotion is strongest when it coincides with enlightened self-interest, as when global citizen states promote democracy to secure peaceful neighbors and better trade partners. But cosmopolitan values can also flourish in areas in which material interests are obscure or ambiguous, like when Sweden strengthens civil society organizations in Africa. And occasionally, states will consciously choose norms at the expense of material concerns—like when South Africa braved U.S. aid cuts to support the International Criminal Court.

IDENTITIES AS INTERESTS

States are political communities that seek values and identities. All nations are "imagined communities"—and "imagined communities are not merely the sum of the beliefs of some national group; regardless of the physical existence of the individuals, they exist in symbols, practices, institutions and discourses" (Adler 1997: 327). "Norms are constitutive components of both the international system and states' interests" (Klotz 1995: 460). In this sense, political identities are self-fulfilling prophecies. Values and mentalities provide the tool kit that frames policy debates (Swidler 1986), " not by directly or inevitably determining them but rather by rendering these actions plausible or implausible, acceptable or unacceptable, conceivable or inconceivable, respectable or disreputable" (Yee 1996: 97).

The realist tradition of international relations identifies national interest as the basis for foreign policy, but constructivism insists that what interests a nation is not always state security. Nations also expend scarce resources in pursuit of identity, which is often formed in international relationships. Prior to defending the national interest, states must *define* the national interest. As Wapner (1996: 142) explains, "No one questions that states act in their own interests. What is less clear, however, is how they perceive those interests."

Why does a particular state construct a particular identity, in this case, as a global good citizen? The answer lies partly in history, partly in structure, partly in the agency of meaning and myth makers, and partly in relations to Others. Internally, human rights promoter states have either a long-established or a newly hard won rights tradition, that is seen as making a crucial contribution to other social goals, such as peace and development. Cosmopolitan political values can come to constitute a part of such a state's domestic legitimacy. Global citizen states are often small to medium sized and highly dependent on interaction, which fosters consensus and proposes a purposeful form of niche foreign policy. Within these societies, at some critical conjuncture charismatic figures or social forces frame salient problems in terms of cosmopolitan norms, and encourage the pursuit of principled foreign policy as a form of "soft power" (Nye 2006).

But foreign policy is also constructed outward. The identities that shape interests are constructed in relation to others. "Identities perform three necessary functions in a society: they tell you and others who you are and they tell you who others are" (Hopf 1998: 175). Construction of domestic and international identities is related, in both directions—national values are projected into international society, and international society socializes states (Klotz 1995, Katzenstein 1996). At the broadest level, constructivists observe that state identities are constructed in relationship to the wider international society (Bull 1995). At another level, states build identities within regional and cultural communities (Brysk, Parsons, and Sandholtz 2002), distinguish national identity from neighbors and enemies, and define the standards of like-minded, Western, or modern foreign policy (Donnelly 1998). "Security communities," whether global or regional, ground membership "not only by the state's external identity and associated behavior but also by its domestic characteristics and practices" (Adler and Barnett, 1996: 76). For global Good Samaritans, these layers of international identity construction are mutually reinforcing. "For example, it would be very difficult for a European state to consistently abuse human rights and still be deemed to belong to contemporary 'Europe'" (Adler 1997: 345).

National identities are historically rooted, but they are not fixed—rather, norms are continuously and dialectically reconstructed. At some points, such identities appear unconscious, when they have become deeply internalized, but socialized norms surface when they are contested by external change or internal challengers. For example, many European states' postwar refugee regimes have been reopened for debate in response to growing numbers of immigrants along with shifting identities of state and regional communities and Others, as well as renewed security threat. The critical point is that external structures and events are always interpreted and filtered through long-standing notions of roles, relationships, and "lessons of history." For global Good Samaritan states, such notions have converged in a specific package of human rights identity and promotion.

Global Good Samaritan Norms

What is the complex of beliefs and practices that constitute a global Good Samaritan? Humanitarian, cosmopolitan norms are introduced, contested, and diffused across the world system, in dialogue with national cultures and experiences. *Human rights* do not comprise a single concrete injunction, but rather an interconnected congeries of beliefs about our duty to protect strangers. These beliefs depend on the dual assumptions that we are rights-holding liberal agents, and that we identify as such with demographically disparate but morally equivalent Others (Tan 2004, Monroe 1996). These norms become accepted and internalized as they are clarified and gain historic status (Legro 2005), framed to fit with prevailing ideologies of liberal modernity (Boli, Meyer, Ramirez, and Thomas 1999) and connect to the humanitarian affective value set of physical threat to innocent victims (Keck and Sikkink 1998).

The observed pattern of *humane internationalism* in foreign policy is defined as a combination of cosmopolitan values, long-term interests, and international projection of a domestic social welfare state (Pratt 1989: 14). Cosmopolitan values, initially articulated by Kant, include moral universalism, the status of individuals as rights-bearing global citizens, the aspiration toward a world community with the power to enforce those rights, and the desirability of democratization of both states and the international system of states (Fossum 2006). Cosmopolitan norms link national interest to universalism as they construct moral and strategic interdependence. The circle of moral identification is expanded from national to international community, as universal markers of human capacity and vulnerability transcend bounded signifiers such as language and kinship. Cosmopolitan doctrines such as human rights and human security assert strategic interdependence across space through a global commons of social action across borders, in which a threat to any touches all (Hampson 2002). Universalism also incorporates the shadow of the future in an intertemporal interdependence of means and ends, so that long-term consequences of an action are built into its deliberation.

Although this value package is based in human rights, it is also legitimated and influenced by a family of related norms with differing levels of national resonance: liberal democracy, social democracy, human security, and specific national historical traumas such as war and dictatorship. Any particular state's set of goals on the scale below will generally be a result of how national values such as social democracy direct a country within the neighborhood of cosmopolitanism. This is a map of beliefs, not behavior. As with all norms, recognition, discourse, and justification often precede full implementation (Risse, Ropp, and Sikkink 1999), although some practice, as well as rhetorical commitment, must be present to qualify a country as holding a norm.

What collection of values characterizes a human rights promoter? Table 2.1 attempts to provide a general checklist of relevant beliefs—a kind of cosmopolitan catechism. The list is organized around a syntax of humanitarian injunctions: in order to fulfill my proper role (in the sociological "logic of appropriateness"), what am I called upon to do? First, which role am I trying to perform: merely a civilized state, a generic liberal democracy, or a self-ascribed global good citizen? Second, what are the kinds of rights an actor in that status has a duty to promote? Third, what are the appropriate and required means to these ends? For example, most

Table 2.1 The Cosmopolitan Creed

Role	*Goals*	
Because we are...	*we should promote...*	
Members of international society	basic human dignity and physical integrity nondiscrimination	
Democracies	elections rule of law civil liberties	
Global good citizens	gender equity children's rights	
European	right to food health rights	
Nordic/Canadian	collective and cultural rights	
Methods		
by some of the following means...	*consisting of...*	*via...*
International law:		
	humanitarian/laws of war	adherence
	international human rights law	mechanisms
	transnational codes of conduct	expanding coverage
Peace promotion:	conflict resolution	diplomacy
	conflict prevention	funding
	intervention	training
	reconstruction	peace-keeping
Bilateral sanctions:	pariahs	diplomacy economic sanctions arms limits
	chronic violators	diplomacy economic sanctions arms conditionality
Direct support to victims:		foreign aid fund and protect NGOs asylum for refugees armed intervention

Targets

and we are responsible...

Where we are connected or implicated (former colonies, trade ties).
When others do.
Wherever it meets a balance of interests and potential impact.
Everywhere possible.

Western democracies promote international law to some degree, but only certain states take on humanitarian intervention on a regular basis, and most debate the efficacy and justification of sanctions. Finally, to whom and under what conditions am I responsible? The Netherlands clearly distinguished its direct responsibility for its former colony in Suriname from more attenuated historic ties to South Africa, where the Dutch waited for multilateral support before pursuing sanctions.

To read the checklist, look down each column as the role becomes more complex and demanding. Once an actor has moved down the column toward a greater range of rights and responsibilities, the new values encompass all previous commitments; human rights promoter states do not generally take on social and economic rights and forget about torture, for example. However, uneven progress along the columns can show us imbalances and contradictions in a particular promoter's progress. For example, a country could favor the full range of rights but be unwilling to employ certain mechanisms to achieve those goals—or conversely be prepared to sanction and intervene, but only to defend against gross abuses such as genocide and crimes against humanity, regardless of chronic discrimination or authoritarian denial of civil liberties. And a state's normative position—not just its record—may change over time. After the failure of humanitarian intervention in Srebrenica, the Netherlands changed its logic of appropriate ends and criteria, not just its military strategy and behavior. As seen in its current engagement in Afghanistan, the second-generation intervention seeks to foster a broader set of rights at the same time that it eschews conventional peacekeeping for a kind of armed reconstruction. By filling in the syntax of the motive, goals, means, and targets of humanitarian action, we can answer the question: what does it mean to say that country X "believes in human rights"?

THE COSMOPOLITAN CREED

All human beings are born free and equal in dignity and rights.
            —Universal Declaration of Human Rights

Constructing Foreign Policy

How do these beliefs translate into the foreign policy practice of states? First, global good citizenship comes to constitute the identity of promoter states, and several domains of international relations, such as foreign aid. Yet reproduction of these roles is not automatic; principled national interests are promoted, selected, disseminated, contested, and reconstructed through political processes (Weldes 1996). These processes operate simultaneously at several levels of analysis—inside and outside (R. B. J. Walker 1993), and they change over time. Some suggest a life cycle of norm promotion, in which "moral entrepreneurs" spearhead persuasion and reframing of new norms (or new interpretations of existing norms, Brysk 2005), followed by a cascade of socialization across states via imitation, belonging to international communities, and a quest for legitimation as modern good citizens (Finnemore and Sikkink 1998).

Thus, at the domestic level, states construct principled foreign policy from inside. "International rules and norms can affect state behavior through the actions of domestic political actors" (Cortell and Davis 1996). Foreign policy elites act as norm entrepreneurs, along with domestic "meaning managers" like churches and social movements. They refer to and promote the legitimacy of cosmopolitan norms such as humanitarian intervention, and bridge them with national traditions and experiences. Moreover, elite initiative and social pressure can lead to the establishment of institutions such as human rights offices of foreign ministries, aid agencies, and international assistance programs with legal institutions and even militaries. These offices, in turn, become advocates as well as implementers of principled foreign policy.

Between state and society, political parties can be promoters or transmission belts for cosmopolitan values. In some cases, this will be linked to a party ideology such as social democracy, which also creates contact with transnational networks. At other times, political parties more generically use humanitarian internationalism as a political resource, to appeal to new constituencies, cement coalitions, or foster national pride in times of challenge on other fronts. For example, McKay shows how divergent political party coalitions made a difference in the application of similar like-minded ideologies by Canada and Denmark to conflict in Iraq (McKay 2006).

The usual suspect for domestic human rights promotion, civil society, also plays a systematic and frequent role in the construction of cosmopolitan foreign policy. Human rights advocates serve as pressure groups, sources of information and expertise, and sometimes implement principled programs like rule of law training abroad. Immigrants, women, and other disadvantaged groups often foster attentive interdependence with transnational peers. Meanwhile, value-oriented civic constituencies like churches play all of these sociological roles as advocates and service providers, as well as expanding moral universalism and legitimacy.

Although domestic political processes foster a supply of human rights foreign policy, external structures and beliefs mobilize the demand side. From outside, states construct foreign policy identities as globalized democracies, as middle powers, and as mentor states. Roles influence policy makers' parameters, commitments, rules, and functions at the global level and in regional or subsystems (S. Walker 1987, Jepperson in Katzenstein 1996). But also, system roles result from and reinforce the expectations of other members that a given state will serve as a broker, fixer, spoiler, or provider of some class of collective goods (such as peacekeeping or disaster relief). Role performance and reactions, in turn, feed back into a new round of self-definition, for example, when the Netherlands faced a crisis of its humanitarian peacekeeping after Srebrenica (Fossum 2006).

Cosmopolitan norms derive from and contribute to perceptions of global interdependence. The objective presence of increasing international flows is interpreted by ideologies of globalization along several dimensions of strategic interdependence that condition national interest. Liberal institutionalists point to all states' increased sensitivity to the actions of others—from trading states to neighbors of countries in crisis (Keohane and Nye 1977), compatible with thin versions of human security and liberal democracy. More critical theorists see an interpenetration of decision-making capacity, resulting in a deeper permeability of sovereignty (Fossum 2006), which tends toward an interdependence of social democratic and full-spectrum versions of human rights. Finally, the aspiration and construction of global governance produces an interdependence of accountability that pushes adherents up the ladder of human rights promotion commitments.

Another layer of cosmopolitan commitment comes from state identities as democracies. As an ideology of strategic interdependence, the democratic peace hypothesis that states that democracies do not make war upon each other directs democratic states toward democracy promotion as a form of peace promotion (and self-protection, as for Costa Rica). But human rights foreign policy may be a more direct expression of liberal democratic identity as a community of values (Risse-Kappen 1995), as stated by the OSCE. In this interpretation, "friends don't let friends discriminate." Moreover, post–Cold War liberal democracies now believe and state that fellow democracies are more market friendly, and thus better economic partners. This perfectly bridges material and value-based interests, although it raises questions about the autonomy of principled promotion efforts by democratic states.

Beyond this, some globalized democracies have the role and mentality of *middle powers*, which contributes yet another set of beliefs and expectations regarding global good citizenship. Middle power status is a loose blend of economic and geostrategic standing and historic foreign policy role, which may be measured globally, regionally, or against an identity-based security community. Middle powers are typically avid multilateralists, and promoters of global governance and international law as a cooperative modality for a range of economic, security, and humanitarian interests. Mid-range global citizen states tend to seek comparative advantage through the roles of catalyst, facilitator, and manager in the international system (Cooper, Higgott, and Nossal 1993: 23). Beyond the process dimension, middle powers generally favor peace, law, and trade, each of which militates toward moral universalism. For such states, their structural position in the world system, role aspirations, and interest perceptions, and the ongoing expectations of others are mutually constitutive. This is one reason that middle power roles can linger decades or even centuries beyond any objective referent, as in the Netherlands.

Finally, the international system now offers a specific niche for principled promoters: the mentor state. "A *gidsland* is a nation that progressively guides other countries locked in pitiful nationalist struggles for power, dominance, and religious zeal to the proper international behaviour consisting of respect for the international legal order, the rights of men [*sic*], and free trade as the best way of ensuring prosperity for all" (Herman 2006: 863). Although the concept originated in the Netherlands, Ann-Sofie Dahl (2006) suggests that it fits Sweden's role as a moral super-power better than conventional cosmopolitanism, and the notion has been applied to Canada by its foreign policy analysts.[1] As Fossum points out, the mentor state model departs from full cosmopolitan norms in that it does not require consistency between a state's internal and external human rights promotion, nor does it address characteristics of the international state system that go beyond critiquing the behavior of individual states (Fossum 2006).

Human Rights as Foreign Policy

Humanitarian foreign policy *is* possible, but it requires the continuous reconstruction of national interest through the constitution and projection of norms of cosmopolitan interdependence. States can become partners in the international human rights regime, but some are more amenable to this role than others. Small, relatively consensual societies are structurally positioned for attention to principled arguments, whereas highly globalized and democratic states are linked to universalist communities of interest.

Ideas matter, but constructivism tells us that human rights norms are always competing with alternative discourses of security threat, parochial nationalism, and narrowly material, short-term calculation. For cosmopolitan commitment to prevail, normative linkage is critical. Notions of human rights must be connected to liberal and social democratic traditions, standards of global good citizenship, and reminders of global interdependence. Domestic and transnational advocates must continually respond to nationalism, fundamentalisms, neoliberal atomization, and postliberal complacency.

Domestic promoters of human rights foreign policy must also remember that good ideas must be mobilized, enacted, and institutionalized by politics as usual. It takes entrepreneurial leadership, calculating political parties, and transnationalized civil society constituencies to strategically mobilize historic norms and persuasively project globalizing logics. Once mobilized, it takes domestic and international institutionalization to maintain states' incentives and momentum for human rights policy.

---

1. Although the classic human rights promoters tend to incorporate social concerns beyond the U.S. liberal model, the mentor state notion is also related to Protestant missionary visions of a "city on a hill" (Hartz 1991). Such multivalent notions have served as a rationale for America's episodes of democracy promotion and humanitarian intervention—which have ranged from sincere projection of liberalism to misguided cultural imposition to legitimation of cynical imperialism (Peceny 1999).

The pathway of principled foreign policy and reconstruction of national interest reminds us of an expanded notion of the political, in which politics is the construction of community (Arendt 1958). The cosmopolitan dream of extending this vision to the global level requires a parallel leap of moral imagination to the nineteenth-century revolution that turned neighbors into citizens (Shafir 1998). In the twenty-first century, it is the lingua franca of human rights that provides a way to make values make sense—whereas taking care of strangers constitutes states as global citizens.

3

The Gold Standard

Sweden

We are not doing this with our hearts, but with our brains, and we have no hidden agenda—we have no reason to help a country like Namibia; we do it because it is important for the world community.
— Swedish International Development Agency (SIDA)
official, June 8, 2004

Sweden sets the gold standard for human rights foreign policy promotion: funding, sheltering, mediating, and advocating for the full spectrum of human rights, all over the world, for several generations. Sweden represents a gold standard in another way as well, in that human rights promotion is grounded in a high level of affluence and security. This means that Sweden has the material and diplomatic resources to influence selected issue agendas and institutions—but it also raises the possibility that only wealthy, safe countries like Sweden may be able to afford the luxury of promoting human rights. Swedish foreign policy generally projects liberal democratic domestic values, even against dominant international trends and occasionally sacrificing domestic interests (Heisler 1990, Sundelius 1989, Goldmann 1986). Yet the question remains *why* and *how* Sweden chooses to expend its various forms of material and political capital in the service of a broader vision of human dignity.

Sweden's 2007 "Human Rights in Swedish Foreign Policy" provides a near-perfect "cosmopolitan catechism" (see chapter 2):

> Promoting and increasing respect for human rights is a priority issue in Swedish foreign policy. Our commitment to human rights is in Sweden's interests and reflects our aspirations for a world in which people can live in freedom and security, free from fear and want.... The principles are: human rights are universal...it is legitimate to react...human rights are the rights of individuals and the responsibility of governments...rights are indivisible....

Sweden's historic diplomatic commitment, multilateralism, and exemplary aid policy have been retained by the Conservative government that took power in 2006 following decades of Social Democratic hegemony—demonstrating that human rights promotion is the ongoing policy of the country, not just a particular government or political party.

The following will document Sweden's contribution to the international human rights regime. Although Sweden's policies have not been as strong and consistent as its rhetoric, the Nordic state has made a significant and sustained impact on bilateral diplomacy, multilateral institutions, and the value-promoting aspects of regional integration. Sweden has also provided impressive economic, organizational, and even military resources to protect human rights and global civil society. Sweden's ready reception of refugees displays an intense humanitarian impact in which domestic resources are expended for the benefit of noncitizens. Finally, security-based contradictions and limitations will be noted, largely through the litmus test of arms exports—in which Sweden's broader national security and financial interests may potentially clash with its stated values.

After mapping Sweden's human rights foreign policy, we will analyze the sources of this strong record of human rights promotion. Sweden's history as a peace-seeking and sheltered small power created an opportunity to project its values, in the hope of creating a like-minded world amenable to stable cooperation and trade. That opportunity was implemented by a collection of willing agents, from charismatic leaders to able diplomats to a receptive public. We will see that this ongoing series of policy choices was enabled and inspired by a collective ideology that reconstructed national interest as global cosmopolitanism.

FOREIGN POLICY ROLES: THE CONSCIENTIOUS CRITIC

As Foreign Minister Carl Bildt took his seat at the newly created United Nations Human Rights Council in 2007, he affirmed that "Sweden must never cease to speak out in criticism of dictatorships that remain and the authoritarian regimes in which human rights protection is weak. We must also have the strength to criticize shortcomings in our own circle." He singled out Sudan, Burma, Zimbabwe, Cuba, Belarus, Iran, and China (Bildt 2007). Sweden has exceeded its peers in the consistent vehemence of its diplomacy, especially on signature issues like the death penalty.

At a bilateral level, Sweden is known historically as the undiplomatic critic of international injustice. Despite a notable domestic preference for dialogue and international contribution to mediation efforts, Sweden has repeatedly and forcefully criticized chronic violations and pariah states. Critics contend that Sweden's human rights diplomacy has been unbalanced, not followed by meaningful action, and sometimes used as a sop to domestic social democrats to cover for a pro-Western military tilt (Dahl 1997). Although Sweden has historically muted its critique of political suppression by liberationist postcolonial governments, and has not systematically linked diplomacy with sanctions, Sweden has ultimately spoken out against governments of every ideology, eventually held even allies like Zimbabwe to account, and has slowly increased participation in multilateral sanctions and aid conditionality.

During the Vietnam War, Sweden extensively condemned U.S. conduct of the war, both directly and in international settings. Swedish Prime Minister Olof Palme compared the U.S. bombings of Hanoi to the Guernica attacks of the Spanish Civil War. Sweden recognized the North Vietnamese government in 1969 and commenced an aid program that continues to this day. Swedish criticism was so harsh that it led the Nixon Administration to adopt some diplomatic sanctions against Sweden (Stenelo 1984: 155), but Sweden was undeterred by superpower disapproval (Jerneck et al. 2005; Stenelo 1984).

Nonaligned, neutral Sweden also condemned human rights violations by the Soviet bloc. The Swedes' 1970s involvement in the European Security Conference "implied an emphasis on questions of human rights in Europe," culminating in the 1984 Stockholm conference (Ekéus/SOU 2002: 394). Sweden in turn criticized Soviet repression of Czechoslovakia in 1968, Poland in 1980, and Afghanistan in 1979 (394).

Sweden's condemnation of South Africa's apartheid regime included numerous statements and policies, over virtually the entire 40-year duration of minority rule. Sweden adopted sanctions on investment in 1978–1979, as well as conditions on loans, trade, and reduced diplomatic relations. Sweden provided aid to the victims of apartheid from the 1950s onward, including supporting key legal aid groups, supporting many ANC leaders in exile, and directing foreign aid preferentially to Southern African "front-line states" (Sevastik 1997).

This foreign policy role of "naming and shaming" has been subsequently institutionalized. For the past 20 years, Sweden has appointed a special human rights ambassador connected to the international law department of the foreign ministry, whose function is to monitor and critique human rights developments across the range of bilateral and multilateral relationships. Ambassador Ulla Strom has participated in bilateral "development dialogues" with politically challenged traditional aid recipients in Southern Africa, Vietnam, and Laos. Although this was not explicit aid conditionality, her presence at aid discussions alongside SIDA and the Swedish Embassy seemed to influence recipient receptivity to donor-suggested projects to enhance land rights, the rule of law, and gender equity. The human rights ambassador is also called upon to meet bilaterally with egregious violators when they are involved in direct trade or diplomatic negotiations with Sweden (interview, June 11, 2004; as an illustration of frequency, she was en route to such a meeting following our interview). Sweden publishes a comprehensive annual report on human rights conditions throughout the world, second in scope only to that of the much larger U.S. State Department.

Currently, this systemic role is supplemented by periodic statements by Swedish foreign ministers that express critical positions on interstate conduct, such as the U.S. approach to the war on terror (Lindh 2003b). Swedish demarches are increasingly channeled via the EU, and Swedish human rights advocates note an overall decrease in bilateral condemnations since the end of the Cold War. However, Sweden still takes strong positions on pariah states and select issues such as the death penalty. In 2006, Sweden sent election monitors to Nigeria to follow contested balloting. In the summer of 2007, Sweden called in Iran's ambassador to protest an execution by stoning in that country.

Although Sweden does not currently follow up its criticism with bilateral sanctions, in a few situations of humanitarian crisis, Sweden has vigorously coupled diplomatic condemnation with a package of humanitarian aid, mediation attempts, and refugee protection beyond the multilateral norm. In Sudan, around 265 million SEK ($40 million) in standing humanitarian aid was matched in 2007 with a renewed diplomatic push for the peace accord via Sweden's ambassador, special support for the Centre for Humanitarian Dialogue to broaden negotiations, peacekeepers, a financial contribution and increased security for the ICRC, support for Médecins Sans Frontières, a UNDP project for legal protection of women in the conflict, and Swedish Rescue Services transport assistance to the UNHCR. Sweden's development minister explicitly cited the "responsibility to protect" norm as support for Sweden's intervention (for a list of Sweden's government reports on Sudan, see bibliography).

Similarly, Sweden followed condemnation of Israel's 2006 invasion of Lebanon with concerted support for Palestinian refugees. Sweden's foreign minister, Carl Bildt, averred: "Israel's repeated attacks on the occupied Palestinian territories, particularly Gaza, are shocking. They are contrary to international law, as is the continued firing of rockets from Palestinian areas. Extrajudicial executions must stop, as must indiscriminate killing that affects civilian populations" (Bildt 2006).

During the Lebanon crisis, Sweden provided tens of millions of dollars in additional humanitarian aid, as well as extensive logistical assistance for displaced persons—from blankets to trucks to doctors. By the following summer, Sweden had pledged special allocations of 5 million SEK to the United Nations' agency dedicated to Palestinian refugees, UNWRA, and 1 million to Save the Children Sweden for refugee camps in northern Lebanon, along with almost 15 million for mine clearance with the Swedish Rescue Service and U.N. Mine Clearance Program (see SIDA reports on Lebanon 2007 in bibliography).

THE INTERNATIONAL HUMAN RIGHTS REGIME: BUILDING INSTITUTIONS

Like Canada, Sweden has been a strong contributor to global institutions through leadership, financial support, initiatives, and the provision of peacekeeping forces. Sweden's official policies and foreign policy personnel seek to strengthen international institutions as multipurpose forums and instruments, for their own sake. Moreover, Swedish contributions to the United Nations have been concentrated in areas relevant to human rights such as the plight of refugees, the rights of children, and conflict resolution.

Sweden has supplied leadership constantly to mediation efforts and international organizational structures. King Gustav's nephew Folke Bernadotte, following leadership of the Swedish Red Cross, played a critical role in the 1948 Israeli-Palestinian conflict. He arranged the first truce supervised by the United Nations, drafted a peace plan that shaped U.N. Resolution 194 regarding the return of refugees, initiated a humanitarian relief program for Palestinians that led to UNRWA, and was assassinated while brokering a second peace plan in Israeli-controlled Jerusalem (Persson 1998). Another key founding figure, Dag Hammarskjöld, served as United Nations secretary general from 1953 to 1961 and helped to strengthen that position and expand the functions of the organization—he also paid with his life for his international service. Former Prime Minister Olof Palme mediated in the Iraq-Iran conflict from 1980 to 1984. Another Swedish leader, 1991–1994 Prime Minister Carl Bildt (who returned as foreign minister in 2006) served as high representative for the reconstruction of Bosnia from 1995 to 1997. In terms of arms control, in 1991 Ambassador Rolf Ekéus was appointed to head the U.N. Special Commission on Iraq (UNSCOM), to monitor the presence of weapons of mass destruction. The successor organization, United Nations Monitoring, Verification and Inspection Commission (UNMOVIC), was headed by another Swede, Hans Blix. Swedish personnel have played a disproportionate role throughout the U.N. legal, refugee, and human rights mechanisms (Swedish Institute 2004).

Sweden has been a major financial contributor to the U.N. High Commission on Refugees, the U.N. High Commission on Human Rights, and UNICEF—in 2003, Sweden donated 72 million SEK to the former and around 700 million to the latter (about $11.5 million and $112 million respectively), in both cases including both project and basic organizational support. Sweden fund s a post at the United Nations Department for the Advancement of Women, helped to promote and fund the establishment of a Permanent Forum for Indigenous Peoples, as well as a special rapporteur on the Right to Education (interview, June 8, 2004). Sweden was an active proponent of the United Nations conferences of the 1990s, providing critical infusions of funding and personnel to the United Nations 1993 Vienna Conference on Human Rights and its precursors (Lindberg 1999). On an ongoing basis, Sweden is the fourth largest donor to the United Nations Relief and Works Agency for Palestine Refugees in the Near East (UNRWA)—a recent annual budget was SEK 242 million, along with SEK 65 million for emergency relief for the Palestinian territories.

Sweden adheres to all the major international human rights treaties, and despite some generic caution regarding new legal commitments,

Sweden has contributed to some innovative mechanisms.[1] In terms of contributions to new treaties, Sweden helped to draft the international convention on disability, and has contributed a special rapporteur, Bengt Lindqvist. Similarly, Sweden has helped to craft the convention on involuntary disappearances, and was one of its first signatories in 2007. Sweden is also part of a working group developing an optional protocol to the International Convention on Economic, Social, and Cultural Rights (ICESCR) (Sweden's Ministry for Foreign Affairs 2003). Sweden actively supports the International Criminal Court, over the opposition of the United States, and encourages ratification of the ICC Statute. As chair of the United Nations General Assembly in 2005–2006, Sweden presided over the conversion of the United Nations Human Rights Commission into a Human Rights Council, and helped to push the establishment of the Peacebuilding Commission (PBC) within the U.N.

Sweden has also been an active sponsor of Security Council and Human Rights Commission/Council resolutions. Every year, Sweden introduces a resolution on the rights of the child and another opposing the death penalty in both the U.N. Human Rights Commission and the U.N. General Assembly. In a typical year, 2003, Sweden's resolutions to the U.N. Human Rights Commission included the rights of the disabled, a protest of extrajudicial executions, and a resolution condemning executions based on sexual orientation. In the Human Rights Council, Sweden has pursued its opposition to the death penalty, highlighted the situation in Darfur, and called for investigations of extrajudicial killings in Sri Lanka (UNHRC 2003).

Sweden has been notably active on gender issues, such as an annual resolution to the CEDAW treaty body protesting the reservations to the treaty. In 1996, when Sweden sat on the U.N. Security Council, it sponsored a Security Council initiative to investigate trafficking in women and peacekeeping, and Sweden also helped formulate and follow up on Resolution 1325 on Women and Peace and Security, adopted in 2000. In June 2006, Sweden adopted a national action plan on gender and peacekeeping, which includes training of personnel in international operations to increase security for women and girls, and inclusion of more women in Sweden's contributions to peace-support operations. Moreover, Sweden has spearheaded implementation of Resolution 1325 in both the European Defense and Security Policy and the OSCE (Sweden 2005/06).

Since the 1990s democratization of Eastern Europe and Sweden's 1995 accession to the European Union, regional institutions have been a growing

---

1. Several participants stated that Sweden may be slow to sign or ratify undertakings that involve new subjects, ironically because implementation is relatively automatic (like the Netherlands). Thus, Sweden has ratified Optional Protocols to CEDAW and the Convention on the Rights of the Child (familiar areas with strong domestic performance), but has been more hesitant on the ILO's Convention 169 dealing with indigenous peoples and the International Convention on the Rights of Migrant Workers.

venue for human rights foreign policy. During Sweden's 2001 presidency of the EU, the EU drafted Guidelines on Torture, a plan for antitrafficking initiatives in Southeast Asia, and issued 30 demarches protesting the death penalty in 20 countries. As a member of the Council of Europe Commission of Experts for the Development of Human Rights, Sweden has helped to reform the European Court and Commission of Human Rights. Sweden proposed Protocol 13 on abolition of the death penalty to the European Convention on Human Rights. Sweden has contributed to EU aid, including human rights conditionality and the Cotonou Agreement targeting the least developed countries. Sweden has also donated expertise, such as Swedish legal experts, in the EU's Georgia Rule of Law project (Sweden's Ministry for Foreign Affairs 2003).

Although both Swedish participants and international observers have expressed concern about the possible dilution of Sweden's strong stance as it is increasingly channeled through the EU's diverse membership, Swedish immersion in the EU coincided with a period of strengthening human rights policy by the wider body. General references to human rights in the EU have increased, with about half of human rights discussion linked to aid conditionality (Stromvik 2005). The EU has maintained ongoing human rights dialogues with China since 1997 and Iran since 2002. In addition, in 2003, the EU passed 10 human rights resolutions on individual countries. The overall EU agenda from around the mid-2000s enlargement has focused more on internal human rights monitoring within Europe than external relations. Nevertheless, Sweden has been involved in an initiative to extend the mandate of the European Monitoring Centre on Racism and Xenophobia in order to convert it into a human rights agency.

Sweden's participation in the OSCE has also provided regional opportunities for human rights activism. Sweden funds and seconds "dozens" of human rights personnel to the OSCE, especially to field offices and law projects (interview, June 7, 2004). In 2001, Swedish Ambassador Rolf Ekéus (former U.N. arms inspector) became the OSCE's high commissioner on minorities. Sweden has supported multiple police training, election monitoring, and antitrafficking projects under OSCE auspices (see chapter 9).

Sweden has been a norm promoter in the international community on several key issues: conflict prevention, smart sanctions, and HIV/AIDS. Sweden planted, diffused, hosted, and funded research, resolutions, and international bodies for conflict prevention at the global and European levels (Bjorkdahl 2002). Later, the Stockholm Initiative for Disarmament, Demobilization, and Reintegration (SIDDR) set a new trend in postconflict resolution modalities (Sweden, Government Communication 2005/06). On sanctions, Sweden hosted and sponsored a study for the Security Council to minimize the humanitarian impact: the 2003 Stockholm Report, "Making Targeted Sanctions Effective" (http://www.smartsanctions.se). This has been followed by several Swedish-funded and Swedish-hosted academic and U.N. projects to design better sanctions instruments. Sweden is described as the driving force behind the establishment of the comprehensive and rights-based U.N. umbrella body UNAIDS; Sweden will chair in 2007, and is one of the largest donors. Sweden's contributions to the AIDS response have increased dramatically in the past few years, and its contribution to UNAIDS in 2006 increased by 33%, from around $20.5 million to $ 27.5 million ("Sweden Standing Up for HIV Prevention").

INVESTING BLOOD AND TREASURE

Perhaps Sweden's most telling investment in international human rights is its willingness to put its own citizens in harm's way in the cause of peace. Since the establishment of the United Nations, more than 70,000 Swedes have participated in peacekeeping operations—and 67 have died (Swedish Institute 1956/2004). Sweden regularly contributes hundreds of millions of Swedish kroner (tens of millions of dollars) each year in voluntary peacekeeping funds, far beyond its compulsory peacekeeping assessment, and several times Sweden's required U.N. budget share. Since the 1990s, Sweden's peacekeeping role has expanded from its origins in the United Nations to include Swedish forces in NATO operations and the beginnings of an EU-based European Defense Force. Sweden recently established a special training academy for peacekeepers, named for U.N. mediator and refugee rescuer Folke Bernadotte, which includes human rights training from the Red Cross and Amnesty International. Several foreign ministry participants stressed Sweden's concern that peacekeeping occur under a multilateral mandate—but also confirmed that Sweden sees participation in peacekeeping operations as a source of credibility and "diplomatic capital" in the international system (interviews, June 2004).

Swedish personnel participate in a majority of ongoing U.N. operations (13 out of 15 one recent year), without regard to region—including Afghanistan, Georgia, and East Timor. Swedish peacekeepers served under NATO in Bosnia and Kosovo. By 2000, Sweden had a total of 911 peacekeepers and 114 civilian police serving abroad (Swedish Institute 1956/2004). In 2004, Sweden sent 240 peacekeepers to the U.N. mission in Liberia. Shortly thereafter, Sweden took over a provincial reconstruction team in northern Afghanistan. As of 2006, more than 200 Swedish police were serving abroad. Beyond Sweden's financial contribution to U.N. peacekeeping, Sweden has also provided funding for regional peacekeeping initiatives—such as SEK 3 million (about $480,000) in 2004 for the African Union's first mission in Burundi ("Sweden to Support Burundi Peace-Keeping Mission," 2004).

Similarly, in Darfur, Sweden via the EU provides the African Union force with staff officers, military observers, police, and funding. The overall numbers of Swedes in the field have fallen in recent years, along with a general

decline in the use of Western peacekeepers in U.N. operations and proliferation of regional rubrics—but like in Canada, proportionally significant
numbers of Swedish troops continue to play critical roles in difficult situations. For instance, in 2007 Sweden proposed sending 160 engineers to a
joint Norwegian force in Darfur, to jumpstart the joint UNAMID operation
slated to take over from beleaguered African Union peacekeepers.

The legacy and promise of Sweden's special role in peacekeeping is
highlighted in the first crisis of the new EU Rapid Response Force. Faced
with early warnings of genocide in a troubled region of the chronically
warring Congo in May 2003, the U.N. needed a replacement for depart-
ing Ugandan peacekeepers. Initially only France volunteered, but needed
European partners. Sweden sent 90 peacekeepers, who played an important role in blunting the assault on civilians (ISIS Europe, July 2003). In
taking on this new and challenging operation, the Swedish foreign ministry was influenced by "humanitarian goals, the desire to show support for
the U.N. (especially during the Iraq War), and Anna Lindh's personal initiative within the government" (former foreign ministry official interview,
July 2004). Subsequently, Sweden has actively promoted the European
force, volunteering an ongoing contribution, and seconding civilian experts
from SIDA, the Swedish police, courts, and prisons bureaus.

RESOURCES FOR HUMAN RIGHTS

Sweden devotes a higher proportion of its GNP to foreign aid than almost
all developed countries. Consequently, Sweden's foreign aid program is
one of the larger sources of assistance for certain areas of the developing
world—and it is among the most clearly oriented toward human rights
promotion. From 1976, Sweden maintained an exemplary 1% aid level
into the 1990s; after dropping to the U.N. recommended target of .7% in
the early 2000s, by 2005 it recouped to .94%. In 2003, this comprised a
total of 15.9 billion Swedish kroner (around $2.56 billion)—11.3 bil-
lion via the official bilateral aid agency SIDA plus a contribution of SEK
757 million to EU aid, as well as a special Eastern Europe fund of
SEK 749 million (SIDA 2003c). Around 15–20% of this total is explicitly earmarked for human rights assistance (focused on civil and political
rights), but most of Sweden's aid programs touch on the broader spectrum of interdependent economic and social human rights, and human
rights is mainstreamed throughout the policy. Sweden's overall Commitment to Development Index is an impressive 6.3, reflecting well-focused
aid and complementary trade and exchange programs.

Most aid is administered through SIDA, an independent agency that
represents a 1995 merger of five bodies that plays an unusually active role
in shaping as well as administering foreign policy alongside the foreign
ministry. Many Swedish embassies in developing countries are staffed—or
even in some cases headed—by SIDA. SIDA has a staff of 580 in Sweden,

plus around 150 abroad; in addition, about 500 Swedish NGO staff abroad are partially financed by SIDA (SIDA 2003a: 10). SIDA works with three levels of partner organizations: international NGOs such as the International Commission of Jurists), local groups in developing countries, and Swedish organizations working overseas.

Most of Sweden's aid traditionally was focused on 40 countries, with the largest single recipients Mozambique, Serbia, Cambodia, South Africa, and Vietnam (SIDA 2003a: 31). In August 2007, Swedish aid was further targeted on a small number of partner countries, notably in Africa, its European neighborhood, and postconflict reconstruction. For example, security sector reform is now concentrated in Liberia, the western Balkans, and Afghanistan. Sweden has also been a leading provider of humanitarian assistance—especially health services—to Palestinian refugees in the West Bank and Gaza, via UNRWA, other U.N. programs, international NGOs, and Swedish church organizations.

Democracy and human rights have been identified as one of six aid targets since 1978 legislation; in 1995 the government instructed SIDA to analyze, unify, and enhance bilateral democracy and human rights aid (Sevastik 1997). In 2003, a new development policy was drafted with eight components; democracy is the first, and human rights is the second. The SIDA Action Program, called Shared Responsibility, is framed by two perspectives: a rights perspective and perspective of the poor (Sweden, Government Bill 2002/03: 122). The development ideology is linked to internationalism in the following terms: "Today, everything is everybody's business....We have a shared responsibility for our world" (6–7). Furthermore, there is an explicit projection of domestic values through global action: "Life is better for everyone when no one is excluded. This is true in Sweden and it is true in the world as a whole" (7). The emphasis on human rights incorporates a low but increasing level of aid conditionality: in Zimbabwe interstate aid was cut in 2001 in response to government restrictions (but support was continued for rule of law NGOs), in India aid was cut after nuclear tests, and aid was reduced from bilateral to project agreements due to "setbacks for human rights and democracy" in Zambia, Eritrea, Ethiopia, Angola, and Nicaragua (Goransson 2002: 18).

Sweden's aid program also supports global institutions. Of SEK 119 million ($19 million) for global institutions, about one-third goes to the U.N. This aid to international institutions is not just a passive grant of resources, but rather an integrated system of involvement in global policy; Sweden sends a joint delegation from the foreign ministry and SIDA to the U.N. High Commission on Human Rights, which includes SIDA's rule of law expert.

Another progressive feature of Swedish aid is integration with private flows. Recognizing the potential undermining of aid goals by the common practice of tying grants or loans to purchases from home country contractors, by January 2002, Sweden untied its aid to LDCs. In a parallel initiative toward the private sector, Sweden also has a Partnership for Global Responsibility Initiative for its multinationals that deepens the human rights commitments outlined in the United Nations' Global Compact subscribed by hundreds of multinational corporations worldwide, with a special emphasis on avoiding child labor in the Swedish norms.

More conventional interstate human rights assistance focuses on police training, legal reform, and election assistance. SIDA funds police human rights training in Nicaragua, Rwanda, South Africa, Sri Lanka, El Salvador, and Ethiopia. About 160 Swedish police serve abroad, and Sweden sent 2 police investigators to work with South Africa's Truth Commission. There are also direct exchanges with police in the Baltic countries through the Swedish National Police Board (Sevastik 1997: 27). One program evaluation shows that Estonian police efficiency and human rights have improved as a result (SIDA 2003a: 102).

Rule of law programs are another focus area. Since 1991, Sweden has had a bilateral accord for legal reform with Vietnam—Swedish legal experts visit Vietnam, Vietnamese visit Sweden and international organizations, and SIDA supports Vietnam's National Legal Aid Agency. There are similar projects with Laos, El Salvador, Nicaragua, Ethiopia, South Africa (Sevastik 1997). These programs exhibit a synergy between interstate and NGO support. For example, rule of law programs are supplemented by Swedish support for "barefoot lawyers" paralegal assistance initiatives. In one specific case, in Ethiopia, the government plan for the rule of law project didn't include civil society organizations, so Sweden and the other donors pushed for their inclusion (interview, June 8, 2004).

Related programs increase government capacity to provide human rights to excluded citizens. In South Africa, Sweden supports an Office of the Status of Disabled Persons. Since 2001, Sweden has provided funding for Peru's Truth and Reconciliation Commission. Sweden has actively supported its signature institution, the ombudsman, in numerous developing countries.

Swedish support for elections was SEK 195 million ($31.2 million) in 1995–1999, including technical support, election monitoring, and voter education (SIDA 2003b: 19). Sweden also funds political parties in LDCs and Eastern Europe, in 2002 for SEK 35 million ($5.6 million). "Funds are disbursed in accordance with party representation in the Swedish parliament." Half of the funds go to small parties with less than 10% voter support, which may be argued to promote democratic pluralism and representation of minorities (SIDA 2003b: 17–18).

Swedish aid has the promotion of civil society as an explicit goal. Support for independent journalism includes a training program for journalists in Russia, an independent journalists' association in Belarus, and a media viability fund for independent media in Ukraine (SIDA 2003a: 100–101). Other human rights programs to foster civil society include support for Uganda's Human Rights Network since 1997, a program to increase the participation of women in the Colombian peace process, and a UNDP program for the Roma in Romania (SIDA 2003a: 28–29). This includes the promotion of civil society *in Sweden*—in 2002, SIDA provided SEK 900 million ($144 million) to Swedish NGOs, which affected 300 organizations working in 100 countries (SIDA 2003c).

Swedish aid has been its hallmark human rights policy, and a sustainable foundation for the international human rights regime. It is parallel in weight and character to the Netherlands' record (see chapter 5).

BUILDING NORMS AND NETWORKS

Another "soft power" aspect of Sweden's human rights promotion policies is civil society outreach. Like Costa Rica, Sweden has hosted numerous intergovernmental and nongovernmental conferences on both traditional and emerging human rights issues that provide education, build networks, and sometimes draft new norms. From 2000 to 2004, a series of four intergovernmental conferences on the Holocaust and genocide took place in Sweden; at the same time, the 2000 U.N. Human Rights Commission Conference of Experts took place in Stockholm. Sweden sponsored the landmark 1996 Stockholm Conference Against the Commercial Sexual Exploitation of Children, which was considered to greatly raise awareness and mobilization on this topic. In 2002, Sweden helped to promote a new issue on the regional agenda, that Sweden considers the next generation of peacekeeping and mediation efforts, through the 2002 Helsingborg EU Conference on Conflict Prevention.

Sweden also hosts several important permanent institutions for training and service in human rights. Sweden was a 1995 cofounder, funder, and host for IDEA: the International Institute for Democracy and Electoral Assistance, a 23-nation consortium that provides technical support and expertise for elections throughout the world. The chair of IDEA's board is Lena Hjelm-Wallen, Sweden's former foreign minister and former deputy prime minister. Lund University's Raoul Wallenberg Institute provides master's programs in human rights and international law for students from around the world in Sweden, as well as joint master's abroad in half a dozen countries including Costa Rica, Thailand, and South Africa. The Wallenberg Institute also hosts a major human rights library, frequent seminars, research projects, and technical cooperation in human rights evaluations. In addition, there are half a dozen treatment centers for the rehabilitation of torture victims in Sweden, serving over 1,000 refugees each year. According to an EU report,

> As the other Scandinavian countries Sweden can be seen as a best practice funding example. Through the county councils and municipalities it provides substantial and reliable funding for the seven rehabilitation centres operating in the country. In 2006 the Swedish Government gave a total of €2.329.230 to these centres. This represents an average of 46 per cent of the six Red Cross centres' yearly budget and 100 per cent of the Kris-och

Traumacentrum's annual funding. (International Rehabilitation Council for Torture Victims, 2007)

The Swedish NGO Foundation for Human Rights, an independent coalition of church groups and international humanitarian organizations partially funded by SIDA, helps to strengthen global civil society in numerous ways—like Canada's Rights and Democracy association. First, the Swedish NGO Foundation for Human Rights provides seed funding for civil society organizations in other countries, especially transitional democracies like South Africa and Latin America (with SIDA funds): currently, it assists 31 organizations in 15 countries. The Swedish Foundation also helps NGOs to address international bodies such as the U.N. Commission on Human Rights and the African Commission for Human and People's Rights. Swedish support helps civil societies in other countries prepare critical "parallel reports" to their countries' official submissions to U.N. human rights bodies, in Nigeria, Uganda, both Congos, Colombia, and Peru. Finally, the Swedish NGO Foundation enhances civic capacities by training partner organizations in lobbying, "opinion making," and legal aid in Botswana, Zimbabwe, Congo, and Uganda (Swedish NGO Foundation for Human Rights, 2001–2002).

SHELTERING VICTIMS: SWEDEN'S REFUGEE POLICY

Reception of refugees is a key area of human rights policy simply because it directly affects the life and death of large numbers of people. It is also a test of commitment to principled policy, because receiving refugees always involves some domestic financial and political costs—in contrast to international rhetorical or institutional activities. Domestic costs will be especially salient in a historically homogenous society like Sweden, where high potential resources for absorption will be weighed against the high per capita impact of diverse and needy populations in a society initially lacking pluralistic institutions or immigrant host communities. Sweden's relatively high responsiveness from World War II through the 1990s is thus impressive. Recent social resistance, declining acceptance rates, Europeanization, and a resulting reexamination of immigration policy somewhat tarnish the luster of Sweden's gold standard in this area—but even a diminished policy keeps Sweden in the top ranks of its peers for refugee reception, and contrasts favorably with the Netherlands' reversals.

From the shelter of its neutrality, Sweden engaged in several extraordinary humanitarian efforts for the victims of repression during World War II. First, in 1943, Sweden welcomed 6,000 Danish Jews who fled in fishing boats across the sound separating Sweden from its neighbor. The following year, Sweden appointed Raoul Wallenberg—a nonprofessional diplomat—to its embassy in Hungary, at the suggestion of the U.S.-based

War Refugee Board. He was granted extraordinary powers to launch a more organized rescue effort for the Jews remaining in Hungary. Prior to his arrival, the Swedish legation in Hungary had issued 700 passports to endangered Jews, and in the spring of 1944, a personal appeal by King Gustav V to Hungary's head of state temporarily halted planned massive German deportations. Wallenberg issued thousands of protective Swedish passports to Jewish victims, and sheltered around 15,000 refugees in Swedish safe houses under diplomatic protection. Wallenberg also employed 340 Jews in his department—which protected them through the war (Larrson 1986). Former Red Cross leader and future U.N. mediator Folke Bernadotte headed another bold and massive relief operation for concentration camp prisoners. Through a series of negotiations with the German authorities, Bernadotte succeeded in releasing more than 20,000 prisoners on "white buses" to Sweden. By war's end, an additional 10,000 survivors were brought to Sweden. Among these 30,000 refugees from throughout Europe (the white buses plus additional survivors, of diverse backgrounds), at least 10,000 were Jews (Persson 1998: 8–9).

Sweden's record during the Cold War was more equivocal, with some groups of Baltic refugees returned and others accepted. But by the 1970s, Sweden was accepting large numbers of displaced Kurds and Latin American exiles—about 12,000 in each case (Sweden, Ministry for Foreign Affairs 2001: 17). Overall refugee admissions during the late 1980s comprised around 146,000 (19). Of the refugees from the Yugoslav wars, around 28,000 per year arrived during the 1990s, and 135,000 remain in Sweden (21). During 1990–1999 about 245,000 asylum seekers entered Sweden; of these, 159,500 were granted residence (23). Since the 1990s, Sweden has had the highest per capita rate of asylum seekers of any country in Europe, and an increasing proportion of asylum seekers who apply after entering Sweden, rather than at the border or from their home states (interview, June 7, 2004)

Current Swedish migration policy permits admission as a refugee on several distinct grounds: the traditional international standard of a "well-founded fear of persecution" on the basis of identity or belief, Sweden's standard of "others in need of protection" from capital punishment or torture regardless of the basis of persecution, protection from a domestic or international armed conflict or environmental catastrophe, and persecution on the basis of sex or sexual orientation (Sweden, Ministry for Foreign Affairs 2001: 35).[2] In addition, persons denied refugee status on

---

2. Although a pioneer in gender-based protection and domestic gay rights, Sweden has been inconsistent in its standards for returning homosexuals to countries where they face the risk of prosecution on the basis of sexual identity. For example, on September 29, 2006, Sweden resumed deporting gays and lesbians to Iran, where they face the death penalty.

these grounds may still be granted residence in Sweden on humanitarian grounds, especially if other family members are present. Significant numbers of applicants are granted residence on this humanitarian basis and other forms of appeal beyond the initial refugee determination. Assessment is by case rather than country conditions, with the exception of Palestinians from the West Bank and Gaza Strip, who are presumed to be suffering persecution by location (resulting in a 100% increase in Palestinian asylum seekers in 2003) (interview, June 7, 2004). In addition, since 1987 Sweden's Migration Board has worked with the UNHCR to transfer and resettle several thousand "quota refugees" per year from refugee camps in conflict regions to Sweden, or sometimes a nearby country (Sweden, Ministry for Foreign Affairs 2001: 40). A recent snapshot is provided by the annual country report of an international advocacy group:

> At the end of 2002, Sweden hosted around 24,900 refugees and asylum seekers. These included about 23,600 asylum seekers with pending claims, about 1,000 refugees resettled from overseas, around 260 persons granted asylum during the year, and 18 persons granted residence on protection grounds due to persecution based on gender or sexual orientation. During the year, over 33,000 persons applied for asylum in Sweden, 40 percent more than in 2001. The largest numbers came from Yugoslavia (5,900), Iraq (5,500), Bosnia (2,900), and Russia (1,500). Some 860 asylum seekers were stateless, mostly Palestinians. The Swedish Migration Board, the initial decision-making authority, issued over 23,600 asylum decisions during the year. Of those, the board recognized around 260 persons (about 1 percent) as refugees under the Refugee Convention, while granting "residence permits on protection grounds" to about 860 persons and "residence permits on humanitarian grounds" to another 4,000 (21 percent). The board rejected any form of protection for 18,500 persons (78 percent). (U.S. Committee for Refugees 2003)

The increasing numbers of asylum seekers, growing difficulties in determining refugee status, concern with harmonization with neighboring European host countries, and social problems in absorbing immigrants eventually resulted in a parliamentary commission of inquiry and review of immigration policy. Asylum rates dropped since 2000 from 23% to 10%, so that 10,500 were admitted in 2000 but only 2,400 by 2004 ("Sweden Grants Fewer Requests for Asylum" 2004)—the report above represents a midpoint. Then, the March 2006 Aliens Act tightened Sweden's policy by strengthening the requirement to document asylum seekers' specific need for protection in Sweden (although it did widen consideration of unaccompanied minors from conflict zones). Nevertheless, Sweden has been the leading European country welcoming Iraqi refugees. "The Scandinavian country took in some 9,000 Iraqi refugees in 2006—over 40 percent of the 22,000 Iraqi refugees who found their way to Europe....Stockholm's asylum policy is the most generous in the West—Sweden accepts some 91 percent of all applications for refugee status [from Iraq]" ("Growing Iraqi Refugee Crisis" 2007).

In July 2006, Sweden appointed a special representative to deal with the growing incidence of trafficking, and has made conscientious efforts nationally and in EU coordination. Among other measures, Sweden revisited its historic liberalism regarding prostitution to criminalize only the *purchase* of sexual services to discourage trafficking and exploitation, while enhancing measures for the protection of victims. Sweden has also funded and designed specific programs for Nordic-Baltic trafficking prevention, enforcement, and repatriation. The United States State Department Trafficking Report puts Sweden in the highest tier of efforts for prevention, protection, and enforcement.

CONSTRAINTS AND CONTRADICTIONS

Sweden's human rights policies have been limited in areas in which traditional notions of national security persist: cooperation with antiterror efforts, and arms exports. Yet in both cases, the broader vision of human security has generated domestic pressure to shift policy to greater consistency with international standards. The antiterror persecutions closely mirror Canada's Maher Arar case, whereas the issue of arms exports is similar to South Africa's dilemma.

Although Sweden has criticized U.S. treatment of a Swedish citizen detained at Guantanamo and three Somali-born Swedes whose assets were frozen under suspicion of funding terrorist organizations, Sweden's own extradition of two terrorist suspects to Egypt has been condemned as *refoulement*—the return of refugees to face persecution—that violates international norms. The two asylum seekers were deported from Sweden to Egypt at the request of the United States, despite the risk that they would face torture. Swedish diplomatic officials did announce their concerns to Egyptian officials, but despite informal assurances, the men and advocacy groups report that they were mistreated once in Egyptian custody, and held incommunicado for five weeks. It was a Swedish investigative television program that revealed the rendition and torture charges, and Swedish NGOs have campaigned vigorously, both within Sweden and abroad. Back home, by the summer of 2004, the migration director stated that there were three parliamentary inquiries on his desk concerning this controversy (interview, June 7, 2004). By May 2005, the U.N. Committee Against Torture (associated with the Convention Against Torture to which Sweden is a signatory) had condemned Sweden's action in one of the cases—in which the asylum seeker remains in prison in Egypt, following an internationally appraised unfair trial in 2004. In November 2006 the United Nations Human Rights Committee (of the ICCPR) castigated Sweden's treatment of the second Egyptian, who was released without charge in Egypt in October 2003, and is currently seeking compensation and repatriation to rejoin his family from Sweden (Human Rights Watch 2007).

A more chronic issue is the structural contradiction of arms exports by a country promoting peace. Sweden is a major arms exporter for its size; in 1997–2002, Sweden was the 10th leading exporter of major conventional weapons, comprising 1.52% of world exports. Swedish arms exports employ 22,162, but many of the companies involved are not wholly Swedish owned and some produce civilian technology as well, diminishing a potential domestic interest group arms lobby. A more significant factor stems from the former deliberate policy of using arms exports to subsidize Sweden's own national defense (over $18 billion in 2003), and part of the "armed neutrality" strategy of national security (Sweden, Government Communication, 2003/2004).

Because Swedish exports were generally expensive, high-tech items rather than light weapons, and Sweden followed international arms embargoes and guidelines against neutral countries providing arms to warring states, there were relatively few cases in which Swedish arms could be implicated in human rights abuse. However, controversies developed during the 1990s regarding a small amount of Swedish exports to Indonesia. Five of Sweden's political parties objected due to events in East Timor. According to the Swedish NGO Peace and Arbitration Society, in 1998 the company involved (Bofors) preempted further criticism by canceling a planned transaction with the Indonesian government. By 1999, the EU had issued a brief arms embargo, and subsequently a regime transition occurred.

During the mid-1990s, Sweden systematized and upgraded its supervision of arms exports, reflecting broader concerns with competitiveness, proliferation, and corruption, as well as human rights—but not responding to any specific scandal or pressure. Thus, since 1996, arms exports have been vetted by an independent agency, the National Inspectorate of Strategic Products (ISP). This agency's criteria list as "absolute obstacles" to export: decisions by the U.N. Security Council, international agreements such as EU sanctions, and international law bans on exports from neutral states during war. The ISP guidelines go on to state, "The human rights criterion must always be taken into account, even in cases involving exports of equipment which in itself cannot be used to violate human rights" (Sweden, Government Communication 2003/2004: 10). In 2003, this agency issued only two denials to Swedish arms exporters, but an extensive system of prior consultation and guidance between the industry and the regulatory body suggests that most problematic requests may be eliminated before they are subject to denial (a common pattern in Northern European regulatory regimes of all sorts). Increasing Swedish military lending (versus exports) and European common arms cooperation make this policy area less traceable and more multilateral, although European regional regulation is developing alongside Swedish standards. Moreover, increased public awareness and pressure seem to have made the policy-making process more accessible in this previously opaque area of "high politics"; the arms export control agency now sponsors public seminars and states that it has "continuous dialogue with interest organizations that work in the field" (Sweden, Government Communication 2003/2004: 8).

SOURCES OF HUMAN RIGHTS PROMOTION

Why and how did Sweden come to play this role as a global Good Samaritan? Sweden's internal development and its place in the international system allowed for the possibility of foreign policy projection of domestic values. A series of influential leaders and a strong civil society enacted this agenda. In a continuous dialogue between domestic ideology and international society, national interest was reconstructed as humanitarian internationalism.

Structure and History

Sweden's role as a peace promoter began as a defensive reaction to its decline from a local power to a weak state and regional balancer by the nineteenth century. Sweden sought to "step out of the war culture of Europe" (interview, July 2004) in part because it could not prevail, and sought to concentrate less abundant resources on its own late industrialization. By the 1920s, Sweden had become a proponent of international law, like many marginal powers seeking international protection from the potential predations of neighbors. Some of these historical limitations were transformed into positive elements of internationalism. Sweden was uninterested in and largely incapable of colonialism, but established strong missionary ties to Africa that formed the initial basis of the foreign aid program. Similarly, massive migration to the United States, driven by rural poverty, eventually fostered a more transnational orientation of Swedish society (Elgstrom and Jerneck 2000, Elgstrom 2000).

> Sweden's rapid transformation from a poor and peripheral state to a prosperous model economy and society was strongly associated with neutrality....While neutrality at the turn of the century had been two rather different things—on the one hand a narrow, realist strategy of national survival, and on the other, a great vision of a totally new, pacific international order—it had by 1945 been forged into a national consensus ideology. (Malmborg 2001: 146)

Like the Netherlands, Sweden was "neutral but not isolated," militarily delinked from international conflict, yet pulled into other forms of international engagement, because Sweden's economic development was early linked to economic internationalization (Kreisler 2004). At home, strong domestic movements for labor, temperance, and religious pluralism (the free church movement) shaped a political culture and development path of social democracy. Between the 1930s and the 1950s, Sweden established its domestic welfare state; this was matched by Third World solidarity by the 1960s. "The national ideal of a welfare society was transferred to the global arena" (Elgstrom and Jerneck 2000: 189).

The Cold War shifted Sweden's stance from strict neutralism toward nonalignment, which was defined by Swedish policy makers to mean "no binding defense guarantees or alliances," despite a notable sympathy for the Western alliance. This permitted partial autonomy from the super-power, along with a resumption of Sweden's role as a balancer within the Nordic region (between Soviet-aligned Finland and NATO member Norway). Within these parameters, Sweden assumed a more active foreign policy gradually from 1950–1975, along with the international opportunities of decolonization and superpower détente, and "the for-mulation of an international ideological vision for Sweden" (Loden 1999: 38–39, Dahl 1997).

The end of bipolarity has allowed space for an even more active foreign policy, along with the partial resolution of the tensions between nonalign-ment and commitment to multilateralism, through Sweden's accession to the EU in 1995. Thus, the post–Cold War period has seen greater latitude for Swedish involvement in peacekeeping, aid conditionality, and crisis management (as well as the emerging strategy of conflict prevention). The Balkan Wars highlighted crisis spillovers and Sweden's "national interest" in rebuilding Europe, whereas the worldwide trend of democratization in the 1990s strengthened Sweden's understanding of the relationship between building rights and Sweden's long-standing interest in development (inter-view, June 8, 2004). Thus, Sweden's ambassador explains the logic of that country's current peacekeeping goals: a combination of geopolitical demands (i.e., the Balkans), next by solidarity with the EU, then by sup-port for the U.N. (for example, in Liberia; interview, September 9, 2004).

Agents of Value Promotion

Sweden's international security niche created an opportunity for interna-tional promotion of domestic values, but it required conscious political agents to shape and enact such policies. Sweden's strong human rights policy benefited from charismatic leaders, a consensual and committed political elite, and a sympathetic civil society.

In every generation since World War II, prominent Swedes in influential positions have promoted a personal vision of humanitarian global gov-ernance. Historically, leadership plays a more prominent role in Sweden than any other case. As a member of the Swedish nobility and a leader of the transnational Red Cross, Folke Bernadotte carried both ascriptive and bureaucratic charisma—which he parlayed into diplomatic influence with everyone from Nazi generals releasing prisoners to British ministers endorsing Middle East peace plans. Dag Hammarskjöld, a former min-ister in the Swedish government before his stint as U.N. secretary-gen-eral, campaigned at home to increase Swedish interest in foreign aid as he lobbied the great powers for a more active United Nations. Gunnar and Alva Myrdal, both ministers and Nobel laureates, were advocates for development cooperation by Sweden, as well as tough-minded critics of civil rights in the United States, increasing Sweden's international credibility as a neutral voice of conscience. Popular politician Olof Palme led the parliamentary working group that crafted the 1962 development cooperation bill. Then, during several terms as prime minister through the 1970s and 1980s, Palme developed the "small-state doctrine" encouraging a more accessible and democratic international system. In the current generation, Foreign Minister Anna Lindh was a strong advocate for internationalism and human security who wielded her tremendous domestic reputation to promote EU membership, peacekeeping missions, democratization, and gender equity. It is worth noting that Bernadotte, Hammarskjöld, Palme, and Lindh were all tragically assassinated, which may have enshrined public respect for their memories and extended the influence of their visions.

In a more general sense, Sweden's diplomatic personnel have several characteristics that seem conducive to the promotion of a principled foreign policy: a small, consensual political elite with democratic socialization and a strong presence of women. Foreign ministers set the major goals, with an annual address to Parliament, and subsequently produce a comprehensive annual human rights report. With a population of only nine million, Sweden's foreign ministry houses about 900 persons, who circulate heavily within posts relevant to human rights. The human rights ambassador Ulla Strom rotated to a post as deputy U.N. ambassador, the head of the migration division was human rights ambassador from 1994 to 1997, the former director of SIDA became ambassador to Kenya, and the former deputy director of SIDA was appointed ambassador to China. The culture and training of foreign ministry personnel produces a high level of consciousness; a former official reports active concern across departments dealing with multilateral bodies with "where to put our human rights energy." This is fostered by education, coordination and mainstreaming of human rights policy: the ministry's human rights representative attends a weekly meeting of the directors of departments, a 1998 government-parliament working group on democratization was created involving SIDA and the foreign ministry, and there are annual two-day courses between SIDA and the foreign ministry's global department.

Sweden's strong record of gender equity is reflected in the presence of five female foreign ministers, who have generally emphasized human rights issues—as well as an informal concentration of women in ministry posts related to peacekeeping. As one example of the influence of these trends, Foreign Minister Leila Freyvalds (2003–2006) coauthored with the female Spanish foreign minister an initiative and public campaign for gender awareness in peacekeeping operations. The gender factor in human rights promotion parallels the experience of Canada, Costa Rica, the Netherlands, and to a lesser extent South Africa.

As in all the global Good Samaritans, the foundation of human rights policy is a sympathetic and influential civil society. Although only 5% of Swedes list human rights as their main concern, periodic large demonstrations and "public opinion storms" on these issues suggest a larger latent base of public support (Goldmann 1986). Indeed, public opinion strongly favors Swedish participation in U.N. peacekeeping even if it involves danger (67%, only 16% opposed), and a similar proportion backs humanitarian intervention (Sweden, Psychological Defense Board 2003). Beyond diffuse public opinion, there are activist organizations: "Sweden is a nation of members" (Holmberg 1989). Between 3–5% in recent years describe themselves as active members of a voluntary organization, with a similar number as passive members (Sweden, Psychological Defense Board 2003). The Swedish NGO Foundation for Human Rights is comprised of the Church of Sweden (World Council of Churches), Diakonia (six independent Protestant churches), Save the Children Sweden (365,000 supporters), and the Swedish Red Cross (370,000 members). Social support for human rights policy is also enhanced by foreign policy makers: SIDA sponsors international education programs in Swedish schools, including more than 70 school trips since 2000 to project countries, and cofinances about 300 Swedish NGOs at 80%; in 2000, it contributed SEK 900 million (SIDA 2003c).

Swedish civil society influences both government policy and global governance. Swedish NGOs participate directly in the United Nations (Lindberg 1999), and the Swedish NGO Foundation for Human Rights drafts position papers for the government prior to U.N. conferences and sat in the ministry's consultative group during Sweden's presidency of the EU (interview, June 7, 2004). At a more general level, the Swedish NGO Foundation for Human Rights sponsors dozens of seminars each year that set agendas and create transnational networks on topics such as Burma, women's reproductive rights, Sharia law, and the International Criminal Court. More directly, the foundation lobbies cabinet officials, MPs, and ministries on topical human rights issues (Swedish NGO Foundation, 2001–2002). Foreign ministry officials, including the U.N. ambassador, cited strong public opinion as a factor in foreign policy, from NGOs, the general public, and political parties (via parliamentary questions to the foreign ministry). However, a former official reports much greater NGO influence in development than security sectors of the ministry (interview, July 2004).

RECONSTRUCTING NATIONAL INTEREST

In all of the like-minded humanitarian internationalist states, national interest is reconstructed as global interest through the introduction of norms that provide explanations, prescriptions, and bridges between power and principle. Human rights norms are intertwined with national democracy through a national ideology of social democracy. Sweden's normative package includes internationalism, solidarity, liberal demo-cratic values, and projection of the Swedish model.

Universalism is deeply entwined with Sweden's post–World War II national identity. As early as 1945, Gunnar Myrdal affirmed that: "We are called upon by history and our external conditions to be the advo-cate of universal interest" (Malmborg 2001: 158). A domestic standard of good governance is to be "a good example for other countries"—for example, NGO critics state that when the government finally agreed to produce a domestic human rights handbook, it was justified "not because we need it ourselves, but for other countries" (interview, June 7, 2004). As the 1977 annual foreign policy declaration averred, "We're not only Swedes but citizens of the world, whose solidarity is not allowed to end at our borders" (Ekéus/SOU 2002, section 5.4). Transgovernmental linkages and the diffusion of internationalization throughout the policy-making apparatus provide a mechanism for universalism: SIDA maintains strong ties to Canada's CIDA and other like-minded donors, whereas Swedish ministries other than the foreign office are highly internationalized, and foreign policy receives unusually high status in the parliament (Lindberg 1999; Sundelius 1989; Stenelo and Jerneck 1996).

The content of an active foreign policy is defined in terms of Sweden's values. The 1968 Riksdag defense resolution (repeated in similar terms from 1969 to 1989) states the following: "We should act outwards for international détente and a peaceful development.... contribute to a world wherein small states also will have the possibility to assert their inter-ests.... [and] defend our democratic freedoms and rights" (Ekéus/SOU 2002: 387–398). Similarly, the 1973 foreign policy declaration explains the "moral dimension of the policy of neutrality" in the following terms:

> Swedish foreign policy during the last years has become more active. This change reflects the stronger concern for the international course of events amongst the Swedish people. One has become aware of the increasing mutual dependence between all people. It is...natural that the government presents its standpoint in the big international issues, especially when these involve the small states' justified demands and the respect for fundamental human rights. Our expressions of opinion in different courses of events are only directed by our own values. (Ekéus/SOU 2002: 446)

Value projection is interwoven with "committed neutrality" (Sundelius 1989).

More specifically, Swedish policy makers seek to export a generalized social democratic model—like in other global Good Samaritan countries, this internalized value complex goes beyond the eponymous political party to constitute a national political culture believed to define "best practices" globally. Sweden's Social Democratic Party ruled from 1932 to 1976, then 1982–1991, then 1994, and in 2002 held around 40% of the parliament. But even domestic dissidents debating the details of the wel-fare state at home shared a vision of a strong foreign aid and human rights focus. Liberal and centrist governments maintained Sweden's 1% aid levels, and differed mainly on selection of partner countries (Holmberg 1989); a right-wing government in 1992 actually wanted more human rights conditionality in aid (Sevastik 1997: 22). The broader linkage between social democracy, national security, and foreign policy is described by one analyst: "The vision is formulated under influence of social democratic ideology and foreign policy tradition....According to this idea increased knowledge in the surrounding world about the Swedish model of society contributes to creating a better, and thus, securer world also for Sweden" (Loden 1999: 38–39).

Swedish policy makers explicitly tie Sweden's national security to good global governance and global human security. The 1983 foreign declaration explains: "What some states perceive as interference in internal affairs, we look upon as respect for superior international principles, which has been laid down in the U.N. Charter, in the European Security Conference's Final Act and in other international law documents. To achieve a passable international order we must criticize violations of these fundamental principles and legal rules" (Ekéus/SOU 2002: section 5.4). In a 2003 speech, Foreign Minister Anna Lindh declared, "Global security must be based on economic and social development, good governance, rule of law and respect for human rights" (Lindh 2003b). Along the same lines, Sweden's U.N. ambassador accounted for humanitarian interventions and principled initiatives in international organizations: "In the globalized world, everything will affect us in the end—so this is part of our national interest" (interview, September 9, 2004).

Finally, Sweden's international projection of human rights values feeds back to deepen domestic democracy—which ultimately strengthens the social support for human rights foreign policy described above. The Swedish NGO Foundation for Human Rights prepares parallel reports to the Swedish government's submissions to the monitoring commissions for U.N. treaty bodies that they use to pressure the Swedish government to do better in both domestic and foreign human rights policy. This currently includes the Committee on the Elimination of Discrimination against Women (CEDAW), the Economic and Social Rights Committee, the U.N. Human Rights Committee, and the Committee for the Convention against Torture (Swedish NGO Foundation, *Newsletter*; interview, June 7, 2004). In a similar dynamic, SIDA uses Sweden's National Human Rights Plan as a model in its consultation with partner organizations—but some of those consultations also reveal areas for further development in Sweden that SIDA carries back home (interview, June 7, 2004). As one specific illustration, Sweden's years of international promotion of protection for sexual minorities led to the 1999 establishment of a Swedish ombudsman against discrimination by sexual orientation.

international system (Cooper, Higgott, and Nossal 1993: 23). For Canada, this translates into an emphasis on agenda setting, institution building, intermediation, norm promotion, and governance innovation. Traditionally Canada was a "helpful fixer," mediating between the United States and Europe, East and West, and even North and South (Cooper 2004; Nossal 1983). A stalwart of the United Nations system, Canada has also participated enthusiastically in a plethora of regional and functional international institutions. Later, moving beyond established institutions with a normative agenda, Canada acted as a "catalytic state," to transcend blocked intergovernmental institutions and bilateral power relations. The beginning of this dynamic was marked by the NAFTA "boomerang" outreach to U.S. environmentalists regarding acid rain, and culminated in Canada's support to the U.S.-based transnational NGO International Coalition to Ban Landmines—including extensive support for advocacy in third countries (Waschuk in McRae and Hubert 2001). Meanwhile, like Sweden and the Netherlands, Canada has simultaneously maintained a more conventional track, consisting of varying levels of bilateral promotion, foreign aid, and civic outreach.

This chapter will document the range of outcomes of Canada's activities as a global Good Samaritan, from global institution building to transnational humanitarianism to bilateral human rights diplomacy. These domains are complemented by strong efforts in peace promotion and overseas development assistance, which provide the resources and sanctions to enforce the rules created by global institutions and diplomacy. Generally favorable refugee reception will be examined as a domestic litmus test, contrasting with some contradictions and shortfalls in human rights promotion in security-related areas. Following this assessment of Canada's record, we will explore how deep democracy shaped the content of Canada's middle-power multilateralism to build a global good citizen state. The social capital of a strong and internationalist civil society was mobilized by Liberal Party elites and associated "moral entrepreneurs" through a series of normative appeals, enduring despite some fluctuations, as a bipartisan ideology that translates global humanitarianism into long-term national interest.

ACTING GLOBALLY

Canada's multilateral human rights advocacy has helped to construct the international human rights regime, through building and acting in global human rights institutions, promoting new norms, and fostering transnational networks and flows. One indicator of Canada's commitment is a relatively high level of personnel and resources within the foreign policy apparatus; in 2005, the Human Rights Division of Foreign Affairs hosted 19 people and a C$500,000 operating budget (exclusive of salaries). Additional staff, funds, and political capital come from the human security program, the office of humanitarian affairs, and the independent development agency CIDA's block grants to multilateral human rights institutions.

As one Canadian foreign policy maker described the Canadian approach, "In a world with strong multilateral institutions, Canada does well; it's a source of comparative advantage for us beyond our military or economic clout" (interview, July 27, 2005). Canada was involved in the establishment of the United Nations, and Canadian John Humphrey was a key figure in drafting the Universal Declaration of Human Rights. Humphrey became the first director of the U.N. Centre for Human Rights, a post he held for the crucial founding generation of 1946–1966. Canada joined the United Nations Human Rights Commission in 1963 despite some initial misgivings, and Canada's U.N. ambassador Yvonne Beaulne became the Canadian representative to the commission from 1977–1984. In this role, he initiated preconference consultations with human rights NGOs, mobilized Canadian provincial legislatures to incorporate international human rights standards, and even brought a Canadian indigenous leader to the U.N. commission in 1978. As a measure of Canada's high level of activism, in 1981 Canada cosponsored a critical resolution for human rights defenders, supported the establishment of the Working Group on Enforced and Involuntary Disappearances (WGEID), and sponsored 5 of 10 country-specific resolutions (Melakopides 1998). Continuing in this vein, at the 1993 Vienna Human Rights Conference, Canada chaired the Western group. Moreover, Canada's former foreign minister Flora MacDonald was an early advocate for expansion of the U.N.'s human rights mechanisms to the establishment of a U.N. high commissioner for human rights (achieved in 1995). Canada currently provides both core and program support to the high commissioner, comprising over $3 million per year and including multiyear commitments.

In a broader sense, Canada's multilateralism has bolstered a wider set of humanitarian institutions, and enhanced the recognition of human rights within these settings. In the 1980s, the civic leadership of the Council of Canadians proposed that Canada "lead the way both financially and politically in fulfilling any responsibilities vacated by the U.S. within the U.N. family" (Government of Canada 1986). From that time forward through the post–Cold War growth of the U.N., Canada has become a major funder for the U.N. Development Program's Governance Department, UNICEF, the U.N. High Commission on Refugees, and gender equity programs in the U.N. Population Fund. In several of these agencies, Canada has sponsored initiatives that enhance the humanitarian mandate. For example, Canada funds a global database and related research on internally displaced persons, helping to expand the international regime for refugees.

Along with financial sponsorship and expertise for global institutions, Canada has provided leadership. When Canada gained a seat on the U.N. Security Council in 1999–2000, Canada's representatives used the first rotating presidency to promote the protection of civilians, via a series of presentations and reports that led the council to adopt Resolutions 1265 and 1296 on humanitarian intervention. Notable features of the process were Canada's invitations to the ICRC and UNICEF to address the Security Council, and coordination with the like-minded Dutch to follow up the Canadian-sponsored report during the Netherlands' presidency. Later in the term, Canada chaired the Angola sanctions committee directing attention to the issue of "conflict diamonds" that eventually resulted in the Kimberly Process for transnational monitoring. Canada has been a member of the Friends of United Nations Reform, and it was Canada's proposal that the new U.N. Human Rights Council be constituted with some sort of peer review mechanism. More recently, Canada helped catalyze the establishment of the U.N. Peace-building Commission. Canada has been an innovator in expanding the U.N. process to take on new issues and expand the agenda of human rights promotion in the areas of accountability, protection of civilians, and the role of civil society.

The International Criminal Court is the most significant institutional innovation for human rights in the post–Cold War period, adding permanent standing, universal jurisdiction, and individual accountability to the emerging archipelago of international human rights law. Establishment of the ICC over U.S. opposition is also a hallmark of the power of counterhegemonic normative coalitions at critical junctures. The conference establishing the ICC was headed by Canadian Philip Kirsch, who later became the first president of the court. Canada chaired the like-minded group of states campaigning for the court, responding to a 1998 appeal by veteran World Federalist Bill Pace. Canada's bilateral diplomatic campaign included Foreign Minister Axworthy lobbying his peers, sponsoring seminars, and paying for a trust fund for poor countries to attend the Rome conference (Axworthy 2003). As U.S. opposition emerged, Canada acted first as "helpful fixer"—but later as catalyzer of "soft power" persuasion to override the hegemon's wishes. Canada sent a legal team to the final 2001 New York meeting to analyze and defend the ICC's juridical framework for peacekeeping forces (the stated U.S. objection to the court), while behind the scenes Canada's representatives negotiated with the United States to stand aside if objections could not be overcome (interview, July 26, 2005). Meanwhile, Canadian Ambassador Paul Heinbecker mobilized an unusual open session of the U.N. Security Council to debate, in which 60 of the 63 participants supported Canada's interpretation over the U.S. position, laying the groundwork for the ultimate majority approval and ratification. Canada has followed up the ICC campaign with numerous assistance programs to partner countries to adopt model implementation legislation, and recently contributed $500,000 to collect evidence for the court of massacres in Sudan.

Canada's support for the protection of civilians in wartime bridged from human rights to international humanitarian law, from disarmament to human security, and intensified the transnationalization of international treaty making. In the pathbreaking 1996–1997 Ottawa Process, Canada catalyzed and hosted an innovative transnational disarmament negotiation, transcending a blocked U.N. treaty in order to limit the use of the antipersonnel explosives that maimed and killed tens of millions of civilians annually. Canada stepped in to support an NGO campaign that had been going on since 1992, and partnered with Norway to host the 1997 negotiation. Another key supporter, Japan's Prime Minister Obuchi, was persuaded to participate through conversations with Lloyd Axworthy (Axworthy 2003). After the treaty was signed by 122 states, Canada led the ratification campaign, such that the treaty came into force unusually quickly, in 1999. Canada then pledged $70 million for demining and started the Canada Landmine Foundation for ongoing support (Matthew 2004, McRae and Hubert 2001).

In similar but much more limited fashion, Canada took an active role in promoting the United Nations treaty on small arms reduction. Canada supported regional meetings before and after the 2001 U.N. Conference, pushed for NGO participation in the U.N. Conference, and funded a 1998 international NGO consultation on small arms action. In a typical year, 2005, Canada funded programs for small arms reduction or exchange in Albania (via NATO), Moldava (the OSCE), and Niger (UNDP).

Building on the new, "people-centered disarmament" and the growing demand for humanitarian intervention, often including Canadian peacekeepers, in the late 1990s Canada crafted and promoted a new international norm: the *responsibility to protect*. First, Canada provided a secretariat and funding for an International Commission on Intervention and State Sovereignty, somewhat modeled on Canadian Royal Commissions on major policy issues. This led to the 2001 report on state sovereignty that was adopted by the secretary-general of the United Nations, endorsed by the General Assembly in 2005, and adopted by the U.N. Security Council in 2006 (Resolution 1674—Protection of Civilians in Armed Conflict). In a 1999 speech to the G-8 by then-foreign minister Lloyd Axworthy rallying intervention in Kosovo, Canada argued, "In states that have failed due to the oppression of a dictator or the actions of a warlord, there must be a new test of accountability, and that new test is human security. The new norm exists—now the United Nations and other international organizations must rise to the challenge of enhancing and enforcing that norm" (McRae and Hubert 2001: 113). Although the implications of the norm are still debated, developments such as the establishment of a United Nations Office of Civilian and Humanitarian Affairs suggest that it has become a fundamental reference point for international society.

In the current era, global institutions are increasingly multilayered, ranging from universal to thematic to geographical. Lloyd Axworthy (2003: 238) remarks, "Some political analysts have commented that Canada is a regional power without a region." Thus, Canada has employed diverse, meso-level international institutions as an additional layer bridging global and bilateral policies, substituting a kind of multiregionalism for the EU venue of its Nordic and Dutch peers.

Canada "belongs" to the OAS by location, the Commonwealth and la Francophonie by origin, and the OSCE by invitation. In the key year 1991, Canada was active in each of these venues: in the OAS helping to draft the Santiago Commitment to Democracy in the hemisphere, promoting the Commonwealth's Harare Declaration, and influencing a summit to establish a human rights/democracy unit in la Francophonie. In the OSCE, since the 1990s CIDA has funded programs for regional institution capacity building focused on the OSCE High Commission on Minorities. Building the institutions, mandate, and activities of the OAS, Canada proposed and headed the OAS Unit for the Promotion of Democracy, as well as funding associated election monitoring and human rights workshops. Canada largely funded the OAS Special Mission to Haiti and headed election monitoring teams in that troubled country in 1996 as well as 2000. In 2004, Canada pressed the G-8 for a statement on violations in Sudan. Finally, Canada has established its own multilateral organization specifically to advance its normative agenda. Along with Norway, Canada cofounded the Human Security Network, a cluster of 15 like-minded humanitarian internationalist states. Canada chaired the group in 2004–2005.

ACTING TRANSNATIONALLY

The Canadian state has also founded, funded, and promoted both Canadian-based and international human rights NGOs, working in concert on specific programs and in multilateral institutions. In 1998, Canada commissioned a study to enhance NGO participation in the United Nations. At the global level, Canada has been a major funder of half a dozen key human rights NGOs, including the International Center for Transitional Justice, IDEA (the 15-nation democracy promotion consortium headquartered in Sweden), Human Rights Internet, and the Coalition to Stop Child Soldiers. In addition, several Canadian organizations have made major contributions to global human rights monitoring, education, and implementation.

The Canadian flagship organization Rights and Democracy was created in 1988 by Parliament as an autonomous, state-funded institution with a mandate to promote global human rights and advise the Canadian government, modeled somewhat on similar bodies in the Netherlands and Nordic states. Although the president is technically appointed by the Privy Council, required multipartisan approval has guaranteed the selection of "notables" with backgrounds in law, diplomacy, or high-level governance. The first president, Ed Broadbent, was an MP and long-standing leader of the New Democratic Party; the second was Warren Allmand, a former Liberal cabinet minister and solicitor general. The current president, Jean-Louis Roy, is a prominent former newspaper publisher who served for almost a decade as the head of la Francophonie. Board members are a mix of 7 Canadians (often including former ministers) plus 4 international representatives, further signaling the organization's prestige and cosmopolitan orientation.

Rights and Democracy has commanded a large budget by NGO standards of just under $5 million/year, which was *increased* 60% by the Canadian government in 2005–2006, in recognition of its success and increasing demands. Averring the body's independence, President Jean-Louis Roy reports that, "in three years, I have never received a phone call from government with pressure on any subject." But Rights and Democracy does lobby the government that pays its bills, visiting House or Senate committees about once a month on human rights issues: for example, in the summer of 2005 they presented expert testimony on the human rights dimensions of proposed security legislation, then on aid to Africa. In addition, the organization sends briefing/advocacy memos directly to the prime minister on issues such as human rights in China and indigenous affairs (interview, August 2, 2005). Rights and Democracy suggests agendas and responds to issue queries from DFAIT, especially in preparation for Canada's annual participation in the United Nations Human Rights Commission/Council. It was Rights and Democracy that drafted Canada's position on reforming that Commission to a Human Rights Council.

The organization also plays a more traditional role implementing government overseas human rights programs, drafting an action plan to coordinate the work of eight Canadian government agencies supervising elections in Burkina Faso, or hosting post–civil war meetings in the Ivory Coast to establish a system of human rights defenders and publications. Rights and Democracy works with CIDA to strengthen civil society organizations in Haiti, and helped DFAIT's Human Security Fund prepare evidence on violence against women for the ICC's Congo inquiry. Rights and Democracy also helps build international capacity, sending four Canadian jurists to assist the African Commission for Human Rights, and funding internships for residents of developing countries at the U.N. High Commission on Human Rights (Rights and Democracy Annual Report 2005–2006).

Reaching out directly to the grassroots of global civil society, the smaller Canadian Human Rights Foundation (renamed Equitas in 2006) has been providing education and training to thousands of human rights defenders around the world from the 1990s. Each year, around 130 participants from 60 countries come to Canada for a three-week human rights course centered on preparation of an action plan for human rights promotion in their home country, followed up by periodic evaluations and some regional or thematic programs. About 15% are sent by national or regional human rights institutions, but around 85% come from developing country NGOs. Current field programs include seminars in Southeast Asia on migrant workers' rights, Central Asian teacher training with women's NGOs and the U.N.'s special rapporteur on violence against women, training for Indonesia's National Human Rights Action Plan with that country's Ministry of Justice, and a Canadian government–Francophonie program to protect West African child domestic workers in 4 countries. All of these programs are largely funded by DFAIT and CIDA. Although the foundation makes the ultimate selection of students, DFAIT sometimes identifies potential participants and facilitates visas; one program officer confirmed that "some of our best friends are in government" (interview, August 2, 2005). Further support and networking exchanges come from the UNDP, UNESCO, UNHCR, Sweden's Raoul Wallenberg Institute, the Soros Foundation, the Helsinki Foundation, and the British overseas assistance agency DFID.

HUMAN RIGHTS DIPLOMACY

In the field of human rights, bilateral relations are a blend of diplomatic signaling and enforcement, which is provided by development assistance and humanitarian intervention (discussed below). As a Foreign Affairs official explained, "To make progress on human rights in a given country, you need two things: political will and capacity. So we need to work on both . . . Foreign Affairs adds will through incentives and sanctions, while CIDA builds capacity" (interview, July 25, 2005). Human rights diplomacy has been mainstreamed in Canadian policy: from the 1980s onward, every foreign service officer gets human rights training. For every country that Canada has relations with, Canada prepares annual human rights reports, which are considered in aid decisions. All exports supported by Canada's Export Development Corporation are theoretically required to be reviewed for human rights impact, and the Foreign Affairs Human Rights Division individually assesses an average of 2–3 export applications each week (interview, July 25, 2005). Although Canada has pressured and sanctioned a series of egregious violators at a level higher than some peer states, bilateral policy has varied over time and across cases, and may be fairly criticized as inconsistent (Scharfe 1996, Pratt 1988, Nossal 2005).

The use of sanctions began with condemnation of South Africa. Canada's Prime Minister Diefenbaker is credited with engineering South Africa's withdrawal from the Commonwealth in 1961 (Melakopides 1998: 65), with systematic economic limitations adopted in 1986. (Conservative) Prime Minister Mulroney defended Canada's use of sanctions against pressure from Margaret Thatcher to lift them—and finally asked his deputy Paul Heinbecker to ask opposition leader Nelson Mandela when Canada should drop its limits, following the lead of the representative of the victims of apartheid over the interests of a powerful ally (interview, July 24, 2005).

Canada's use of sanctions was widespread during the 1980s, encompassing 22 countries (Nossal 1994), but had become more selective by the 1990s. In the strong case of Indonesia, two Canadian investors (Babcock-Wilcox and Alcan-Inco) appealed to Mulroney to lift sanctions, and the prime minister again resisted interest-based pressure, instructing Heinbecker to draft a letter stating, "When they change their policies, we'll change ours" (interview, July 24, 2005). The Nigerian dictatorship garnered the stick of a 1993–1995 block on visits, arms, military training, and aid, along with the carrot of a $2.2 million Democratic Development Fund. Following the execution of dissidents, Canada cosponsored a 1995 U.N. General Assembly Resolution against Nigeria, a 1996 fact-finding mission, and sought to strengthen Commonwealth sanctions such as voluntary oil import restrictions (Black in Irwin 2001). Similarly, Canada led bilateral and multilateral sanctions against Angola during the 1990s. In 1999, Lloyd Axworthy chaired the U.N. Security Council's Angola sanctions committee, and Canada's ambassador Robert Fowler supervised two expert reports on arms and diamond smuggling, lobbied DeBeers and European diamond merchants, and eventually led the transnational Kimberley Process for monitoring the illicit export of conflict diamonds (Donaghy 2003). Finally, Canada participates strongly in multilateral sanctions programs such as U.N. limitations on exchange with Burma, and Commonwealth condemnation of Zimbabwe.

But during the 1990s, Lloyd Axworthy—the same Liberal foreign minister promoting innovative multilateral programs—systematized a policy of "principled pragmatism," eschewing trade limitations with some human rights violators in exchange for their acceptance of human rights assistance. Canada arranged such a package with Cuba in 1996, and in 1997 granted $500,000 to Indonesia for its National Human Rights Commission and NGOs. Critics point out that sanctions were focused on states with low economic ties (like Nigeria), whereas principled pragmatism was reserved for important trade partners like China, which was Canada's leading aid recipient in 1994–1995 (Smith in Irwin 2001). In 1997 Canada initiated an annual two-day bilateral human rights dialogue with China, pressed for visits by Canadian religious groups, and in 2000 set up a treaty implementation cooperation program with the University of Ottawa Human Rights Center—but then stopped sponsoring the U.N. Human Rights Commission resolution against China (Mendes and Lalonde-Roussy 2003).

In an interesting revival of the assertion of "Canadian values" over globalized interests by a Conservative leader, since 2006 Prime Minister Stephen Harper has repeatedly critiqued China on its human rights record, over the objections of Canadian business constituencies. In November of that year, Harper contended, "I think Canadians want us to promote our trade relations worldwide. . . . But I don't think Canadians want us to sell out our values, our beliefs in democracy, freedom and human rights. They don't want us to sell that out to the almighty dollar" (Mendes and Lalonde-Roussy 2003). A recent poll showed that 76% of Canadians agreed that human rights, not trade, should be the main priority in Canada's relations with China ("Human Rights Now Tops the Agenda" 2007). In a related move, Canada's secretary of state for multiculturalism invited the Dalai Lama to Canada. After heated response from China and some attempts to smooth trade relations, Harper renewed his critique in February 2007 over the case of a Canadian citizen imprisoned in China for alleged involvement in terrorism while traveling in Uzbekistan, warning China that it has "more to lose" from economic reductions, and stating, "When the rights of a Canadian citizen need to be defended, I think it is always the obligation of the government of Canada to vocally and publicly stand up for that Canadian citizen" (Sallott 2007). After Canadian Foreign Minister Peter MacKay visited in May and pressed this case, China accused Canada of "harping on human rights" (York 2007).

Although 1986 export guidelines clearly prohibit arms sales to regimes with a "persistent record of serious violations of the human rights of their citizens," during the mid-1980s Canada sold military supplies to Chile, Guatemala, Pakistan, the Philippines, South Korea, and Indonesia (Regehr in Matthews and Pratt 1998). Although controls have been tighter since the 1990s, as late as 2005 Canada was supplying military equipment to Saudi Arabia and the Philippines. Similarly, in the late 1990s Canada found itself unable to block investment by Canadian oil giant Talisman in Sudan, despite a global civil society campaign and a critical official investigation (the Harker Report). In part because Canada's legislation requires a multilateral platform for sanctions, Axworthy's exhortations to Talisman resulted only in the adoption of a voluntary code of conduct, but no bilateral sanctions (Donaghy 2003).

FUNDING RIGHTS

Canada is a significant but underperforming provider of humanitarian aid and good governance assistance at both the global and bilateral levels. Canadian policy makers envision and promote both aid and peacekeeping as protecting Canadian interests. On the positive side, Canada's $4.1 billion contribution in 2007 puts it in the top 10 donors, and the absolute total has increased each year since 2001. But Canada's ODA contribution *rate* is only fair: historically around .25% of GNP, peaking at .34% in 2005 (OECD, "Development Cooperation Report," 2006). This stands in contrast to the international benchmark of .7% proposed by the World Bank–sponsored Commission on International Development, led by Canada's own Lester Pearson in 1969. The international norm has been achieved by the Nordic states and Netherlands, although Canada's aid ratio is almost twice that of the United States. During some periods, aid has been too highly tied to Canadian providers and too focused on middle-tier potential trade partners rather than the neediest states (Pratt 1988; Keenleyside in Matthews and Pratt 1998). Although Canada has not used aid cuts and conditionality extensively, notable suspensions of assistance over human rights conditions have included dictatorial Uganda in 1973, Guatemala in 1981 at the height of that country's civil war, and Sri Lanka in 1985 over construction of a dam displacing local residents. The leading current recipients of Canadian aid are Afghanistan and Haiti, which some analysts praise as a synergistic approach to peace promotion alongside intervention, but others criticize as a security-biased diversion from pure poverty reduction (Hodgson 2006).

Although Canadian aid comprised only 3% of the global total in 2004, CIDA's budget averages over one-third for support of multilateral institutions (mostly core funding) and an additional 15–20% for governance and rule of law programs. In 1996, CIDA adopted a landmark policy, "Human Rights, Democracy, and Good Governance." A human rights policy unit provides thematic guidance, coordination and review with a staff of 5 and a budget of C$400,000 per year. Implementation is centered in the human rights and participation policy branch, comprising around 12 people (roughly the size of the China desk), and emphasizing child protection and children's rights. Canada's aid presence and human rights focus are also multiplied by coordination with like-minded donors. Numerous programs are partnered with the Nordics or Netherlands, such as a recent Canadian-Dutch initiative to fund the establishment of ombudsmen offices throughout Latin America. At a multilateral institutional level, Canada chaired the first two meetings of the OECD's Development Assistance Committee's Human Rights and Development Task Team seeking to strategize and promote rights-based development.

Specific CIDA programs provide governance support in impoverished, war-torn, or transitional states. Canada supports important legal and judicial reform programs in Ethiopia, Rwanda, Afghanistan, and Vietnam. A judicial exchange with China brought 40 Chinese judges to Canada for eight months, then 4 Canadian legal academics to China—1 participant cited the impact of the Canadian program in stopping previously routine pretrial consultations with appeals courts as they were demonstrated to violate international norms (interview, July 29, 2005). Canada has increasing placement of police and corrections officers abroad in post-conflict reconstruction, training, and funding roles, notably in Afghanistan and Haiti (around 120 Canadian police currently serve there). Although refusing to participate in the U.S. military operation in Iraq, Canada chairs the International Funders' Group for reconstruction of that country and donates around $300 million per year. Similarly, Canada has provided Sudan $14 million over two years. Multilateral programs for governance supported by Canada include the UNDP's work with the Nepal Human Rights Commission, the World Bank's Cambodia program for land administration, UNICEF's demobilization of child soldiers in Sri Lanka, and an ILO program on child labor.

Besides funding and administering multilateral and bilateral programs, Canada also sends its citizens to promote development. The long-standing CUSO volunteer program is roughly equivalent to the U.S. Peace Corps. In 1997, an additional Canada youth international internship program was established, with around 1,850 placements per year, about one-third in the area of human security (Axworthy 2003). Finally, the Canada Corps was launched in 2004, with international volunteers all focused on governance.

ENFORCING HUMAN SECURITY

Human security means individuals' right to freedom from fear, whether fear of oppression by their own state, internal or international war, failure of government protection, or humanitarian crisis. States that take human security seriously usually participate in peacekeeping, but not all peace-keepers protect civilians, and peacekeeping is not the only or always the best modality of peace promotion. Canada's promotion of human security has developed beyond border control for warring states to multifaceted programs for humanitarian intervention, conflict prevention, and postcon-flict reconstruction. In this regard, Canada contributes to the enforcement power of global governance, when human rights must be guaranteed by coercive authority. At the same time, Canadian scholars show how assuming an international peacekeeping role has bolstered Canada's domestic legitimacy, contributed to nation building, and fostered international recognition of domestic diversity (Thomsen and Hynek 2006).

One indicator of Canada's commitment to human security is the institutionalization of such functions in the foreign policy apparatus. Interventions generally involve participation by Foreign Affairs, the development agency CIDA, the Defense Ministry, often Elections Canada, and increasingly the Royal Canadian Mounted Police and Corrections Canada. Foreign Affairs has been reorganized to create a new director general for Human Security, with a START Fund (Bureau for Stabilization and Reconstruction) of $100 million per year for five years. The Humanitarian Affairs section, which has grown from three to a staff of nine, works with the geographic desks for demarches, treaties, and programs for violations that arise in conflicts and natural disasters (for example, the safety of aid workers in Afghanistan). In addition, the Peace-building unit receives about $10 million per year to works on emerging issues such as small arms reduction (Haiti), economic dimensions of conflict (the Kimberly Process), corporate social responsibility, "women, peace, and security," and children and armed conflict.

Canadian Prime Minister Lester Pearson won the 1957 Nobel Peace Prize for his role in establishing a U.N. peacekeeping force to settle the Suez Crisis. Since that time, Canadian forces have been a stalwart of U.N. peacekeeping operations, although current numbers have fallen drastically in the 2000s. By the early 1990s, there were around 4,000 Canadians in the field, comprising around 10% of the global total (Keating 2002: 164). That number has now declined dramatically, with Canada providing a mere 56 U.N. troops and military observers (outside Afghanistan, which is a NATO operation)—outnumbered by 85 Canadian police working under U.N. auspices (Valpy 2007). Although current force levels are light, some observers point to continuing influence because numerous Canadian troops beyond the core "blue helmets" work under additional command structures such as NATO, and Canada's peacekeepers in small missions are usually skilled officers providing critical training and supervision for more numerous troops from developing countries. Canada is one of 10 members that belong to the U.N. Stand-by High Readiness Brigade, a promising but rarely used new mechanism, and chaired that group in 2003.

In a situation of intense humanitarian crisis and governance failure, the U.N. presence in Haiti in 1995 was enabled by Canada sending its effective and bilingual troops—and paying its own contribution. Canada again sent around 500 troops to stabilize Haiti under U.N. auspices in 2004. In addition, there are currently 65 Canadian police officers in Haiti, both RCMP and Quebec, and the police commissioner for the mission is Canadian (Morneau 2006: 80). Peace promotion is coupled with aid; Canada is the second or third leading donor in Haiti, just after the United States and/or EU, depending on the year. Canada has contributed over $700 million to Haiti in recent decades, and has recently pledged an additional $520 million through 2011 (Canada, Standing Committee 2006: 14, 2). Small but significant governance projects include a $5 million match with Canada's Parliamentary Centre to strengthen the Haitian legislature, as well as Rights and Democracy's ongoing work strengthening civil society rights advocates. Canada's ambassador to the United Nations, John McNee, heads the Economic and Social Council's advisory group for Haiti. There are about 100,000 Haitian families living in Canada, and numerous Haitian solidarity groups, and analysts report that the Haitian intervention was strongly influenced by the concerns of Montreal's Haitian community (Keating in Irwin 2001).

A failed attempt at altruistic intervention was Canada's involvement in Zaire in 1996. At the request of the U.N. and apparent urging of the United States, Canada was asked to lead a multinational force in collapsing Zaire to defuse a refugee crisis resulting from Rwandan cross-border, postwar flows. Canada's willingness to undertake this extremely challenging mission was said to stem from a historic sense of insufficient attention to Rwanda, sparked by Canadian General Romeo Dallaire—who had presided over the U.N.'s failure to protect civilians from the genocide over his protests, and then returned to Canada publicizing the world's shame. In addition, the U.N. had designated Canada's U.S. ambassador Raymond Chrétien—the nephew of then-prime minister Jean Chrétien—as a special envoy. Canada was designated the lead in a multinational force in November and arduously assembled a 13-nation force prepared to intervene. Then, in December U.S. intelligence reported a strange dispersion of the endangered refugees before the Canadian force could act, causing the U.N. to withdraw the mandate under disputed circumstances (Axworthy 2003, Hampson 2002, McRae and Hubert 2001).

The 1999 Kosovo crisis marked Canada's promotion of human security even over its commitment to multilateralism, as Canada overcame the lack of U.N. Security Council authorization and participated actively in the NATO campaign. It is estimated that Canada provided 19% of the bombing for NATO forces. In his memoirs, Lloyd Axworthy cites reading a report on the failure in Rwanda as a factor in motivating his support for the intervention, and he played a key role in drafting the U.N. Security Council resolution ensuring that the KFOR occupation force would cooperate with the International Criminal Tribunal for the former Yugoslavia. That tribunal was headed by Canadian judge Louise Arbour, who appears to have coordinated her indictment of Milosevic with the intervention, to influence that dictator to halt his repression. Later, Canada contributed postconflict reconstruction through a demining program, exchange of 200 police, and construction of a new prison system in Kosovo.

About 2,000 Canadians currently serve in Afghanistan, up from several hundred since the 2001 U.S. invasion. Furthermore, Canada patrols the most conflictual area: Kandahar. Most of the Canadians participate in civil-military provincial reconstruction teams, with an additional presence of Corrections Canada personnel seconded to the U.N. As of June 2007, 54 Canadian soldiers and 1 diplomat had been killed in Afghanistan. As the Afghanistan mission has incurred significant casualties, Canadians have begun to debate the price of peacekeeping, including opposition party proposals in Parliament to reduce the Canadian presence and academic critiques (Byers 2006). Following a bloody attack in 2005, one commander of a provincial reconstruction team (PRT) argued for public support for the increasingly costly and interest-free mission, "We hope that Canada does that gut check and says, 'Hey, it's all about values we espouse'" (Oziewicz and Harding 2006).

In 2007, another aspect of the Afghanistan mission provoked a human rights debate: the abuse of Afghan detainees, captured by Canadian troops, by Afghan authorities. Although Canada signed an agreement in December 2005 to turn its captives over to Afghan authorities and inform the Red Cross, there were no provisions for monitoring nor specifications regarding Canada's obligations under the Geneva Conventions and its own Charter of Rights (which some Canadian courts have found applies to Canadian personnel overseas). As evidence of widespread torture and mistreatment began to emerge, including the report of the U.N. high commissioner for human rights (Canadian Louise Arbour) and at least one beaten detainee rescued by Canadian troops, Amnesty International took the Canadian government to court. There had also been allegations of some isolated but serious cases of detainees who "suffered an odd pattern of injuries in the custody of Canadian soldiers" in April 2006, which led to a Canadian military commission of inquiry. A House of Commons ethics committee held hearings, and opposition MPs vigorously questioned the defense minister. After a series of contradictory government statements about the evidence of abuse, the standing of the charter, and the role of the Red Cross, on May 3, 2007—under threat of a court injunction—the Canadian envoy to Afghanistan signed a new protocol for prisoner exchange guaranteeing Canadian officials access to detainees and pledging Afghan authorities to halt the abuse of prisoners (*Globe and Mail* 2007: February 21, March 9, April 12, April 21, April 23, April 24, and May 4).

In yet another agonizing conflict zone, Sudan, Canada has had a more limited and indirect presence. In the 2005 Darfur conflict, Canada sent $170 million in military and technical assistance to the African Union peacekeepers, as well as $28 million in humanitarian aid through the U.N., and $500,000 to the ICC. This commitment has been criticized as slow, partial, subject to Sudanese government caprice, and discreditably diminished by domestic politics. Some of the impetus for this package came from campaigning by ex-Rwanda commander, Senator Romeo Dallaire, and some from a crusading Liberal MP who had been secretary of state for Africa (David Kilgour), who was a swing vote on government budget issues but lost his clout and some elements of a stronger proposed package when he defected from the Liberal Party to become an independent. Meanwhile, Dallaire acquiesced in the more limited involvement when he was appointed as part of a team of special peace envoys (Nossal 2005). Some Canadian peacekeepers have been present in the separate long-standing conflict in Southern Sudan, where a Canadian is the deputy force commander. Meanwhile, despite declining support for Canada's intervention in Afghanistan, in 2007 two-thirds of the Canadian public wanted Canada to take a leading role in Darfur, with 52% specifically endorsing sending troops as a peacekeeping force (Whittington 2007).

Disarmament and weapons control are another aspect of Canada's peace promotion activities. There are numerous programs, such as an RCMP exchange with several Central American countries, to model legislation and technical training for the control of small arms. The most extensive program is a follow-up of the Ottawa Accord landmines ban with information, resources, and technical assistance. Canada has sponsored a 1998 global survey, funded a planning consortium for the 10 most affected countries, and coordinated monitoring by Land Mine Monitor, funding from the World Bank, expertise from Vietnam Veterans of America on mine clearance, and victim assistance from the Red Cross and Handicap International. From 2004 to 2007, Canada contributed $21 million to the Voluntary Trust Fund for Assistance in Mine Action, and is the second leading donor (after the EU).

REFUGEES

Reception of refugees represents both a substantive form of assistance to the victims of human rights violations, and a litmus test for willingness to bear domestic costs for international principle. Although Canada, like its neighbors, often failed to provide refuge to the first wave of contemporary victims of the Holocaust, since the establishment of the international human rights regime Canada has maintained a fairly strong record compared to its peers. Because Canada is a historic zone of high migration that has generally made an economic contribution, and cultural differences have historically been processed under a model of multiculturalism, receiving refugees is not as costly for Canada as it is for more homogenous or less developed countries. Refugee reception can be assessed in terms of numbers admitted, appropriate openness to disparate sending zones, fair and accountable determination procedures, and provisions for support during and following determination of asylum status.

Since the 1950s, Canada has admitted significant numbers of refugees, from zones reflecting need rather than affinity. Following Soviet repression of dissident movements in satellite states, in 1956–1957 Canada took in 38,000 Hungarians and in 1968–1969 13,000 Czechs. In response to Id Amin's expulsion of Ugandan Asians in 1972–1973, Canada admitted 5,600. During the Pinochet dictatorship, thousands of Chilean exiles were welcomed—after initial reluctance—4,500 in 1976 alone (all from Melakopides 1998: 112). During the 1970s and 1980s, Canada absorbed the victims of America's wars: from 1975 to 1980 over 60,000 Indochinese, and from 1984 to 1988 around 21,000 Central American refugees came to Canada. Overall, by 2004, Canada admitted 32,685 refugees (of a total of 235,824 migrants) (Towse 2005).

The process of refugee determination has been more complex and contested. Canada's refugee policy was not institutionalized until the passage of a new Immigration Act in 1978. As a socially concerned Liberal minister of employment and immigration from 1980 to 1983, Lloyd Axworthy established a Task Force on Refugee Issues, whereas a 1985 Supreme Court case challenging the basis of refugee denials led to more changes. Attention to international norms was strengthened, and a new body was created in 1988 to monitor the Immigration Service and represent refugee rights, although the net effect was more restrictive, and critiqued by the Canadian Council of Churches (Thompson 2005). The nonpartisan, autonomous, quasi-governmental Refugee Status Advisory Commission was initially headed by refugee advocate and Axworthy confidante Joe Stern. A mixed body of ministry and civil society representatives, the commission works closely with NGOs, unions, churches, and bar associations. As a result, through the 1990s there was a general expansion of the transparency of refugee determination, the bases of recognized persecution, and asylum seekers' opportunities for appeal and review. A 2001 Immigration and Refugee Protection Act did establish the possibility of merit reviews of denials, but by 2006 the government had not established or funded the new appeals mechanism (Amnesty International Canada 2006).

One noteworthy and pathbreaking feature of Canada's refugee policy is the recognition of gender discrimination and sexual violence as a basis of persecution. Since 1988, Canada has sponsored Women at Risk, a program establishing this important principle but reaching relatively small numbers (30–50 per year). Canada also funds a senior position at the UNHCR on this issue. In 1993, the Immigration and Refugee Board adopted guidelines regarding gender-related persecution that were replicated by Australia and New Zealand (Cooper 2004: 134–135).

On the other hand, during the current decade, general social support for migration has declined, security concerns have increased, and bilateral coordination with the United States has resulted in a shifting balance away from refugee rights. The most significant restriction has been a 2002 policy limiting asylum seekers to their country of first refuge. The Safe Third Country Agreement with the United States means that the roughly 11,000–12,000 asylum seekers per year who arrive in the United States first, due to geography, finance, or family ties, who could formerly appeal to Canada if they did not meet U.S. refugee criteria or required social support not available in the United States, will now be denied admission by Canada. Moreover, post-9/11 security standards have resulted in half a dozen contested deportations despite the risk of torture, more restrictive interpretations of international admission standards, and the issuance of indefinite "security certificates" of restricted movement and supervision for a handful of applicants deemed threatening who cannot be deported due to the threat of torture (Thompson 2005; Amnesty International Canada 2006). The security certificate system was struck down in February 2007 by Canada's Supreme Court, which directed Parliament to draft a new regime compatible with due process and Canada's Charter of Rights and Freedoms (Austen 2007).

CONSTRAINTS AND CONTRADICTIONS

Despite a generally strong record across the spectrum of human rights foreign policy, Canada does suffer from constraints and contradictions. The two main sources of insufficiency are institutional features of the foreign policy apparatus and contemporary challenges of counterterror policy.

Inconsistencies in human rights promotion are often related to generic structural features of the foreign ministry. Standard three-year rotations disrupt the cumulation of expertise and attention about critical issues and regions. At higher levels, changes in the foreign ministry and directorates may influence the priority of human rights in the basket of foreign policy goals. Interviews confirm that the standard division of interests between thematic units with a human rights mandate and more commercially focused and partner-invested geographic desks holds in Canada, not only in DFAIT but also CIDA. One of the changes specifically noted to undercut promotion was that following 9/11, some human security staff members were moved to more conventional security programs.

Canadian counterterror policies have resulted in scattered but severe violations of the rights of refugees, migrants, and even Canadian citizens. Although Canada remains a strong supporter of human rights at the international level, bilateral pressures from the United States and domestic security elites seem to exercise a pernicious influence on the maintenance of international standards and even the domestic rule of law.

In the notorious Maher Arar case, Canadian intelligence and security officials apparently collaborated, by negligence and illicitly providing erroneous intelligence to U.S. authorities, in the kidnapping/"rendition" of a Canadian Syrian national in transit in the United States back to his home country, where he was imprisoned and tortured for almost a year—and eventually released for lack of evidence. A Canadian inquest does suggest some measure of accountability for this violation, along with a $9.75 million settlement and a formal apology. But several similar cases of Canadian citizens tortured in Syria and Egypt suggest that this was not a wholly isolated violation (Krauss 2005b, Adelman 2007). In contrast to the British and Australian governments, Canada refuses to advocate for the sole Canadian citizen imprisoned at Guantanamo, Omar Khadr—the son of an Al-Qaeda member who was captured on an Afghan battlefield at the age of 15 and has now been imprisoned without trial for 5 years (Koring 2007).

At the same time, Canada maintains meaningful multilateral commitments in this area. Canada has supported the establishment of a special rapporteur on counterterror in the U.N. Human Rights Commission, funds OSCE and OAS workshops on counterterror that include safeguarding human rights, and has refused security cooperation for counterterror when there are serious questions about human rights in the host country (for example, Canada would not provide RCMP training in Uzbekistan) (interview, July 29, 2005). It can only be hoped that negative public reaction to the revelation of these cases and continuing international socialization will provide some corrective to these disturbing lapses.

SOURCES OF HUMAN RIGHTS FOREIGN POLICY

What makes a global Good Samaritan? Canada fits the profile of necessary conditions: a secure, democratic middle power, usually possessing a parliamentary system, with low social stratification and strong multilateral ties. The factors that transform this potential into a fully realized human rights policy are leadership, civil society influence on foreign policy, and the construction of a conducive ideology that motivates and guides humane internationalism.

Middle-Power Multilateralism

Canada has one of the most globalized economies and societies in the world. International trade generally comprises about two-thirds of national income. Canada has experienced high flows of immigration for several generations, and the Department of Foreign Affairs and International Trade (2007) reports that 2.7 million Canadians (of 30 million) live outside Canada. Canada has diplomatic representation in 80% of the world's 192 independent states. Canadians have numerous channels of global linkage and awareness, from very high rates of international travel to a multilingual educational system to nearly universal Internet access. As former foreign minister Bill Graham (2001: 17) put it, "Canadians are global citizens drawing on a distinct set of values and a diverse culture....It is in our interest, then, to promote cultural diversity."

Canada's structural position can best be characterized as a protected middle power, freed of the security dilemma by U.S. hegemony—at the price of perpetual junior partnership in an involuntary alliance. Martin Wight points out that middle powers are often ardent multilateralists, because they have interests in managed world order and channeling capabilities through institutions. Canadian John Holmes adumbrated Canada's multilateralist vocation before its full flowering in the post–Cold War period: "There is nothing particularly high-minded or unselfish about a strongly internationalist policy on the part of a country that so obviously cannot protect its people and its interest except in collaboration with others" (both cited in Keating 2002: 10). As Lloyd Axworthy described his own strategy two generations later, "When I came to office as Foreign Minister with a mandate to protect Canadians, I thought, 'I'd better find some friends'" (interview, February 11, 2005). At the same time, Keating reminds us that "multilateralism becomes important as a counterweight to an exclusively continentalist [U.S.-dominated] foreign policy" (Keating 2002: 12).

Consequently, as Liberal senator and children's rights advocate Landon Pearson puts it, "Canada belongs to every club that will have us, from ASEAN to the Circumpolar Conference" (interview, July 27, 2005). One policy linkage is the presence of 12 international associations in Parliament, including intergovernmental associations of the Commonwealth, la Francophonie, the Interparliamentary Union, and the EU Parliament. Canada is also linked to international human rights jurisprudence: Canadian courts refer to European Human Rights Court decisions over 40 times, even though Canada is not a member. Similarly, 14 Canadian court decisions cite the Convention against Torture, and 64 cases use the Convention on the Rights of the Child (Piper and MacKay in Mendes and Lalonde-Roussy 2003).

Another kind of influence of multilateralism on human rights policy can be seen in the constant flow of what we might call "humane transgovernmentalism" (Slaughter 2004)—meso-level policy networking among the foreign policy bureaucracies of like-minded states. One participant described this as a conscious strategy: "We have a kind of policy development by stealth; instead of going up the ranks on our own, we reach out to foreign counterparts and IGO contacts, initiate something that comes back as a success story, and then get political authorization" (interview, July 25, 2005). One specific example of this dynamic was the U.N. Resolution on the Protection of Civilians.

Canada's low level of social stratification and welfare state policies influence international promotion in a variety of ways. First, the projection of social democratic policies helps shape the content of international development assistance. Second, a relatively egalitarian society opens wider possibilities of policy innovation and representation of marginalized people who may identify with international peer groups, such as migrants and women. Generally, such a society provides a high level of education, which reinforces a strong civil society, an attentive and informed public, and a relatively higher influence of expertise versus interest groups than Canada's pluralist but stratified southern neighbor.

Agency and Leadership

Agency and advocacy for human rights foreign policy in Canada starts from the top and permeates key institutions down to the implementation level. Individual prime and foreign ministers have provided a succession of initiatives over decades, increasing the cumulation and sustainability of Canadian policy. Prime Minister Lester Pearson set the template for internationalist Liberal foreign policy when he helped resolve the 1956 Suez crisis with a U.N. peacekeeping force, and his influence is cited by succeeding generations of policy makers (Axworthy 2003). By the 1970s, Pierre Trudeau was generally considered an advocate for progressive causes, globalism, and solidarity with developing countries. Even a minister who did not share the Liberal Party affiliation, Brian Mulroney, was notably supportive of democratic struggles in South Africa and beyond during his later tenure.

Finally, Lloyd Axworthy, foreign minister from 1996 to 2000, was a dedicated policy entrepreneur who came to power with a vision of cosmopolitanism and explicit human rights promotion. Educated at Princeton by human rights legal scholar Richard Falk, Axworthy had unusual latitude vis-à-vis Prime Minister Chrétien due to his long political experience and independent power base (interview, February 11, 2005). Seeking to implant a broadened human security agenda, Axworthy explicitly drew on a vision of soft power outward (Axworthy 2003), and increased the activism of the foreign service by greater use of academic expertise. The activist foreign minister recruited around a dozen young globalist expert outsiders to the ministry, placing them in key positions with longer mandates and empowering them to start new programs that would transcend the rotational civil service.

Such domestic circulation, along with international socialization of notables, also helped to sustain human rights policy, albeit at a lower level, during periods lacking strong high level leadership. A lull in human rights promotion following the exit of Axworthy was recaptured somewhat by Foreign Minister Paul Martin—inspired by the U.N.'s 2004 High-Level Panel on Threats, Challenges and Change. Throughout the 1990s, Canadian policy entrepreneur Maurice Strong promoted U.N. conferences and in turn strengthened Canadian linkages. The U.N. commander who unsuccessfully campaigned to increase international response to the

Rwanda genocide, Canadian General Romeo Dallaire, eventually returned to Canada as a senator, a role that has served as a bully pulpit for further international promotion as well as continuing Canadian consciousness regarding the importance of humanitarian intervention.

As in Costa Rica, Canada's foreign policy professionals play an independent mid-level role in enhancing human rights promotion. Describing the overall ethos in which Canada's international civil servants understand their roles, one replied to a question about bureaucratic incentives for value promotion simply, "When you join Foreign Affairs Canada, you know you're going to do human rights" (interview, July 21, 2005). The creation and circulation of a human rights–friendly talent pool has permeated Canadian policy. Even a single individual *can* make a difference—if he or she is in the right place at the right time. One notable example of this is foreign policy advisor Paul Heinbecker. After starting his career in the like-minded Swedish Embassy during the 1960s, Heinbecker served as minister in Washington in 1985–1989, defending Canadian principled values and peace promotion against hegemonic pressures during the Reagan era. As chief foreign policy advisor to Mulroney from 1989 to 1992, he helped to hold the line on sanctions, then became assistant secretary to the cabinet for foreign policy during the next government. As assistant deputy minister for global and security affairs, Heinbecker headed the task force that determined the Kosovo intervention in 1999. Then, in 2000 he became Canadian ambassador to the United Nations, including the ICC negotiations. It was Heinbecker's personal initiative to catalyze the R2P Commission on State Sovereignty, and he picked Gareth Evans to head the body (interview, July 24, 2005).

In a similar circulation pattern, the career of Axworthy's protégé Heidi Hulan illustrates how mid-levels carry the torch. Hulan began as a peace and security advisor to Lloyd Axworthy—for example, she wrote Axworthy's last speech to the U.N. General Assembly in 2000. Throughout the 1990s, she was assigned to various task forces on crises and interventions in Zaire, Iraq (1998), Kosovo, Sierra Leone, and Burundi. In 1999–2000, Hulan worked with Heinbecker when he was U.N. ambassador, launching particular promotion efforts when Canada chaired the Security Council. Back in Canada, she worked with fellow globalists Don Hubert and Rob Macrae to include "responsibility to protect" language in the International Policy Statement. In 2005, she transferred to Canada's U.N. mission in New York (interview, July 26, 2005).

Canada's version of the parliamentary system provides one additional source of human rights leadership and accountability. As in the Netherlands and Nordic states, Canada's Parliament provides tight monitoring of foreign policy through a daily question period for ministers. But Canada also hosts U.S.-style committee hearings on salient issues, with active human rights committees in both House and Senate that have held hearings on issues from trade with China to the social responsibility of Canadian mining companies. Government must respond to House reports within 150 days; for example, a critical report on Colombia's human rights led to changes in CIDA's aid program in that country (interview, July 27, 2005). The Canadian Parliament is also seen as an important source of socialization on international issues for key government figures: former foreign minister Bill Graham chaired the Standing Committee on International Relations for seven years, whereas Development Minister Eileen Carroll also served on this committee.

Canadian senators play a special role as "policy entrepreneurs" rather than party representatives, and the appointed Senate is traditionally composed of around one-third socially active notables (although it also hosts many political appointees). Thus, Senator Landon Pearson had been a children's rights advocate for decades, and a foreign ministry advisor on children since 1976, when the prime minister appointed her "to represent children's issues" (interview, July 27, 2005). Senators have independent budgets of around $100,000 for research and issue promotion, and can commission reports and call hearings. Other senators active on human rights issues include Romeo Dallaire, former U.N. commander in Rwanda; Rarell Andreychuk, Canada's former representative to the U.N. Human Rights Commission; Mobina Jaffar, who was appointed Special Envoy on Women, Peace, and Security; and Sharon Carstairs.

Civil Society

Canada's civil society is a "best case" for human rights promotion; it is dense, internationalist, and well connected to channels of influence on foreign policy. The presence of advocacy NGOs may be considered a necessary condition for the emergence of a human rights foreign policy, whereas receptive public opinion and political parties facilitate its implementation and tip the balance in assessing trade-offs. Beyond these generic characteristics, Canada's historical configuration grants space to several sectors with an affinity for humanitarian ties.

Canada's NGOs are plentiful, rights-oriented, globalist, and linked to the foreign policy apparatus. The Canadian Bar Association sponsors numerous overseas missions, and works closely with the International Bar Association and the International Commission of Jurists. Former minister of justice Irwin Cotler (who represented Andrei Sakharov and Nelson Mandela as an international human rights lawyer) has been active in this professional NGO, as has Canadian U.N. High Commissioner for Human Rights Louise Arbour (formerly of the International Criminal Tribunal for the Former Yugoslavia). Another nexus between human rights academics and government is the Human Rights Centre at the University of Ottawa, which was very active in creating networks for U.N. conferences during the 1990s (Cooper 2004), and has organized human rights dialogues with China.

The relationship is mutual, as Foreign Affairs sponsors an annual preparatory meeting for NGOs prior to the meeting of the U.N. Human

Rights Commission that draws around 250 people for three days. Foreign Affairs officials state that this meeting not only provides information,
but shifts their agenda—for example, three to four Canadian NGOs suggested to Foreign Affairs a strategy and language to promote sexual orientation rights at the United Nations (interview, July 25, 2005). Foreign
Affairs also regularly includes NGOs in international delegations, both
at the United Nations and even in bilateral settings such as the China
Dialogue. Staff circulation is another mode of influence, especially at the
CIDA development agency, where staff members often come from NGO
backgrounds and maintain ties to development advocacy or implementation groups. At higher levels, there are cases of humanitarian circulation,
such as former minister of defense David Pratt, who now serves as head
of the Canadian Red Cross.

Although there is no systematic influence of religious groups on politics in Canada, the liberal Protestant United Church (Canada's largest
denomination, with around three million congregants) may contribute
in several ways to humane internationalism. The UCC founded, peopled,
and contributed financially to some development watch groups (Pratt
1988), as well as the Inter-Church Committee on Refugees. The social
gospel of the UCC has inspired various forms of humanitarian international exchange; Lloyd Axworthy cites the influence of church-sponsored
delegations to Central America on his views as an MP, and his policies
beyond. More specifically, he describes how he debated the ethics of
the Kosovo intervention as a "just war" with his United Church minister
(Axworthy 2003).

Conversely, traditional interest groups such as business and arms man-
ufacturers play a relatively weak role in determining Canadian foreign
policy. Rather than lobbying their government, Canadian small arms man-
ufacturers went with the Canadian delegation to a U.N. meeting on arms
limitation. The Canadian company most implicated in overseas human
rights violations, Talisman oil in Sudan, was unable to push Canadian government policy—instead, Foreign Affairs was able to push the company,
albeit to a limited extent (interview, July 24, 2005).

The general climate of Canadian public opinion serves as an inspiration
and guide for policy makers to prioritize humane internationalism. Polls
consistently show support for "assertive internationalism and core Canadian values of democracy, peacekeeping, and human rights" (Irwin 2001:
5; also see Howard-Hassmann 2003). Foreign Affairs has conducted focus
groups around new programs such as the land mines initiative, which generally show wide support for humanitarian outreach. It can also tip the
balance in times of crisis. A policy advisor cited the role of politicians' perception of public opinion in bolstering Canadian intervention in Kosovo,
pointing to an opinion poll conducted at the height of media attention to
"ethnic cleansing" that showed Canadians' humanitarian allegiances overcame the lack of historically valued multilateral validation. The current
DFAIT Web site takes credit for serving Canadians by promoting human

rights, citing a 2005 University of Ottawa poll that says that 87% of Canadians see their country as a human rights promoter (http://www.tbs-sct. gc.ca/rpp/0708/fait-aeci/fait-aeci01_e.asp). In 2002, Canada was the only one of 44 developed countries surveyed in which a strong majority (77%) said that immigrants were a *positive* influence (Adams 2003: 66–67).

Thus, it is not surprising that the historically dominant Liberal Party is generally receptive to humane internationalism, by conviction and electoral incentive. Liberals define their own ideology as somewhat akin to "new" social democrats—one longtime party figure defined his group as "socialists who aren't in a hurry." But beyond their beliefs, as a practical matter, because the Liberals have usually comprised around 40% of Parliament, they have generally sought coalitions or to capture the constituency of the more traditionally leftist New Democratic Party, which controls as much as 20% of the vote. This has been especially important in the prairie states with a legacy of progressive populism, such as Lloyd Axworthy's electoral base in Winnipeg. Since Liberal governments began to enact fiscally conservative policies in the 1990s, Canadian analysts contend that international value promotion has provided a way to balance the party's appeal to the left side of their electorate (as in South Africa's "talk left, walk right" strategy detailed below).

The other major party, the Conservatives, have usually ruled in minority governments. Their ideology of limited government is fully compatible with the promotion of individual civil and political rights, they share the overall Canadian emphasis on rule of law, and their closer embrace of U.S positions tends to emphasize the democracy promotion agenda as a balance to compatriots' accusation of subservience to savage capitalism. Moreover, even if Canada's Conservatives eschew specific Liberal notions like "human security," minority Conservatives also have electoral and governability incentives to appeal to Liberal and Quebec minority parties on internationalist values via some of the relatively popular and low-cost humanitarian policies. Conservative Stephen Harper's electoral campaign included a pledge to *increase* foreign aid—an invisible issue or unthinkable position for the budget-cutting aspiring national leader of most developed democracies. Similarly, Harper used a summer 2007 trip to Latin America to push a philosophically liberal agenda of freer trade *and* rule of law.

Canada's historical multiculturalism and social equity empower at least three groups that tend to reach out transnationally to protect disadvantaged peers: women, migrants, and Francophones. As in the other social democratic states of Sweden, the Netherlands, and Costa Rica, welfare state policies and egalitarian commitments have produced relatively high participation of women in foreign policy making. Women in Canada have played notable roles as senators, ministers of development, and currently comprise four Supreme Court justices. Women have elected and been promoted for participation in rights-relevant international posts; as one CIDA official averred, "We put women front and center in all the human rights machinery." Canada's mobilized women, domestic expertise, and interest translated into international leadership on issues of gender equity. For example, Maureen O'Nell, the director of the federal Status of Women Canada bureau, became the head of the western group and a key player in the United Nations' Nairobi conference on women. In 1988, a Canadian woman became the Director of UNIFEM (Cooper, Higgott, and Nossal 1993: 161). Louise Fréchette, Canada's former U.N. ambassador and deputy minister of defense, became the deputy secretary-general of the United Nations. Canada's former Supreme Court justice Louise Arbour is currently the United Nations' high commissioner for human rights.

One in five Canadians was born abroad, and this fact is noted prominently by the Department of Foreign Affairs and International Trade in its policy plan (2007). Migrants have played a role in advocating for the rights of their diasporic peers, as well as generally favoring development assistance and human security programs in sending regions. Lloyd Axworthy reports being lobbied as foreign minister by groups such as the East Timorese, Tamils, Sikhs, Palestinians, Somalis, and Armenians (Axworthy 2003; interview, February 11, 2005). Haitians and Sri Lankans from conflict-ridden states have been especially attentive to Canadian aid and peace promotion programs. Axworthy's staff established an outreach program on land mines, and found that this form of protection of civilians resonated strongly with "new Canadians" and put a human face on disarmament (interview, July 20, 2005). In a similar vein, a participant in the OSCE minorities program reports that that multilateral involvement was "pushed by Canadian migrants" (interview, July 27, 2005).

Finally, the French connection has bolstered Canada's humane internationalism. At the most general level, multicultural compromise is mentioned frequently by policy makers as an important root of Canada's international role as a bridge builder. This has strengthened Canadian involvement in the international promotion of cultural rights and cultural conflict resolution: the UNESCO Diversity Convention, Sri Lankan peace negotiations, and programs for the Kurds in Northern Iraq. The political profile of Francophones is even more social democratic and postmodern than the Canadian liberal norm, as affirmed in public opinion and political values surveys (Adams 2003). Quebec even has its own Ministry of International Relations. Again, this strengthens electoral incentives for humane internationalism; Lloyd Axworthy cites a Quebecois staffer urging him to prioritize human security issues as an appeal to the Francophone constituency's internationalism. Among other measures, this led to the establishment of a French branch of the Pearson Peacekeeping Centre in Montreal (Axworthy 2003). Through linguistic affinities, Francophones have been especially attentive to the troubled regions of Haiti and West Africa—and bilingualism has given Canadian interveners a comparative advantage there. CIDA originated as a Francophone agency, and is located on the Quebec side of Ottawa. Key programs are led by Francophones: the current president of Rights and Democracy, Jean-Louis Roy, was head of La Francophonie in 1989–1998, presiding over an increase of half the budget to human rights issues (interview, August 2, 2005).

THINKING GLOBALLY

Canada's commitment to humane internationalism has been articulated by policy makers and civil society as an expression of Canadian values that enables an enlightened form of national interest as global good governance. Liberal theoretician Michael Ignatieff has written that Canadian foreign policy should be guided by a projection of Canada's national slogan "peace, order, and good government" (Ignatieff 2004).

Lloyd Axworthy made the link between humane internationalism and national interest, labeling human security as "the New Testament of security"—a necessary recognition of interdependence in a globalized world (Axworthy 2003). Long-standing components of Canadian political culture and identity have directed its human rights focus, with the newer human security ideology expanding and institutionalizing the pursuit of global interest.

The most salient internal element of Canadian political culture for human rights foreign policy is Canada's identity as a rule of law society. The origins of this identity lie in Canada's history as "British North America," loyal to the Commonwealth but also the first colony to gain "responsible government." This underlies the difference between the Canadian focus on democracy as rule of law from the U.S. emphasis on democracy as freedom, with consequences for the domestic welfare state and foreign policy projection.

> What then is distinctive about the Canadian political tradition is the idea that the state creates the nation, that government action is a precondition both for economic development and the creation of a political community. At the same time as we believe in government we are a free enterprise country. Social democracy has had a huge influence on our politics and so has the history of free trade unionism, but we have never been socialist. (Ignatieff 2004)

The 1982 Canadian Charter of Rights and Freedoms, which was referenced by every policy maker interviewed and posted on the wall of many government offices, reinforces the notion of rights as norms. Louise Arbour, Canada's chief prosecutor for the ICTY and later U.N. high commissioner for human rights, stated, "I believe that the contribution that Canada has made on the international scene, particularly in the past decade, reflects our new identity, born of charter awareness, about the universality of rights and the imperative of enforcing those rights" (Arbour 2002: 1). A more strategic policy maker consciously recognized the projection of this fundamental Canadian value complex as the comparative advantage of a middle power, concluding, "We talk about the rule of law because we don't have aircraft carriers" (interview, July 20, 2005).

Most of the Canadian public, some policy makers, and most civil society organizations advocating for humane internationalism *believe* that Canada has a unique identity as a moral superpower—even if this is operationalized inconsistently, the belief motivates and legitimates policy initiatives. One Foreign Affairs official summarized this animating vocation, found throughout government discourse and documents: "Canada has something to bring to the world" (interview, July 23, 2005). The slogan of CIDA is "Canadians making a difference." Lloyd Axworthy (2003: 6) positions Canada as the "value-added nation" in the international system, and the phrase is a constant refrain in DFAIT. More specifically, a Canadian security official considering trade-offs between security and values asserted that "part of being Canadian is to feel obligated to defend human rights" (interview, July 29, 2005).

Like all identities, this discourse is relational—it does the important work of differentiating Canadians from their culturally similar but richer and more powerful neighbors. In a previous era, Canadian historian J. L. Granatstein called anti-Americanism Canada's state religion (Keating 2001). In a more constructive update for an era of globalization, Lloyd Axworthy affirms in his 2003 political autobiography: "The values we express internationally help define who we are when other distinctions are being erased" (p. 1), continuing "We are not Americans. We have our own destiny to fulfill…to march to the beat of our own international drummer" (p. 34). This has strategic and substantive implications for foreign policy. A foreign policy official articulated Canada's global strategy of expertise and norm innovation, "We have to be smarter than the U.S., to protect Canadian values" (interview, July 20, 2005). Substantively, a survey of Canadian civic leaders reports that, "Not being Americans—having better qualities than Americans, being accepted in Europe more readily than Americans—was important to them.…Canadians are characterized by moderation, compromise, and tolerance.…[One summarized,] 'We get involved in world affairs in a good sense, in a peacekeeping sense'" (Howard-Hassman 2003: 37–40).

The human security concept builds on these elements to broaden the linkages between governance and development gaps in failed states and humanitarian crises and Canadian interests. The International Policy Statement explicitly links the threat of terrorism to failed states, and Lloyd Axworthy (2003: 41) projects global "freedom from want" with the Canadian welfare state experience of public health and education as the basis for social development and democracy. The notion of human security in Canada was conceived by foreign policy professionals to get beyond the limits of human rights, in a turn to international humanitarian law over human rights law, and peace enforcement over norms. As one put it bluntly, "When I am in the middle of a genocide, I don't want to talk to a Special Rapporteur—I want to talk to a military force that can stop it" (interview, July 27, 2005). The Kosovo intervention was the first test of such ideas in a contested situation, and a participant in the 1999 Cabinet debate on intervening in Kosovo without U.N. Security Council authorization recounts that the humanitarian argument trumped the strategic (interview, July 26, 2005). In a similar kind of linkage, Canada's commercial interest as the world's third leading producer of diamonds was harnessed to global humanitarian stability through the Kimberly Process for monitoring the trade in conflict diamonds (interview, July 26, 2005). A national security policy maker tasked with threat analysis describes how the human security vision makes a difference in assessing national interest; in order to strategize threats to Canada, this security office looks for linkages (countries with Canadian investments and tourists), then "countries where we can make a difference," then prevention of terrorism through long-term conflict resolution and good governance (interview, July 29, 2005).

CONCLUSION

We have seen that Canada's humane internationalist potential as a deeply democratic and highly globalized middle power was activated by progressive elites and a supportive civil society, animated by cosmopolitan values and a benign form of liberal nationalism. Canada's international projection has strengthened democracy at home and abroad, and contributed to the construction of the international human rights regime.

Canada's human rights foreign policy has deepened democracy at home by tightening linkages to the international human rights regime, and by stimulating the growth of civil society. Already by 1978, Canada's secretary of state indicated that international involvement had stimulated Canadian human rights legislation and agencies at the federal and provincial levels (Nolan in Matthews and Pratt 1998: 110). In a specific case, in 1985 Canada responded to questions in the U.N. regarding military exports to the Chilean dictatorship with a modification in its Export-Import Control Act (Matthews and Pratt 1998). Canada undergoes regular review by the full range of U.N. human rights monitoring bodies, and has signed the Optional Protocols to the ICCPR and the Convention against Torture. A strong area of domestic policy—children's rights—has become a specialty of international projection, and in turn, the Canadian Action Plan for Children references the Convention on the Rights of Children in both norms and implementation.

Human rights promotion by a strong civil society creates a feedback loop in which state actors seek out and enhance civic partners in policy making. DFAIT helped to establish a national Working Group on Women, Peace and Security to support their agenda building on this issue, drawing on and strengthening the position of Canadian women's organizations. Foreign Affairs also organized a series of cross-Canada consultations before major U.N. conferences, like the Cairo Plus Five population meeting. Canada's International Policy Statement (2005) pledges to "engage Canadian diasporas," to "seek regular input from Canadian NGOs, labour unions, business groups, academics, and professional bodies," and specifically names the aid advocacy group International Development Resource Center, the Forum of Federations, and Rights and Democracy.

The study of Canada's principled foreign policy supports a constructivist interpretation of international relations, in which the meaning and interpretation of social conditions filter actors' perceptions of their interests. Global Good Samaritanship is in some sense a form of cosmopolitan identity politics, giving participants orienting roles and ideological maps in the international system. Canada also needs the world, to establish its niche as a moral superpower.

Although Canada's human rights policies are well institutionalized, and the international human rights regime and human security agenda are growing, they are not immune from challenges. Worldwide trends of declining civic activism, increasing preoccupation with conventional security in the face of terrorism, and defensiveness vis-à-vis migration are shared by Canada, with the potential to diminish Canada's humane internationalism. More specifically, the loss of Liberal Party hegemony, the growing human toll of peacekeeping, and stagnation in key United Nations bodies may cause Canadians to question and rethink established modes of humanitarianism. Nevertheless, Canada's international reputation and growing coordination with like-minded states across a variety of settings should maintain Canada's core agenda of promoting "peace, order, and good government."

5

The Little Country That Could

Costa Rica

Human rights is our national interest.
—Costa Rican foreign ministry
official, June 2003

Costa Rica provides an interesting case study of good global citizenship, because it lacks the resources or security of a Sweden or Canada. Although Costa Rica's human rights promotion clearly represents a projection of domestic democracy, this principled peripheral state has pursued human rights at the cost of antagonizing neighboring countries and sometimes contradicting the policies of the U.S. hegemon. The reconstruction of national interest through civil society, international norms, and leadership initiatives has expanded Costa Rica's marginal structural opportunity to create an international niche as a global Good Samaritan. The power of such socialization is clear when Costa Rican foreign ministry officials from a span of administrations spontaneously aver that human rights is "a part of our national identity" (interviews, June 2003). Yet Costa Rican policy makers spoke of human rights promotion pragmatically as a source of "moral power," "comparative advantage," and "long-term security" in the international system. As one put it, "The promotion of peace in Central America, environmental conservation, human rights, and democracy all make the world a better place—and that makes the world better *for Costa Rica*" (interviews, June 2, 2003).

COSTA RICA: "THE LITTLE COUNTRY THAT COULD"

Our foreign policy is like the bumblebee—it's really too heavy to fly, but the bee doesn't know this, so it just keeps moving its wings and stays in the air anyway.
—Ambassador Rodrigo Carreras, former vice minister of
foreign affairs

Costa Rica has an enduring, multifaceted, and meaningful record of international promotion of human rights. Costa Rica's contribution is sustained—it can be assessed over numerous administrations of varied political coloration. Human rights policy has been pursued in a broad array of multilateral, regional, bilateral, and transnational settings. And Costa Rica has made a meaningful contribution to globally significant initiatives.

Multilateral Promotion

Costa Rica's influence in multilateral institutions has helped to frame and ratify treaties, create and staff institutions, monitor and sanction offenders, and introduce new understandings of rights to the global agenda. A recent foreign minister (Ricardo Rojas, 1998–2002) summarized Costa Rica's role: "The policy of promotion and respect for human rights and democracy is not only internal but has become the active, constant, and priority goal of Costa Rica's foreign policy in the major international organizations" (Costa Rica, *Memoria Annual* 2001–2002: 6).

At the United Nations, Costa Rica has played a part in virtually every major human rights initiative and institution—vastly disproportionate to its size, wealth, and power. Costa Rica was an early and active advocate of global institutions, and a founder of the international human rights regime. Costa Rica served as the cochair of the London preparatory conference for the San Francisco meeting that established the United Nations itself. Costa Rica's first ambassador to the U.N., Fernando Soto Harrison, was vice president of the founding Human Rights Commission (Soto Harrison often presided, because the official chair was also the prime minister of New Zealand and thus distracted by national responsibilities). Soto Harrison, who had been involved in the establishment of Costa Rica's Supreme Electoral Tribunal—a pathbreaking domestic democratic institution—worked closely with Eleanor Roosevelt in drafting core procedures and documents of the human rights regime. Costa Rica's Soto Harrison recalls that small countries were assigned to the seemingly insignificant Third Committee, but determined to use the emerging institution as a platform for a broader global vision (interview, June 5, 2003). Costa Rica also sought to block Franco Spain's membership in the U.N. on principled grounds throughout the 1950s, despite common cultural ties and regional ambivalence (Rhenán Segura 1999).

Costa Rica has been an institution builder and stalwart of the key committees. Costa Rica was a founder of the United Nations Children's Fund, and the first country to sign the 1966 International Covenant on Civil and Political Rights and the Covenant on Economic and Social Rights. The same year, Costa Rica's long-standing diplomatic advocate for human rights, Fernando Volio Jiménez, became president of the U.N. Human Rights Commission. Costa Rica consistently sought election to this body, and held a seat in 1964–1967, 1975–1977, 1980–1988, 1992–1994, and 2001—an unusual span for a single small country (Rojas 2001; Vargas Garcia 2001). Although Costa Rica's own activities and positions within the commission followed a consistent and positive line (see below), it would occasionally support the membership of human rights violators on the commission—as in 2005, when Costa Rica supported the ascension of Cuba in February, while voting to condemn Cuba's human rights record in April. During one of the "lulls" in commission membership, 1988–1990, two Costa Ricans (Luis Varela and Jorge Rhenán Segura) headed the U.N. Human Rights Sub-Commission for the Prevention of Discrimination and Protection of Minorities—keeping a hand in this priority policy area. In May 2007, Costa Rica was elected to the Executive Committee of the U.N. High Commission on Refugees (UNHCR/ACNUR 2007).

Perhaps most significant, Costa Rica helped create the U.N. high commissioner for human rights (established in 1995). The establishment of a high commissioner was based on an initial proposal introduced by the indefatigable Fernando Volio Jiménez in 1965 and renewed at periodic intervals. Costa Rica's campaign for the new institution resumed in 1980, but gained critical mass in 1993, when Costa Rica hosted the Latin American regional preparatory conference for the Vienna Human Rights Conference. Then-foreign minister Bernd Niehaus, U.N. veteran and minister of justice Elizabeth Odio, and former human rights commission representative Jorge Rhenán Segura exercised multiple levels of diplomacy—and Costa Rica's influence was magnified when it was designated vice-president of the Latin American regional caucus at the Vienna Conference itself.

As far as activities within these bodies, Costa Rica has been an active proponent of resolutions and treaties, and has a solid voting record on human rights measures. As a measure of activity level, in 2000 alone, Costa Rica cosponsored 34 thematic and country-specific human rights resolutions in the General Assembly and voted for 70, while cosponsoring an additional 45 measures in the Human Rights Commission (Costa Rica, *Memoria Anual, 1999–2000*). In 1994, Rhénan Segura proposed a Decade for Human Rights Education in the U.N. Human Rights Commission (1995–2005), which was inaugurated with a San José workshop (Vargas Garcia 2001). In 2005, in the Third Committee of the General Assembly, Costa Rica submitted draft resolutions on the following: rights of people with disabilities, strengthening the United Nations Crime Prevention and Criminal Justice Programme, violence against women, improvement of the situation of women in rural areas, rights of the child, indigenous people, torture, International Covenants on Human Rights, protection of human rights and fundamental freedoms while countering terrorism, human rights in the administration of justice, Declaration on the Right and Responsibility of Individuals, Groups and Organs of Society to Promote and Protect Universally Recognized Human Rights and Fundamental Freedoms, human rights mainstreaming in the U.N. system, the right to food, and the protection of and assistance to internally displaced persons (United Nations General Assembly 2005).

Costa Rica has played a key role in proposing, drafting, and lobbying for the treaties that sit at the pinnacle of international human rights law. Costa Rica's campaign for the Optional Protocol to the Convention against Torture, which was adopted by the U.N. in December 2002, attests to the significance of the country's multilateral initiatives. As Costa Rica's minister of justice, Elizabeth Odio Benitez pushed for the establishment of a working group to draft an optional protocol—a body she was designated to head once it was established a decade later. After consulting with the International Commission of Jurists and sympathetic European ambassadors in Geneva, Costa Rica presented the proposal—mandating periodic inspection visits to detention facilities—to the U.N. Human Rights Commission. Costa Rica then lobbied its hemispheric neighbors through the regional U.N. grouping of Latin American and Caribbean states (GRULAC), and sent diplomatic notes to the embassies of its fellow members of the Human Rights Commission. Costa Rica maintained leadership of the working group for most of the 1990s: Jorge Rhenán Segura chaired in 1992–1994, Carlos Vargas Pizarro in 1995–1998, and in 1999 leadership returned to Elizabeth Odio Benitez (Vargas Garcia 2001). Costa Rica is widely recognized as the leading state in this successful campaign for a key measure enhancing the protection of fundamental human dignity.

In other measures of special regional salience, Costa Rica was again a key player. Costa Rica was a strong supporter and active negotiator of the International Convention for the Protection of all Persons from Enforced Disappearance, and was one of the original signatories in February 2007 (United Nations Human Rights Council 2006). Similarly, Costa Rica actively promulgated treaties on disability rights at the global and regional levels (see below). The Convention on the Rights of Persons with Disabilities was adopted on December 13, 2006 during the 61st session of the General Assembly by resolution A/RES/61/106. The convention and its optional protocol opened for signature in March 2007. Costa Rica signed both. Costa Rica has been a cosponsor of the U.N. Declaration on the Rights of Indigenous Peoples, approved after a decade of debate on September 13, 2007.

From the 1990s onward, Costa Rica has also been active on emerging human rights concerns and agenda expansion at the U.N. In 1995, Costa Rica proposed expanding the membership of the Committee on the Rights of the Child (Ministerio de Relaciones Exteriores 2001). In 1999, Gabriela Rodriguez Pizarro from Costa Rica was appointed special rapporteur for migrants by the Human Rights Commission.[1] Costa Rica played a particularly active role in the U.N.'s Durban Conference on Racism, partially

---

1. Gabriela Rodriguez Pizarro serves as an "independent expert," not an instructed representative of the Costa Rican government; she is a Chilean exile who settled in Costa Rica as a refugee during the 1970s. However, Rodriguez Pizarro is tied to Costa Rican civil society and foreign policy networks: she runs an NGO with rural development and microcredit projects for Nicaraguans in Costa Rica, cofounded by Costa Rican jurist Elizabeth Odio.

inspired by the leadership of Vice Minister Elayne Whyte—Costa Rica's first Afro-Latina foreign ministry official.[2] Costa Rica has been an active proponent of new multilateral mechanisms linked to broad understandings of human rights, including the International Criminal Court, Land Mines Treaty, attempts to limit small arms, and campaigns against child soldiers.

Between terms in office, Oscar Arias worked with a network of 17 other Nobel laureates to draft and promote the Nobel Peace Laureates' International Code of Conduct on Arms Transfers (1997). Costa Rica was vice president of the preparatory commission, and the Arias Foundation coordinated with Costa Rica's foreign ministry and U.N. ambassador. After several years of unavailing transnational promotion, the network redrafted the code as a binding international convention, based on the Geneva Convention and the Universal Declaration of Human Rights (Arias Foundation 1997–1999; interview, June 3, 2003). The measure would ban arms transfers that contribute to conflict and human rights abuse. The seven country sponsors include Costa Rica and Canada, and talks opened in October 2006 (Oziewicz 2006). Moreover, the corollary Costa Rica Consensus of 2007 is a framework norm that seeks to reward countries that shift resources from weapons and troops to education and health with debt forgiveness (Cordero 2006).

Costa Rica's voting record in the U.N. is actually a crossover measure of bilateral as well as multilateral relations, as most of the recorded resolutions are country-specific condemnations. The Community of Democracies' U.N. Democracy Caucus scorecard voting project reports the following recent results for Costa Rica:

Table 5.1 U.N. Member Votes, Human Rights Resolutions, 2005

	Cuba Resolution	Belarus—no action motion	Belarus resolution	North Korea resolution
Costa Rica*	Yes	No	Yes	Yes
Canada	Yes	No	Yes	Yes

*In 2006, Costa Rica anomalously abstained on half a dozen country resolutions. In a press release, the Democracy Coalition Project notes that Costa Rica usually votes with other leading democracies on country resolutions. Costa Rica abstained on all but one in 2006 because they argued that these resolutions should be brought up before the new Human Rights Council.

"Democracies Secure UN Censure of Worst Human Rights Violators," December 18, 2006, http://www.democracycaucus.net/pdf/Scorecard%202006%20Analysis%20FINAL.pdf.

2 Her appointment in itself signified Costa Rica's growing awareness of racism, because blacks constitute a socially marginalized but numerically small and electorally insignificant population in Costa Rica.

Like the Netherlands, Costa Rica's bilateral record on Middle East issues balances a historic commitment to Israel as an embattled democracy of Holocaust survivors with an increasing recognition of Palestinian concerns. Thus, Costa Rica has abstained on blanket condemnations of Israel in the U.N. Human Rights Commission (Brenes Zy 2005)) but supported more concrete critiques and humanitarian measures for Palestinian civilians (United Nations Office at Geneva 2007a, 2007b).

In parallel fashion to the global institutions, Costa Rica has helped construct the inter-American system, which is among the strongest regional regimes, and served as an advocate for human rights treaties, institutions, and enforcement within that system. Costa Rica played a key role in establishing both the Organization of American States' Inter-American Court of Human Rights and the independent Inter-American Institute of Human Rights, and now hosts both institutions. Costa Rican president Trejos Fernandez initiated the 1969 San José (Costa Rica) conference that drafted the hemispheric keystone: the Inter-American Convention on Human Rights. The historic conference was chaired by Costa Rica's foreign minister. Costa Rica was the first country to ratify the convention, and the first to accept the jurisdiction of the Inter-American Human Rights Commission, as well as the subsequent Inter-American Human Rights Court (Pasqualucci 1995). Costa Rica was one of the founding members of the (Washington-based) Inter-American Human Rights Commission in 1960, and Costa Rican Angela Acuña Braun was one of the seven original commissioners. Fernando Volio Jiménez also served on the Inter-American Human Rights Commission, in between his human rights work at the United Nations and domestic posts in Costa Rica.

In his 1978 inaugural address, Costa Rican president Rodrigo Carazo Odio offered Costa Rica as the site for a regional human rights court. Costa Rica's foreign minister then initiated a resolution in the OAS to host the court, which was approved at a meeting chaired by Costa Rica's ambassador to the OAS (Ventura 1983). The following year, Costa Rica's OAS delegation helped to draft and lobby for a budget for the new court. Costa Rica secured a special session of the OAS to designate judges, and proposed two of the initial seven jurists (Rodolfo Piza, Costa Rica's former U.N. ambassador, and U.S. legal scholar Thomas Buergenthal, who had worked in and with Costa Rica for many years). Costa Rica was the first state party to submit a case to the court (1981). In 1988–1995, Costa Rican law professor Sonia Picado became the first female judge on the court, and a particularly active presence in Inter-American jurisprudence. Picado took on contentious cases, and increased the enforcement power of the court (Pasqualucci 1995).

Although the Inter-American Commission provided monitoring and the Inter-American Court enforcement, hemispheric activists and scholars envisaged a third pillar for the emerging human rights architecture: an inter-American institute for human rights research, education, and promotion. OAS judge Thomas Buergenthal discussed his vision, modeled on the Rene Cassin Institute in Strasbourg, with Costa Rican colleagues Son a Picado, Rodolfo Piza, Fernando Volio (then at the University of Costa Rica School of Law), and Elizabeth Odio (at that point, minister of justice and acting foreign minister). This network crafted a new institution, and in 1980, Costa Rica signed an agreement with the OAS to host the Inter-American Human Rights Institute. Since 1987, Sonia Picado has directed the institute, expanding its mission to include election monitoring and substantial technical assistance to emerging democracies (interview, June 3, 2003). A new body, CAPEL, was created for this purpose.

In 2000, Costa Rica introduced a set of ambitious proposals to strengthen the inter-American human rights institutions. An ad hoc working group on human rights met in San José, with Costa Rica as its secretary. This group recommended a bigger budget and permanent sessions for the court, independent standing before the court for victims (via an optional protocol), and enhanced enforcement of court decisions through linkage to sanctions by the O.A.S. political institutions (Despouy 2001). When Costa Rica served as president of the OAS Permanent Council, the small state used its influence to get the Judicial and Political Affairs Commission to set aside a week for the Costa Rican institutional reform proposals, and arranged a technical coordination and planning summit between the Inter-American Court and Commission with the OAS Administration and Budget Committee (Vargas Garcia 2001). The Inter-American Court and Commission have begun to hold periodic joint sessions, including a special session on human rights and terrorism in Costa Rica in August 2002, as discussion of structural reform continues.

Meanwhile, Costa Rica has also advanced numerous human rights initiatives in the wider ambits of the O.A.S. When Fernando Volio Jiménez served as Costa Rica's foreign minister from 1982 to 1986, Costa Rica presented resolutions for an additional protocol on social and economic rights to add to the American Convention. Costa Rica also helped sponsor an inter-American declaration on the rights of prisoners, a resolution on the rights of migrants, and the 1999 Declaration on the Rights of Indigenous Peoples. As president of the OAS Permanent Council, Costa Rica sponsored meetings with Costa Rica's Ministry of Justice and the United Nations Crime Prevention Unit to contribute to the prisoners' rights declaration (Rojas 2001, Vargas Garcia 2001).

A notable Costa Rican initiative that demonstrates the small state's role in catalyzing new issues is the Inter-American Convention on Discrimination against the Disabled. In 1994, Costa Rican OAS official Hermes Navarro del Valle presented the convention. Navarro worked closely with his ex-law professor Rodrigo Jiménez Sandoval, who was the president of Costa Rica's federation of "Limitados Funcionales" and an officer of Disabled Peoples' International. Sonia Picado supported the proposal through the Inter-American Institute, and by 1995, the OAS had created a working group to study the measure. In 1998, Costa Rican Jorge

Rhénan Segura (formerly of the U.N. Human Rights Sub-Commission) became president of the Working Group. By 1999—record time by OAS standards—the disability rights convention had passed. And of course, Costa Rica was the first member state to sign it (Vargas Garcia 2001).

Costa Rica has a long-standing tradition of support for democracy and democratic freedoms, in the hemisphere and beyond. The culmination of Costa Rican diplomacy for democratization came in 2001, when Costa Rica hosted the 31st meeting of the OAS General Assembly, with the special theme of human rights. Costa Rica used this occasion to help sponsor a Carta Democrática, a region-wide system of reciprocal support for democracy and sanctions for its abrogation (such as a cut-off of Inter-American Bank loans). Costa Rica emphasized coordination with nongovernmental organizations, sponsoring preparatory meetings and representing civil society positions to the interstate forum. A current Costa Rican proposal in the O.A.S. for a "peace dividend" would provide matching funds from international aid for Latin America's diversion of military spending to social programs (Vargas Garcia 2001, interviews with foreign ministry).

The campaign for democracy drew on and stimulated other forms of inter-American diplomacy, beyond the OAS. In the same year of 2001, Costa Rican president Rodriguez proposed a similar democratic guarantee clause at the Summit of the Americas (Latin America, the United States, and Spain). Costa Rica also joined the subregional Rio Group in 1999, and became president of that institution in 2002. Through this group, Costa Rica coordinated efforts with Chile and Peru to promote the Carta Democrática, as well as the Colombian peace process (Ministerio de Relaciones Exteriores 2001, interviews with foreign ministry).

Costa Rica's advocacy for the interlinked themes of human rights, democratization, and peace bridges the global, hemispheric, and Central American regional levels. The culmination of this policy was Costa Rica's leadership of the 1980s Central American peace process, which garnered the Nobel Peace Prize for then-president Oscar Arias. Costa Rica convened and brokered the only successful negotiations of the region-wide crisis, resulting in the Esquipulas Accords that resolved civil wars in El Salvador, Nicaragua, and Guatemala. The Costa Rican peace plan provided for mutual disarmament of government and guerrilla forces, withdrawal of external combatants and peacekeeping by the United Nations, civil society commissions coordinated by the Catholic Church to guarantee peace and address underlying conflicts, and human rights accountability to the extent possible in each country.

The transition from the Monge administration (1982–1986) policy of neutrality and passive support for U.S. proxy wars to Arias's peace plan shows a conscious change to a risky policy of defiance of the hegemon, based on a transformed vision of national interest. Arias had campaigned on a peace platform against an unpopular interventionist opponent, citing the impact of regional conflict on Costa Rica through loss of investment and a refugee crisis as the basis for a necessary new vision. He predicted a painful loss of U.S. aid, but successfully rallied the Costa Rican public to absorb this sacrifice in the name of national values of peace, democracy, and regional self-determination (Hey and Kuzma 1993, Rojas Aravena 1992).

Since Oscar Arias left office, the Arias Foundation—a policy-oriented think tank similar in stature and orientation to the U.S. Carter Center—has followed up the peace plan with ongoing programs for demilitarization and democratization in the region. The foundation coordinates a network of dozens of peace, human rights, and development groups in each country. In 1997, for example, this *Dialogo Centroamericano* sponsored a study and workshops in El Salvador on reintegration, with hundreds of ex-combatants (who in many cases have continued to threaten public order). In Guatemala, where the military itself continues to threaten public order, the Arias Foundation has commissioned and disseminated courageous studies of Guatemalan military spending, and the military's business connections throughout Central America (Arias Foundation 1997–1999).

The foundation has also spearheaded broader multilateral efforts for ongoing disarmament in Central America. The foundation's study, "The Invisible Arsenal," helped to frame regional arms trafficking as a concern of national police and foreign ministries—as well as securing international aid. The Arias group then held training seminars with Central American police forces, along with a study comparing U.N. and O.A.S. standards to Central American national laws and mechanisms. As this brought state-level attention to bear, the network of experts, aid officials, police, and ministries approached the militaries in each country. Regional efforts on arms trafficking continue (interview, June 5, 2003).

In a few cases, Costa Rican influence has actually led to full-fledged demilitarization—following the model of Costa Rica's own definitive democratization concurrent with the elimination of its army in 1948. Neighboring Panama was invaded by the United States and defeated in 1989, in the waning years of the Central American crisis and Arias's presidency. Arias initially approached the new president of Panama and suggested elimination of the military associated with defeated dictator Manuel Noriega. Although the suggestion was deferred, when Arias returned as a private party with international funding for a referendum in 1992, Panama's next administration was willing. Even though demilitarization was not approved in that referendum, the idea was planted and adopted by civil society organizations—some fostered by the Arias Foundation. Thus, two years later, Panama did eliminate its army, assisted strongly by its peace-promoting neighbor (interview, June 6, 2003).

In Haiti, the relationship was more direct and demilitarization was effected more quickly—although ultimately less successfully. In this case, Arias himself simply persuaded new reforming leader Bertrand Aristide to demilitarize, and hired a Costa Rican polling firm to gauge social support for the measure. Haiti's elimination of its army was announced at a joint press conference with Aristide and Nobel laureate Arias. However, the structure of Haiti's Constitution has required repeated ratification of this policy, and the prevalence of police and paramilitary violence in Haiti limit the scope of demilitarization (interview, June 3, 2003).

Within Central America and beyond, Costa Rica's reception of refugees constitutes a litmus test for human rights policy. The generosity and tolerance of all nations is tested by the arrival of vast numbers of needy strangers. Although Costa Rica sits in the middle ranks of developing nations, its resources are limited, so that support of refugees is in some sense a surrogate for foreign aid for struggling neighboring states. Support for refugees is also a transfer of resources to the direct victims of human rights violations. Costa Rica's conscientious efforts to shelter refugees in accordance with international standards place it in the top tier of state practice historically, even though there are ongoing shortfalls in the treatment of migrants by civil society, some lagging government agencies, and a contested and problematic 2006 immigration bill.

Costa Rica has a long-standing tradition of granting political asylum to dissident democratic political figures, even at the cost of annoying neighboring governments. Through the dictatorships of the 1970s and 1980s, the inter-American institutions based in Costa Rica also sheltered some grassroots exiles and human rights workers. The Inter-American Institute of Human Rights currently invites Cubans for special scholarships (interview, June 3, 2003), and the IIDH is just starting a program to host persecuted judges from Colombia—about 20 each year (interview, June 10, 2003).

But massive flows of migrants, generated by the Central American wars, posed far deeper challenges. During the 1980s, hundreds of thousands of poor Nicaraguans (and some Salvadorans), flooded Costa Rica (total population then around three million). A positive sign of civil society support was the establishment of one of Costa Rica's first human rights groups in 1980—on behalf of refugees (Comité Ecuménico Pro Refugiados). At the same time, the United Nations High Commission on Refugees opened a regional office in Costa Rica during the 1980s. Costa Rica provided short-term shelter and humanitarian services for these refugees, although it strongly encouraged voluntary repatriation and the Arias Peace Plan included provisions on repatriation.

During the 1990s state policy and social attitudes were significantly more ambivalent regarding continuing flows of economic migrants, as well as those who chose not to return to their countries of origin. Costa Rica's 2000 Census shows 240,000 Nicaraguans, and experts estimate true numbers up to 400,000—which would be around 10% of Costa Rica's current population (Casasfranco Roldán 2001, Acuña González and Olivares Ferreto 2000). Migrants are eligible for social services, and can even safely denounce exploitative labor conditions. But undocumented Central Americans can be deported, and are subject to social and employment discrimination. Costa Rica's ombudsman has a special program to track the treatment and access of migrants, and a migration amnesty was declared in 1999–2000 in response to Hurricane Mitch. Costa Rica continues to participate in multilateral coordination processes that aim to foster both enforcement and relief, such as the Puebla group regional migration conferences (along with the United States, Mexico, and the remaining Central American states). By 2005, social tensions with Nicaraguans reached the point that several were killed in unofficial altercations, leading Nicaragua to bring a case against Costa Rica for discrimination in the Inter-American Human Rights Court; in March 2007 the case was ruled inadmissible (Murillo 2007).

Meanwhile, Costa Rica has been visited by a new flow of refugees during the late 1990s: Colombians, usually traveling overland over the narrow Isthmus of Panama from Latin America's bloodiest country to its most peaceful. The UNHCR has registered about 8,000 Colombians in Costa Rica (with estimates up to 30,000) (interview, June 9, 2003, UNHCR 2003)—this gives Costa Rica the highest number of recognized refugees in Latin America (interview, June 3, 2003). Accordingly, the UNHCR has reopened the regional office that had closed during the 1990s. Although the Colombians generally have more education and resources than Central American refugees and thus less of a social service impact, their presence has created new security problems in Costa Rica, through transnational reprisals by Colombian persecutors crossing into Costa Rica.

Costa Rica's response to this population has been concerted. When over 1,000 Colombians arrived in 2000, the Costa Rican foreign ministry began meeting with the International Red Cross, and by 2001, Costa Rica had coordinated a refugee status determination program with the UNHCR. After the UNHCR contributed computer equipment and training to Costa Rica's migration department, about half of that year's 5,800-plus arrivals were granted refugee status. The UNHCR has even mounted training programs with Costa Rican border guards to refer rather than apprehend anyone declaring refugee status. Costa Rica's migration department automatically issues one-month residency permits to refugee applicants, and does not sanction illegal entrants who later apply for refuge. As numbers rose into the thousands, Costa Rica did introduce a visa requirement for Colombians, which may have had a chilling effect on refugees with fewer resources and facing more immediate threats—but for those who make it to Costa Rica, refugee approval rates rose to almost 70% by the mid-2000s. Refugee assessment is coordinated with international standards, including UNHCR information on country situations and plausible grounds for claims of persecution (for example, the high incidence of nongovernmental violence in Colombia). Finally, there is an appeals process for refugee applicants, and they are not detained or deported for the duration of this process (interviews June 2, 3, and 9, 2003, UNHCR 2003).

However, continuing social backlash led to the approval of a harsh new immigration law under the Pacheco administration in 2005. Domestic NGOs and the U.N. High Commission for Refugees challenged the law, but did not receive a hearing until President Oscar Arias took office in 2006. Social Democrat Arias did attempt to have implementation of the law postponed to December 2007 to allow time to consider changes, but failed to secure legislative approval for the delay ("Assembly Derails Attempt" 2006)). When Arias's attempts to postpone implementation failed, he created a technical team in 2007 to propose reforms to the law to guarantee respect for human rights and greater participation by immigrants in society (Roberson 2007).

Besides multilateral institutions and flows, Costa Rica has also participated in various forms of transnational networking, training, and education to promote human rights. These activities range from hosting international conferences to establishing NGOs, from exporting democratic institutions to promoting alternative models of security. All involve initiatives of Costa Rican civil society, usually working in partnership with the Costa Rican government at some level, and targeting foreign NGOs and states alike.

The early landmark experience was Costa Rica's sponsorship of the First World Human Rights Congress in 1982, an epochal event attended by over 5,000 representatives from all over the world. Under the Monge administration, a group of professors from the University of Costa Rica decided to commemorate the centennial of Costa Rica's abolition of the death penalty, inviting representatives of all the states that had followed suit (including France, Venezuela, and Spain) and the main international human rights NGOs (Amnesty International, the Red Cross, and Human Rights Watch). It was thus one of the first mixed human rights gatherings of government representatives and NGOs. Monge gave the academic organizers an office in the presidency and contact lists, issued a special postal stamp to fund it, and sponsored some delegates from poorer countries. The gathering took over the university town of Alajuela, to the extent that the mayor blocked traffic in the town for an entire week, and housed many delegates with Costa Rican families. Afterward, the academic organizers published 24,000 proceedings—the biggest printing in Costa Rican history, and issued the "Carta de Alajuela": a standard-setting document that discusses torture, the death penalty, neutrality, and Costa Rica's early proposal for an international criminal court. The special postal stamp was so popular in Costa Rica that a surplus was raised beyond the conference expenses, so they established a small foundation to issue an annual human rights prize and foster more human rights courses at the National University. Subsequently, lead organizer Dr. Nestor Mourelo was appointed Costa Rica's ambassador to UNESCO (1984–1986), and used his post to distribute copies of the proceedings and the "Carta de Alajuela" to all the delegates in all the U.N. languages (interview, June 5, 2003).

In a continuation of this role, Costa Rica was designated by the United Nations in 1978 to host the University of Peace. This multinational educational program conducts research and training on conflict resolution and sustainable development under U.N. auspices, and is based in San José.

During the 1990s, the Arias Foundation has worked to provide technical training and capacity building to NGOs embodying the "culture of peace" throughout the region. They have specialized in women's groups, following a vision that links militarism to machismo and women's empowerment to democratization. Representative projects include publication and region-wide dissemination of a bilingual (Spanish–Maya) children's edition of the Convention on the Elimination of All Forms of Discrimination against Women, advocacy training workshops on land rights for rural women across Central America, and training for government officials on citizen participation and women's issues. The current director of the foundation summarized this transnational networking: "Our most important accomplishment has been the creation of a network of NGOs in Central America: first of all, for gender equality. The creation of networks has also been important for control of arms trafficking, connecting Ministries, academics, police, customs, military intelligence, across the region." The Arias Foundation has also helped to draft legislation for citizen participation in Guatemala, Nicaragua, and Costa Rica (interview, June 5, 2003, Arias Foundation 1997–1999). A current project promotes exchange among women's peace groups in the region, with outreach to women's organizations in Colombia.

Diffusion and networking have also touched the democratic institution most intimately linked with the defense of citizen rights—the ombudsman. Costa Rica established an ombudsman in 1993, with the power to investigate any government agency on behalf of citizens' rights. The Costa Rican ombudsman has worked with transnational federations at all levels: from the regional Consejo Centroamericano de Procuradores to the transatlantic Federacíon Iberoamericano de Ombudsman to the hemispheric Red de Instituciones Nacionales de Promocíon y Proteccíon de DDHH del Continente Americana (affiliated with the U.N. High Commission on Human Rights). Costa Rica is one of the four regional representatives to the U.N. Coordinating Committee of Ombudsman, and recently hosted a meeting of this group with the disability rights theme. Along with Costa Rica's general promotion of migrants' rights, the Costa Rican ombudsman has introduced migrants' rights discussions to the Central American and Ibero-American coordinating bodies. Furthermore, these networks help threatened Ombudsman offices in neighboring countries; they have lobbied for peers threatened with closure or devastating budget cuts in Nicaragua, Colombia, and Venezuela (interview, June 4, 2003).

Alternative visions of state security and accountability are the other side of the promotion of civil society and its rights. The Costa Rica–based Inter-American Human Rights Institute thus has launched an education and training program in the administration of justice—for example, fostering the establishment and development of a public defenders program in Guatemala (where the vast majority of defendants are indigent). Most of the advisors to this program are Costa Rican, providing training, models, and networks to courts, legislatures, and law schools throughout the region (interview, June 9, 2003).

Similarly, Costa Rica's former minister of justice Lara Chinchilla, a staff member of the Arias Foundation, has done studies on police reform disseminated throughout the region. The foundation held a series of important meetings on Central American disarmament and police reform (Zárate, Jiménez, and Barrantes 1999)—including a 1998 direct transfer of a Costa Rican community security program to El Salvador (Arias Foundation 1997–1999). As a result, Costa Rica has begun to exchange community policing training with El Salvador and Honduras (interview, June 10, 2003). Following demilitarization, Costa Rica helped Panama to professionalize its police force.

Costa Rica's experience as regional peacemaker has been consciously analyzed and diffused at the global level as well. A Dutch agency invited the Arias Foundation to prepare a comparative study of "Lessons from Central America," working with partner target groups in Southern Asia and West Africa. Subsequently, Oscar Arias himself traveled to Africa to promote demilitarization. The Costa Rican group has participated in a series of World Bank and UNDP conferences in West Africa on conflict prevention, demilitarization, and regional peace processes (Arias Foundation 1997–1999). As an Arias Foundation–sponsored study concludes, "Central Americans have paid a very high price to learn that the security of a people lies not in the protection of national sovereignty, but in sustained development and personal liberty" (Isacson 1997: 181).

CONTRADICTIONS AND LIMITATIONS

Although Costa Rica's policies have been positive on balance, it is important to acknowledge the contradictions and limitations of even this best-case human rights advocacy. The reconstruction of national interest is an ongoing and contested process, and traditional realist considerations periodically persuade policy makers to pursue more conventional strategies of power that ignore human rights. As a principled peripheral, Costa Rica sometimes simply lacks the resources to participate effectively in the international human rights regime. And intertwined with these limits, principled policies in a small state are catalyzed by a limited cadre of dynamic individuals—and such leadership inevitably evokes rivalries.

Even principled proponents of Costa Rica's human rights policies acknowledge that their small agile statecraft has sometimes foundered on the shoals of realism. During the mid-1990s, Costa Rica aspired to greater levels of multilateral leadership—and traded off some human rights policies to achieve it. Between 1994 and 1998, Costa Rica campaigned for the vice presidency of the U.N. General Assembly, the presidency of the G-77, the U.N. Security Council, and the U.N. Human Rights Commission. During these campaigns, Costa Rica abstained on some human rights resolutions at the U.N., and specifically improved relations with the Philippines, Zambia, and Indonesia—ignoring generally acknowledged human rights concerns within those countries. While seeking a seat on the U.N. Human Rights Commission, Costa Rica voted for arch-violator Libya. Costa Rican president Abel Pacheco offered the U.S. support for the war in Iraq as a trade agreement was pending with the northern hege-mon, despite widespread opposition among Costa Rica's traditional allies and general population.[3] After 63 years of support for Taiwan, explicitly based on shared political values of democracy and human rights, in May 2007 Costa Rica shifted diplomatic relations to China, on the basis of trade relations (Cody 2007).

Nevertheless, Costa Rica continued to regularly condemn Cuba despite nationalist skepticism from fellow nonaligned nations. Costa Rica persevered in its idiosyncratic, historically based commitment to Israel, which is framed by Costa Rican policy makers as a principled defense of self-determination for the victims of the Holocaust but has cost Costa Rica support in the G-77 and nonaligned movement (interviews, Vargas Garcia 2001). Most recently, President Arias condemned the closure of RCTV (Venezuela's Radio Caracas Television) by Hugo Chavez as a "mortal blow" to democracy, while other Latin American governments were silent ("An Opposition Gagged," 2007).

Lack of resources can also limit human rights policy. Costa Rica's foreign ministry human rights team consists of three or four individuals—only one specifically designated exclusively to human rights—who cannot possibly track all relevant developments, attend all relevant meetings and conferences, or even hold their own internally with the trade and regional integration offices (Vargas Garcia 2001). Travel budgets are so limited that Costa Rica's ombudsman could not afford to attend the U.N. Durban Conference on Racism (interview, June 4, 2003). Government officials frequently hold simultaneous academic or even private posts, diffusing attention to policy making. Costa Rica's Foreign Service only recently professionalized, which has held back policy learning and continuity until now, but should improve future coordination and consistency (Rhenán Segura 1999).

Finally, Costa Rica's human rights policy is ironically clouded by one of its sources—the dedication of a small circle of key individuals. When human rights promotion is a source of domestic and international prestige in a small country with limited opportunities, internecine rivalries sometimes undercut the potential for international leadership. Multiple informants point out that 1990s president Figueres Olsen failed to back Oscar Arias's proposed presidency of the O.A.S., partly due to a general downgrading of human rights diplomacy during his 1994–1998 term, but also in part from fear the rival politico would use the international post as a launching pad to return to national power.[4] Similarly, President Pacheco refused to support

3. Because Costa Rica has no army and limited economic resources, support for the U.S. campaign would be largely rhetorical and thus perhaps a less significant trade-off than it may first appear.

4. President Jose Figueres Olsen was the son of founding father president Jose Figueres Ferrer, but pursued a different agenda in several areas—including human rights promotion. In terms of anticipated potential rivalries with ex-president Arias, although Costa Rica's Constitution historically specified no reelection, a 2005 reform permitted former presidents to run again, and Arias was returned to office in 2006.

human rights superstar Elizabeth Odio's candidacy for the International Criminal Court from personal motives, a decision so potentially injurious to Costa Rica's international prestige that elements in the Foreign Service broke ranks with the president to quietly secure her appointment as the first female jurist on the court (anonymous interviews).

These contradictions and limitations are real. But Costa Rica's overall record as a global Good Samaritan is substantial and persistent. The sources of this positive role thus merit further analysis.

HUMAN RIGHTS AS NATIONAL INTEREST

Costa Rica's human rights policies result from a blend of historical political culture and continuing policy choice. Although Costa Rica has been blessed with a location and demography conducive to democracy, the decision to project democracy outward has been a strategy of conscious leadership influenced by powerful ideas. Furthermore, the deepening of Costa Rican democracy has improved human rights promotion—and international promotion has enhanced human rights at home.

Costa Rican Democracy: From Structure to Culture

Costa Rica is a special place, but it is not wholly exceptional or magically gifted with a democratic culture. The structural parameters permitting the development of democracy were Costa Rica's inconvenient location for colonization, sparse indigenous population, and lack of mineral or plantation wealth, producing light colonial settlement and the development of agricultural production by independent smallholders rather than large labor-exploitive plantations. The relative dispersion of agricultural wealth meant that slowly emerging elites had to negotiate political arrangements more widely among themselves, whereas Costa Rica's colonial-era backwardness reduced church and military presence. Thus, Costa Rica was spared the classic oligarchy-military-church triumvirate of Latin American dependency. Furthermore, Costa Rica fell at the fringes of U.S. attention during its formative years (Booth 1998; B. Wilson 1998; Yashar 1997).[5] Although recent national scholarship suggests that Costa Rica was more socially stratified, more militaristic, and less educated than previously believed, revisionist accounts affirm that scarce labor and the

---

5. However, Costa Rica was not born pacifist: it possessed a substantial military through the nineteenth century. The military waned during the first half of the twentieth century, and was abolished in 1948. "By the early 1980's, however, Costa Rica—under heavy U.S. pressure—was obliged to strengthen and militarize its Civil Guard to the point of it resembling a counterinsurgency force....Costa Rican president Oscar Arias (1986–1990) reversed much of the national police force's creeping militarization" (Isacson 1997: 7, 12).

relative weakness of entrenched oligarchies allowed an unusual latitude and incentive for gradual democratization (Quesada Camacho 1999).

As a result, Costa Rica made a series of progressive policy choices. Early presidents, who were often teachers or jurists with European education and aspirations, established the region's first universal primary education (1869), abolished the death penalty (1882), allowed legitimate political competition (1889), and established the first international court (1907–1918). Labor rights and universal social services were introduced early in the twentieth century, as a conscious strategy to modernize the country. When the Depression decimated the region's export economies and fueled social unrest, instead of responding with the dictatorships of its neighbors, Costa Rica introduced a minimum wage, smallholder associations, and labor negotiations. Even before its mid-century democratic breakthrough, Costa Rica had securely institutionalized basic human rights and civil liberties in its constitution (Masís Iverson 1999).

José Maria Figueres emerged as a muscular ideological heir to Costa Rica's classically Liberal tradition. By 1943, he had published a republican manifesto (*Ideario Costarricense*) and urged the creation of a "Caribbean legion" to spread democracy throughout the region. After an electoral dispute in 1948 unexpectedly escalated into a brief but bloody civil war, the horrified Costa Rican elite established a pact declaring Figueres founding president of the second republic, further institutionalized political competition, and abolished the military—so that it could never again become a tool of political violence (B. Wilson 1998; Eguizabal 2000).

The year 1948 was a "critical historical juncture" in world as well as national terms: key elements of the U.N. were established, and the declaration of the State of Israel focused attention on the Holocaust by the emerging Costa Rican republic's founding fathers (interviews, June 5 and 9, 2003). After the 1948 Revolution, a National Constitutional Assembly established an Electoral Tribunal as an independent fourth branch of government, reformed Costa Rica's judiciary to separate legal investigations from law enforcement, and granted several state and civic institutions autonomy—including the University of Costa Rica (Masís Iverson 1999). Costa Rica has regular free and fair elections, and respect for civil liberties is in the top rank worldwide.[6]

Costa Rica's only guarantors of public order and "monopoly of legitimate force" are its police and border guards, democratic civic education of the general population is intense (Rodriguez et al. 1998), and the "generation of '48" political leadership made a conscious decision to rely on international institutions for their national security. One measure

6. In one area of slippage, Reporters without Borders found that Costa Rica had gone down 20 points on the Reporters without Borders scale in 2004 compared to 2002. The freedom of the press scale is based on measures of the ability of citizens to give and receive information freely, the existence of legislation that protects journalists, and the level of harassment of the press that exists (Vizcaino 2005).

of the success of the reconstruction of domestic security comes from Chief of Police Walter Navarro, the country's maximal armed force commander, who favors the social welfare model over the power and influence of his own institution. In his vision of national security, "The secret of the triumph of Costa Rica is that we invested in hospitals and schools instead of armies" (interview, June 10, 2003). Costa Rican police and prisons are generally accountable; limited abuses are sporadic and generally ameliorated. Another measure of the culture of law is that the ombudsman's nonbinding recommendations to government agencies are followed voluntarily the "vast majority" of the time, particularly if they cite international obligations or standards (interview, June 4, 2003).

On the external front, Costa Rica has made collective security work. The small state appealed successfully to the O.A.S. regarding border disputes with Nicaragua (including resolving a 1949 Nicaraguan invasion). Costa Rica has balanced military protection and independent principle in its relationship with the United States. And along with multilateral promotion, Costa Rica has modestly diversified its security relationships and defense assistance—from U.N. aid to resettle refugees, to OAS assistance with mine removals, to Spanish funds for community policing.

A final structural/historical factor that increases the scope for policy choice and leadership is Costa Rica's small political elite. "Small is beautiful" for principled foreign policy, because it creates tight networks, easy access, and a bipartisan consensus. Fernando Soto Harrison, whose influence spanned from U.N. ambassador during the 1940s to U.S. and O.A.S. ambassador during the 1980s, is the great-grandson of the founding father who had abolished the death penalty. Similarly, former director of foreign policy Rodrigo Carreras is the son of "Generation of '48" hero Benjamin Nuñez, and grew up with "Uncle" *Don Pepe* (President José Maria Figueres). Luis Guillermo Solís has bridged the Arias Foundation, foreign ministry, and political party leadership. The foreign ministry human rights secretary started out her career in Costa Rica's ombudsman's office, and maintains a good relationship with that agency (interview, June 4, 2003). The foreign ministry's legal director (who deals most with refugee policy) is an international law professor at the University of Costa Rica who studied with Fernando Volio, and has worked in turn with the UNHCR, UNDP, and Costa Rica's National Migration Council prior to her position with the ministry (interview, June 9, 2003). Even the opposition party Pacheco administration was forced to draw on Social Democratic PLN members for many posts, due to the small number of qualified candidates in a small country, and in any case there are numerous personal and professional ties among educated elite members of the major parties. Thus, Soto Harrison, reflecting on his half century of foreign policy service, concluded that this has knit together Costa Rica's policy choices: "There has always been a consensus among the political tendencies in Costa Rica over human rights....The differences between administrations were not over human rights or democracy" (interview, June 5, 2003).

RECONSTRUCTING NATIONAL INTEREST

From these structural roots and the historical experience of policy choices, human rights values have been incorporated in national identity. Virtually every person interviewed for this study, and even ordinary Costa Ricans, describe human rights as "a question of [their] culture." Internalized national interest follows a constructivist logic of norms, in which actors seek guidance from roles and values in dialogue with calculation of material gains (Jepperson, Wendt, and Katzenstein 1996). For example, when asked to explain recent decisions to promote new human rights agenda items and invite NGOs to interstate bodies, a foreign ministry official replied, "Because we knew it was the *correct* thing to do" (interview, June 2, 2003). On this basis, Costa Rica has made a continuous series of choices to use its scarce foreign policy resources to project democracy and human rights. As Soto Harrison put it, "I own some stock, and even if I am a minority shareholder, I always go to the meetings. Because even if you don't own much, if you are at the table they may listen to your ideas, and you may change the agenda. This is the same idea behind Costa Rica's international vision" (interview, June 5, 2003).

The agents of reconstruction of national interest were charismatic leaders with big ideas, along with a committed cadre of diplomats, all anchored in a highly sympathetic attentive public. They constructed Costa Rica as not merely a generically Good Samaritan, but more specifically as a regional "island of peace"—a role that reinforced principled policy with international rewards. Costa Rica's highly legitimate international role also allowed a tiny state in a bad neighborhood to somewhat diffuse and balance its relationship with the regional hegemon.

Foreign policy in Costa Rica is initially framed by presidential prerogative; although its history proposed a principled foreign policy, men of vision disposed Costa Rican internationalism at critical junctures. Former foreign policy vice minister Rodrigo Carreras recalls that José Maria Figueres was inspired by H. G. Wells's utopian vision of a society without an army (interview, June 9, 2003). Fernando Soto Harrison knew and admired Eleanor Roosevelt, before arriving at the nascent U.N. with unusual latitude from his president in the organization's founding period (interview, June 5, 2003). Oscar Arias is the scion of highly influential and unexpectedly progressive wealthy coffee planters, who became enamored with the British Labour Party during his European education.

Between trailblazers, within the broadly supportive parameters set by more routine presidents, career diplomats like Facio Gonzalez, Fernando Volio, Sonia Picado, and Elizabeth Odio pushed the human rights agenda and leveraged their domestic political capital to promote progressive internationalism. The outstanding contemporary example, Elizabeth Odio Benitez, began her U.N. career on the Sub-Commission for the Prevention of Discrimination (1980–1983), then moved into a concurrent post as special rapporteur for religious discrimination (1982–1987). She was later elected vice president of Costa Rica and served as minister of justice in another Costa Rican administration (1980). Odio Benitez then became a judge on the United Nations War Crimes Tribunal for the Former Yugoslavia, and currently serves as a jurist on the new International Criminal Court. In between these posts, she was the president of the United Nations Working Group for an Optional Protocol to the Convention against Torture (1990–1991).

Since 1948, a transmission belt and attentive public for democratic foreign policy has been Costa Rica's dominant Social Democratic party, Partido Liberación Nacional (PLN). Although political parties do not play a formal role in shaping Costa Rican foreign policy (as in some European parliaments), and there are not huge party-based swings in policy between administrations, the PLN has helped shape Costa Rica's human rights consensus. PLN leaders like Sonia Picado and Luis Guillermo Solís, as well as grassroots activists such as most of the country's academics, are disproportionately aware of and committed to human rights principles. The PLN has produced a strong intellectual elite with a strong foreign policy orientation who have served in most administrations—a number are international lawyers. Although the PLN is a member of the Socialist International, it is a Social Democratic party whose positions are generally more centrist and anti-Communist than the international body (interview, June 6, 2003). However, the Social Democracy International has facilitated networks with European policy makers, who have consciously sought to balance U.S. influence and provided aid in the region from the Arias era onward (Rhenán Segura 1999).

Ideas gained further purchase, and civil society greater input, through the strong influence of academics on Costa Rica's foreign policy. The democratizing 1948 Revolution was largely crafted at the Center for the Study of National Problems. Once the University of Costa Rica (UCR) was established, it became the country's talent pool and source of expertise—particularly on legal matters. Assessing this relationship, a UCR law professor who served in several governments—including a term as minister of justice—asserted, "the [Costa Rican] legal system was formed by the UCR" (interview, June 4, 2003). By the 1970s, the more professional-technical National University (UNA) had also developed an interest in human rights, and later established a master's-level international relations program with close ties to the Foreign Service. Many countries at Costa Rica's size and level of development barely have one university, yet Costa Rica has two high-level institutions that grant graduate degrees, including a law school at UCR that draws students from throughout the region. This has all been supplemented by international education of policy-making elites, which further diffused democratic values and created cosmopolitan networks. Ambassador Rodrigo Carreras studied theories of democracy in the Ph.D. program in political science at University of California–Berkeley; Luis Guillermo Solís analyzed alternative modes of foreign policy making in the international relations program at Tulane. Sonia Picado met OAS judge Thomas Buergenthal when he was the dean of American University and she was the dean of UCR's Law School.

Costa Rica's resulting national identity as global Good Samaritan has been constructed in relation to other states (Barnett 1998). Costa Rica's regional niche fostered principled policy, and principled policy in turn secured the regional role. Costa Rica is considered, and considers itself, an island of peace in Central America. One reason Costa Rica hosts the inter-American institutions is that it is safe, stable, and can even shelter participants from more troubled nations. Sonia Picado recalls that as a Costa Rican, she had enhanced maneuverability as director of the Inter-American Institute, in that she could travel anywhere (interview, June 3, 2003). In similar fashion, Costa Rica also hosts the regional offices of UNICEF, UNESCO, the UNHCR, the ILO, the UNDP, the Red Cross, the International Organization for Migration, and the International Court of Arbitration. The presence of these institutions brings personnel, conference and tourist income, and reinforcement of internationalist and humanitarian values to Costa Rica. Peace pays—tourism is Costa Rica's leading source of income, and the safe, educated country has recently garnered significant high-tech investment. By the 1990s, some policy makers consciously sought to expand this role in response to chronic economic decline; they proposed making Costa Rica "the Geneva of Central America" (interview, June 6, 2003).

Costa Rica's international legitimacy as a global Good Samaritan has also given that country occasional autonomy from the U.S. pressures that unremittingly dominate its Central American neighbors. A key policy maker explains, "Although in fact Costa Rica almost always supports the U.S., it would be unpopular to say this. So we avoid it and label this as 'support for Western democracy and values.' But sometimes that makes a difference" (interview, June 9, 2003)—especially at moments when U.S. policies reflect realpolitik rather than our own self-proclaimed support for democracy. Oscar Arias was "allowed" to pursue his peace plan and resist U.S. militarization because he had impeccable humanitarian credentials, good contacts with congressional Democrats skeptical of Reagan's policies in the wake of the Iran-Contra scandal, and European support (Rhenán Segura 1999, Isacson 1997). Costa Rica has criticized U.S. economic sanctions on Cuba—yet has independently repeatedly criticized Cuba's human rights record. Costa Rica follows an independent line at the United Nations, and has broken with the United States over principled issues such as the International Criminal Court; one tally shows only a 28% overlap with the U.S. voting record (Murillo 2005).

Deepening Democracy

The pathway of alternative national interest ultimately reconstructs the national identity that inspired it. Costa Rica's democratic foreign policy reflects a deepening democracy at home. International projection, in turn, returns to Costa Rica as new norms and mechanisms that consolidate human rights at the national level.

Although foreign policy is usually the policy area most insulated from social influence, Costa Rica's foreign policy makers work closely with NGOs. The Arias Foundation is first among equals in this regard, setting regional security agendas, jointly administering programs with state and foreign agencies, and harnessing state representatives to lobby for particular initiatives in multilateral settings. Former Arias program officer Carlos Walker recounts that he had "incredible access—we could call the Foreign Ministry and be sitting talking with someone two or three days later" (interview, June 3, 2003). Other NGOs are consulted by the foreign ministry for information on local human rights conditions to prepare reports mandated by international treaties, as well as briefings on global human rights problems and proposals that correspond closely with Costa Rica's eventual positions on these issues. Costa Rica's participation in the U.N. Torture Convention Optional Protocol, OAS Disability Convention, and Durban Conference on Racism showed particularly strong NGO influence. One indication that this is a principled rather than interest group relationship is the foreign ministry's fluid interaction with transnational as well as domestic human rights organizations: they will "call Amnesty to figure out what the issues are" (interviews, June 2, 3, and 4, 2003).

Costa Rica has even gone further, to foster NGO participation and promote democracy in global governance. Several days before the OAS 2000 meeting in Costa Rica, the foreign ministry met with a coalition of national and international NGOs and the Inter-American Human Rights Institute to prepare proposals. As the host, Costa Rica got a broader group of NGOs invited to OAS events, beyond the officially accredited list—a practice that was carried over into subsequent OAS meetings elsewhere. Within the interstate forum, Costa Rica made a commitment to present NGO human rights proposals, as it has continued to do in the OAS and other international institutions (interview, June 2, 2003).

Another aspect of Costa Rica's democracy that strengthens its human rights role is the strong presence of women as foreign policy makers. Women's education, social status, and political participation are generally higher in Costa Rica than most developing countries. Women are particularly visible in academics and the PLN, two notable sources of government officials. Costa Rica's electoral code mandates a gender representation quota of 40% for both political party posts and parliamentary tickets. Costa Rica has had female deputies, ministers, and even vice presidents (Barahona Montero 1999, Masís Iverson 1999). Within the Costa Rican government, women seem to be concentrated in rights-relevant posts. The foreign ministry's human rights director is a woman, the director of the Inter-American Human Rights Institute was the first female dean of UCR's Law School, and Costa Rica provided the first female judge on the International Criminal Court. Costa Rican women active in human rights policy attribute their focus on rights partially to their own experience of gender inequities; as Sonia Picado said, "Remember, my experience with human rights started with the fight for women's rights" (interview, June 5, 2003, also see Pasqualucci 1995). Accordingly, Costa Rica's human rights policies have been particularly sensitive to gender issues and discrimination.

Human rights foreign policy deepens democracy in Costa Rica, as it brings international standards—including many promoted by Costa Rica—back home to bear on domestic behavior. Costa Rica has signed every major international human rights treaty, and after some delay due to understaffing now provides all reports mandated by these instruments (Vargas Garcia 2001). This continual self-monitoring serves to strengthen domestic reform initiatives and identify underserved populations. For example, the ombudsman's office describes the 1993 establishment of their institution as an "internalization of international politics and domestic conscience." The Special Protection Department's mission is to monitor groups lacking access to the legal system, which are also populations Costa Rica has advocated internationally—migrants and minors (interview, June 4, 2003). Similarly, after the self-scrutiny required for participation in the Durban Racism Conference, in 2001 Costa Rica's president issued a formal apology for the "errors of the past" (such as residential/regional discrimination against the small Afro-Latino population). Along with activism in the U.N. and O.A.S. indigenous rights declarations, Costa Rica has included indigenous groups in its census and registration process (Whyte 2002). While he was foreign policy director, Luis Guillermo Solís commissioned a study on religious discrimination in Costa Rica following a U.N. resolution on the theme, as well as a visit to Costa Rica by a Baha'i delegation (interview, June 6, 2003). Responding to a wave of global efforts for gender equity and its ratification of the Convention on the Elimination of All Forms of Discrimination against Women, in 1990 Costa Rica passed sweeping and regionally unprecedented equal rights legislation (Rojas 2001). In keeping with the children's rights theme, Costa Rica has created a special department for children, and launched a vigorous campaign against child prostitution (unfortunately facilitated by high tourism). Regional efforts at security reform have articulated with a 2000 professionalization of Costa Rica's own police, including better training, higher salaries, a civil service structure, and human rights instruction (interview, June 10, 2003, Zárate, Jiménez, and Barrantes 1999).

GLOBALIZING GOOD SAMARITANS?

To what extent can the elements of Costa Rica's experience transfer to other developing nations? Some of the features that built Costa Rica's human rights policies are fixed legacies or resources. Small scale, dispersed wealth, visionary leaders, and generations of democratic institutions all contributed to Costa Rica's democracy and foreign policy, and they are not available to any country. However, Costa Rica's tools for the reconstruction of national interest are latent resources in many: persuasion by ideas, openness to civil society, socializing participation in international institutions, dedicated diplomats, and alternative regional and global niches. All of these factors are amenable to choice, all can be assisted externally, and all help to strengthen democracy at home as well as abroad.

Costa Rica did not require wealth or power to afford the luxury of pursuing a principled foreign policy. National identity and international society produced a significant and surprising contribution to global human welfare by a country at the periphery of global governance. But Costa Rica's democratic, internationalist political culture was made, not born, and it struggles to survive the shifting tides of globalization and hegemony. This means that other societies can reconstruct foreign policy in positive directions—but it also means that cultures of peace must be continually renewed.

6

Globalization and Its Discontents

The Netherlands

One peace is better than countless victories.
—1648 medallion, struck by the City
of Amsterdam to celebrate the
Treaty of Munster

The Government shall promote the development
of the international legal order.
—Article 90 of the Dutch Constitution

The Netherlands has been renowned for a long tradition of humanitarian internationalism, seeking a combination of "peace, profits, and principles" through foreign policy strategies historians identify as "maritime commercialism, neutralist abstentionism, and internationalist idealism" (Voorhoeve 1979). Holland's historic projection as a small power using international law to protect its borders, business, and values defies the predictions of realpolitik and standard counsels of foreign policy (Baehr and Castermans-Holleman 2004), suggesting the utility of a constructivist analysis of foreign policy roles and norms that link long-term national interest with the commonweal. Yet the evolving Dutch mix of moralism and pragmatism in the exercise of human rights policy shows that global citizenship is a constructed and constantly renegotiated paradigm, not an effluence of altruism. The limitations of the Netherlands' best-case promotion policies also show the boundaries of commonsense cosmopolitanism when it meets countervailing aspects of globalization, such as trade and migration patterns.

The Netherlands has made a conscious, concerted, and multifaceted effort to promote human rights for several generations, crystallized in both a 1979 Policy Document on Human Rights and a subsequent 2001 Memorandum on Human Rights Policy. Human rights is described as "a cornerstone" of Dutch foreign policy, although these documents ultimately call for pragmatic promotion "wherever possible"—without incurring a break in diplomatic or trade relations. Accordingly, the Netherlands has been a strong advocate in multilateral settings with a much more mixed record in bilateral relations—a profile similar to Sweden or Canada. Within the domain of multilateralism, the Dutch seem to emphasize international law more heavily, and are somewhat less active on transnational linkages than the other classic promoters. The Netherlands' aid record is stellar, in terms of volume, focus, and sustainability. Migration presents the biggest shortfall as well as the biggest change in Dutch policy; the general leveling off of global promotion efforts since the 1980s is exceeded by massive and controversial reversals in refugee reception.

The roots of this record roughly parallel the Netherlands' peer group of humanitarian internationalist states. Like the Nordic countries, Canada, and Costa Rica, the Netherlands is a globalized middle/regional power, with a strong history of domestic democracy, a moderate level of development, and a demilitarized or neutralist security niche. These necessary conditions are activated by a slightly different balance of similar agents than the typical global Good Samaritan, with less emphasis on leadership and more on an internationalist and mobilized civil society. The Netherlands' humanitarian ideology departs from the standard cosmopolitan consensus, but with a more system-building and pragmatic flavor, rather than the transformational social democracy of Sweden and Costa Rica or the vision of national distinctiveness found in Canada and South Africa.

HUMANITARIAN INTERNATIONALISM: THE DUTCH RECORD

"The Cornerstone": Global Institutions

The Netherlands has consistently sought to promote universal rights of the person in multilateral institutions in a variety of ways, from providing funding and expertise to developing new norms and mechanisms. The government's residence of that country, The Hague, has also served a unique role as the "legal capital of the world"—hosting most of the relevant judicial institutions (Van Krieken and McKay 2005). Within an unusually active small-power Dutch diplomacy, human rights plays an especially prominent role.

Like Sweden and Canada, the Netherlands is a founder and funder of the U.N. Multilateral support accounts for around one-third of the foreign ministry's aid budget, comprising approximately 6 million euros in the United Nations unit alone in 2006. The Netherlands gives especially strong support to the UNDP, Office of the High Commissioner for Human Rights, the United Nations' Human Rights Commission (now Council), and women's agencies.

The Dutch pioneered the use of special rapporteurs and working groups to focus on particular countries or patterns of violation more actively than the generic U.N. committees, notorious for their slow pace and diplomatic horse-trading. An estimated 30% of U.N. special rapporteurs have been Dutch or Dutch-educated, and the Netherlands' Theo van Boven played a pathbreaking role as both director of the U.N. Human Rights Center during the era of Latin American dictatorships, and special rapporteur on torture since 2001. Dutch former under-secretary of foreign affairs Peter Kooijmans also served as special rapporteur on torture. Dutch expert Cees Flinterman has been renowned for his vigorous promotion of women's rights at CEDAW (the Convention on the Elimination of Discrimination against Women). The Netherlands, along with Canada and Australia, promoted the establishment of the Working Group on Forced Disappearance in response to the situation in Argentina, and served on the body from 1984 to 1993 as its work expanded to other regions.

The Netherlands served on the United Nations' Human Rights Commission in 1961–1966, 1970–1975, 1980–1985, 1992–1997, and 2006. The Dutch have been slow but stalwart supporters of standard setting, joining Swedish initiatives for the Declaration and later Convention against Torture, actively promoting the Second Optional Protocol to the ICCPR, and initiatives on the death penalty as well as conscientious objection. Beyond sponsoring its own country and thematic resolutions, the Netherlands coordinated with like-minded states in the commission; for example, in 1985, the Netherlands took over sponsoring resolutions on Guatemala from Canada, after the kidnapping of Canadian nuns in Guatemala complicated Canada's advocacy (Baehr, Castermans-Holleman, and Grünfeld 2002). Although Dutch activity in the commission and treaty bodies has slowed considerably since the 1990s, there are some areas of notable ongoing promotion, such as gender issues. In the U.N. Third Committee, the Netherlands tabled the first resolution on female genital mutilation (FGM), and has sponsored initiatives on "honor crimes" and domestic violence throughout the U.N. system.

However, the Netherlands has been criticized by advocates and even allies as a fussy fellow traveler on substantively worthwhile juridical initiatives that may conflict with its precise vision of international law (such as the appropriate phase and venue for the proliferation of standards). The 1979 Memorandum on Human Rights and Foreign Policy states that the Netherlands considers the framework of international standards more or less complete, a conclusion reaffirmed in the 2001 policy guide. Hence, Dutch diplomats dropped back from joint promotion of the torture convention with Sweden on architectural grounds during the 1970s, rejoining in 1980 only after Amnesty International NL wrote to the Netherlands minister of justice and lobbied Parliament. In the end, the treaty was adopted in 1984—and the first chair of the monitoring committee was the Dutch Herman Burgers (Baehr in Everts and Walraven 1989). Similar patterns of legalistic hesitancy in norm promotion reappear in regard to the Convention on Forced Disappearance, the Optional Protocol to the Convention against Torture, and a monitoring instrument for the Convention on Economic and Social Rights (ICESR). Regarding the Convention on Forced Disappearance—which some Dutch officials argued messily overlapped with existing treaties—once again, pressure and publicity from two Dutch NGOs (HOM and HIVOS) reactivated the foreign ministry to support the measure on substantive grounds (interviews).

Nevertheless, the Netherlands has helped to foster a kind of global civil service and expertise on human rights in global institutions. Some have circulated and carried relevant experiences between institutions; for example, Peter Kooijmans moved from the United Nations Human Rights Commission to the foreign ministry to the International Court of Justice. In contrast to customary state practice of staffing the core committees with nationalist diplomats, until 1994 the Netherlands had a tradition of appointing an independent outsider (sometimes a former government official) as head of the U.N. Human Rights Commission delegation—for example, Cees Flinterman was head from 1993 to 1994 after he had returned to being a law professor at Maastricht University. He states that this civic status of Dutch representatives generally encouraged strong consultation with NGOs, even in the practice of interstate human rights diplomacy. A veteran of numerous international human rights posts, Flinterman stresses the Netherlands' commitment to providing independent global expertise. After serving the Human Rights Commission, he was nominated by the government (twice) to CEDAW, but never "instructed." He also served as an alternate (to Theo van Boven) on the U.N. Sub-Commission on Prevention of Discrimination and Protection of Minorities, and in that role once voted against companies trading with South Africa, which was opposed to the Dutch government's position at that time. "There were absolutely no consequences; there is a general feeling that Dutch independent experts on treaty bodies reflect well on Dutch international relations—precisely in their expertise and independence" (interview, July 4, 2006).

The story of one such expert, Theo van Boven, is in different respects both a microcosm and a pinnacle of Dutch human rights diplomacy. Van Boven began his diplomatic career in 1960 as the founder of the human rights desk in the international organizations department of the foreign ministry, a post in which he remained until 1976. Since human rights was then considered "a small subject with low interest," he wrote his own instructions, with the exception of a few sensitive areas: Israel, South Africa, and the former Dutch colony of West Irian/New Guinea as it transferred sovereignty under U.N. supervision. During those years, the foreign ministry gave him wide latitude to promote new standards, mechanisms, and country initiatives—even over the concerns of the geographic desks: "the general position was, if you can find two European supporters, go ahead" (he usually called Dublin and Copenhagen) (interview, June 28, 2006).

Later, when he needed to find allies at the U.N. on Latin America, he could count on Canada and the Nordic countries—and the United States during the Carter years (interview, June 28, 2006). In 1977, van Boven was appointed director of the United Nations Human Rights Center, a role he controversially expanded for the next five years—until he was removed under pressure from targeted violator states, especially dictatorial Argentina, regrettably acting in concert with Reagan's U.N. ambassador Jean Kirkpatrick (Guest 1990). Van Boven campaigned for resolutions, working groups, hearings, and other forms of pressure against the Latin American dictatorships. The Dutch government diplomatically acquiesced in his removal in 1982, but he returned home an inspiration to the Netherlands' civil society: Parliament adopted a motion supporting him, the media lauded him as a hero of conscience, and 40 Dutch NGOs signed a statement praising his service. Academic colleagues also active in the foreign service, like Cees Flinterman, state that they were influenced in their own promotion efforts by van Boven's book on his experience (interviews, June 28, July 4, 2006).

After a period of "academic exile" as a law professor, van Boven returned to international service as the Netherlands' head of the International Criminal Court delegation, then the registrar for the International Criminal Tribunal for the former Yugoslavia housed in The Hague, and finally the special rapporteur on torture. However, he is disappointed by the Netherlands' declining level of interventions in the U.N. Human Rights Commission, which he feels is diluted by coordination with the EU—for example, the mid-2000s votes on Guantanamo, in which the Dutch deferred to the EU, which then declined to vote. A further example of the perils of regionalism came when van Boven was invited to Spain as special rapporteur on torture to investigate allegations concerning mistreatment of ETA prisoners. When he discovered "some real problems," Spain campaigned against him and refused the traditional dialogue with the rapporteur, the EU closed ranks to defend a member state, and the Netherlands defended "my independence but not my findings. Only Switzerland, Norway, and Canada supported me in that case" (interview, June 28, 2006).

As in Sweden, Dutch human rights advocates and scholars complain that EU membership is a double-edged sword for pioneering human rights promoters. An academic included in the Dutch delegation to the EU echoed van Boven's complaints about a lowest-common-denominator trend in the U.N. Human Rights Commission—this time on the issue of China, particularly hamstrung by France's demurral (interview, July 4, 2006). Similarly, the director of an NGO that participates in Dutch policy implementation critiqued a broader mixed record when the Netherlands chaired the EU in 2004. On the one hand, the Dutch presidency was unable to get EU resolutions on China or several other country cases, and the "summits" the Netherlands led with Russia and ASEAN were closed to civil society and had no specified human rights content. On the other hand, the EU presidency did provide a modest opportunity for dissemination of a human rights defenders handbook and other policy tools and networks (interview, June 27, 2006). Moreover, the Netherlands used the 2004 presidency to push for the establishment of an EU special representative for human rights (Javier Solana).

Like Costa Rica, the Netherlands has played a special role in hosting global institutions—in this case, courts and tribunals. Holland has long hosted the International Court of Justice (ICJ), which deals with inter-state disputes, and the International Court of Arbitration. During the 1990s, the Dutch volunteered to host the International Criminal Tribunal for the former Yugoslavia, contributing physical facilities, extensive security and legal personnel, and over $3 million per year. The International Criminal Court (ICC), which prosecutes war crimes and crimes against humanity worldwide, is now hosted at The Hague. This role as the "legal capital of the world" has permeated Dutch society, from the extremely high presence of international law in Dutch academics to the notion of Dutch domestic accountability to international legal standards.

A key clause of the Dutch Constitution directs the government to promote the international legal order. In addition, according to 1953 and 1956 Amendments to the Dutch Constitution, Article 63, the government can make international legal agreements—even if they are contrary to the national constitution—with the consent of two-thirds of Parliament. Once passed, international agreements supersede national law.

It was in this spirit that the Netherlands recently joined the small set of countries seeking to implement universal jurisdiction for crimes against humanity in national courts. In April 2004, a Congolese torturer residing in Holland was convicted in Dutch court under the Dutch Torture Convention Implementation Act. In December 2005, a Dutch businessman was sentenced to 15 years for war crimes—selling chemicals for weapons to Saddam Hussein. Dutch officials stated that this prosecution was prompted in part by the opening of the International Criminal Court in The Hague. Similarly, in June 2006, a Dutch arms trafficker was charged with war crimes, and convicted of smuggling weapons to Liberia breaking a U.N. arms embargo (Simons 2005, 2006b, 2006c). Increased screening of asylum seekers for possible human rights violations in conflict zones and some of the additional legislation that enabled the domestic prosecutions for crimes against humanity as well as war crimes were proposed by the Dutch section of Amnesty International, in concert with a Social Democratic MP who had also been a prosecutor (interview, July 10, 2006).

The Netherlands has been a major force behind the OSCE minority rights regime. The Dutch initiative to establish a high commissioner for minorities was inspired in part by post-Srebrenica loss of international reputation and in part by growing realization of regional security interdependence, resonating further with traditional Dutch values of religious toleration. The first high commissioner was Dutch, the organization has been based at The Hague, and the Netherlands has provided a significant proportion of the finance (Reiding 2007: 396–397).

Finally, the Netherlands has contributed to "soft law" through the development and dissemination of human rights compliance standards and evaluation methodologies for businesses, NGOs, and bilateral programs. The Dutch humanist NGO HOM specializes in impact assessment instruments and training, including a set of business standards developed by the Danish Human Rights Institute now adopted by Dutch multinationals such as Shell, TNT, ABM, and Heineken. The Dutch foreign ministry has commissioned extensive evaluations of its own country programs and global NGOs supported by Dutch assistance (Biekart et al. 2004, Zwamborn et al. 2006, Landman and Abraham 2004). These modalities have been exchanged with foreign ministries, business groups, and NGO promoters in the United Kingdom, Canada, and Nordic countries.

Dutch diplomacy is highly developed: the Netherlands, a nation of around 15 million, has representation in over 150 countries. All of these Dutch embassies receive a human rights syllabus and voluntary biannual human rights trainings, all new diplomats receive several days of initial training in human rights and international law in their three-month course, and periodic in-service expert briefings are organized by the home office of the foreign ministry on human rights. The three divisions of the foreign ministry that deal with human rights at The Hague collectively comprise around 70 people, distributed among human rights, good governance/peace building, and humanitarian affairs (roughly similar to Canada's structure). The humanitarian affairs division alone supervises around 600 projects.

The human rights division administers aid to international organizations, nonpartner countries, supplementary human rights project assistance to partner countries, and global human rights NGOs. Although geographic desks within the foreign ministry are primarily assigned to answer parliamentary questions, any question concerning human rights must be signed off by the human rights unit. The human rights unit also coordinates with Dutch delegations to international organizations, briefs ministers and geographic desks on human rights issues before country visits, and brokers international law and policy discussions with other relevant ministries. Interministerial coordination has included peacekeeping policies by the Ministry of Defence for Afghanistan, which resulted in a memorandum of understanding (MOU) with that country regarding prisoners that limited transfers and detention conditions in accordance with international humanitarian law. Another significant relationship has been the Ministry of Justice participation in U.N. treaty negotiations and domestic ratifications, with the foreign ministry generally seeking to foster greater support and incorporation of international law. The human rights division has also engaged in special projects designed to enhance networking and dissemination of Dutch human rights diplomacy, such as translating a United Nations study of violence against women into Turkish and Arabic to distribute to local women's groups in the Middle East (interview, June 29, 2006).

Like Sweden, the Netherlands has a human rights ambassador, but does not have a broader national human rights institute (as do Denmark and Germany). The Dutch human rights ambassador travels extensively to express Dutch concerns abroad, maintains a liaison with civil society and Parliament, and builds linkages with homologous European ambassadors. He meets two to three times a year with the umbrella group for Dutch NGOs, the Broad Front for Human Rights, for "agenda setting," and "explaining" human rights and governance aid allocations in the Parliament. Since late 2005, the human rights ambassadors of the Netherlands, France, Spain, and Sweden have met several times with the Human Rights Committee of the Council of Europe to coordinate some joint initiatives: thus far, combined visits to Cambodia and the Philippines (interview, June 29, 2006).

"Wherever Possible": Bilateral Relations

Although multilateral promotion efforts have been the predominant venue for the Netherlands, bilateral pressures have been exercised in a series of cases since the 1970s. One aspect of the preference for multilateral channels on cases of fellow middle/regional powers like South Africa and Turkey is a realistic assessment of the Netherlands' relative lack of bilateral leverage; as one human rights scholar put it, "At this point, the only country the Netherlands *can* influence bilaterally is Suriname" (interview, July 4, 2006). In a few such cases, the Netherlands has actually been able to catalyze EU efforts (notably Indonesia), but more commonly the EU has been a brake on Dutch concerns (as in China) (Zwamborn et al. 2006). Bilateral efforts have moved from mainly sanctions and conditionality to an increasing preference for dialogue and training programs. The 2001 memo indicates that Dutch policy should prioritize countries with massive or serious violations, EU applicants, and countries with special historic ties to the Netherlands. Overall, bilateral diplomatic initiatives are less institutionalized and more variable than the multilateral program; as one Dutch diplomat observed, a notable embassy-based promotion program in Guatemala declined in the early 2000s in part due to staff rotations (also see Biekart et al. 2004), even as new personnel rotating into China energized a human rights program for that country (interview, June 29, 2006).

As in Costa Rica, the Netherlands' bilateral human rights policy begins with a postwar special relationship with Israel and support for associated refugee issues. From 1967 to 1990 the Netherlands represented Israel in Moscow, issuing 600,000 Israeli visas to Jewish émigrés. Although this mediating relationship may have restrained some bilateral criticism of the USSR, the Dutch did issue demarches for Anatoly Sharansky and other cause célèbre, and did carry lists of dissidents during visits and disarmament talks in 1985–1986. Furthermore, the Netherlands led the Human Dimension Mechanism at the Helsinki Conference, which contributed to the Helsinki Accords' human rights understandings (Baehr, Castermans-Holleman, and Grünfeld 2002).

On more direct relations with Israel and the Middle East conflict, the Netherlands steered an uneasy course between the dictates of post–World

War II guilt,[1] colonial obligations to Muslim Indonesia, Dutch Labor party linkages to Israeli trade unions and their Labor party counterpart, contravening pressures from allies (U.S. pro-Israel versus French pro-Arab sympathies), and dependence on Middle East oil supplies. Thus, the Netherlands cautiously avoided action from the 1948 establishment of the Jewish state through the 1956 Suez War, but by the 1973–1974 Arab oil embargo supported Israel on principle—despite marked economic losses. Eventually a pattern developed in which the Netherlands supported Israel on the *Arab*-Israeli conflict with neighboring states, but Palestinians on questions of the Israeli occupation, *Palestinian* rights, and Israel's obligation to participate in a comprehensive settlement. Hence the Dutch assisted Yasir Arafat in exile, provided numerous assistance projects in Gaza, hosted part of the Oslo Agreement negotiations, and criticized Israel's 1998 invasion of Lebanon (Grünfeld 1991, interview, June 28, 2006).

A more comprehensive bilateral human rights policy was catalyzed in 1973, under the van der Stoel administration, in response to the Pinochet dictatorship in Chile. Chile was a "best case" for human rights mobilization—a globally recognized violent overthrow of a democratic government followed by massive assassinations, torture, and imprisonment of political opponents, in the era of emergence of the international human rights regime. The murdered democratic president, Salvador Allende, had links to the Dutch Labor Party, and "in the case of Chile, NGOs were almost part of the government itself. In a previous episode of his life, [Dutch Cabinet minister] Mr. Pronk had been a cofounder of the Chile Committee" (Baehr, Castermans-Holleman and Grünfeld 2002: 1006). The Dutch campaign was a combination of measures in all available venues. Following the 1973 coup, the Netherlands ended financial credits to Dutch companies doing business with Chile, official loans, and arms sales. In 1974 the Dutch cosponsored a U.N. resolution (with Britain and Sweden), in 1975 a U.N. commission inquiry, in 1976 and 1977 further resolutions, in 1978 a working group, in 1979 a special rapporteur, and in 1980 further measures in the U.N. Commission on Human Rights. But critics note that in the similar case of Argentina, despite Dutch leadership of U.N. condemnation, the Netherlands did *not* coordinate multilateral castigation with bilateral measures, and continued to trade heavily with that dictatorship and even export arms (Baehr, Castermans-Holleman, and Grünfeld 2002).

---

1. Despite the Netherlands' international image as the conscientious rescuers of Anne Frank and other Holocaust victims, the broader pattern is that Dutch Jews were deported at the highest rate in occupied Western Europe. "Tens of thousands of Danes— politicians, pastors, fishermen, ambulance drivers—helped smuggle 7,300 of the country's 7,800 Jews into Sweden. Many more helped by not betraying the operation. Only 116 Danish Jews, or 1.5 per cent of the total, died in the Holocaust. The other extreme in western Europe was the Netherlands. More than 100,000 Dutch Jews—three-quarters of the total— were massacred. This was nearly twice the proportion killed in Belgium, where Jews had far more chance of finding hiding places, and three times as high as in France" (Kuper 2005).

Continuing this trend of mixed action, along with the growth of regionalization, the Dutch led ambiguous pressure on Turkey limited to the EU. Linkages are tight, as Turkey is one of the Netherlands' leading export markets and an estimated 300,000 Turks live in the Netherlands. In 1982, the Netherlands filed a state complaint against Turkey under the European Human Rights Convention (joined by Denmark, Norway, Sweden, and France) and issued a critical 1983 policy memo—but continued to export arms. By 1987, these pressures had induced Turkey to a "friendly settlement," involving some reforms. The Netherlands participated in a further 1995 Council of Europe Parliamentary resolution against Turkey, but since 2000 Dutch policy toward Turkey has emphasized positive promotion of legal aid and training programs without criticism or sanctions (Baehr, Castermans-Holleman, and Grünfeld 2002).

A cluster of cases with close historic ties to Holland show similarly mixed efforts with variable responses. Suriname and Indonesia were both Dutch colonies, which devolved into dictatorships receiving significant Dutch aid. In Suriname, one wave of political executions in 1982 led to a suspension of Dutch assistance to that small, isolated country, followed by some regime accountability. However, massive oil-rich Indonesia was not amenable to Dutch leverage. After the mid-1960s massacres, a generation of chronic political repression, and occupation of East Timor, ongoing Dutch diplomatic pressure—catalyzed by NGOs—culminated in several aid suspensions and reductions in the late 1980s and early 1990s. One such cut, coordinated with Denmark and Canada in response to the Dili massacre in East Timor, resulted in an Indonesian investigation. But by 1992, the Indonesians simply spurned Dutch aid, after a more definitive attempt at conditionality in that year (Baehr in Forsythe 2000a, van den Berg 2001).

After Indonesia democratized, the Netherlands became more active in promoting rule of law and accountability, under a February 2000 bilateral Memorandum of Understanding. The Netherlands, via the EU and U.N., pressed for peacekeeping in the Moluccas and East Timor, leading to an arms embargo and multinational force in the latter case. The Dutch provided extensive support for human rights tribunals, especially on East Timor—although the unprecedented attempt at accountability was internationally judged to be incomplete at best. Similarly, the Netherlands has supported the multilateral Partnership for Governance Reform along with the UNDP, World Bank, and Asian Development Bank (Zwamborn et al. 2006).

South Africa, even more than Israel, presented the Netherlands with a quandary of competing values and interests, with an ambivalent policy also evolving over several decades. An illustration of the salience of this issue in Dutch politics is that debates on South Africa sanctions brought on Dutch Cabinet crises—twice. The Dutch core commitment to tolerance and nondiscrimination clashed with "family ties" to a pariah state founded by (Afrikaner) Dutch settlers with strong religious links to the Dutch Reformed Church, supplemented by an estimated 43,000 Dutch migrants to South Africa following World War II. In a classic expression of postcolonial identity politics, in 1953 a Dutch prime minister referred to white-ruled South Africa as the Netherlands' "adult daughter" (Baehr, Castermans-Holleman, Grünfeld 2002: 196; Brysk, Parsons, Sandholtz 2002). Some observers point out that the "common kinship" argument cut both ways; inspiring some Dutch governments to refrain from criticism, even as Dutch civil society argued that the Netherlands had a special historical responsibility to contest oppression committed by their coethnics (Baehr, Castermans-Holleman, and Grünfeld 2002).

Thus, until 1963 the Netherlands abstained from U.N. resolutions against apartheid, although it followed the U.N. optional military embargo. By 1965, without adopting sanctions on the South African government, the Dutch allocated positive financial support for legal aid to the victims of apartheid, and in 1968 issued a timid policy declaration based on dialogue. In 1973, as human rights policy strengthened across the board, the Netherlands ended Dutch government investment in South Africa and pushed Dutch private corporations to adopt voluntary codes of conduct. A further escalation occurred in 1977, with a diplomatic push for a *mandatory* U.N. arms embargo, cancellation of bilateral export credits, and a symbolically significant downgrading of the Dutch–South African cultural agreement (Voorhoeve 1979).

During the 1980s Dutch policy toward South Africa became more vigorous, although mostly multilateral. After early 1980s parliamentary sanctions debates, the Netherlands used a stint on the U.N. Security Council to try to secure a U.N. oil embargo. By 1986, as chair of the (then-) European Community, the Dutch did succeed in a policy of no *new* investment in South Africa by member states, as well as no exports of iron and steel (Kremer and Pijpers in Everts and Walraven 1989). In the later 1980s, several Dutch NGO campaigns against the death penalty led to Dutch embassy monitoring and appeals regarding a series of political executions in South Africa (van den Berg 2001).

Currently, Dutch government and society debate appropriate relations with the same human rights violators targeted by the like-minded promoter states: China, Iran, Indonesia, and U.S. counterterror campaigns. The general trend has been persistent agenda setting but declining and selective activity. As a comprehensive study by a trio of long-standing scholars and policy participants concluded, "Has the Netherlands become less outspoken on the subject of human rights during the last quarter of the twentieth century? On the basis of the cases studied, our answer would tend to be affirmative" (Baehr, Castermans-Holleman, and Grünfeld 2002: 233).

The contemporary case of China shows the familiar pattern of declining leverage, ineffective attempts to channel criticism through multilateral venues, a preference for incentives over sanctions, and inherent ambivalence (in fairness, shared by Sweden and Canada). After the Netherlands did orchestrate some criticism of China in the U.N. through the 1990s, in 1997 China froze economic relations in protest (Baehr, Castermans-Holleman, and Grünfeld 2002). The Netherlands has used official visits to regularly express concerns on the death penalty, freedom of religion, rule of law, and individual cases: in 1999 during a visit by the queen to China, at a 2001 economic delegation, in 2004 run-ups to the Netherlands' EU presidency, as well as several additional missions by the human rights ambassador. However, when a Dutch foreign minister planned to include a meeting between the ambassador and the persecuted religious group Falun Gong in a 2001 tour, the Chinese authorities pressured the Dutch, and the visit was "postponed." On the individual cases, the Chinese authorities have begun to be somewhat more responsive with information, but in only one of an estimated 80 demarches was an individual released from government custody (Zwamborn et al. 2006). The Netherlands now plays a major role in the EU's annual human rights dialogue with China, and the Netherlands embassy finances a special additional cooperation fund earmarked for human rights implementation (of standards China has ratified), such as judicial training.

Although China has been notoriously impervious to most forms of international pressure, the Netherlands has achieved occasional successes in concerted campaigns with other contemporary cases. In Iran, Dutch-led EU pressure has produced moratoriums on stoning and the execution of juveniles, despite continuing structural abuses and persecution of women and religious minorities. Dutch dialogue, 16 million euros per year of governance assistance, and interventions under a bilateral memo of understanding have helped Rwanda to modify its justice system for prosecution of those implicated in the 1994 genocide and defended the independence of a handful of NGOs. However, combined Dutch and EU pressure was unable to achieve accountability for political opponents who "disappeared" prior to the 2003 elections, leading to the suspension of the Netherlands' 250,000 euros of election assistance to Rwanda (Zwamborn et al. 2006).

PUTTING YOUR MONEY WHERE YOUR MOUTH IS: DUTCH DEVELOPMENT AID

The Netherlands was one of the first countries to provide overseas development assistance in 1949, and this small country quickly became one of the world's leading donors of humanitarian aid—in both absolute and relative terms. ODA grew about 24% from 1963 to 1976, from .26% to .82% of GNP (Voorhoeve 1979)—from the mid-1970s to the mid-1980s, the Netherlands led the OECD in aid levels. Dutch aid reached the U.N. target level of 1% of GNP by 1971—after a cabinet minister threatened to resign unless it was raised—and later on to 1.5% by 1976 (Malcontent 2000: 32). Levels in the 1990s stabilized at 1.1% total foreign assistance, of which 0.8% was reserved for pure development aid

(Malcontent 2000: 53).[2] Besides direct funds, the Dutch have provided notable development expertise and technical assistance bilaterally and through the U.N. agencies, and participated in almost every World Bank country-specific aid consortium (Nekkers and Malcontent 2000). In addition to the high gross levels and proportion of development assistance, the Netherlands ranked first in the world in 2006 and 2007 on the complex Commitment to Development Index incorporating aid, trade, investment, migration, environment, security, and technology assistance to the global poor—including complementary policies such as tropical timber imports and anticorruption efforts (http://www.cgdev.org). In 1999, the Netherlands provided 7.1 billion guilders in foreign aid.

Although mainly a principled policy, Dutch aid represented a mix of values and interests; in the early years, it was perceived as a vehicle for postcolonial international prestige, export promotion, and technical overseas employment. Although by the early 1970s colonies were receiving only 22% of aid, three-time development minister Jan Pronk stated, "On the one hand, aid was an attempt by the former colonizers to preserve their political influence and economic advantages under changed constitutional circumstances. At the same time, it reflected a certain sense of guilt for the suffering caused in colonial times and therefore included an element of atonement" (Malcontent 2000: 33–34). A powerful coalition of "merchants and clergymen" lobbied for the Dutch aid program. For the former, a significant proportion of aid was tied to Dutch suppliers through the 1970s—for the latter, co-financing for the Catholic, Protestant, and Humanist development NGOs had risen to 359 million guilders by 1990 (Malcontent 2000: 12, 18, 23–24). A key marker of the evolution toward a more principled policy was Dutch support for structural change in the international economic order, such as increased prices for the raw materials produced by developing countries, as early as 1962 and continuing through vigorous advocacy of UNCTAD North-South talks, the New International Economic Order, and import promotion of developing country products (Malcontent 2000: 28–29).

Since the 1990s, Dutch aid has been reformed to provide better targeting and greater governance focus. The number of aid partners was reduced to "17 + 3," funds were introduced for *peacemaking* to complement Dutch peacekeeping, and in 1993–1994, the Netherlands signed a model Sustainable Development Agreement with Benin, Bhutan, and Costa Rica. Following the 2001 Memorandum on Human Rights Policy, the government sought better integration between human rights and development policy, assigning greater weight to "good governance" programs, and

---

2. On a cautionary note, the proportional formula for aid allocation produced two unintended consequences: budget poaching from questionably affiliated policy areas and unplanned reductions due to national budget fluctuations. In the first regard, development funds have been raided at times to pay for refugee reception, export promotion, and even occasionally military expenses related to peacekeeping.

greater coordination with United Nations standards, as well as parallel German, British, and Swedish experiences. Furthermore, the Netherlands now contributes to the EU's cofinancing European Initiative for Democracy and Human Rights (125 million euros in 2004) (AIV 2003).

Dutch official aid is distributed through a minister for development cooperation (attached to the foreign ministry, in contrast to the independent Swedish SIDA and Canadian CIDA), the foreign ministry via embassies, thematic units such as the Human Rights Office, contributions to multilateral development organizations, and some partnerships between relevant domestic ministries and foreign counterparts—such as the Ministry of Justice for rule of law programs. Direct humanitarian aid, which would generally be focused on social rights and empowerment of disadvantaged groups, is decentralized and administered in country. Dutch NGOs, such as the Humanist Committee (HOM)—now called Aim for Human Rights, have an open tender to administer some of these programs and are often involved. In addition, designated Dutch development NGOs—currently HIVOS, NOVIB, ECO, PLOM, and Cordaid—receive an independent set-aside from Parliament of 10% of the Netherlands' annual 0.8% of GDP aid target (interview, June 27, 2006). Dutch aid is coordinated with a like-minded network including the OECD Donor Action Committee Human Rights Task Force; the Swiss, Swedish, German, Canadian, and British aid programs; the EU's COHOM; UNDP; UNIFEM; and the World Bank.

The human rights unit of the foreign ministry provides targeted aid exclusively dedicated to human rights projects for 15 million euros per year in development partner countries (restricted to nongovernmental recipients), with an additional 1 million euros per year for non-ODA countries (such as Iran). This unit also provides major support to five international human rights NGOs: the Geneva-based International Council for Human Rights Policy, the International Service for Human Rights, the Federation pour les Droits de l'Homme, the Association for the Prevention of Torture, and the Religious Tolerance World Forum (interview, June 29, 2006). Dutch support for nine international human rights NGOs, including the World Organization against Torture, Penal Rights International, the International Commission of Jurists, Minority Rights Group, Anti-Slavery International, and the Helsinki Federation, totaled 5.3 million euros between 1997 and 2001. Such aid generally provides 5–15% of the organizations' budgets, in some cases core as well as program support. An independent evaluation showed that all of the transnational organizations were efficient, accountable, and effective in producing research reports, educational resources, contribution to standard setting in international forums, and even occasional direct improvement in human rights abuses—such as prisoner releases (Landman and Abraham 2004).

The funding criteria for country selection for Dutch human rights aid includes the recipient's international relevance and political relationship with the Netherlands, the projects' strategy and timeliness, and the fit with Dutch promotion priorities. These include the following issues: the struggle against impunity, violence against women, protection of human rights defenders, the death penalty, torture, children in armed conflict, freedom of expression, and religious intolerance (these and other goals are coordinated with the EU Guidelines and COHOM) (interview, June 29, 2006).

In a best case of Dutch will and influence to support development on principle, results were decidedly mixed. When Suriname gained independence in 1975, the former colony was offered massive, treaty-based, Dutch aid, partly designed to stem a mass exodus of residents to the Netherlands, which had already begun. The 3.5 billion guilder aid package made the country of 350,000 people one of the world's leading aid recipients. In 1982, when the dictator assassinated 15 opponents, the Netherlands suspended aid (Malcontent 2000: 34, 47). Although the enormous infusion of Dutch resources did increase income levels and improve health conditions in the former colony, it was insufficient to reduce an ongoing brain drain, and did not produce sustainable development or noticeably improve human rights conditions (van Galen 2000).

On the other hand, Guatemala—one of the top recipients of Dutch governance assistance but with lower overall aid levels—yielded some real gains, despite a forbidding political context of wavering governability and attempts to block mandated reforms. Beginning in the waning days of the civil war, in 1992 the Netherlands dedicated 7.6 million guilders to aid programs for Guatemala's most marginalized groups—Indians and women, along with 12.5 million to support human rights NGOs, co-ops, and refugees. Following the signing of the 1996 peace accords, this aid was doubled to support the peace process and reconstruction (Baehr, Castermans-Holleman, and Grünfeld 2002). A government-commissioned evaluation of the 1997–2003 (approximately $14 million per year) governance program in Guatemala found generally positive results. Five programs supported by the Dutch played a significant role in the peace process, including demobilization of ex-guerrillas (via the United Nations' MINUGUA), a truth commission, forensic anthropology team, and land registration service. Dutch diplomatic pressure protected the director of the controversial land program from removal by the minister of agriculture—and the replacement of the recalcitrant minister instead. Dutch support for women's rights and initiatives on domestic violence played a unique role in Guatemala, albeit slower to yield measurable results. Rule of law programs focused on peace judges and civilian models for security forces (Biekart et al. 2004).

The Netherlands does apply human rights conditionality to its humanitarian aid program. Aid was suspended to Pakistan in 1971 in response to its conflict with Bangladesh, and to Uganda because of Idi Amin's dictatorship; in 1979 aid to Vietnam was reduced due to the invasion of Cambodia (Malcontent 2000: 33, 40–41). Overall guidelines were first applied widely during the 1980s political conflicts in Haiti, El Salvador, and

Guatemala (Baehr, Castermans-Holleman, and Grünfeld 2002). Aid has been completely denied due to prohibitive levels of human rights abuse and state involvement in Syria, Burma, Zaire, and Kazakhstan. Deteriorations in rights were met with aid cuts in Chile, Sri Lanka, Sudan, Niger, Mali, and Mauritania. Positive incentives of increased aid were provided to support more recent improvements in human rights in Cambodia, Haiti, Malawi, Chile, and Guatemala (Baehr in Forsythe 2000a).

PEACEKEEPING: THE THIN BLUE LINE

As in Sweden, peacekeeping is the raison d'être of the Dutch military, but less numerous Dutch forces have experienced more serious challenges than their Nordic counterparts in the key conflict zones of the post–Cold War period. The first sentence of the Netherlands Ministry of Defence's (2004) briefing booklet on Dutch security policy reads, "The Netherlands maintains an active peace and security policy. It attaches great value to the promotion of the international rule of law and has long demonstrated wide concern for human suffering and a strong commitment to combating human rights violations," and goes on to state that the Dutch armed forces have three tasks: national defense, "promoting the international rule of law," and humanitarian aid. Peace operations must have a mandate from some international organization, such as the U.N., NATO, the OSCE, or the EU, and must be approved by Parliament under the "Frame of Reference for Decision-making for the Deployment of Military Units Abroad." An advisory report on failing states commissioned by the Dutch ministries of foreign affairs, defense, and cooperation to consider Dutch international legal frameworks for intervention links a Dutch "duty" of humanitarian intervention when requested by the United Nations to the Dutch Constitution's Article 90 exhortation for the government to promote the international legal order. It goes on to state that Dutch military availability for "missions at the upper end of the spectrum of force" is important to give the Netherlands a seat at the table in international political debates on problem regions (AIV 2004b: 62, 66).

Since 1963, Dutch forces have been sent on United Nations' missions to Angola, Cambodia, Mozambique, and Lebanon. Since the 1990s, the Netherlands' troops have played central roles in Macedonia and Afghanistan, with a Dutch commander for the U.N. force in Ethiopia and Eritrea (2000). Current deployments include around 1,000 Dutch soldiers in the Balkans, along with about 1,300 in Iraq.

The presence and inaction of Dutch peacekeepers in Srebrenica during the 1994 massacre of 8,000 has been a blot on the national conscience. The Netherlands had sent 630 peacekeepers, later reduced to 430, to guard the United Nations–designated "safe zone" in the former Yugoslavia. But overwhelmed Dutch forces with an unclear mandate failed to protect the refugees from Serb gunmen, and stood by as enemy forces murdered

thousands of men while abusing women and children as part of a strategy of "ethnic cleansing." Although the Dutch government requested a
United Nations' investigation in the aftermath, when the U.N. refused,
the Netherlands commissioned its own inquiry—via an obscure but thor-
ough research institute for the documentation of World War II–era war
crimes (Netherlands Institute for War Documentation 2002).

In 1995, following news of the massacre, the then-minister of defense
offered to resign, but the prime minister insisted he remain until completion of the report. When the report finally emerged after numerous delays
in 2002, under the same prime minister, parliamentary and public debate on
the report's establishment of Dutch negligence led to the resignation of the
entire government, which took responsibility for the massacre and their command of the failed Dutch peacekeeping operation (Voorhoeve 1979). After
the Srebrenica debacle, the Netherlands' peacekeeping criteria and peacekeepers' rules of engagement were revised by the Ministry of Defence and
foreign ministry, in close consultation with international law. In addition, the
Netherlands developed perhaps the world's most active program on military
ethics via its national defense academy. The academy itself gives mandated
ethics courses for officers, including features such as the use of Canadian
U.N. commander in Rwanda Romeo Dallaire's book, lectures from anthro-
pologists researching conflict zones, visits to refugee reception centers, and
training on sexual harassment and peacekeeper-sponsored prostitution. In
concert with the Ministry of Defense and sometimes international military
bodies such as NATO, the Netherlands Defence Academy sponsors regular conferences on issues such as child soldiers and "asymmetrical warfare,"
as well as publications including a multivolume study, *Military Ethics: The
Dutch Approach* (Van Baarda and Verweij 2006, interview, July 5, 2006).

The twenty-first century Dutch deployment of about 2,000 forces in
Afghanistan has raised renewed concerns about the criteria for humanitarian intervention, the conduct of counterinsurgency, and the tensions
between Dutch and allied human rights standards. The Dutch Parliament
has regularly debated the basis, risk, and exit strategy for the Dutch presence in Afghanistan; as in Canada, the Dutch left is critical of potential
neocolonialism or service to U.S. imperialism, whereas centrist governments and internationalist militaries support the interventions as the
promotion of national values and liberal international norms ("Dutch Parliament" 2006). As far as the conduct of counterinsurgency, Dutch peacekeepers in Afghanistan emphasize reconstruction and training activities
(like the Canadian Provincial Reconstruction Teams), but the Dutch also
openly avoid combat in the most contested zones. "We're not here to fight
the Taliban," said the Dutch commander, "We're here to make the Taliban irrelevant" (Chivers 2007: A1). Upholding internalized international
human rights standards over the practices of U.S. allies and Afghan hosts,
the Netherlands refuses to transfer Afghan prisoners captured in their
operations to Afghan national or NATO forces without guarantees and
monitoring of possible inhumane detention, torture, and rendition. An

early 2006 memo of understanding on detainee policy for the Dutch military mission, drafted by the Netherlands Ministry of Defence, was revised and toughened in June of that year—after the Dutch section of Amnesty International lobbied Parliament and launched a public debate insisting, in the words of a supportive MP, "you must guarantee they do not end up in Guantanamo" (interview, July 10, 2006).

The smaller, more routine Dutch operation in Iraq has been marred by one controversial case of a civilian death in the field. After Dutch soldier "Erik O" killed an Iraqi civilian during a military operation, the Netherlands' civil prosecutor brought charges of improper use of force in 2004. The Dutch soldier was ultimately cleared by a higher court. The trial and public debate were replete with conflict between the Ministry of Defence and Ministry of Justice concerning legal and authorized responses to unconventional conflict in a multinational operation, which may ultimately have some repercussions for the understanding of future Dutch deployments—but thus far it remains an isolated case (Deiben and Deiben 2005).

Direct Dutch military intervention is supplemented by peace-building support for the training and finance of national or regional military forces, as well as complementary postconflict police training, election support, and reconciliation activities. Much of this support comes under either the 1996 Directorate of Crisis Management and Humanitarian Aid or the 2000 peace-building division of the human rights office of the Ministry of Foreign Affairs, although there are also direct training programs under the Ministry of Defense and a Dutch Centre for International Police Cooperation. Most of these multidonor and often multilateral programs are concentrated in Africa and the Balkans. In sample year 2002 the Netherlands dedicated 10 million euros to 20 activities, including training Nigerian soldiers for African peacekeeping, restructuring the Bosnian army, and support for the Afghan police (Frerks et al. 2003).

MIGRATION: "A DUTCH DILEMMA"

Just as Gunnar Myrdal labeled race "an American dilemma"—when national identity conflicts clash with national values of liberal institutions—migration could be considered the parallel, transnational Dutch dilemma. From the end of World War II, Dutch refugee policies were famously liberal, for victims of dictatorships from all regions and ideologies. For example, by 1989, there were 2,500 Chilean refugees in the Netherlands (Baehr, Castermans-Holleman, and Grünfeld 2002). But from the 1970s to the 1990s, massive waves of economic migration by Muslims from Turkey and Morocco, originally invited by Dutch companies, created cultural tensions and strained the social policy capacities of the shrinking Dutch welfare state. Although national immigration figures rose to a historically unprecedented but manageable 10–15% (similar to Sweden), immigrants comprised as much as 40% of the population of Amsterdam. Dutch liberals' multicultural commitments were tested by increasing crime, gender-based abuses such as "honor killings" on Dutch soil, and Islamic fundamentalist violence. Political violence by immigrants included the assassination of gay anti-immigrant politician Pim Fortuyn, as well as the murder of a Dutch filmmaker, Theo Van Gogh, who had controversially criticized Islam in his work. As one Dutch human rights scholar explains,

> When massive immigration started in the 1960s, migrants were simply allowed to erect their own "pillars" to foster *their* culture and ideas, and were benignly neglected by the traditional Dutch inhabitants. It is this neglect that has exploded in Dutch society's face at the beginning of the 21st century when radical elements in the Muslim pillar made clear that they did not adhere to the elaborate collective bowl of norms and ostentatiously stuck to their own. In return, the traditional Dutch did not allow for the freest possible spirit of tolerance anymore. (Herman 2006: 865)

At the same time, by the 1990s, larger numbers of more troubled refugees from the Balkans, several African conflicts, and the Middle East complicated asylum standards originally based on individual political dissidents and refugee reception based on integration. There was spillover migration as other EU countries tightened their borders; for example, in 1994 the Netherlands received 19% of all EU asylum applications (Bocker and Havinga 1997: 43). The Netherlands developed a huge backlog of applications, a restive and marginalized immigrant population, and Dutch citizen discontent with widespread perceptions of immigration abuse and newcomers' violations of Dutch liberal norms.

In 2000, the Netherlands adopted a new Aliens Act, followed in 2002 with a new accelerated procedure for adjudicating asylum claims. The new act regularizes but tightens refugee policy: reducing asylum status to one category with an annually renewable maximum of five years of temporary protected status, shifting primary claims to an administrative review with judicial appraisal only for appeals, and obliging officials to follow bloc rulings without discretion for humanitarian exceptions. About half of all asylum cases are now processed and usually deported under the accelerated procedure, which gives authorities 48 working hours to determine status—although under Article 3 of the European Convention and article 33 of the International Refugee Convention, the Netherlands does refrain from "refoulement," granting temporary nondeportable status to a sizeable subgroup not deemed to meet the refugee criteria who would be personally endangered by return to their country of origin and cannot be resettled in a safe third country (interview, June 30, 2006).[3]

---

3. Ever mindful of international standards, Dutch parliamentary rights advocates proposed in 2002 that the Netherlands' new immigration policy should be modified by Dutch adherence to the Council of Europe Convention on Minority Rights, but opposition by the Parliament's First Chamber and Migration Minister Rita Verdonk resulted instead in a downgrading of *which* minorities the Netherlands would consider covered by the Convention—in the end, limited to the tiny group of native-born Frisian-language speakers of one province.

Government data shows that most asylum seekers since 2000 do come from conflict zones; recently Iraq, Somalia, Angola, and Afghanistan are the leading source countries for refugee applicants (AIV 2004c: 24). Overall, the EU, Turkey, Morocco, China, and the postcolonial areas of Antilles, Suriname, and Indonesia are the main sources for overall migration. Although asylum seekers held steady at 8–12% of total migrants, asylum approval rates ranged from only 7.3% in 2002 to 10.8% in 2004 (AIV 2004c: 18).

In the same year as the Alien Act, the Netherlands established a new Ministry of Alien Affairs and Integration within the Ministry of Justice, the only such hydra-headed "ministry without portfolio" except for the foreign ministry's relationship with the Ministry of Development Cooperation. The new ministry was headed by rising Conservative politician Rita Verdonk, dubbed "Iron Rita" for her relentlessly restrictive policies— for example, in 2006, she attempted to deport 26,000 asylum seekers who had overstayed their temporary status. With this institutional move, the Netherlands also combined the functions of immigration (screening and border control) and integration (the opposite of U.S. reform of the I.N.S. around the same time, which separated enforcement under Homeland Security and reception under Health and Human Services). Formerly, the Netherlands' Integration Department had been located in the ministry of home affairs and was thus more oriented toward social welfare, often generating proposals to strengthen migrants' legal status as recipients of programs. Appeals of immigration status were shifted to the quasi-judicial Aliens Chamber of the executive Council of State, which has limited itself to review of procedure and insisted on Ministry of Justice and Immigration Service establishment of facts. This functional limitation of due process has resisted not only the appeals of Dutch migration lawyers, but even the 2003 Said ruling by the European Court—which asked for full reconsideration of the facts of that case by the Dutch appeals body. Finally, in 2006 Parliament began debate on a bill on integration, which would reform naturalization and citizenship tests in a manner Dutch rights advocates contend is culturally discriminatory, and institutionalize ongoing differential treatment standards for native and naturalized Dutch citizens (interview, June 30, 2006, Human Rights Watch 2003).

These changes have been so prejudicial to the rights of migrants and asylum seekers that they caused Human Rights Watch to issue its first-ever report on the Netherlands. The international human rights watchdog group points out that the accelerated procedure is applied with inconsistent criteria, inadequate safeguards, and ultimately rejects at least 60% of asylum seekers. Although accelerated processing is supposed to be limited to applicants from safe countries, it is commonly applied to those from war-torn countries, especially if they have reached the Netherlands indirectly. Moreover, at least 30% of child asylum seekers are processed in the 48-hour track, which systematically denies their access to counsel, child welfare services, and family reunification efforts, and sometimes even translation. Human Rights Watch warns of the negative implications of a reduction in the arrival of around 7,000 unaccompanied minors in the Netherlands in 2000, by about one-third to one-half with the introduction of the new procedure—cited by Dutch authorities as a success, it more likely represents a chilling effect and denial of refuge to the most powerless claimants (Human Rights Watch 2003).

The human rights NGO also criticizes the provision of inadequate food and housing for refugee applicants pending their claims, including more long-term applicants who may spend weeks or months in government reception facilities. This picture of substandard conditions for refugees is expanded by the report of a recent Dutch ombudsman that about 16–19% of his complaint caseload concerned migration procedures and living conditions in asylum reception centers. The Dutch ombudsman institution, established in 1982 and incorporated in the Dutch Constitution in 1999, represents one of the only loci of accountability for non-citizens and, like in Costa Rica, seems to serve as an effective extension of Dutch democracy. His nonbinding recommendations, within a narrow mandate, are generally followed by executive agencies, and in the last instance pursued by Parliament. A recent ombudsman reports that on migration, at one point, he recommended 95 changes in conditions of asylum centers—and the government eventually followed them all (interview, June 30, 2006).

The cause célèbre of Somalian-born Dutch parliamentarian Ayaan Hirsi Ali displays some of the contradictions of Dutch refugee policy, and the intensity of the globalization debates around migration in the Netherlands. As former ombudsman and Amnesty International chair Roel Fernhout points out, it also shows the implications of these debates for Dutch democracy: the right to citizenship is not absolute in the Netherlands, and decisions of the executive can be used to change the composition of Parliament (interview, June 30, 2006).

After gaining political asylum in the Netherlands in 1992 and citizenship in 1997, Ms. Hirsi Ali rose from housecleaning to parliamentary representative on a neoliberal, assimilationist program that included extensive criticisms of Islam's treatment of women. Following death threats from Islamic fundamentalists against Hirsi Ali in 2002, government protection, and attendant controversy, the legislator's background and political ambitions came under increasing scrutiny by the press and public. Coverage of her case culminated in a critical documentary alleging that the parliamentarian had lied in her application for asylum, which was based on fleeing an arranged marriage. As a result, Ali's former ally, the politically ambitious hard-line immigration minister and fellow Conservative Party feminist Rita Verdonk cancelled Hirsi Ali's Dutch citizenship, stripping her of her seat and subjecting her to deportation. The move paralleled a cluster of around 50 similar asylum revocation cases, and it is reported that Verdonk was at pains to show evenhandedness, in the broader context of her program to deport 26,000 asylum seekers who had overstayed their appeals. But the outcome and conduct of this case provoked parliamentary rebellion and a Cabinet crisis, including controversy on the government's proper use of documents and "who knew what when." In the event, the autumn 2006 elections produced a new coalition government, parliamentary condemnation of Verdonk—and her refusal to resign, defying customary Dutch political practice. After months of further debate over immigration policy, Hirsi Ali immigrated to the United States (Simons 2006). Finally, in December 2006, after Cabinet resignations in protest, Prime Minster Balkenende removed Verdonk from the immigration portfolio (although allowing her to continue as minister of youth). Moreover, deportation proceedings were suspended against asylum seekers who had been resident more than five years in the Netherlands.

THE ROOTS OF THE DUTCH RECORD

Structural Conditions: A Grotian Democracy

The Netherlands is perhaps the classic globalized middle power, although like Sweden, the middle power ranking is more historical, regional, and aspirational than a contemporary geopolitical reality. The Dutch economy has been the most open in Europe, with trade around two-thirds of GNP and multinationals providing around one-fourth of jobs. Correspondingly, tiny Holland is number 5 in the world in membership in IGOs (number 2 according to Voorhoeve 1979). The foreign ministry receives around 4.5% of the national budget, and development cooperation around 80% of that, including the maintenance of hundreds of embassies (Everts and Walraven 1989). There is an interesting comparison with neighboring Belgium, which has been much less generous in aid and much less active in international law: "Belgium was much more industrialized and geared more to the European market than the Netherlands, which had always been a maritime trading nation" (Kuitenbrouwer 2000: 187).

In security terms, the Netherlands has positioned itself as a pragmatic peace promoter from an early period. "Missionaries were not the only ones with a mission, however.... Writing on the eve of the Great War, [Dutch legal scholar C.] van Vollenhoven, for example, argued vehemently that the Netherlands—being a small, neutral country—should form an international police force to act like a latter-day Joan of Arc in maintaining the rule of law around the world" (Kuitenbrouwer 2000: 198–190). This is reminiscent of Costa Rican president Jose Figueres's democracy-promoting "Caribbean Legion."

Since the era of Grotius (the father of modern international law), Dutch policy makers have interpreted the Netherlands' structural position as an incentive for humane internationalism—regardless if this is accurate, it has become a self-reinforcing foreign policy niche. As one scholar points out, "We believe that international law brings peace, and in peace we prosper as a trading state.... We believe that human rights gives us a role and helps us make a difference. This leads to the development of a large influential sector of international lawyers and development agents, who are a self-sustaining industry that want to sell their ideas, and an institutionalization in the Foreign Ministry and beyond" (interview, July 4, 2006). Externally, this cadre of experts becomes a diplomatic resource: as one Dutch scholar/diplomat recounts, the Netherlands' influence in multilateral institutions rests on expertise, which includes languages, education, and knowledge of diplomatic strategy. "Historically there has been a tradition that we send our best to the global institutions" (interview, July 4, 2006). At the system level, by 1973, Dutch political party leader Bas de Gaay Fortman was writing about the foreign policy position of the Netherlands—as an example to the rest of the world. Similarly, as a new minister for development cooperation took office in 2000, with shrinking budgets and growing pressures, she promised to maintain aid levels and programs, stating, "The Netherlands has a reputation to keep up" (Kuitenbrouwer 2000: 175, 192).

Like the other global Good Samaritans, the structure of Dutch democracy links a cosmopolitan foreign policy niche with a liberal internationalist program. Muscular Dutch democracy means a strong role for Parliament in foreign policy and a significant influence for globally minded epistemic communities.

The Dutch Parliament has budgetary, monitoring, legislative, and international treaty-making powers relevant to human rights promotion. The most frequently cited parliamentary role in human rights policy is the three to four parliamentary questions monitoring human rights issues *per week* directed to the foreign minister. The foreign minister also sends agenda letters to Parliament before all United Nations meetings, leading to debate on goals, and files reports with Parliament after the international summits. Parliament works with the minister for development cooperation to pick the Netherlands' partner countries for aid, and approves specific programs. Parliament requests the generation and publication of information on human rights issues and treaties from the foreign ministry, often via the advisory council (below). Finally, Parliament passes specific motions on Dutch policies on countries and issues, sometimes to the point that foreign ministry officials complain of micromanagement (such as one MP's insistence on sponsoring a satellite dish in Iran, an impractical measure that was eventually merged into a broader Dutch program on freedom of expression). The Ministry of Foreign Affairs often includes MPs in delegations to international conferences and negotiations. Individual MPs act freely as "policy entrepreneurs" and vehicles for NGO input in human rights policy, across party lines (interview, June 29, 2006).[4]

---

4. Currently active individual MPs include: Koenders (Labour—subsequently minister for development cooperation), Halsema (Green), Szabo (VVD), and De Haar (CDA).

Dutch democracy has traditionally included numerous advisory councils in a variety of policy areas, composed of independent experts who provide research, transmit opinion, and work to shape ministries' programs. By the 1970s, there were around 300 such bodies, including several with international relations mandates. In 1979, a specific Advisory Commission on Human Rights and Foreign Policy was established, with around one dozen "independent experts" and two members of the foreign ministry. This measure was announced by the foreign minister as a "necessary step in making our democratic system more perfect" (Baehr and Castermans-Holleman 2004). A consolidation of the advisory council system during the 1990s limited each ministry to one council, but foreign affairs chose to create four subcommittees for its council, transferring the human rights commission to a committee of the international relations advisory board, parallel with peace and security, development cooperation, and European affairs.

The members of the AIV (Advisory Council on Human Rights) are nominated by its own secretary and current commission, and appointed by the minister of foreign relations. The AIV functions and is considered a kind of central bank of human rights expertise: the first chair was Peter Baehr, Theo van Boven has been a member since 1982, Cees Flinterman since 1980 (and chaired for twelve years), Roel Fernhout before and after his term as ombudsman, and Renée Jones was the first human rights ambassador. They do not hold government posts while on the council, but may serve on national or international NGOs—when AIV chair Peter Baehr was a candidate for the Executive Committee of Amnesty International, the Dutch government did not object to the potential dual role, but Amnesty did.

AIV's main task is to issue reports, at the request of the ministry or Parliament (in most cases)—although potentially at their own initiative. Their annual work plan and agenda are approved by the Cabinet, and in return, the Cabinet must respond to AIV reports on any given issue within three months. Among other measures of autonomy, the council's lump sum budget is allocated by the secretary—not government. They have all the sources of information of NGOs, but also access to embassy reports and most internal policy memos and government documents. AIV has regular meetings with the Parliamentary Standing Committee on International Affairs (interview, June 21, 2006).

The impact of this body can be seen in agenda setting, consciousness raising, specific reports, and citation of expert opinion in policy debates. The AIV has introduced issues or aspects of human rights that become subsequent permanent referents. The current secretary estimates that about 60% of the recommendations in their reports have been adopted, for example, many parts of the report on coordinating human rights and development policies. As an indirect effect, the AIV's report on the death penalty led to a more active Dutch role in EU discussions, which in turn helped shape EU policy guidelines on the death penalty and interventions with the United States. As far as the use of expertise in policy debates, in a recent parliamentary debate on peacekeeping, the council was cited 20 times (interview, June 21, 2006).

Agency: The Global Village Begins at Home

The classic formula for activating internationalism applies in the Netherlands: leadership, civil society, and a linking ideology. Civil society seems to weigh even more heavily here than in similarly situated states such as Sweden, leadership is less prominent, and ideas are more of a mentality than a political program.

Like the other promoters, the Netherlands benefits from a tight and integrated foreign policy elite. One 1976 study estimated that the Dutch foreign policy elite was around 800 people, plus 5–15% of the attentive public. Of this group, 47% believed that international should supersede national interests, and 46% wanted development aid to *surpass* the United Nations' 1% target. Even mass publics showed majority (50–60%) "support for LDCs" (Voorhoeve 1979).

Several Cabinet ministers such as Jan Pronk (minister of development, 1973–77 and 1989–98) and Max van der Stoel (foreign minister, 1973–77) presided over significant upgrades in Dutch policy, but prime ministers have not played the catalytic role of an Olof Palme or an Oscar Arias. The political orientation of foreign ministers has not seemed to shape the Netherlands' relatively institutionalized consensus policies, although foreign ministers' standing within the Cabinet and vis-à-vis Parliament has influenced their ability to promote any relevant initiatives. Mid-level diplomatic circulation was important for figures such as Cees Flinterman, Peter Kooijmans, and Theo van Boven, but there has not been a notable wave or cadre of human rights promoters in the middle ranks. As a cultural characteristic, observers note that many of the people who are individually prominent in human rights promotion come from committed Protestant backgrounds, even though the Protestant Church as such has not played an institutional role in foreign policy.

The real star of the Netherlands' story is an egalitarian, engaged, internationalist civil society. The historic pattern of consociational representation to bridge sectoral and religious differences gave Dutch civil society a special seat at the table of foreign policy making, whereas the modernization of those identities and "depillarization" of Dutch society has filled that chair at the table with global citizens. (Once again, this contrasts with neighboring Belgium's more conservative corporatism and less-value-promoting foreign policy, Kuitenbrouwer 2000: 188.) Dutch civil society is a hotbed of support for human rights, from half a dozen major national NGOs to a dense cosmopolitan academe to liberal church and labor groups. The four major political parties all converge on civil libertarian human rights (Liberal, Labor, Christian Democrats, and even centrist

D66—self-described as "radical liberals").[5] As in Canada, potentially competing interest groups do not lobby in the foreign policy arena—in this
case, Dutch multinationals concentrate on foreign governments.

At the base of the Dutch human rights network, the Netherlands' dozens of campaign and country solidarity groups were established as early
as the 1950s, reaching 174 separate groups by 1982 (Malcontent 2000:
20). The large and influential "development lobby" is anchored by several church-based development groups: NOVIB (nominally secular but
founded by a breakaway minister and priest), Catholic CEBEMO, and
Protestant ICCO. Decolonization of the 1960s shifted the missionary
movement to a secularized version of humanitarian outreach—according
to a former missionary, "Suddenly, the word 'missionary' had become a
dirty word. If you wanted to move with the times, you called yourself
a development worker instead" (quoted in Kuitenbrouwer 2000: 188).

At its peak, the Netherlands hosts the world's largest national branch
of Amnesty International, comprising almost 1% of the entire population of the country. Minister Jan Pronk, many Dutch diplomats, and the
current secretary of the AIV have been prominent members of Amnesty.
AIV secretary Tiemo Oostenbrink was a lobbyist for Amnesty from 1983
to 1992, along with a team of 15. Summarizing his experience during
that decade, Oostenbrink recounts that "9 out of 10 times, the government did what we wanted, but we had to raise the issues" (interview, June
21, 2006). Amnesty NL currently has a paid staff of 120, with a total of
200 personnel, of whom 12–15 concentrate on external relations: 3 in
political affairs—including an EU coordinator, 3 in press, and several dedicated to the Dutch government. Using standard tactics of letters, calls,
media appeals, and meetings with Parliament and the foreign ministry,
the current director of external affairs estimates that he visits the ministry an average of three times each week. Amnesty has systematic contacts beyond the human rights division with peace and security thematic
units, as well as country desks; human rights advocates complain that
the problem these days is not finding foreign policy contacts, but rather
keeping in touch with the plethora of relevant players. As an illustration
of Amnesty's generalized influence on Parliament, when the foreign ministry approached Parliament for input prior to the meetings of the new
United Nations Human Rights Council, several MPs replied that they
had to wait for Amnesty to issue their policy letter before forming their
own positions (interview, July 10, 2006). Moreover, there is circulation
between Amnesty and governmental and diplomatic posts. The Amnesty
lobbyist for universal jurisdiction for torture later joined the Ministry of
Justice, whereas the Netherlands' state-appointed representative to the

5. Although all of the parties support human rights actively, at one point, the
Labour Party foreign policy commission took the extra step of issuing a report with MP
Bert Koenders, Leiden law professor Nico Schriguer, and U.N. veteran Cees Flinterman
as experts, which led to a policy memo that may contribute to election platforms
and government plans.

United Nations' Working Group on Torture later joined the board of the Netherlands' Amnesty International (Reiding 2007: 421).

In the meso-layer, the Dutch legal group NJCM—a national affiliate of the International Commission of Jurists—quietly bolsters the rule of law component of human rights foreign policy. The organization was established by Cees Flinterman in 1972 at one of the nation's leading law schools, Leiden University, so that many prominent graduates active in the organization have circulated for 30 years through the ministries of justice, foreign affairs, home affairs, the Dutch judiciary, European Court, and Parliament. During the critical years 1979–1982 there was a strong relationship with the foreign ministry—all the members of the human rights desk were NJCM members. About 1,500 passive members are attentive to the NJCM's main publication, a human rights law review, and dozens of yearly contacts on critical foreign policy issues of international law as they arise. In terms of casework, the organization consciously seeks to complement Amnesty, thus concentrating on bringing proceedings in Dutch courts using international law, with only about 20% international advocacy. However, on the international side, through the 1980s the NJCM argued for a complaint against Cambodia under the Genocide Convention (interview, July 6, 2006).

To complete the panorama, it is interesting to note a sector of civil society that has *failed* to influence human rights policy: refugee NGOs. Although this sector of the human rights movement is less historic and professionalized, the Netherlands does host several groups that represent or advocate for refugees. These include the national Refugee Council, mainly focused on providing legal assistance and some services in concert with local governments, and an umbrella group for country-based refugee associations—the Federation for Displaced Persons. Neither has secured a hearing with the Ministry of Immigration or Foreign Affairs, nor with Parliament. Amidst substantial Dutch academic debate and critique of national migration policy the traditional "independent experts" have been similarly unavailing, despite the existence of an Advisory Committee on Alien Affairs structurally similar to the Human Rights Advisory Council. This reinforces the idea that migration as an issue has other characteristics that overwhelm agency: not just countervailing interests, but also ambivalent norms.

The ideology that animates agency in the Netherlands is a combination of a long-standing humanist mentality with some contemporary inflections of complex interdependence. Although the Netherlands' cosmopolitan norms are similar to those of its peer group of principled promoters, ironically Dutch human rights norms are so embedded that they are less responsive to contemporary challenges than more forcefully articulated social democratic ideologies, and fall back on national values more than explicit universalism.

The cultural base of the Netherlands' outward-looking idealism is a Protestant ethic that morphed early on into a strongly normative humanism. Dutch moralism is rooted in a combination of "Scandinavian-style Calvinism with post-colonial guilt" (Baehr in Forsythe 2000a). But Holland's geography and demography forced a constant negotiation of tolerance and exchange (contrasting with U.S.-style missionary

Protestantism), along with a healthy skepticism toward centralization and state authority. Dutch authors on a range of political issues often cite the humanist credo, "Man does not exist for the state—the state exists for man." From the 1960s modernization of Dutch society, this humanist foundation assumed a more active internationalist flavor. As one analyst put it, "Perhaps the ideals of mundialism have taken over a part of the role of religion as a selection principle in Dutch politics. In the age of secularization, different concepts of an ideal world give various political groupings new identity" (Voorhoeve 1979: 10). By a 1971 public opinion poll, 90% of the Dutch public favored foreign aid, describing their motives, in descending order, as moral duty (54%), to promote peace (37%), mutual interest (32%), and colonial guilt (11%) (Voorhoeve 1979: 249).

The increase in globalization following the Cold War inspired a new wave of construction of a cosmopolitan vocation less tied to projection of national values and more linked to external conditions. Specific ideology guiding development was detailed in a series of crucial policy documents by Minister Jan Pronk, beginning with the 1991 post–Cold War white paper "A World of Difference," which focused on interdependence and a more comprehensive need for humanitarian internationalism. This was followed by the peace-building guide "A World in Dispute" (1993), advocating integration between development aid and foreign policy. Pronk's influential views were further developed in a widely cited 1996 "Princeton speech" (at a UNHCR conference), which concludes that the lesson of Rwanda is "Humanitarian action cannot substitute for political action" (Frerks et al. 2003: 8–10). The interdependence argument for a shifting Dutch role is articulated clearly in a foreign ministry study of the grounds of "solidarity" and "stability" for intervention in failing states: "Ultimately, there is a certain overlap between these grounds and self-interest, certainly in the case of Western countries such as the Netherlands: a stable world is the best environment in which to promote economic interests, to maintain the international legal order, and to combat crime, disease, environmental hazards, and terrorism" (AIV 2004b: 87).

These norms set the template for policy decisions by setting agendas, empowering claimants, setting priorities, and legitimating actions. Human rights is the default mode, and often a trump card, in Dutch policy making. AIV secretary Tiemo Oostenbrink, who has spent over a decade lobbying his government as an independent expert following a decade lobbying as an activist, summarized the experience recounted by various Dutch human rights advocates with a deeply embedded norm that meets the criterion for "prescriptive status" of the "spiral model" of human rights reform (Risse, Ropp, and Sikkink 1998). "I'm not sure how to answer your question about making arguments to connect human rights to interests. We don't have to justify ourselves that way normally. Human rights is so established in Dutch discourse that you just refer to it; there are no specific arguments. If you identify the issue as a matter of human rights, the standards, and some instruments, they have to listen" (interview, June 21, 2006).

On the rare occasion when the norm is openly challenged, the response is generally based on national values, not universal standards. Thus, ethics professor Verweij countered a Dutch general's call in a military journal for a more hard-line counter-terror policy by chiding his abandonment of "the Dutch approach" rather than citing international human rights standards. "I argued that 'we don't want to become like Nazi Germany'—that is the powerful, definitive argument in the Netherlands" (interview, July 5, 2004).

But it is precisely this return to national values, in the face of the contradictions of globalization, that fosters the normative side of the Dutch dilemma on migration, and opens the door to a wider regression. Projecting humanism abroad is different than negotiating universal rights for radical Others who may reject the fundamental Dutch ethos of tolerance and consensus. International standards are thin on migration, and in this case the Dutch embrace of multilateralism—such as harmonization of EU migration policy—pushes toward a lowest common denominator in principle as well as practice.

Overall, the Netherlands' human rights advocates warn that the combined pressures of terrorism, migration, and EU integration tensions have begun to deconstruct Dutch cosmopolitanism. Fringe anti-immigrant political parties and crusading migration ministers are just the tip of the iceberg, as public debate on a range of issues shifts from "Is this good for the world?" to "What does it mean for us?" (interview, July 4, 2006). As one advocate put it, "I'm afraid we may lose our way, because when people are afraid, they want to go back to the village" (interview, July 10, 2006).

CONCLUSION

The Dutch record as a global Good Samaritan is broad, sound, and sustained. In the usual pattern, Holland's humanitarian internationalism was made possible by its niche as a small, peaceful trading state that developed a vocation for international law. Once the torch was lit, it was carried forward by a vigorous community of global citizens. Their pragmatic humanism inspired decency around the world.

The Dutch have been leaders in constructing global governance, humane diplomacy, and providing resources for development, relief, and the rule of law. Mixed efforts have been less effective in bilateral leverage, whereas an earnest contribution to peacekeeping has clashed with the harsh realities of contemporary conflict. In an era of globalization, declining Dutch direct influence abroad has been matched by the growing challenge of migration that strains national resources and tests national values.

As the Netherlands' cosmopolitan contradictions come home to roost, that country stands at a crossroads. Will the oldest Good Samaritan retreat into passivity, isolation, or even xenophobia? Or will Dutch decency be reconstructed for the twenty-first century, reinforcing one small country's dike against the new tides of intolerance and abuse?

7

Peace without Justice

Japan

Human security as a human-centered approach to global issues is close to Japanese thinking. We learned from the loss of the war that military approaches don't solve global problems, and that military means lead to the destruction of the state.
—Japan's ambassador for human security, April 2006

In the generation of globalization, Japan has moved from being a politically passive trading state to a major proponent of humanitarian internationalism, as an expansion of postwar peace policies. Japan initially appears as a missing case for several generations, in which the most developed, most democratic, and most globalized state in a region avoided engaging in principled internationalism. However, Japan also shows the recent emergence of efforts to enter new multilateral arenas, reframe nascent democratizing and humanitarian programs through the lens of "human security," and serve as a bridge between regional reluctance to address human rights and the Western/Northern liberal consensus. In November 2006, Foreign Minister Taro Aso announced the furthest extension of these efforts in a new, "value-oriented" foreign policy:

> We are aiming to add a new pillar upon which our policy will revolve. First of all there is "value oriented diplomacy," which involves placing emphasis on the "universal values" such as democracy, freedom, human rights, the rule of law, and the market economy as we advance our diplomatic endeavors. And second, there are the successfully budding democracies that line the outer rim of the Eurasian continent, forming an arc. Here Japan wants to design an "arc of freedom and prosperity." Indeed, I believe that we must create just such an arc. (Aso 2006)

The brief and controversial leadership of Prime Minister Shinzo Abe (2006–2007) was associated with rising nationalism, denials of historic abuse, and regional resentment. Yet recent administrations have also increased their association with the democratizing global agenda, and explicitly linked the promotion of liberal values to global citizenship and participation. In early 2007, the prime minister associated global values with Japanese interests: "Abe said he hopes to strengthen ties with countries that share similar views on democracy and human rights during a trip to Europe that begins next week. 'I hope that Japan will gain trust through international cooperation. I think that would lead to Japan's becoming a permanent member of the U.N. Security Council in the future,' he said" (Watanabe 2007).

How much has Japan's ambivalent human rights policy accomplished—and even more, how and why? The timing, variance, and provenance of Japan's efforts as a human rights promoter are significant: Japan is a late developer, with a lopsided emphasis on aid and multilateralism, heavily inspired by exogenous influences. Japan's global citizenship also exhibits an uncoordinated mix of peace promotion, the developmentalist version of human security, and human rights content. The following will assess Japan's late-breaking principled foreign policy, and the unhappy marriage between human rights and a more instrumental version of global citizenship.

IS JAPAN A GLOBAL HUMAN RIGHTS PROMOTER?

Japan has been a leading aid provider and multilateralist, but a slow and even reluctant human rights advocate. Unlike the more long-standing internationalists, Japan's global citizenship emerged largely in response to exogenous post–Cold War challenges. In contrast to more recent developing-state sponsors of human rights, like Costa Rica and South Africa, Japan's activities have centered on resources rather than diplomacy—and been organized predominantly under the rubric of peace or its successor doctrine of human security. Although some countries such as Canada attempt to consciously coordinate different modalities of influence, for Japan policies are relatively independent for multilateral human security versus bilateral human rights, aid versus intervention, and even international support compared to domestic acceptance of refugees.

Multilateralism

Multilateral human rights policy can be measured by a blend of norm promotion, institutional support, diplomatic initiatives, and the construction of networks in global organizations. Multilateralism has been a strong and growing venue of Japanese foreign policy, with financial support, norm promotion, and even some institutional innovation. The Ministry of Foreign Affairs' human rights officer stated, "We believe the United Nations is the main arena for promoting human rights" (interview, April 20, 2006).

Historically, Japan has been among the top contributors to the United Nations budget, with particular support for rights-relevant multilateral bodies and humanitarian programs such as the UNHCR and UNICEF. Japan has provided an average of around $1 million per year to the U.N. human rights offices—in a recent year 32 million yen to the Office of the

United Nations High Commissioner on Human Rights, with additional allocations for projects such as international tribunals (approximately $700,000 to Rwanda [HRFOR] and $111,000 to former Yugoslavia). In a more specific example, in February 2003 Japan cosponsored a UNICEF symposium on trafficking children for $470,000, along with an associated project in Myanmar. Multilateral funding priorities are guided by Japan's ODA Charter, which includes human security as a pillar, and set by the head of the Ministry of Foreign Affairs Multilateral Department—previously Yukio Takasu, current ambassador for human security. Japanese funding for the UNHCR increased when that agency was headed by Japanese diplomat Sadako Ogata.

In terms of standard setting, Japan has been a member of the Human Rights Commission from 1982 to 2002, again in 2005, and will join the successor Human Rights Council in 2008. Japanese diplomat Fumiko Saiga played an important role in crafting and helping to ratify CEDAW, the Convention on the Elimination of Discrimination against Women. In 2005, she was appointed Japan's ambassador for human rights, although her mandate appears limited to U.N. conferences, and she was simultaneously assigned as ambassador to Norway and Iceland. Japan has traditionally been slow to condemn human rights violators on a country basis in the U.N. commission. However, in 2003 Japan cosponsored its first resolution on human rights in North Korea, and was the main sponsor of a resolution on human rights in Cambodia. Japan has also sponsored multilateral human rights dialogues with Sudan and Cuba.

Although Japan has been a relatively passive participant in international networks, Japanese civil society has begun to play an advocacy role in the multilateral domain. The Japan Federation of Bar Associations (JFBA) lobbied the Ministry of Foreign Affairs (MOFA) for the establishment of the U.N. Human Rights Council and increased aid to the U.N. high commissioner on human rights, and a multisectoral coalition of Japanese NGOs has engaged in joint advocacy for U.N. reform and a more human rights-oriented approach to global activities.[1]

Japan's multilateral innovation has come in the promotion of a norm, commissions, projects, and funds for human security. In December 1998, Prime Minister Keizo Obuchi announced the creation of the Trust Fund for Human Security. During the September 2000 Millennium Summit, his successor established the international Commission on Human Security,

---

1. The coalition includes Peace Boat (PB), Japanese International Volunteer Center (JVC), Shimin Gaikou Centre (SGC, Citizens' Diplomatic Centre for the Rights of Indigenous Peoples), Network for Indonesian Democracy (NINJA), and Jubilee Kyushu on World Debt and Poverty. The human rights components include universality, a rights-based approach, remedies for vulnerable groups, nondiscrimination, and review of national law by international standards. Structurally, they advocate the Human Rights Council, a special rapporteur on counterterrorism and human rights, human rights review of the Peacebuilding Commission, more powers for treaty bodies, a high commissioner for human rights budget increase, and human rights education for U.N. staff and personnel.

cochaired by Japan's Sadako Ogata, which issued an influential report in 2003. Japan's contribution to the Trust Fund for Human Security from 1999 to 2006 has totaled 31.5 billion yen. In 2005, 14 billion JPY was dedicated to Grant Assistance for Grassroots Human Security Projects (Japan 2006). As a promotion and dissemination effort, Japan's foreign ministry has sponsored a series of symposia on human security themes: in July 2000, December 2001 (on human security and terrorism), February 2003—including members of the commission, December 2003—with release of the report, and July 2004.

Bilateralism

Bilateral human rights policy is usually demonstrated by some combination of sanctions, incentives, and diplomacy. Japan's bilateral activities have been quite limited and selective. There have been scattered efforts at aid conditionality (below), relative inactivity on regional pariahs such as Burma, and "quiet diplomacy" on China. Because bilateral sanctions ultimately depend on some form of leverage, it is fair to recall that demilitarized Japan's relationships with its neighbors come mostly in the form of trade and aid, so delinked diplomatic condemnation would be relatively unavailing in the region. One of the few historical cases of sanctions was a short-lived Japanese aid cut to China following the 1979 Tiananmen Square Massacre, reportedly imposed at U.S. request (Arase 1993).

A foreign ministry official affirmed that human rights is seen as a political matter for bilateral relations, whereas human security goals are applied to foreign assistance (below). Japan's foreign ministry human rights officer states that although human rights are universal, Japan prefers quiet diplomacy and multilateral activities to implement those standards.

> Asian countries are ashamed to be criticized internationally, and since we are Asians, we understand this. So we assist human rights by simply sharing our experience regarding prisons, police, and similar matters. We try to be partners rather than instructors—often using ODA and technical assistance for democratization. I wouldn't say we use leverage, but we try to send the message that "if you continue to be a violator you will be criticized"—and Asian countries want to avoid being criticized. (Interview, April 18, 2006)

Concretely, over the past 10 years Japan has sponsored bilateral dialogues with China, Iran, Myanmar, Cambodia, and Indonesia over human rights and democratization.

Japanese NGOs critique the limits of this approach. Amnesty International's representative has tried to press her government for standard diplomatic condemnation on Indonesia and Myanmar and has been told, "We have our own approach" (interview, April 4, 2006). Even in cases of violations affecting Japanese interests with clear leverage points, Japan has been reluctant to exercise its power. The Japanese-based environmental advocacy group Mekong Watch asked Japan as the major donor to pressure the Cambodian government, when a British NGO monitoring a resettlement program was forced out of that country and Cambodian NGO partners of the Japanese aid program were arrested. Both the foreign ministry and the Japanese embassy refused to act—although the less affected U.S. and Australian embassies were protesting the persecution of NGOs on principle (interview, April 7, 2006).

Foreign Assistance

Foreign assistance for democracy promotion, governance, and human rights can play a role in building mechanisms for the protection and empowerment of vulnerable populations. Overall, Japan has provided a high level of assistance, with an emerging focus on governance and human security. Aid must be considered as both a positive contribution and a potential source of leverage, as aid conditionality has been an important channel for human rights policy in other cases.

Aid plays a particularly strong role in Japanese foreign policy. As Keiko Hirata states, "In Japan, ODA is the central foreign policy issue facing the government and the public. Since 1991, Japan has been the largest single aid donor in the entire world" (Hirata 2002: 3). Although aid levels peaked in 1995 and the level of ODA declined for the following decade, the emphasis on humanitarian aid, democratization, and U.N. support is increasing. Japan is still the second leading donor, providing about 25% of world ODA, and is the top donor to 55 countries. About one-third of aid is multilateral (Katada 2004). Japan is the largest donor for many neighboring countries, notably Cambodia and Vietnam. Even beyond the region, humanitarian aid has increased to Africa and South Asia—Japanese aid to Africa reached $1.333 billion by 1995 (Hirata 2002). A 2005 funding pledge aims to recoup some of the previous aid level, adding $10 billion by 2010 (http://www.jica.go.jp).

Japanese aid has evolved from a top-down program to provide infrastructure for Japanese trade and investment to a more participatory and humanitarian mode. Between 33% and 40% of Japanese aid is for infrastructure, and loans dominate grants (Katada 2004). But changes were triggered in waves by the regional crisis of 1970–1980s Indochinese refugees, Japan's own 1995 Kobe earthquake and emergent civil society, and the establishment during the 1980–1990s of Japanese branches of transnational humanitarian organizations such as CARE, Greenpeace, MSF, and Oxfam (Hirata 2002). After 1989, the ministry of foreign affairs established an NGO assistance division and increased funds to NGOs 10 times. Japan also founded the Japan Overseas Cooperation Volunteers (JOCV), "staffed by young experts who volunteer to assist developing countries in nation building." As of September 2007, "JOCV has dispatched more than 16,000 men and women to some 63 countries around the world" (http://www.zm.emb-japan.go.jp/jocv.html).

Following the 1997 Asian economic crisis, Prime Minister Obuchi used the human security concept to justify a new kind of ODA. This included the development of the Japan Bank for International Cooperation as an offshoot of previous funding mechanisms under the Ministry of Finance (Hirata 2002). In 2001, a financing scandal in the foreign ministry led to a reorganization of that body, with an associated increase in humanitarian aid focus to recapture public support (Katada 2004). A 1992 introduction of democratization criteria into Japan's ODA Charter achieves full fruition in the 2003 version, which includes poverty reduction, sustainable growth, global issues, and peace building as primary goals of aid. This is explicitly linked to Japanese interests, as the 2003 charter says the purpose of aid is to "contribute to peace and development of the international community, thereby help ensure Japan's own security and prosperity" (Katada 2004: 179).

Governance assistance has been concentrated in electoral and judicial activities in neighboring countries or zones of postconflict reconstruction. For example, Japan has provided technical assistance for the establishment of a legal framework in Vietnam, a 1999 election in Indonesia, and the drafting of a constitution for Afghanistan. The Japanese role in Cambodia has been particularly multifaceted, with strong participation by the Japanese Federation of Bar Associations. A joint project between Japan's foreign ministry, Japan International Cooperation Agency (JICA), Ministry of Justice, and Supreme Court is helping to draft civil law in Cambodia; this complements Canadian, U.S., and French assistance with criminal law. The JFBA is running a legal training center, mainly for paralegals and defenders, and a Cambodian law school is funded by JICA. The JFBA has recently started a research mission to assist with the Khmer Rouge tribunal project, which will receive Japanese government assistance and probably JFBA observers (interview; http://www.mofa.go.jp/policy/oda/category/democratiz/1999/index.html).

Some new streams of aid and redirection of aid programs focus on human security. This reorientation has been especially pronounced since around 2004, when former UNHCR director and coauthor of the Human Security Report Sadako Ogata took over JICA. Examples of new projects expanding Japan's traditional aid include assistance for ex-combatants in Sierra Leone, street and trafficked children in Vietnam and Cambodia, and reconstruction in Sri Lanka and Afghanistan (JICA report, "Poverty Reduction and Human Security," March 2006).

In addition, new human security and peace-building units have been created within the aid agency. A four-person human security team reviews existing projects, provides training for JICA's technical experts and field staff, and fosters donor coordination in this area (especially in Vietnam). About 200 existing projects have been identified as human security programs, with 27 selected as models, and some internal sensibility that a human security emphasis will help to garner approval for proposed future projects. Although most such projects are simply extensions of a grassroots approach to community development, such as well maintenance in Senegal, others have a distinctive orientation to conflict resolution—like a program for Afghan refugees (interview, April 26, 2006).

A final area of human rights relevance for overseas development assistance is aid conditionality, which has been promoted by Japanese and international NGOs. Following increasing criticism of Japanese aid projects on environmental and social grounds, the 1992 revision of Japan's ODA Charter includes democracy as a guideline, whereas the Japanese Bank for International Cooperation established an ombudsman-like inspection panel to review the impact of aid, followed by new guidelines for JICA in 2004. Campaigns by Japanese NGOs blocked Japanese aid to the World Bank for the controversial Narmada Dam in India in 1990, and suspended projects involving locally contested pesticides to Cambodia in 1992 (Hirata 2002). Similarly, a Laos/Thailand river project was cancelled in 2001 after pressure by Mekong Watch—but repeated requests to suspend projects in Burma that involve exploitation, resettlement, and repression of local populations were ignored by MOFA (interview, April 7, 2006). A Japanese-funded Asian Development Bank project for a Cambodian national highway experienced similar resettlement problems from 2000, and was finally audited by the Asian Development Bank in 2004 after NGO complaints—resulting in JICA pressure on the Cambodian government in the successor national Route 1 project (Sugita 2005). Japan-based Mekong Watch brought the UNHCR to the contested resettlement site, and approached the World Bank and Asian Development Bank (with some help from Japanese representatives in this recent case) to increase compensation and decrease government threats to local resisters, despite a general pattern of passivity on multilateral conditionality (interview, April 7, 2006).

At a broader policy level, NGO pressure has led to the creation of a JBIC monitoring mechanism modeled on the World Bank Inspection Panel, feeding into April 2004 JICA Guidelines. NGOs state that this has had a positive preventative impact despite a low level of claims and enforcement, with greater contact and responsiveness in project design from government aid agency "staff scared of us filing a claim" (interviews, April 7 and 17, 2006). On the negative side, the Japan Volunteer Committee (JVC) challenged Japan's 2004 ODA review regarding fulfillment of the United Nations' Millennium Goals and participation in Iraq reconstruction. As part of the Japan Afghanistan NGO Network and Peace-Building Inter-sectoral Group, they have lobbied MOFA and presented a joint letter to the January 2006 donor conference requesting greater Afghan security sector assistance to protect NGOs and aid workers, as well as more transitional justice in that country. Japanese NGOs have been protesting military-based Provincial Reconstruction Teams' aid projects in Afghanistan that blur neutrality and undercut development NGOs' credibility with local populations—to the point of endangering their workers (interview, April 17, 2006).

Two additional issues affect the future of Japanese aid and its impact on human rights: structural reform and rival donors. Japan's aid bureaucracy has evolved through several divisions of labor among the Ministry of Foreign Affairs (MOFA), the Ministry of Finance, the Japan International Cooperation Agency (JICA), and the Japan Bank for International Cooperation (JBIC). Even as Japanese foreign aid has developed a stronger relationship with NGOs as humanitarian service providers, homologous with other donors (Reimann 2003), diffusion of institutional responsibility has complicated civil society leverage and accountability. In 2006–2007, Japan's ODA was reorganized yet again, in response to a shift in the funding formula based on privatization of the postal savings system. JBIC loans and MOFA grants have been centralized under JICA. At the same time, a 10-year package of aid increases coupled with consolidation are slated to produce an overall annual budget of $8.5 billion. But NGOs complain that the process of reform has been lacking in transparency—and the role of civil society in monitoring and participation remains uncertain (interviews, April 17, 2006).

Finally, just as Japan has finally begun to adopt some governance assistance, human security goals, and human rights conditionality, its position as a regional donor is being eclipsed by China. Humanitarian organizations from several sectors and even some government sources cited situations in which authoritarian Southeast Asian governments frustrated by Japanese or multilateral monitoring turned to China for funding for infrastructure projects or concessionary investment, with "no questions asked" about labor conditions, displacement, or environmental damage (interviews, April 4, 7, and 17, 2006).

Peace Promotion

Peace promotion includes conflict mediation, peacekeeping with a human rights mandate, governance-oriented postconflict reconstruction, and weapons control. Japan has played a limited role in conflict mediation, mostly in multilateral settings such as the six-party talks regarding North Korea's nuclear program. Although initially reluctant, Japan ended up playing a critical role in the transnational mobilization that resulted in the 1997 Convention on the Prohibition of the Use, Stockpiling, Production, and Transfer of Anti-Personnel Mines and on Their Destruction. (Mekata 2000). Japan has participated occasionally in postconflict peacekeeping and reconstruction, with an unarmed training mandate. Since the end of the Cold War, Japan has struggled to find a path to peace promotion consistent with its post–World War II foundational commitment to demilitarization and nonintervention, memorialized in Article 9 of the Japanese Constitution, which has been interpreted as forbidding overseas military deployment.

Japan's participation in the 1990 Persian Gulf War marked a turning point in the possibility of military presence and the necessity of burden sharing for increasingly multilateral global governance. The 1992 peace-keeping law, reportedly drafted in part in response to U.S. pressure, shifted the mission of Japan's Self-Defense Force (SDF) and established threshold conditions for intervention, but still forbade participation in peace enforcement or the use of force. In general, Japanese intervention was limited to U.N.-authorized or humanitarian relief operations. A diplomatically oriented government screening agency for participation in multilateral peace operations, the International Peace Cooperation Headquarters, includes the Minister of Foreign Affairs as deputy director and the chief cabinet secretary.

The first major application of Japanese peacekeeping under the new law was sending 283 SDF personnel to guard Rwandan refugees in Zaire in 1994, after an appeal from the UNHCR—then headed by Japan's Sadako Ogata. Japanese involvement in election monitoring grew apace during the 1990s: in Namibia 1989, 1990–1996 in Nicaragua, 1992 Angola, 1994 ONUSAL (El Salvador), also Cambodia, Mozambique; and independent of U.N. presence in Russia 1993 and South Africa 1994.

Japan's most comprehensive and controversial peacekeeping operation was during the early 1990s in Cambodia, where the United Nations supervised postconflict reconstruction, governance, and recovery from genocide for most of a decade. Japan originally sent 8 military observers, 600 SDF engineers, and 75 Japanese police to supervise the Cambodian police regarding human rights. After this mission was expanded to guarding political parties prior to a contested and intermittently violent election, the Japanese government asked UNTAC to reassign Japanese forces because of risk. Nevertheless, a Japanese police officer was killed in a May 1992 ambush, which produced public shock in Japan. Subsequently, the Japanese government refused to send police requested by the U.N. to Mozambique and Bosnia in similar situations (Heinrich, Shibata, and Soeya 1999).

A 2004 law now identifies peacekeeping operations as the main task of the Self-Defense Forces, whereas a 1997 guideline includes regional and global stability as intervention rationales. Japanese forces have now participated in operations in East Timor, elections in Kosovo, and relief in Afghanistan. In Afghanistan, Japanese participation in joint military-civilian Provincial Reconstruction Teams, headed by U.S. military, NATO, or sometimes Canadian forces, has been controversial due to concerns about lack of neutrality, transparency, and coordination. In 2005, for example, a Japan International Volunteer Cooperation clinic was taken over by the U.S. military, and JVC asked the ICRC (Red Cross) to intercede with the U.S. military to discuss the violation of neutrality. Similarly, when Canada asked Japanese volunteers to join its military-led reconstruction efforts, JVC dialogued with the Japanese embassy to discourage them, and Japan withdrew after some of the Canadians were killed (interview, April 17, 2006). The character of contemporary conflict zones will continue to complicate Japan's attempt to expand its humanitarian intervention without the use of military force.

Transnationalism

Transnationalism is a modality of humane internationalism that fosters the growth of global civil society, usually complementary with more interstate forms of multilateralism. Incorporation of domestic NGOs as foreign policy actors, support for foreign NGOs, hosting of headquarters and conferences of international movements, and promotion of private sector social responsibility and resource transfers are all mechanisms of principled transnationalism. This has been a very limited area of Japanese activity, although there are some emerging linkages.

Japan's domestic NGOs are relatively sparse, and Japan's foreign policy institutions have been relatively slow to incorporate them. There are semiannual meetings with MOFA, some consultation before filing treaty reports, and a single case of the inclusion of a Japanese disability lawyer in the official delegation for the Convention on the Rights of Persons with Disabilities from 2002 on. The rising number of Japanese overseas volunteers (over 20,000 by June 2000) has been influential for aid policy, and a number have gone on to serve in domestic or transnational NGOs.

Although the Japanese government does not support foreign NGOs, it does sometimes respond to them. In early 2006, after the Japan International Volunteer Center invited Cambodian NGOs to Japan along with Amnesty International and the Cambodia Civil Society Forum, the Japanese government issued its first statement regarding Cambodian persecution of NGOs. Similarly, a landmine advocacy coalition comprised of the Japanese Coalition to Ban Land Mines, transnational NGOs, and a few sympathetic Diet members pressured MOFA, the Japan Defense Agency, and then-prime minister Keizo Obuchi. As a result, Japan not only joined the treaty process, but hosted a demining conference in 1996–1997. Japan also hosted the 2001 Second World Congress against Commercial Sexual Exploitation of Children in Yokohama, and a key March 2006 conference on human security and the rule of law.

The most significant private sector contribution to human rights— catalyzed and supported by the Japanese government—has been the Asian Women's Fund. The fund for survivors of military sexual slavery during World War II has been praised by some as the beginning of a reparations process for civilian victims of Japan's war crimes, but criticized by others as a private deflection of government responsibility. After decades of international pressure, in 1990 questions were raised in the Diet on Japan's abuse of so-called comfort women drafted into forced prostitution from surrounding countries. Specific forms of international attention to the issue included a 1994 U.N. report and Hague Permanent Court of Arbitration case, a 1997 ILO report, and a U.N. special rapporteur on violence against women report (E/CN.4/1996/53/Add.1) that recommends that the Japanese government take legal responsibility, issue a public apology, pay compensation, and engage in full disclosure.

The Japanese government commissioned an investigation, released on July 6, 1992, and August 4, 1994. Later that month, Prime Minister Tomiichi Murayama (from the receptive Social Democratic Party) issued an apology and established a government subcommittee on the issue. The following year, the Asian Women's Fund was established as a nonprofit foundation; after leaving office, Murayama became its second president on Sept. 1, 2000. The foundation sponsors health and welfare projects in the Philippines, Korea, Taiwan, Indonesia, and the Netherlands for affected women and communities, and has issued direct payments of about 2 million yen in the Philippines, Korea, and Taiwan (http://www.awf.or.jp). It was disbanded in March 2007, following the disbursement of all designated funds.

Meanwhile, in a related development, in April 2007 Japan's highest court rejected two sets of compensation claims by former wartime sex slaves and forced laborers from China. The claims were directed against both Japanese corporations and the Japanese military. The court affirmed the historical record and government responsibility for about 38,935 Chinese laborers—nearly 7,000 killed by slave-like conditions, and at least 50,000 sex slaves, contradicting Shinzo Abe's galling denials. But postwar reparations were deemed to have exhausted legal liability (Onishi 2007).

Immigration Policy

To counter the argument that "talk is cheap," all avowed global Good Samaritans should be examined for some national interest litmus tests, in which principled promotion is likely to conflict with domestic interests. Moreover, issues such as refugee policy, arms exports, and regulation of multinationals are independent potential contributors to transnational human rights violations that undercut promotion efforts. Refugee policy is a particularly crucial area for human rights, because it provides a remedy for foreign direct victims, whereas overall immigration policy is a test venue for discrimination. Immigration policies can be described in terms of the numbers, admission standards, legal process, and official and social treatment of the foreigners seeking access to a developed, democratic country.

Unfortunately, immigration policy is Japan's least successful area. Domestic policy flatly contradicts international standards, and is clearly driven by domestic economic interests—but even more by competing domestic principles of national identity, in a kind of negative constructivism. The key problem areas are resistance to admission of refugees, tolerance of human trafficking, and chronic discrimination and legal exclusion of Japan's immigrant Korean minority.

Japan currently accepts fewer than 50 refugees each year, and international human rights organizations such as Amnesty International regularly point out Japan's deviation from international standards in both procedure and results (Human Rights Watch World Report 1999, Amnesty International Annual Report 2002, Amnesty International Report 2007). Most recognized refugees in Japan are from Burma: in 2005, 43 of 46. There is a separate system of humanitarian protection run by the Ministry of Foreign Affairs for a few dozen legal entrants, mostly from North Korea, and occasionally members of China's Falun Gong religious group. As recently as the 1990s, the refugee approval lag time was four to five years, but by the current decade decisions are generally made within one year. When Sadako Ogata became the U.N. high commissioner for refugees in 1994–1998, Japan was admitting about 1 refugee per year; however, after Ogata met with the Ministry of Justice, refugee immigration increased up to 15–16 per year (interview, April 25, 2006).

Most advocacy and reform of refugee policy has come through Japanese lawyers' groups. There is an overarching group, Japan Lawyers' Network for Refugees (JLNR), as well as country-specific organizations such as the (largest) Lawyers' Group for Burmese Refugees, with similar groups for Kurds, Falun Gong, and Afghanis. These organizations grew out of transnational networks and resistance to government policy. For example, following a 1991 Asia–Pacific Law Network meeting, the Japanese members wanted to bring Burmese lawyers to Japan but were blocked by the Ministry of Justice. So the Japanese lawyers traveled to the Burmese border to meet with their counterparts, and in 1992 started the JLNR—now comprising about 70 lawyers (interview, April 25, 2006).

Around 2000, the lawyers began to introduce international refugee law in Japanese courts, and worked to raise awareness of overseas cases among Japanese judges. They invited the vice president of the International Association of Refugee Law Judges (Alan Mackay of the U.K. Appeals Court), who testified for two days in a Japanese court. Another influence for reform was a 2001 case featured by the Japanese media, in which a family of North Koreans sought protection at the Japanese consulate in China, and Japanese guards let the Chinese arrest the asylum seekers. Media, lawyers, and public pressure combined to push the Diet for change.

The changes sought included independent review, suspension of detention and deportation for asylum seekers with expired visas, and abolition of a requirement to apply for asylum within 60 days. In 2004, Japan's refugee appeals system was changed, introducing consultation with independent refugee counselors. The 19 adjudication counselors are selected by the Ministry of Justice, including some suggestions from the lawyers and UNHCR, but also pro-government former ambassadors and prosecutors—all trained by the Immigration Bureau. Although it is difficult to assess impact, under the new system annual recognitions went from 15 to 46. The 60-day rule was abolished in 2005. For the few cases pursued to the highest level, the third instance (appeals court) has been even more favorable; around 15% admissions on appeal for refugees overall, and more than half for the Burmese. An unresolved issue is work permits while cases are pending; last year about 50 of 400 refugee applicants received some support but otherwise were forbidden to work and had no other source of funding—some subsisted on support from a few church groups. Lawyers' groups state that their biggest challenge is anti-immigrant public opinion, including policy elites, which they counter with an emphasis on the international law status of refugees and the connection to human security (interview, April 25, 2006).

Drastically limited legal migration, regional economic disparities, and a sexually exploitive culture of gender inequity have combined in Japan to produce a high level of sex trafficking. An estimated 50,000 undocumented immigrants come to Japan each year, at least one-third women doing sex work, with many coerced, duped, and/or exploited (Neary 2002). Hurights Osaka estimates that Japan's sex industry brings in U.S. $90 billion each year, and a significant proportion of sex workers in Japan are undocumented foreign women and girls (personal communication; see also http://www.hurights.or.jp/index_e.html). The U.S. State Department has placed Japan on its trafficking watch list, and the Colombian embassy filed a complaint in 2005 after over 60 trafficked women fled to its shelter during that period (Onishi 2005).

The Japan Network Against Trafficking in Persons (JNATIP) was established in January 2003 following an Asia Foundation international symposium in Tokyo—in response to the gap between international attention and domestic indifference to the problem. As of April 2005, the network included 27 Japanese organizations and over 100 individuals, and events are regularly attended by the Thai and Colombian embassies, National Police Agency, public prosecutor, and Ministry of Justice. Its activities have included a May 2004 survey, a January 2004 working group with the Japanese Federation of Bar Associations to draft new laws, and an April 2004 liaison team with the government. JNATIP lobbied the Oct. 2004 Diet session meeting, leading to the formation of committees on trafficking within the LDP, Democratic Party, Komeito, Japan Communist Party, and Social Democratic Party (http://www.jnatip.org; interview).

A new law in December 2004 increased definitions and penalties for trafficking, following an Inter-Ministerial Delegation to the Philippines and Thailand as well as hearings in Japan. The more meaningful scrutiny of 80,000 "entertainer" visas per year—notoriously abused by traffickers—did not take place until 2005. In addition, the immigration code was revised to allow a stay of deportation and witness protection for trafficked women to testify. A Cabinet office on antitrafficking has been established (Onishi 2007). In January 2007, Japan's foreign ministry sent a delegation to Cambodia and Laos to foster greater cooperation to combat trafficking. But the U.S. State Department continued to place Japan on its Tier 2 Watch List and noted, "While prosecutions and convictions under Japan's 2005 trafficking in persons statute increased significantly this year, fewer victims of trafficking were identified and assisted by Japanese authorities. The 58 victims found by the government in 2006 were less than half the number identified in 2005" (http://www.state.gov).

Chronic legal and social discrimination against Japan's minority Korean population is another blot on Japan's domestic record with international implications; for most purposes, Japan refuses to recognize ethnic Koreans as a minority because it labels even Japanese-born ethnic Koreans as "foreigners." Japan's current community of around 800,000 Koreans are the descendants of several waves of immigrants, from early twentieth-century economic drift to wartime massive import of forced labor to refugees from the Korean War to contemporary economic migrants. Probably the majority derive from wartime laborers, who ironically lost citizenship in 1945 when Japan decolonized Korea, and were then forced to register and excluded from possible postwar benefits and employment. This led to further transnational complications, as both North Korea and South Korea established competing educational, credit, and social welfare groups for Koreans in Japan. The Northern-sponsored support was so successful, and conditions in Japan so unwelcoming, that by the 1960s over 80,000 Koreans voluntarily repatriated to the impoverished and repressive North—some anticipating reunification. When Japan established relations with South Korea in 1965, it required ethnic Koreans regardless of origin to acquire South Korean nationality for travel and social welfare benefits; but the majority of the Korean community refused, so that many now carry North Korean nationality without Japanese *or* South Korean citizenship—stateless in the country of their birth (interview, April 10, 2006). Koreans became eligible for some benefits and permanent resident status in 1979, when Japan ratified two U.N. treaties, but continued to suffer employment and educational discrimination, as well as required registration, fingerprinting, and potential deportation as perpetual "foreigners." Through the 1980s and into the 1990s, Japan and South Korea slowly abolished the more onerous registration conditions (Neary 2002). Ongoing waves of tension between Japan and North Korea regarding nuclear weapons (1994), abductions (2002), and the World Cup—vividly detailed in the Japanese media (Onishi 2006)—have been associated with occasional physical attacks on Koreans in Japan and boycotts of Korean-owned small businesses.

A second generation of Korean political mobilization, originally based in Korean language schools and social welfare organizations, has pursued legal and international remedies. A series of court cases in the 1980s contested Japan's fingerprinting policies, employment discrimination by Japanese corporations, and lack of recognition of Korean schools' educational credentials. A law student refused admission to the Japanese bar won his suit and became the first Korean lawyer in Japan. After the Association for Human Rights of Koreans in Japan became frustrated with the Ministry of Justice's lack of response to complaints about language education, harassment, and bullying in Japanese schools, they turned to the U.N. in 1995.

Through Korean NGO representations to the Human Rights Commission, the subcommission on discrimination, and counterreports to treaty bodies, Japan was cited by the Committee on the Rights of the Child (June 5, 1998 and February 26, 2004), Human Rights Committee (November 18, 1998), Committee on the Elimination of Racial Discrimination (April 27, 2001), and Committee on Economic Social and Cultural Rights (September 24, 2001). Japanese government attention has improved, and the U.N. special rapporteur on racism paid a visit to Japan in 2005. Koreans pushed to mobilize as "foreigners" have enlisted the support of both North and South Korean governments at the U.N. to critique Japanese treatment of coethnics; the Korean Human Rights Association translates Japanese materials into Korean for both delegations, and sometimes sits together at U.N. meetings. Despite some gains in recognition, Japanese reforms for ethnic Koreans have been slower and weaker than historically disadvantaged ethnically Japanese Buraku and indigenous Ainu, who are not considered foreign (interview, April 10, 2006).

WHAT FACTORS FACILITATE AND WHICH IMPEDE JAPAN'S PRINCIPLED FOREIGN POLICY?

Japan fits most of the structural and historical conditions that are necessary for humanitarian internationalism. Japan is a globalized middle power and a developed demilitarized democracy. However, each of these enabling conditions contains a caveat that can be traced to limitations of Japan's global citizenship, and compounded by a lack of sufficient sources of agency to promote human rights systematically. So, Japan is structurally positioned to be a human rights promoter, but struggles to realize its potential due to contradictions and shortfalls in globalization, democracy, and cosmopolitanism.

Although Japan is highly globalized, the dimensions of globalization are more uneven for Japan than for the typical middle power. For example, the Netherlands emerged simultaneously as a promoter of international law and a trading state, whereas Japan remained an "economic giant and political pygmy" (Hook 2001) until the 1990s. Although a growing multilateralist in passive roles, Japan is a consumer rather than a generator of international law, and international law has been imported by civil society groups rather than systematically adopted by government as a constitutive feature of national identity (as in the Nordic states).

Structural globalization is not matched by cultural globalization, so that international socialization does not follow automatically from high levels of global flows (as most theorists of transnationalism would contend, contra Rosenau 1990). One key indicator is language use. A strikingly small proportion of Japanese traders, travelers, bureaucrats, and opinion leaders operate comfortably and consistently in English, which means they have less access to international information and are less influenced by international public opinion than their Western peers. At the grassroots level, activists report language barriers in networking across a region lacking a lingua franca, where organizations from less developed and more authoritarian Southeast Asian nations usually have better command of English—a reversal of the global pattern of language use correlation to national influence. One of the monitoring roles of Mekong Watch has been to take JBIC and JICA staff to the field to increase understanding of project impact; they report that the Japanese agencies don't generally study World Bank or Asian Development Bank project histories prepared in English—so the more internationalized activists have also translated and summarized project reviews into Japanese, in order to raise consciousness with their own international government agencies (interview, April 7, 2006).

Although Japan is a demilitarized developed democracy, it is not a deep democracy. Japan's weak Parliament was dominated for decades by a single nonideological party, and there are few channels for ordinary citizens to influence government. Japan has been slow to ratify the major human rights treaties, filed brief and unresponsive reports to treaty bodies through the 1980s, and has not joined the International Covenant on Civil and Political Rights (ICCPR) protocol that allows citizen appeals to the U.N. Human Rights Committee (Neary 2002). Similarly, demilitarization was shallow—Costa Rica's demilitarization was the result of a domestic elite consensus that it is proud to export, whereas Japan's demilitarization was externally imposed, currently contested, and thus poorly adapted to international humanitarian intervention.

With the 1990s came the nascence of some domestic human rights culture in Japan underpinning international promotion efforts, with better reports, accession to CEDAW, the Convention on the Rights of the Child, CERD, and the Convention against Torture. In 1995, the prime minister created a Human Rights Commission; 1997 saw the Ainu Culture Promotion Law; and 2000, the Human Rights Education Law (Neary 2002). However, a proposed comprehensive 2003 human rights protection law was dropped after the Diet dissolved without treating it. International reframing as human rights has increased issue attention and legislation for culturally controversial gender-based violations, such as domestic violence, reproductive rights, "comfort women," and child prostitution; a Japanese bureaucrat told one scholar that on these issues now "Japan cares where it stands internationally" (Chan-Tiberghien 2004:139).

Japan's media have also been a critical and growing but limited source of democratic deepening and human rights culture. From the era of globalization, an increasingly independent and lively Japanese media have provided coverage of human rights cases, situations, law, and international context. Activists report regularly lobbying and securing favorable media attention that can press the government into action, even on sensitive issues such as refugees, citing support from the Asahi Shimbun, TBS, and NHK news services. Even mass-circulation *Playboy* Japan has slipped in critical social commentary with a civil libertarian perspective. The unfortunate exception is on the issue of nationalism, particularly disputes with North Korea, in which the Japanese media fan the flames and promote an uncritical acceptance of right-wing government and party views (Onishi 2006).

A final structural/historical factor that complicates Japan's potential as a global citizen is its regional placement. Although Japan has the objective resources of a middle power, it lacks the customary strategic vocation to project internationalism due to unresolved concerns with its wartime aggression and historic human rights violations. In contrast with Germany, which has overcome its historic handicap through regional integration, Japan is part of a region that lacks both institutional architecture and value consensus for a common project. Constant tensions over Japanese textbook accounts of wartime atrocities, provocative visits by Prime Minister Koizumi to a shrine honoring war criminals, and disputes over recognition of military sexual slavery have led to riots against Japan in China and South Korea, as well as bilateral diplomatic breakdowns—to the point that a Japanese foreign minister had to express "deep remorse" for wartime behavior prior to an ASEAN summit to ensure China's participation in bilateral talks (Brooke 2005). A Japanese foreign ministry human rights official noted that Asia now has the basis for a regional human rights mechanism, with the establishment of national human rights bodies in Thailand, the Philippines, Malaysia, and Indonesia, as well as joint ASEAN-EU meetings (elsewhere in the region, national commissions also exist in Nepal, South Korea, Sri Lanka, Fiji, and Hong Kong). Although Japan supports and could provide institutional as well as financial resources and expertise for a regional human rights body, the official remarked with frustration that Japan is unable to function as a regional promoter "for historical reasons" (interview, April 18, 2006).

Shortfalls of Agency

The mixed picture of a promising internationalist underachiever can also be traced to shortfalls of agency in Japanese foreign policy. Multilevel leadership, cosmopolitan civil society, and mobilizing ideology for human rights are not entirely absent, but weak and inconsistent. These factors interact with shallow democracy, unbalanced globalization, and parochial mentalities to produce a variable and limited human rights policy.

Leadership

We have seen in cases as varied as Sweden, Costa Rica, and Canada that principled foreign policy requires at least one key charismatic national leader, and often a middle-level network of foreign policy entrepreneurs across relevant institutions. Prime Minister Obuchi began to play this role in Japan but was cut short by an untimely death, and his top-level successors have not focused on humanitarian issues. The leading individual figure associated with human security, former UNHCR director Sadako Ogata, has made progress internationally but lacks sufficient national stature and domestic traction.

In many parliamentary democracies, like the Netherlands and Canada, entrepreneurial MPs and receptive social democratic parties have catalyzed human rights foreign policy and held their executives to account. In Japan, Parliament and political parties play a very limited role in international relations, and only a handful of parliamentarians can be identified as sources of passive support when lobbied by activists.[2] On the other hand, human rights activists state that the few inquiries from the Diet are one of their only channels of influence over the ministries. The relatively new and good governance-oriented New Komeito Party is generally deemed the most accessible, whereas the ideologically sympathetic Social Democrats and Communists are often limited in influence by their position in opposition. On the issue of refugees, Sadako Ogata established a League of Parliamentarians for the UNHCR, headed by former prime minister Yoshiro Mori.

There is a small circle of key figures in the foreign policy elite who have helped to introduce and develop the human security concept, and their influence shows both the potential for mobilization through mid-level leadership and its limitation to the peace and development package. In the 1990s U.N. ambassador Owada, a former U.S. ambassador with ties to the royal family, carried the human security concept to Japan and back. Later vice minister of foreign affairs, he authorized initiatives such as a $300,000 rule of law program in Cambodia. Former university professor Takemi Keizo, 1990s vice foreign minister, introduced human security to Prime Minister Obuchi. Current human security ambassador Yukio Takasu, then director general of the Ministry of Foreign Affairs Multilateral Department, suggested to Prime Minister Mori placing Ogata and Sen on the Human Security Commission—and went on to supervise the subsequent establishment of the United Nations Trust Fund (interviews, April 17, 20, and 26, 2006). Japan's former U.N. ambassador, Yasushi Akashi, served as under-secretary-general (USG) for humanitarian affairs and emergency relief coordinator (ERC) of the United Nations from March 1996 to December 1997, after U.N. service in the former Yugoslavia and Cambodia. He presided over the restructuring of the Department of Humanitarian Affairs (DHA) as the Office for the Coordination of Humanitarian Affairs (OCHA).

There is little or no activist circulation to government, but the few consistent implementation figures show strong international socialization. Yasonobu Sato, head of the unique and prestigious Human Security Program at Tokyo University and influential peace-building advisor

---

2. MP Mizuho Koshima (Social Democrat), Minister of Finance Tanigaki (LDP), and MP Toyoyama (Komei) were the most widely cited parliamentary humanitarians.

to MOFA and JICA, attended Harvard Law School and worked for the United Nations Center for Human Rights, UNHCR, UNTAC (Cambodia mission), and European Bank for Reconstruction and Development. The young official heading the Ministry of Foreign Affairs human security desk, Jun Yamada, studied at York University, served in Japan's Canadian embassy and the local Canada desk, and states that his interest in human security started in Canada (interview, April 18, 2006). A high proportion of the NGO leaders and legal reformers in Japan have been educated overseas.

Civil Society

Japan's civil society does not meet any of the conditions that have fostered human rights policies in other nations. Civil society is not very strong domestically, most policy-relevant interest groups are not internationally oriented, and there are few channels into foreign policy that influence political decision makers. Slow changes and issue-specific exceptions to these conditions mark the few areas of relative success for humanitarian internationalism.

As the head of Japan's national bar association reflected with distress, "I'm not sure Japan can be called a democratic country...civil society is very weak. We don't think democracy is really working, and political parties are not the voice of civil society in this system." She pointed out that the Japan Federation of Bar Associations is a compulsory corporatist professional association, not a value-oriented NGO comparable to the American Civil Liberties Union, and its principled influence only operates in parallel fashion with the organized interest groups that form the pillars of Japanese society. By contrast, Japan's national Amnesty International is one of the smallest in a developed democracy—with only about 5,000 members. They complain that Japanese civil society is "not mature enough" to support challenges to state policy, and that the Japanese government regards them as an enemy rather than a partner—at best inviting them occasionally to NGO roundtables in which the government listens but does not respond (interviews, April 4 and 21, 2006).

Overall, Japan hosted up to 400 development NGOs by the 2000s, but the government framework is inhospitable—it was very difficult to incorporate as an NGO until 1998, and nonprofits are still highly regulated by government and not tax exempt (Hirata 2002). Furthermore, the sectoral concentration of NGOs is largely in development, with smaller but significant clusters for peace and environment, and very few true human rights organizations. Much of Japan's civil society, and especially human rights organizations, emerged under international influence. For example, the pathbreaking International Movement Against All Forms of Discrimination and Racism (IMADR) that unites Buraku, Ainu, Okinawans, and Koreans was founded with the assistance of the United Nations Human Rights Center and the International Abolitionists

Federation (interview, April 17, 2006). General public opinion is usually salient only on development, with occasional episodes of interest in refugee crises. Through the 1990s, public opinion on ODA was stably favorable at 42–44%, but in the current decade a falling percentage favor an increase (about 40% down to less than 20%) and more favor a cut (from around 10% to 25%) (Katada 2004).

Lawyers are usually a natural constituency for international promotion of the rule of law, but most Japanese lawyers see international human rights as a way to improve human rights *in Japan*, with the exception of a small network of true globalists—usually a result of international education or foreign policy experience (interview, April 21, 2006). The JFBA *has* taken active civil libertarian positions on domestic issues such as immigration law reform, national security/privacy issues, fingerprinting of foreigners, and "losers pay litigation." During the 1990s, Amnesty International and the Japan Civil Liberties Union linked up to prepare alternate treaty reports to pressure the Japanese government on domestic compliance, as Japan subscribed to six of the seven monitored treaties (ICCPR, ICESR, CERD, CEDAW, CRC, CAT). Starting in 1993, when the Japanese bar started attending the ICCPR in Geneva and realized its impact, as well as the Vienna Human Rights Conference, they expanded to all six treaties and now work as an ongoing network with Amnesty on alternate treaty reports.

Perhaps the most influential international human rights organization in Japan is actually an environment and development advocacy group, operating transnationally—Mekong Watch. The Japan-based regional network works with Friends of the Earth, OXFAM, Rivers Watch, and Thai groups—but few Japanese environmentalists, "who tend to focus narrowly on Japan." Using classic transnational pincer tactics, Mekong Watch lobbies Japan via the Asian Development Bank, the Asian Development Bank via Japan's minister of finance (sometimes with support from a Diet member), and sits on the Board of JBIC (interview, April 7, 2006).

Several recent organizations and networks are laying the groundwork for a more sustained and broad-based human rights constituency. HURIGHTS Osaka is a human rights information center for Asia based in Japan, established in 1994 with international NGO and Osaka municipal support. Based on the appeal of U.N. human rights officer Yo Kubota, who died on a 1989 election mission to Namibia, Hurights Osaka was catalyzed by a 1992 Asia-Pacific human rights conference in that city. Osaka is a local node of human rights receptiveness due to that city's experience with Buraku mobilization, labor movements, and Yokohama foreign residents.

At a national level, several leading Japanese NGOs launched an August 2005 human security public forum including ministry and public participation. Key conveners are the JVC development group, influential Peace Boat movement, and the Kamimura Civil Forum Center. Through a series of regular meetings that continued in 2006, they seek to provide a regular channel for civil society input into U.N. reform, peacekeeping, and

ODA reform, with a stress on government foreign policy accountability to Japanese taxpayers.

Ideology

A linking ideology is a final factor in the formula for global good citizenship. To mobilize political will and public resources, policy makers must articulate and promote some package of ideas that link national interest to global interest, overcoming the altruist dilemma. Social democracy, universalist religious humanitarianism, class-based solidarity, and human security are all modes of thinking that make doing good make sense. Such concepts provide generative and orienting rationales for foreign policy doctrines, programs, institutions, and initiatives, and serve as a domestic source of legitimation for internationalist leaders. This is the factor that has been most vexing for Japan, and represents the key challenge for human rights promotion.

Japan's postwar reconstruction of national identity inscribed the universal values of *peace* and *democracy* as long-term guidelines for the pursuit of national interest, but did not address individual liberal civil rights or humanitarian internationalism. This can be compared with Germany, where civil rights was an additional key component of postwar ideology (Katzenstein 1996). Unresolved aspects of Japan's cultural globalization and consequent nationalist backlash additionally combine with neighbors' claims of Asian values that contradict universal human rights as a Western imposition. Japanese analysts point out that because Japan did not craft its own constitution, the Japanese people "did not fully digested [*sic*] vested rights as their own natural rights." Furthermore, the construction of Japanese cultural identity as homogenous intrinsically excludes foreigners and minorities (Higashizawa 2001). Moreover, the overarching Japanese value of social harmony (*wa*) is difficult to reconcile with the standard liberal, legalist model of individual rights acquired through adversarial universal institutions.

Although Japan's foreign ministry formally subscribes to universal human rights, human rights as such receives little resources or attention—only a handful of staff in the foreign policy office and international law. Japanese human rights activists report that "MOFA is keen on human *security*, but the Ministry of Justice, the security agencies, and the LDP [dominant party] resist the concept and agenda of 'human rights'" (interview, April 4, 2006). Within the Diet, the right wing has challenged the definition of human rights as they debated the establishment of a national human rights commission, and nationalist groups explicitly complain that human rights is an imported concept. Even Japan's recent sponsorship of United Nations human rights resolutions against North Korea are a response to the kidnapping of Japanese citizens rather than concern for the fate of Korea's own brutalized citizenry. Human rights is used by the Japanese government mainly as a strategic discourse for multilateral democracy promotion and postconflict reconstruction, as part of the Western alliance.

Japanese policy elites have consciously promoted the human security concept as an alternative. As MOFA veteran and current human security ambassador Yukio Takasu stated, human security is helpful in that focal ideas like "sustainable development" can orient new waves of global action when we establish and spread a concept, link it to "personalities," then follow with policies and "operational norms" that can give a "moral dimension to development." He contrasts human security with human rights as easier to work with, because it is not treaty based like human rights. "Human security is more a perspective than a single norm that provides accountability and a common understanding so that different countries can take different initiatives without universalism" (interview, April 26, 2006). The content of that perspective is roughly a stance of humanitarian interdependence that mandates policies to protect vulnerable communities from problems that spill across borders that governments cannot handle alone.

In this respect, human security has tremendous potential for Japan as a discursive bridge to humanitarian agendas that is collective, speaks to global commons, and thus finesses the issues of sovereign and regional resistance to intervention and liberal cultural values. However, human security addresses only acute human rights crises that spill across borders—it is silent on stable authoritarianism, discrimination, and institutional empowerment of marginalized citizens and groups to make their own claims. Furthermore, Japan's limited developmentalist version of human security contrasts with the more comprehensive "responsibility to protect" promoted by Canada, and adopted by the frontline global Good Samaritans (Krause 2005). Human security does provide a linking ideology for Japan's internationalism—the question is whether it provides a sustainable reconstruction of national identity that can address the range and roots of contemporary abuses of human dignity.

CONCLUSION AND IMPLICATIONS

What does Japan teach us about the emergence and limits of an aspiring global Good Samaritan? Perhaps the most important measure is to socialize and network lagging states. International socialization has been tightly linked to most of the progress in Japan thus far. It is critical to educate and empower civil society *within* unduly passive democratic developed states; social capital is just as important for deepening democracy in underperforming internationalist states as for promoting development in the periphery. Dialogue and debate on normative constructions of interdependence may foster more positive responses to globalization, and greater linkage between universal human rights and national interest.

Humanitarian democracies still need greater attention to and accountability for less visible aspects of their own foreign policies that may undermine their promotion efforts in multilateral forums. Exploitative foreign investment and refusal of refugees contribute to root causes or impede responses to human rights violations. Only global civil society and growing monitoring via global institutions will help to address these contradictions.

Japan's record shows that multilateralism matters—and that the pursuit of peace is not enough to secure human dignity. As Ambassador Takasu observed, the pursuit of peace is part of Japan's quest to regain full membership in the international community. When Japan was readmitted to the U.N., 10 years after the war, the foreign minister linked the Japanese Constitution to the U.N. Charter—the right to live in peace, and the duty to act as a member of the global community (interview, April 26, 2006). The next stage for Japan to act globally is to foster the linkage between peace and justice—and to appreciate that a region is only as strong as its weakest link.

8

From Pariah to Promoter

South Africa

Human rights will be the light that guides our foreign policy.
—Nelson Mandela, 1994

South Africa's historic transformation from dictatorship to democracy is paralleled by an equally remarkable transition in foreign policy: from realist supporter of regional instability and unholy alliances to principled exporter of global human rights. South Africa provides a role model for other emerging regional powers, demonstrating that underdevelopment, non-Western culture, and historic divisions are not necessarily impediments to an active and principled foreign policy role. However, the new South Africa has experienced limitations in its human rights program and vocation—due to a combination of the normalization of national interest as a globalizing middle power, along with countervailing rational values.

The hand of history lies heavy on South Africa's international relations. That country's systematic policy of institutionalized racism and minority rule led to international exclusion. South Africa withdrew from the British Commonwealth in 1960, and was prevented from occupying its U.N. seat in 1974 (Wheeler 2004: 83). Through the 1980s, the international community condemned apartheid via a series of U.N. resolutions and commissions, bilateral and multilateral economic sanctions, and various cultural and athletic boycotts. At the same time, transnational antiapartheid movement solidarity sustained the black South African movement through decades of repression, and ultimately provided critical leverage for the transition to majority rule in 1994 (Klotz 1995). South African scholar Jack Spence summarizes South Africa's

> influential legacies from the past: a pattern of economic relations with trading and investment partners in the West, dating from the apartheid era; a diplomatic corps which had spent much of its energies trying to capitalize on those relations and defeat the sanctions regime; a defence force geared to cope with an alleged "total onslaught from the Soviet Union"; and finally, the heady expectations of ANC supporters of a new deal in which the defence, extension and consolidation of human rights would be given pride of place in both domestic and foreign policy. (Spence 2004: 36)

Another ambiguous legacy is that South Africa was transformed to a democracy "with the backing of an array of states whose political ethos in the main contradicted these same values" (Habib and Selinyane 2004: 49).

Nelson Mandela came to power with an ambition to transform South Africa's foreign policy liabilities into strengths, as well as an extraordinary level of personal principle, charismatic leadership, and international legitimacy. Francis Kornegay, at the South Africa-based Center for Policy Studies, reflects the new stance: "South Africa punches above its weight in foreign policy. The key to this is South Africa's unique moral high ground—and its role as a regional African power" (interview, November 17, 2006). This resulted in an initial push for reintegration and promotion, followed by a gradual retreat in some areas and realignment in others. South African scholars have labeled the foreign policy periods since the transition as follows: 1994–1996 "heroic," 1996–1997 recalibration, 1998–1999 routinization, and 1999–2000 African (Nel, Taylor, and van der Westhuizen 2001).

Multilateral promotion by South Africa has most clearly reflected this shifting trend from universalism to regionalism, whereas aid and peace promotion have showed more persistence and even growth. As with most of the other countries in this study, bilateral relations have been checkered and limited in impact. Sound institutional efforts on refugees have been undercut by social conditions and governance shortfalls. In the era since Mandela, South Africa has been caught between the global values of its increasingly distracted civil society and the regional realities and historic loyalties embodied by its centralizing leadership. Like the consolidation of domestic democracy, for South Africa the construction of cosmopolitan internationalism remains a contested and fragile process.

SOUTH AFRICA AS GLOBAL CITIZEN

Like Costa Rica, South Africa has been a multilateral innovator at both global and regional levels. South Africa has also specialized in hosting international events and institutions, similar to both Costa Rica and the Netherlands. South Africa has been less consistent in multilateral diplomacy and institution building, but has played a unique role as advocate for Africa.

The new democratic South Africa burst from its isolation to emerge as a global citizen. Between 1994 and 2000, the new government signed 70 treaties and joined 40 institutions. Postapartheid South Africa played prominent roles in the 1995 Nuclear Non-Proliferation Treaty, the 1997 Ottawa Process on land mines, and the 1998 Rome Statute of the International Criminal Court. South Africa moved beyond membership to leadership roles: from 1995 to 1999 as chair of the regional organization SADC, from 1996–1999 as president of UNCTAD, simultaneously heading the Non-Aligned Movement (1998–2001), U.N. Human Rights

Commission (1998–1999), and Commonwealth (1999–2002) (Nel, Taylor, and van der Westhuizen 2001). Since 2006, South Africa now sits on the United Nations Security Council as a nonpermanent member.

South Africa's support for multilateralism extended to accepting negative consequences for its principled promotion of international law. In 2003, South Africa refused to sign an impunity agreement with the United States to exempt it from the ICC, choosing a reduction in U.S. aid over defecting from the international accord (Cornelissen 2006). A former Cabinet minister recalls that South Africa's top policy makers favored this stance collectively and unanimously (interview, October 27, 2006).

South Africa hosted an unprecedented series of global and regional conferences. Major world events in South Africa included the 1996 UNCTAD conference, 1998 Non-Aligned Movement meeting, 1999 Commonwealth Summit, UNAIDS 2000, the United Nations' Conference on Racism 2001, the 2002 founding meeting of the African Union, and the United Nations' World Summit on Sustainable Development in 2002. South Africa has hosted world championships in cricket, rugby, and soccer (slated for the 2010 World Cup), as well as numerous major academic and development conferences, and the 2005 Socialist International. In addition, South Africa funds and provides the site for the Pan-African Parliament, comprising twice annual, weeklong meetings of over 250 MPs, as well as supporting facilities and staff.

There are further intergovernmental linkages: South Africa's minister of public service and administration currently chairs the Commonwealth Association for Public Administration and Management, and a recent minister of environment headed the International Union for the Conservation of Nature. The Department of Foreign Affairs participates in the Community of Democracies, Alliance of Civilizations, Human Security Network, and Helsinki Process on Globalization and Democracy (Finland/Tanzania), as well as IDEA (the international institute for election monitoring).

Yet after an initial wave of almost routine support for a variety of U.N. human rights initiatives, South Africa began to waver by the mid-2000s. Breaking with the Europeans, South Africa supported "no action" motions on both China and Zimbabwe on the U.N. Human Rights Commission. In 1996, South Africa abstained from a vote against Iran, and in 2003 abstained and later returned a negative vote on a Canadian resolution against Iran—both in the Third Committee. Moreover, South Africa supported violator Libya's designation as chair of the U.N. Human Rights Commission (Wheeler 2004: 97). Once serving on the U.N. Security Council, South Africa disappointed international supporters by voting in January 2007 against a resolution condemning Myanmar. Shortly thereafter, South Africa opposed a Security Council briefing on the decline of neighboring Zimbabwe (Wines 2007).

The government had a similarly equivocal record on transnational human rights governance processes, leading some but eschewing others.

On the positive side, South Africa played a major role in crafting the Kimberley Process for the regulation of "conflict diamonds," whose illicit trade had underwritten some of Africa's bloodiest civil and regional wars. South Africa, a major producer of legitimate diamonds, hosted the key conference in 2000, pushed national producer De Beers to participate, helped to draft the 2003 Certification Scheme, and introduced the United Nations' General Assembly Resolution A/RES/57/302. Making the link between global citizenship and national interest, Mandela said, "Rather than boycotts being instituted it is preferable that through our own initiative the industry takes a progressive stance on human rights issues" (Cornelissen 2006: 45). On the negative side, the Mbeki government took a surprising stance *against* the international reparations campaign for corporate social responsibility for apartheid—purportedly fearing a chilling effect on critical infusions of current foreign investment. At the request of the U.S. government, South Africa went so far as to file amicus briefs for the corporate plaintiffs in July 2003 at New York trials (Bond 2004: 50–52).

Meanwhile, South Africa began to play a role as an advocate for African interests in aid, development, and conflict resolution at the Non-Aligned Movement, the G-8, and G-77. South Africa's role is credited with increasing Tony Blair's Commission for Africa, strengthening campaigns for debt relief, and introducing more human security priorities within the Non-Aligned Movement. South Africa began to promote "post-Western" principled alliances, hosting a 2006 Third Way conference with Brazil's Lula, India, and some Nordic states. South Africa helped to establish and advance the more strategic counterhegemonic IBSA (India-Brazil-South Africa) and BRICSA (Brazil-Russia-India-China-South Africa) coalitions (Kornegay 2006).

This global role as "mouth of the South" served as a bridge to regional governance initiatives. South Africa used its chair of the Non-Aligned Movement in 1999 to push for a new economic plan for African development at the Sirte Summit of the OAU. When specially invited to the 2000 G-8 meeting, Mbeki then took a prototype Millennium Partnership for African Recovery Programme to the conference. When South Africa became chair of the reconstituted African Union (former OAU) in 2002, Canada invited four African regional leaders to the 2002 G-8. South Africa carried the latest version of the continental development initiative to this meeting, so the G-8 formed the Africa Action Plan. This plan included a substantial earmark for Africa from the earlier Monterrey conference $12 billion global pledge (but no new funds), and the African Peer Review Mechanism (APRM) (Sidiropoulos and Hughes 2004). Although initiator South Africa almost dropped the ARPM in October 2002 to secure regional consensus, Mbeki was pressed to carry it through by Canada's prime minister Chrétien (Bond 2004: 96).

The African Peer Review Mechanism of NEPAD is a pioneering governance initiative, intended to regionalize accountability, deepen nascent democracy, and transcend bilateral donor conditionality. It is run by African member states, hosted by South Africa and implemented by South African nongovernmental agency SAIIA, and funded by donors such as the EU, Britain's DFID, the Nordic states, and Canada. The APRM is a monitoring mechanism that provides states with guidance on compliance with international standards for good governance and human rights as well as recommendations for best practices. Although the peer review may serve as a reference point for donor planning, there is no explicit linkage built into the process. So far, Rwanda, Ghana, and Kenya have undergone systematic reviews, with South Africa in process. In addition, there have been eight-country thematic reviews of peacemaking and human rights under parallel rubrics (Sidiropoulos 2004).

In a similar vein, it was South Africa that pushed the OAU for a 1999 clause forbidding unconstitutional change of government. After a military coup later that year, Côte d'Ivoire was suspended under the provision. Later on, in the process of reformulating the OAU into the African Union, South Africa again stood for stiffer regional support for human rights. Although the AU retains the OAU's nonintervention norm, charged with historically blocking meaningful regional action on African states' violations, the new African Union introduces a basis for emergency action. At South Africa's urging, Article 4(h) provides a right for the organization to intervene in cases of war crimes, genocide, and crimes against humanity (Sidiropoulos and Hughes 2004).

DIPLOMACY AND ITS DISCONTENTS

South Africa has played a variety of diplomatic roles around the world and across the continent, from modeling to mediation to attempts at leverage. As with most of the countries studied, there has been an overall trend away from global bilateral linkages toward regionalization of focus and increasing use of multilateral mechanisms. South Africa has concentrated on fellow African regional powers and ailing neighbors. Beyond the promotion of bilateral interests and global norms, democratic South Africa has an additional bilateral norm of responsibility to repair the damage caused by successive apartheid governments to the frontline states, which were often sheltering ANC resistance fighters (Sidiropoulos and Hughes 2004: 61).

Along with the initial flurry of multilateral support for global human rights, South Africa provided diplomatic succor and institutional modeling to beleaguered peoples and young democracies. South Africa welcomed the Dalai Lama, sent peace advisors to Sri Lanka, and promoted the model of its Truth and Reconciliation Commission in Rwanda and beyond. The South African Human Rights Commission has been involved in most new African constitutions for the past decade.

South Africa's one ongoing global diplomatic engagement has been with the Middle East, where a plethora of interests and norms collide, just as for the Netherlands and Costa Rica. On the whole, South Africa tilts more toward Arab and Palestinian positions, with a lack of negative Holocaust historic ties supplemented by a positive history of PLO solidarity and leadership linkages during the antiapartheid struggle. In terms of more material interests, "President Nelson Mandela acknowledged in 1999 that the ANC had received $10 million each from Saudi Arabia and UAE for the 1999 elections and $50 million each from Saudi Arabia and Malaysia for the 1994 elections" (Jhazbhay 2004: 284). But on the other hand, Israel is South Africa's largest export market in the Middle East.

In the post-Oslo Middle East peace stalemate period, South Africa attempted to broker a mediation through an inconclusive 2002 dialogue process with Israeli and Palestinian representatives held at Stellenbosch. As the Israel-Palestine conflict deepened in recent years, and Mandela's vision of "balance" waned in favor of Mbeki's pan-African tilt, South Africa has become harshly critical of Israeli military initiatives, violations of international law, and conditions of occupation. For example, in December 2003, the minister in the presidency condemned the West Bank security fence as an "apartheid wall." However, he carefully distinguished Palestinian solidarity from anti-Semitism, reminding South Africans, "Ninety-five percent of the whites who supported our struggle against apartheid were Jews" (Jhazbhay 2004: 288–289).[1]

But attention and resources generally focused closer to home, as sub-Saharan Africa's crises and South Africa's regional capability rose in tandem. South Africa's first regional foray resulted in failed leverage in Nigeria during the mid-1990s, and the turn from bilateral sanctions to regional quiet diplomacy. Following the 1995 globally castigated executions of Nigerian dissident Ken Saro-Wiwa and his Ogoni colleagues, Nelson Mandela called for Nigeria's expulsion from the Commonwealth and the imposition of sanctions. Initially, Nigeria was suspended and South Africa formed a Commonwealth Ministerial Action Group and recalled its ambassador. But other LDCs in the Commonwealth refused to back South Africa, so in 1997 South Africa withdrew from the CMAG. No sanctions were imposed (Black in Nel, Taylor, and van der Westhuizen 2001). In a candid assessment, South Africa's international affairs advisor to the office of the deputy president summarized that country's lessons from Nigeria:

> In 1994, the newly elected South African government…had no choice but to become involved in the Nigerian crisis because a political refugee spillover from that country would adversely affect South Africa. The US and the

---

1. Although this figure is a rhetorical exaggeration, it does accurately reflect the strong presence of South Africa's large and notably liberal Jewish community in the antiapartheid movement. Although many South African Jews emigrated to Israel in the wake of the 1994 transition, those who remained have been less tied to Zionist policies than their counterparts elsewhere (such as those in the United States), and thus have not constituted an attentive foreign policy interest group.

UK pressured South Africa to criticize and even sanction the Nigerian military regime. However, Thabo Mbeki, who has spent many years in Nigeria and who knows the Nigerian political and social landscape well, realized that sanctions would have little, if any, impact on the situation.... When Nelson Mandela called for sanctions at the Commonwealth Heads of State Summit in 1995 and failed to get any support for his appeal, the South African government also learned that no country can call for sanctions successfully without the backing of a coalition. The government therefore started engaging in low-level or quiet diplomacy with the Abacha regime. (Majola 1998: 51)

Under Mbeki's more pan-African leadership and sympathy toward his country of exile, South Africa even denied visas to persecuted Nigerian activists during the mid-1990s (interview, October 30, 2006).

A series of African mediations carried mixed results. Mandela's solidarity-era relationship with Libya's Muammar Gaddafi combined with his interest in peacemaking allowed him to broker a pathbreaking resolution of the Lockerbie affair, helping bring outlier Libya back into the international community (Jhazbhay 2004: 286).

However, in Côte d'Ivoire, although a South African mediation produced a truce, disarmament plan, and election framework—in the end, the intervention failed over rebel suspicion of South Africa's alignment with the government and unresolved questions of immigration and France's role (Ikome et al. 2005).

South Africa's contradictory interventions in the DRC exemplify what some analysts label the "schizophrenic" qualities of South Africa's bilateral relations. "During the 1997 Zairean debacle in the twilight of Mobutu's kleptocracy, the South African state played a double role: it mollycoddled the regime in Kinshasa while simultaneously fostering contacts between South African companies and the rebels in Lubumbashi, thereby risking its credibility as a catalyst for regional stability" (Habib and Selinyane 2004: 56–57).

But a short time later, South Africa intervened constructively: "In November 1999 South Africa pledged R1.2 million [South African rand] towards a joint military commission in the DRC, and for more than a year the minister of local government, Sydney Mufamadi, was responsible for bringing the belligerents together...after the Rwandan and DRC presidents...had signed a deal on 30 July 2002 brokered by Mbeki and Kofi Annan...in December 2002 the final agreement was concluded" (Habib and Selinyane 2004: 56–57). The Sun City Inter-Congolese Dialogue was funded by South Africa for $8.5 million (Aning et al. 2004: 75). Although the 2002 U.N. Report of the Panel of Experts on Illegal Exploitation of Natural Resources in the DRC named 14 South African companies (including Anglo-American and De Beers) as war profiteers, South Africa followed up its aid and mediation with 1,300 peacekeepers for the MONUC U.N. force in June 2003 (Williams 2006).

President Mbeki visited the DRC in August 2004 to stabilize renewed tensions with Rwanda following a massacre of Tutsi refugees in Burundi.

Subsequently, South Africa sent its Independent Electoral Commission to the DRC and provided police training, capacity-building assistance in local government, census and public administration, and integration of armed forces. This involved an initial contribution of R25 million through the African Renaissance Fund (Pahad 2006). South Africa even printed and distributed ballots in the DRC's 2006 elections.

Yet South Africa's weakest bilateral effort—in the crisis at its doorstep—defies both humanitarian principle and many readings of national interest, as it eschews opportunities to criticize, sanction, or otherwise leverage neighboring Zimbabwe. Through the 1990s, anticolonial leader Robert Mugabe has slid into a repressive dictatorship with disastrous economic policies, generating an estimated three million migrants to South Africa, as well as spillovers of crime, disease, and smuggling across the long border. Mandela and Mbeki's reluctance to criticize a liberation leader from a frontline ally in the struggle against apartheid combined with fears of border instability, so that South Africa even propped up the ailing regime, providing economic assistance including credits for power provision and intermediation with international lenders, in the belief it would prevent more refugees. South African critics contend that politically, "the ANC government's real fear regarding the MDC [Zimbabwean opposition] is that its coming to power in Zimbabwe would embolden the populist and union element within the tripartite alliance in South Africa that seeks a fundamental departure from current government policy" (Sidiropoulos and Hughes 2004: 78, 82). After years of international and domestic criticism of South Africa's passivity, the policy of constructive engagement and quiet diplomacy culminated in another failed attempt at leverage, when South Africa offered to lend Zimbabwe $1 million to meet a World Bank loan in exchange for the formation of an electoral study commission. Instead, Zimbabwe secured the loan from its Chinese trading partner, and turned down the South African package ("China Comes to Zim's Rescue," September 14, 2006, http://www.news24.com). There are widespread allegations that South Africa has traded silence on Zimbabwe for its vote in various international organizations with regional voting blocs, both at the reformulation of the OAU to AU, and most recently when South Africa sought a seat on the U.N. Security Council.

STEPPING UP TO THE PLATE FOR PEACE

South Africa's postapartheid director-general of foreign affairs told the South African military that the new government sought "to transform ourselves as a nation into a global player that is capable of making a meaningful and significant contribution.... There is naturally great expectation that this country should increasingly be involved in peace-keeping, peace-making and peace-enforcement operations, especially in Africa." By 2003, the chief of the military concurred that "South Africa has involuntarily been thrust in a leadership role, which ultimately serves South Africa's national interest." The linkage between participation in peace missions and international voice is echoed in the 1998 White Paper on South African Participation in International Peace Missions, which also stresses South Africa's interest in regional stability for trade, development, and spillovers such as crime and refugees (Neethling 2004: 140–141, 143). Some critics point out that peacekeeping serves the political interests of channeling a government revenue surplus and providing secondary missions for a military demobilized from its repressive role (interview, November 6, 2006), whereas others stress that South Africa's interventions have occurred only in situations of military coups or government collapse, but not "stable tyrannies" (Hamill 2006). Nevertheless, by 1999, there were 6,000 South African soldiers in various venues of peace operations (Williams 2006). In addition, South Africa contributes over $2.5 million to the AU's peace fund (Aning et al. 2004: 75–76).

Beyond serving within multilateral forces in the DRC and elsewhere, South Africa's largest and most controversial intervention was in neighboring Lesotho. In Lesotho, a disputed election in 1997–1998 led to a regional legal experts' commission of inquiry, headed by the South African Constitutional Court's Pius Langa. But contested results of the inquiry produced rioting, mutiny, and widespread disorder in the capital. Thus, South Africa sent in a military force at the request of the sitting government (Adebajo and Landsberg 2003). The original force of 600 SANDF soldiers encountered surprising resistance in 1998, and 9 were killed, along with scores of local civilians. The unexpected deeper conflict led South Africa to increase its force to around 4,000 troops for several years, but this peace enforcement operation was criticized for operating with no wider multilateral mandate.[2] Eventually, South Africa helped to broker a mediated settlement and vowed not to repeat the ill-prepared, reactive intervention even in a modestly equipped neighboring power (Williams 2006; Shelton 2004; Lambrechts 1999).

By contrast, South Africa's much smaller presence in Burundi was tightly focused on human rights and generally judged successful. In that ethnically conflicted country, Nelson Mandela mediated a series of agreements from 1999, eventually joined by Mbeki's deputy and current vice president Jacob Zuma. As part of that settlement, from 2001 to 2003 South Africa sent 700 troops to protect returning Hutu exile politicians, to allow multiethnic power sharing as part of the conflict resolution. As a follow-up to this presence, in 2003–2004 South African peacekeepers joined the African Union mission, with 900 South African troops of 2,154 total (Williams 2006).

---

2. South Africa eventually claimed it entered Lesotho under the auspices of SADC (the Southern African Development Community)—an economic development multilateral organization.

South Africa's Institute for Security Studies plays an unusually strong role as an administering agency in region-wide peace promotion initiatives. The ISS has directly advised the South Africa government, drafting several white papers and some security legislation during the 1994–2000 period, and the government draws on data collected by the ISS Research Department and Early Warning Center. But in addition, the ISS has trained regional organizations in demobilization and light weapons management (recently in Mozambique), trained AU peacekeepers, coordinated police training exchanges, and worked with MPs to analyze defense spending (interview, November 1, 2006).

At the global level, South Africa has emphasized weapons control and peace promotion consistently, from nuclear nonproliferation to land mines to child soldiers. Its most prominent role was as a regional leader on the elimination of land mines. In 1997, South Africa hosted the first Continental Conference of African Experts on Landmines, and South Africa's U.N. Representative Jackie Selebi was nominated by Canada as chair of the global process. South Africa is credited with keeping the African coalition together in the negotiations, and was the third country to sign the accord—after Canada and Norway (van der Westhuizen in Nel, Taylor, and van der Westhuizen 2001). This peace promotion initiative especially reflects South Africa's civil society; the government was pushed into land mines by local NGOs and "the government's realization that assuming a leading position in an international moral campaign would carry great political benefits" (Cornelissen 2006: 42). South Africa's large concerned community had already established in 1995 the Ceasefire Campaign, which included over 100 NGOs that catalyzed South Africa's 1997 domestic ban and international promotion drive (Naidoo 2004: 186–187).

SOLIDARITY: GOVERNANCE ASSISTANCE

Although developing South Africa lacks sufficient national resources to sponsor a comprehensive foreign assistance program and does not have an overseas development agency, that country has generously provided significant flows of governance resources and training to its less fortunate neighbors. Such programs are often linked to conflict resolution processes in the region. South African aid flows include foreign affairs grants, matching programs between South African ministries like justice and their foreign counterparts, and South African NGO trilateral partnerships with foreign donors for third-country programs. Although there is no centralized coordination or record of these diverse programs, a 2005 treasury department study concludes that South Africa transferred at least 9.5 billion rand (about $1.3 billion) to Africa in 2002, and R15.2 billion in 2004. The largest proportion of reported transfers came from the defense department to support peace operations, and the majority of funds went to neighboring countries in the SADC region (http://www.dcis.gov.za).

In addition, South African president Thabo Mbeki established a special African Renaissance Fund to promote regional development and global pan-African relations. Established in 2000 with an estimated $30 million (Adebajo and Landsberg 2003), and supplemented by presidential appropriations around $18 million each year, it has funded regional mediations like the DRC dialogue, pan-African meetings, and even African diaspora conferences in Senegal, Haiti, and Jamaica.

On a bilateral basis, South Africa's minister of public service and administration Geraldine Fraser has provided extensive assistance in administration and governance to the DRC and Burundi, along with the ministry of local government and the social welfare department. The South African ministry of justice has provided judicial training directly in the DRC and to several southern neighbors, and South Africa receives Swedish and Dutch aid to train the DRC police. In the destroyed DRC, the South African Department of Local Government constructed physical facilities for the new national assembly; as one program director remarked, "this is literally institution-building" (interview, November 19, 2006). Seeking to remedy apartheid-era police militarization of frontline states as well as coordinate regional security, the South African police have engaged in bilateral projects in Mozambique for post–civil war disarmament and Southern Africa tracking of conflict diamonds, as well as training programs in Mozambique, Sierra Leone, Burundi, Tanzania, Uganda, and Kenya (Wannenburg 2004). "Operation Rachel" with Mozambique lasted over six years, and although South Africa had some interest in keeping light weapons from crossing its own borders, much of the demobilization of mortars and grenades was clearly disinterested peace promotion.

An integrated South African assistance initiative of critical importance is the implementation of Sudan's North-South peace accord. Since 2004, South Africa has chaired the African Union's Ministerial Committee on Post-Conflict Reconstruction of Sudan. In that capacity, Mbeki has also visited that country three times, lately seeking to encourage greater multilateral presence in the Darfur conflict. South Africa's foreign affairs ministry with the national university UNISA manages a large capacity building project in the new autonomous region of Southern Sudan: including one month courses in international relations, local government, public administration, and computer technology for Southern officials. South Africa also contributes to the United Nations' Trust Fund for Sudan.

South African NGO IDASA, founded by white dissident MPs to resist apartheid, has, since the transition, moved gradually from domestic advocacy to regional rule of law promotion and training. With international funding and a staff of around 100, IDASA has region-wide projects on public opinion (the Afrobarometer conducts surveys in 18 countries), migration, budget, information, legislative strengthening, and community empowerment. Through a regional office in Nigeria, there are programs on election violence, as well as citizens and local governments in the Niger Delta. They have played a planning role on police reform in the DRC, a channeling role for Japanese aid agency funds, and provide briefings for the ministry of foreign affairs on democratization processes in smaller countries such as Sierra Leone, Swaziland, and the Central African Republic. Although IDASA cautions that they no longer see elections as the center of democracy, they sent several election observers to the DRC and a few to Zimbabwe. But in Zimbabwe, they have been targeted for government repression due to their civic education and work with opposition parties; Mass Public Opinion Institute (MPOI) pollsters, an Afrobarometer partner of IDASA, were badly beaten (interview, November 19, 2006).

In similar fashion, South Africa's Centre for Conflict Resolution has become increasingly pan-African: in this case, in both composition and program focus. With a Nigerian executive director and program officers from Zimbabwe, Zambia, Uganda, Kenya, and Cameroon, the Cape Town organization now promotes linkages to the West African Peace Network, ECAS, the AU, SADC, and NEPAD. Specific projects on capacity building in pan-African institutions and civil society complement this mandate, and thematic work on women and peace building is supported by UNIFEM and gains greater national acceptance via African organization norms and networks. Finally, the CCR program on mediation support services works in South Africa primarily with immigrants (interview, October 23, 2006).

XENOPHOBIA: THE NEW RACISM?

A South African refugee advocate and scholar, himself a victim of the Congo conflict, reminds us that refugees represent a triple test for the assessment of human rights policy: as a product of human rights violations in their home country, as a test of the host country's admission commitment to rule of law and international norms, and as their treatment once admitted reflects the state of rights for noncitizens (interview, October 30, 2006). South Africa's problems with refugee policy center around the last criterion; it is in some ways a "worst best case."

With the transition to democracy in 1994, South Africa made the parallel transition from being a source to a host country for refugees. The postapartheid South African Constitution and Refugee Act are unusually progressive and rights based, but refugees' legal entitlements are unrealized due to a combination of administrative discrimination, bureaucratic negligence, and social opposition. The UNHCR arrived in South Africa in 1991 to resettle returning exiles, and helped to stimulate democratic South Africa's incorporation of international rights standards. The new government subscribed to the 1951 Refugee Convention, an African Union Refugee Convention, and in 1998 passed a Refugee Act that guarantees some civil and social rights, protects refugees from *refoulement*, and limits the use of detention. South African court decisions have even interpreted this to include the right to work for refugees. South Africa does not house refugees in camps nor systematically detain them—thus most settle in cities like Johannesburg, which now hosts as many as 25% foreign-born residents in the poor neighborhoods of the city center (Landau 2006).

Of a total estimated current migrant population around 500,000 (more than 1% of the nation), South Africa hosts almost 140,000 asylum seekers, along with 30,000 recognized refugees. The largest group is from the Democratic Republic of Congo, with over 10,000 already granted asylum—but over 19,000 more are still awaiting a decision. Zimbabwe is another leading source for both refugees and economic migrants, but large numbers of migrants also come from Nigeria, Somalia, and Angola (Landau 2006)—all repressive or war-torn countries.

Delay and years of legal limbo in asylum determination are one key source of immigrants' suffering in South Africa. The Department of Home Affairs responsible for status determination and issue of critical documents is described as "one of the most corrupt departments during the apartheid period, administrative incompetence and irregularities flourished between 1994 and 2004 under the former Minister, Mangosuthu Buthelezi" (Landau 2006: 10). In response to charges of corruption and violence in the processing of refugee claims, this office closed in 2005—under a court challenge by Lawyers for Human Rights, it reopened under very limited conditions and with immense backlog. Because of a combination of lack of documents and social/administrative discrimination, refugees are unable to access basic education, emergency health services, and employment. Finally, a significant number who cannot document their status are improperly detained or even deported at a notoriously abusive privatized detention facility, the Lindela Repatriation Centre. Because this facility is not part of the state prison system, it is not subject to the regimen of inspection and access specified in democratic South Africa's legislation (interview, November 3, 2006). Francophone refugees face systematic additional barriers, and local governments outside of Johannesburg that control refugees' safety and access to social services are generally less sympathetic and less responsive to international standards—or even South African norms (interview, October 30, 2006).

Refugees are also caught up in wider problems affecting all immigrants, and the crisis in Zimbabwe increasingly brings a large population of unrecognized refugees fleeing a combination of economic hardship and generalized political violence—without necessarily qualifying for a personal history of persecution. Migrants to South Africa, including refugees, are inaccurately linked to the increase in crime in South Africa. Thus, they are harassed, extorted, and sometimes brutalized by police as well as neighborhood residents. The problem became so severe that the South African Parliament held special hearings on xenophobia in 2004, and the government has launched a public education campaign. Incidents of beatings and lynching of migrants around Johannesburg continued, and were shortly matched by the murder of around 30 Somali shopkeepers in the Cape Town area in August 2006, with responsibility popularly attributed to rival South African shopkeepers of South Asian origin with reported links to complicit local police (Landau 2006b). Finally, in 2008, as economic conditions in South Africa's townships continued to deteriorate, resentment against immigrants erupted in riots that killed dozens and displaced thousands. In one horrendous televised incident, a man was burned alive (Bearak 2008).

Government response has been part of the problem, not a solution. In 2005, close to 200,000 immigrants were deported from South Africa with minimal due process, most to neighboring Zimbabwe and Mozambique, and it is estimated that at least 10–20% are asylum seekers or refugees (with a higher proportion of those sent back to the DRC). In a 1998 report, Human Rights Watch says that about 20% of the deportees are actually undocumented South Africans, especially rural speakers of minority languages that overlap with neighboring countries' (Human Rights Watch 2006). The bureaucratic incompetence of the asylum system guarantees that a high proportion of asylum seekers are detained by police before they can apply or even receive temporary documents showing they have applied, because there are queues of thousands, the main asylum office in Johannesburg is now open only one day each week, and appointments are booking into the next year. Human rights organizations like Black Sash and Lawyers for Human Rights have done some police training to try to improve treatment, as well as bringing some court cases regarding illegal detention and deportation. Several of these cases have been settled by the government—achieving scattered individual remedy well short of policy change (interview, November 3, 2006). Although the South African government condemned the 2008 spasm of anti-immigrant violence and police eventually arrested hundreds of perpetrators, the xenophobic lynchings and beatings, along with the tardy response, highlighted the lack of government protection of this vulnerable population (Bearak 2008).

CONTRADICTIONS: ARMS AND THE MAN

Unusually for a developing country, South Africa has struggled with the human rights contradictions of its exports of arms and armed men. Its apartheid-era pariah security niche conflicted with the new democracy's aspirations as a peace promoter, while the white minority government had fostered both open and illicit military-industrial complexes, including a state-subsidized arms industry to evade U.N. export sanctions. By 1994, South Africa was the world's tenth arms producer, and weapons were the country's second leading export, generating 50,000 jobs. But the new government, sensitized by a 1995 incident in which South African arms destined for Lebanon ended up in a conflict in Yemen, appointed a commission of inquiry headed by Judge Cameron, and set up a National Conventional Arms Control Committee. Under the new regimen, South

Africa blocked arms to military-dominated Nigeria, although not to controversial governments in Rwanda or Congo-Brazzaville (Alden and LePere 2003).

Former minister of education Kadar Asmal, one of the drafters of the South African Constitution, chaired the Arms Control Committee from 1994–2004. It included nine ministers and deputies plus the secretary, striving to apply 9 or 10 key principles, such as no arms to countries that were at war, *systematically* violating human rights, spending vastly disproportionate budgets on arms, or violating U.N. Security Council resolutions (like Turkey's illegal occupation of Cyprus). Asmal states that the committee's deliberations were clearly influenced by human rights considerations in the cases of Sri Lanka (an Amnesty International report), Nigeria (the Saro-Wiwa case), and more generally on Sudan and Pakistan. Arms sales to Colombia were questioned, but eventually approved due to its nominal democracy and leadership of the Non-Aligned Movement ("this case was my only regret"). Some other controversial cases had competing principled logics; for example, although Rwanda had a questionable record in some respects, they argued that in the aftermath of the state collapse following the genocide and facing ongoing border incursions, the government had a legitimate need for South African weapons to rebuild Rwanda's national defense (interview, October 27, 2006).

However, civil society activists question the transparency and accountability of these new security policies, and point to further dubious transfers. In the 1995–2000 transition era, the arms control commission and defense ministry lacked capacity on security policy, such that Parliament rejected administratively inadequate drafts prepared by the defense department and later the ministry of foreign affairs. This meant that long-standing CCR analyst Laurie Nathan, apartheid-era founder of the End Conscription Campaign, and IDASA's Richard Calland ended up preparing many of the commission's guidelines, as well as the later implementing legislation (not passed until 2002). Those guidelines specified annual reports to Parliament, and the creation of a secretariat in the ministry of defense to review applications. The civil society draft included extensive parliamentary oversight and potential veto of arms sales, but the chair and defense ministry insisted on removal of this mechanism. Hearings of the committee are now closed, and no report has been provided to Parliament since 2002. Besides the questionable cases of Colombia, Rwanda, and Turkey in some periods, arms control advocates are concerned about incidents such as the delivery of arms to beleaguered Haitian president Jean-Bertrand Aristide—who later received asylum in South Africa—in a murky conflict scenario before his ouster, at the command of the executive over the objections of the arms control secretary (interview, November 10, 2006).

Mercenaries comprised another pernicious transnational flow from South Africa, originally fostered by the apartheid-era government as a paramilitary instrument of regional destabilization, but later an autonomous private industry. The flow of mercenaries increased after the transition, as downsized South African military and police officers exported their repressive skill sets to neighboring conflicts. South Africa had signed the 1985 OAU and 1989 U.N. conventions on mercenaries, and the new government was further sensitized by a CCR study and muckraking article by Laurie Nathan on former South African Special Forces paid in mineral rights in Angola, Sierra Leone, and the DRC. The government invited civil society experts to draft legislation, which was passed smoothly in 1998 (interview, November 10, 2006). In March 2004, a group of South African mercenaries were arrested in Zimbabwe with South African cooperation for plotting a coup in Equatorial Guinea. There have been a total of five convictions under South Africa's legislation, including cases in Guinea and Côte d'Ivoire. After the legislation, the largest private military recruiter, Executive Outcomes, left South Africa. Nevertheless, gray areas in an increasingly transnational and privatized military world have required a new 2005–2006 act to tighten and clarify South Africa's policy, such as South Africans serving in Commonwealth armies, as well as private security contractors in Iraq.

SOUTH AFRICA'S STRUCTURAL OPPORTUNITIES

We can explain this uneven but fundamentally positive record of human rights promotion with the same factors seen in the comparative cases. Despite South Africa's lower level of development, non-Western culture, and recent transition to democracy, it basically fits the profile of necessary conditions for a global Good Samaritan. South Africa is a globalized middle power that occupies a demilitarized security niche. It is a stable and functioning democracy, although as in Japan, a lower level of democracy in foreign policy making is linked to shortfalls in human rights promotion.

South Africa meets the requirements for an emerging middle power outlined by analysts: a stable domestic base, "respectable" military capability, sizeable economic capacity, a functioning democracy, and a "reasonably hospitable regional or continental environment." But South Africa also embodies the difference between the classic middle powers such as Canada and the Nordic states and *emerging* regional powers. Status quo middle powers do not aspire to transform the global system (Spence 2004: 43–45), whereas South Africa has become famous—and embroiled in contradictions—as the "mouth of the South." At a population of around 46 million, South Africa is bigger than Canada, the Netherlands, or the Nordic states. Its GDP of over $200 billion comprises around 40% of Africa's income, and despite vast poverty and inequality, per capita income of around $5,000 puts South Africa in the middle-income tier of developing countries. South Africa's demilitarized security niche began with the 1991 voluntary termination of its nuclear weapons program, culminating in 1995's leadership at the Nuclear Non-Proliferation Conference (Wheeler 2004: 88).

Furthermore, South Africa is globalized, and its increasing economic engagement in the region pushes toward a more pan-African policy and ideology. "In the category of countries with populations exceeding 20 million, South Africa ranked 18th among the 59 listed countries in terms of international economic competitiveness" (Neethling 2004: 137). South Africa's exports to the continent have more than quadrupled since the transition, and Africa now comprises South Africa's second-leading export market. Similarly, FDI has grown threefold, with notable ties of South African firms to key sectors of neighboring countries: the national railroad in Cameroon; power plants in Mali and Zambia; banks and supermarkets in Tanzania, Mozambique, and Kenya; telecommunications in Nigeria, Uganda, and Swaziland; and mining in Ghana (Naidu 2004: 211–215).

The structural dimension that is weakest, although well past the principled foreign policy threshold, is democracy. On the positive side, South Africa has a remarkably stable, law-governed democracy that functions as a full citizen of the community of nations. The mandate of democratic foreign policy is described as to "consolidate and extend the country's international role in the interests of all South Africans, as well as the people of the region, the continent and the developing South" (Chikane 2001).

However, South Africa lacks the deep democracy of the historic promoters or even Costa Rica, so that Parliament and even the foreign policy bureaucracy are overrun by presidential prerogative. Mandela's charismatic personal leadership was succeeded by Mbeki's institutional reorganization of the presidency under the Chikane Report, which created executive policy clusters beyond the Cabinet and parliamentary committees. As the former head of South Africa's Institute for International Affairs summarized the situation, "The institutional losers...are parliament and the ANC" (Spence 2004: 41).

Most foreign ministers have been party loyalists without an independent vision or political standing. The Department of Foreign Affairs is institutionally weak and divided between the old, largely Afrikaner foreign service and the new generation of black South Africans. Although large sectors of the ANC were exiled and moved into key policy positions in other sectors of the new government, the new Department of Foreign Affairs was largely staffed with activists from the independent "homelands" administrations (as they call themselves, "inziles"). As one newly minted diplomat candidly recalled, "We had to learn on the job in a globalizing era; there was a real skill deficit. Can you imagine, I went from the Transkei to the United Nations?" (interview, November 20, 2006).

Parliament plays an oversight and promotional role in foreign policy, but is not a source of leadership or accountability. Parliament approves and can request earmarks in the Department of Foreign Affairs' budget, but does not control the significant presidential, ministerial bilateral, or African Renaissance funds. A member of the parliamentary International Relations

Committee explained the agenda-setting role of committee hearings, such as the xenophobia hearings in 2004, and inspection visits (for example, she had recently toured South African forces in Burundi with a delegation of MPs at the defense ministry's request). South African MPs participate in democracy promotion and modeling: they have observed elections in Zambia, Tanzania, and the DRC, and they have sent Pan-African Parliament conflict resolution delegations to Darfur, Uganda, and Mauritania. South Africa's representatives have pressed human rights issues at the twice-yearly SADC Parliamentary Forum and training programs (interview, October 25, 2006). But South Africa's parliamentary committees lack the research capacity and independent political base of their Canadian counterparts, in an underfunded institution with a party list system.[3] ANC dominance prevents the kind of norm challenge or civil society representation shown by the Netherlands' or Sweden's vocal legislatures. Human rights foreign policy is thus more fragilely dependent on a smaller circle of leadership, and civil society on extra-governmental influence.

ACTIVATING THE POTENTIAL: LEADERSHIP

South Africa was blessed with a visionary, focused, and internationalist leadership in the initial period of transition. But the routinization and regionalization of foreign policy have also diminished the ranks of cosmopolitan activism. The initial influence of Nelson Mandela cannot be overstated, as a torchbearer of universal human rights values, advocate of multilateralism, and broker of interdependence in tandem with democracy. In his inaugural foreign policy statement, directed to an international audience during the transition to democracy, Mandela stated the following:

> The pillars upon which our foreign policy will rest are the following beliefs:
>
> - that issues of human rights are central to international relations and an understanding that they extend beyond the political, embracing the economic, social and environmental;
> - that just and lasting solutions to the problems of humankind can only come through the promotion of democracy worldwide;
> - that considerations of justice and respect for international law should guide the relations between nations. (Mandela 1993)

As in Sweden, Canada, and Costa Rica, top-level leadership was supplemented by mid-level diplomats and internationally active policy makers.

---

3. In the late 1990s, an MP named Raymond Sutner, who was chair of the Foreign Affairs Committee, tried to remedy this by getting outside funding for parliamentary research from the Ford Foundation. He was rebuffed by the government, and posted off as an ambassador (interview, October 2006).

Key figures of the South African transition such as Desmond Tutu, Richard Goldstone, and Chief Justice Pius Langa projected South Africa's human rights package internationally. Tutu promoted South Africa's Truth and Reconciliation Commission model in dozens of countries, Goldstone served as prosecutor for the international tribunals for the former Yugoslavia and Rwanda, and Langa consulted on constitutional review commissions in Sri Lanka, Zimbabwe, Rwanda, and Tanzania. Following the model of the 1994 transition talks, lead ANC negotiator Cyril Ramaphosa got involved in second-track diplomacy in Sri Lanka, Northern Ireland, and Palestine. Mandela advisor Nicholas "Fink" Haysom joined international agencies in Sudan and Afghanistan to assist in conflict resolution.

Some mid-level leadership continued in subsequent years. Jackie Selebi, who represented South Africa at the Non-Proliferation Treaty and Ottawa Process on land mines, became the director-general of foreign affairs, and South Africa's representative to the U.N. Human Rights Commission. Barney Pityana—now the principal of UNISA—began with South Africa's Human Rights Commission, and was seconded to the African Human Rights Commission. In that regional post, he is credited with increasing the level of expertise and women's representation (interview, November 19, 2006).

But human rights leadership waned as successor president Thabo Mbeki shifted from a universalist to a pan-African and counter-Western agenda, in part based on his own exile experience setting up anti-apartheid linkages in Africa and the developing world. As a former Mandela foreign policy advisor, Mbeki became a hands-on foreign policy president. But his more interest-based vision of the cultivation of better relations with Nigeria—his country of exile—or China—Africa's rising trade partner—dictated a renewed emphasis on sovereignty and strength and a downgrading of principle and multilateralism. This change in the tone of leadership away from cosmopolitanism may have represented a response to the challenge of rival nationalist figures within the ANC, such as populist vice president Jacob Zuma.[4] Human rights policy in South Africa has persisted in large part due to the efforts of civil society.

MAINTAINING MOMENTUM: CIVIL SOCIETY

Although civil society in South Africa does not have the kind of institutionalized channels of influence into foreign policy of the Nordic countries, the Netherlands, Canada, or Costa Rica, it has played important roles of agenda setting, advocacy, and implementation. South Africa's diversity and globalization have produced a relatively cosmopolitan civil society,

---

4. For example, Zuma reinforced South Africa's internationally castigated AIDS denial with his statement in a trial for raping an HIV-positive woman that he had taken precautions by showering after having unprotected sex.

with uneven but significant levels of transnational, urban, and traditional-sector social capital. Broadly supportive public opinion, highly capable research and implementation NGOs, and labor movement international-ism have all been resources for human rights promotion. As in Costa Rica, a regionally anomalous level of feminist ideology and women's participa-tion have also enhanced humanitarian internationalism.

Although there is little systematic research, sporadic public opinion polls indicate that two-thirds to three-quarters of the South African mass public is very concerned about human rights abuses in other countries and favors South African participation in peacekeeping (Nel 1998, in Nel, Taylor, and van der Westhuizen 2001). Similarly, 78% supported a policy of human rights promotion in 1997–1998 (Alden and LePere 2003). Many waves of in- and out-migration by South Africa's white, Indian, and Jew-ish populations maintain a high level of international awareness in those groups, and the transnational ties forged during decades of anti-apartheid activism foster a high level of global consciousness and linkage in the politically mobilized urban black community. Over one million South African Indians, the largest population outside of India, played a bridg-ing role in both the struggle and the new democracy; out of 28 members of the first Cabinet, 6 were South Africans of Indian origin, and several Indian vice ministers of foreign affairs have been influential.

In a similar way, women's strong roles in resistance to apartheid have fostered an ideology of gender equity. The interracial 1955 women's march against pass laws was a turning point in the campaign, and the Black Sash movement of anti-apartheid white feminists was a keystone of the South African human rights movement. The ANC adopted gender equality as a central goal alongside nonracialism, and has an influential women's group, as well as quotas for party and legislative representation. Although the *national* conditions of South African women leave much to be desired, they generally lead regional trends,[5] and are superseded by aspirational foreign policy promotion. In 1996, the new South African government created gender focal points in all departments, including eight in foreign affairs. A woman, Nkosazana Dlamini Zuma, became foreign minister in 1999. As chair of SADC from 1997 to 2000, South Africa pushed gender issues (Schoeman and Sadie 2004). South Africa has been an active sup-porter of women's human rights throughout the U.N. system.

South African think tanks and implementation NGOs (like IDASA and CCR) are capable and relatively influential in the Foreign Affairs Department. The DFA policy research unit meets with research organi-zations in a forum 3 to 4 times each year, and regularly contracts studies. The partially state funded Institute for Global Dialogue was founded in 1994 by the ANC after Mandela met with Helmut Kohl, as a think tank

5. South African women have better incomes, literacy rates, personal freedoms, and political participation than most neighboring countries. The notable exception to this is sexual violence; South Africa has been estimated to have the highest rate of rape in the world.

and policy advisor to reposition South African foreign policy. In addition to voluminous foreign policy studies, the IGD seconds staff to the AU, and has coordinated second-track diplomacy in the DRC, Burundi, Nigeria, Lesotho, Sudan, and Côte d'Ivoire. The Institute for Security Studies has been important for drafting security sector reform within South Africa, as well as planning disarmament and demobilization programs in the region (Alden and LePere 2003, LePere and Vickers 2004: 69–70). The private-sector-funded South African Institute for International Affairs played a significant role in drafting the 1996 foreign policy discussion document and has had input on other white papers. Deputy Foreign Minister Aziz Pahad regularly cites publications by ISS, SAIIA, and IGD.

As far as challenger international human rights advocacy, labor internationalism has played the role that South Africa's weak opposition parties and refocused historic human rights groups cannot. Because the ANC governs in a trilateral coalition with the labor federation COSATU and the Communist Party, COSATU as a labor movement is in a linchpin position. Within the coalition, there is a struggle for the soul of the ANC, as it has moved from oppositional social movement to realist wielder of state power. COSATU has maintained a more social democratic identity; far from being co-opted into a corporatist alliance, the labor entity has found its members squeezed by its coalition partner's neoliberal policies. So labor internationalism on antiglobalization and global labor rights issues has become a major focus of COSATU contestation. COSATU by 2004 had more than two million members (Naidoo 2004: 190).

A COSATU representative points out that its differences with the ANC over Zimbabwe fall within a broader range that includes privatization policy, and formerly HIV/AIDS (COSATU worked with the Treatment Action Campaign to pressure the South African government to provide antiretroviral treatment). The one area in which COSATU's opposition has secured a change in government policy was in contesting proposed antiterror legislation they contended would chill legitimate protest, which was modified by Parliament. COSATU's differences with the ANC as government have led it to seek a change in the parliamentary representation formula to mixed constituency representation, to enshrine more accountability to opposition. But in an interesting twist on the dynamic between the party as government and its social movement opposition, when COSATU representatives met with Deputy Foreign Affairs Minister Aziz Pahad regarding human rights in Palestine, he said he agreed with COSATU but found it difficult for the government to take a stand without visible civil society pressure, inviting the opposition-partner to force his hand (interview, November 6, 2006).

Mandla Rametsi, the international relations director of COSATU, explains that although he sits on the National Executive Council of the Tripartite Alliance, he has stopped attending the meetings because the ANC sets the agenda—especially on Zimbabwe—without consulting COSATU (interview, November 6, 2006). His position in specific

COSATU-ANC-SACP talks on Swaziland and Zimbabwe policy has been that South Africa should expel Zimbabwe's high commissioner and withdraw the South African ambassador. Meanwhile, on the ground, COSATU has maintained strong links with its labor federation counterpart, the ZCTU, and a steady stream of border protest. After the Zimbabweans attempted to organize a protest march in September 2006, its leaders were arrested and beaten at the assembly point (filmed by the AFL-CIO Solidarity Center)—a few escaped to attend the COSATU Congress in South Africa days later, displaying their injuries to the world press. A series of regular visits between the ZCTU and COSATU was disrupted two years ago, when the COSATU delegation to Harare was deported and its general-secretary "banned for life." Last year, *all* internationals were sent back from Zimbabwe, leading to an ILO ruling against Zimbabwe (interview, November 6, 2006).

COSATU has also maintained an agenda of concern with labor repression in Swaziland, a lesser-known, much smaller, and more dependent neighbor whose quasi-feudal monarchy has been less condemned by the international community. In August 2003, South African unionists mounted a Swaziland border blockade in solidarity with internal protests (Naidoo 2004: 192). More recently, renewed political persecution led to April 2006 blockades by South African unionists of the Swazi border.

South Africa's leadership and society have been influenced in many ways by its history and transition to become bearers of human rights values, which have been projected abroad as South Africa reengaged with the world—just as the world came across its borders through globalization, conflict, and migration.

FROM LIBERALISM TO LIBERATION: THE SHIFTING NORM PACKAGE

In many domains, South Africa's diversity is both a strength and a challenge—and this extends to the diverse ideological sources of humanitarian internationalism in that country. The main sources of norms include liberal human rights, interdependence solidarity, and identity-based liberation. The value package that converged around resistance to apartheid loosened into parallel strands in the decade that followed. As in Japan—where the collective human security approach can sometimes undercut universal human rights—South Africa's overlapping humanitarian values can pull in different directions in complex situations. Moreover, different sectors of human rights promoters are mobilized by different elements of the value package, so that some kinds of challenges will unite, whereas others divide South Africans seeking a better world beyond their borders. In the constructivist reading of foreign policy, norm promotion becomes possible when a country defines what it means to be itself in terms of universal roles and identities. For

South Africa, the construction of identity is actually a three-part question: What does it mean to be South African? What does it mean to be *African?* What does it mean to be human?

South Africa's history of struggle for basic freedoms and personal integrity for its majority of black citizens implanted universal liberal human rights as a fundamental referent of political culture and national identity. South Africans recall that although their country has the continent's newest democracy, that democracy was crafted by Africa's oldest liberation movement, dating from 1912. That movement later appealed to classic human rights norms—but black South African struggles earlier helped to *create* the values of human rights, in documents such as the 1923 African Bill of Rights that *predate* the post–World War II Universal Declaration (later developed in the ANC's 1955 Freedom Charter). South Africa's majority framed their claims in global terms as early as 1943, when they responded to the Allies' Atlantic Charter with the anticolonial manifesto, "We Fight for World Democracy." International recognition of apartheid as a crime against humanity in turn led to an extraordinary level of international normative validation, notably the OAU's 1989 Harare Declaration and the United Nations' International Convention for the Suppression and Punishment of the Crime of Apartheid. It is notable that even those in the armed wing of the ANC adhered to the Geneva Conventions in their guerrilla struggle, and called upon the apartheid government to do the same (Asmal 2005).

For the internationalized political class of South Africans of color, as well as the remaining white activists and academics, national values *are* universal. When asked about her human rights platform, multiply exiled parliamentarian Fatima Hajaig said—"As an ANC MP, human rights is part and parcel of who I am" (interview, October 25, 2006). The Department of Foreign Affairs Human Rights Office stated that South Africa's leading international resource is "moral authority," and that their main mission is to share best practices and externalize the lessons of South Africa's democracy (interview, November 20, 2006).

But following the transition from liberation movement to governing party, South African policy makers discovered an overlapping but distinct rationale for humanitarian internationalism: interdependence. President Thabo Mbeki articulated South Africa's national interest in African solidarity in 2002: "I don't think you can have sustainable and successful development in this country if the rest of the continent is in flames" (Hamill 2006: 120). On the security side, this reasoning parallels Costa Rica's early version of "democratic peace" theory, in which a country that is an "island of democracy" realizes a national interest in stabilizing poorly governed neighbors who may become regional aggressors or generate spillovers of refugees and social deterioration. But the interdependent solidarity norm differs from human rights, in that it dictates conflict resolution but not necessarily democracy promotion, and it encourages a regional more than a universal focus.

This state-based logic of interdependence meets evolving international norms in the human security agenda, which has assumed increasing salience in South Africa. The United Nations Commission on Human Security involved two South Africans, including a former speaker of the South African Parliament. The doctrinally influential Institute for Security Studies has positioned itself as "human security for Africa" since 1996, and the language of interdependence, social roots of conflict, and integrated conflict resolution is used by all the major think tanks and some NGOs. However, outsider movements and intellectuals more linked to transnational movements insist on the language of human rights, and point out the inconsistencies on issues such as Zimbabwe. As interdependence trickles down to the Department of Foreign Affairs, they express the linkage in strikingly similar terms to those used by counterparts in Costa Rica: "A better South Africa makes a better Africa, and that makes a better world" (interview, November 20, 2006).

But the same political actors add a third element to the package that is unique to South Africa, diffused across distinct sectors of decision makers, and has different implications than human rights, human security, or other countries' social democracy. The Department of Foreign Affairs explains, "All of this, human rights and international solidarity, is based in our *African* values. We have *umbuntu;* it means a kind of humaneness—there was a tradition that you take care of your neighbor's house" (interview, November 20, 2006). The same history that inculcated South Africa with a hunger for human rights also planted a thirst for African identity—as apartheid separated black from white inside South Africa, it also put barriers between that country and its continent. Pan-Africanism has been both an affirmative agenda for South Africa's reconstruction of national identity and a defensive response to continental estrangement and resentment of South African hegemony. When South Africa prodded Nigeria for universal human rights in 1995, a defensive Nigerian foreign minister famously criticized South Africa as a "white state run by a black President" (Lee, Taylor, and Williams 2006).

Shortly thereafter, President Mbeki announced his African Renaissance program, which has reoriented South Africa's multilateral engagements and resource flows. Although the African Renaissance is centered in regional development, Mbeki has tried to bridge African pride to both democracy and core humanitarian values. In his 1997 announcement of the African Renaissance, which took place in a corporate investment forum in the United States, Mbeki emphasized democracy as part of self-determination: "The one-party states and the military governments will not work. The way forward must be informed by what is, after all, common to all African traditions—that the people must govern! ... This generation remains African and carries with it a historic pride which compels it to seek a place for Africans equal to all the other peoples ... it must resist all tyranny, oppose all attempts to deny liberty by resort to demagogy" (Mbeki 1997). The following year he added a plea for humanitarian solicarity in Africa's continuing crises based on Other identification: "Both of these—the harbingers of death and the victims of their wrath— are as African as you and I. For that reason, for the reason that we are the disemboweled African mothers and the decapitated African children of Rwanda, we have to say enough and no more. . . . And by acting to banish that shame, remake ourselves as midwives of the African Renaissance" (Mbeki 1998).

Pan-African solidarity has appealed to the more nationally based sectors of the ANC and mass public, some think tanks like the Center for Political Studies, and some South African NGOs who see African regionalism as a strategic channel for the promotion of universal values such as gender equity. Conversely, identity-based internationalism undercuts the acceptance of some universalist actors—such as civil libertarian IDASA, which was referred to by several policy makers as "that *white* NGO."[6] Self-determination is the core norm of pan-Africanism, which more globalized activists critique as fundamentally agnostic concerning governance and prone to culturally relative rationalizations of human rights abuse, as suggested by the limits of the African Peer Review Mechanism. Some left and social democratic analysts even see pan-Africanism as part of a broader "false consciousness" identity politics, intended to distract South Africans from neoliberal disempowerment at home and semiperiphery subimperialism on the continent.

When the values of human rights, human security, and African solidarity come together, like in the DRC, South Africa can play its most constructive role as a humanitarian internationalist. When they conflict, as in Zimbabwe, South African policy becomes inconsistent or neglectful. Maintaining a balance of South Africa's triple norms of national, regional, and universal identity—and the influence of their attendant constituencies—is the key to consolidating South Africa's global citizenship.

CONCLUSION: SAMARITANS FROM THE SOUTH

South Africa's contributions to international human rights promotion make it an instructive study of the potential and limits of a non-Western, developing, recent democracy as global Good Samaritan. First, the case of South Africa demonstrates that multilateralism matters, as determinant and arena of human rights promotion. But in the second generation, South Africa shows that multilateral linkages are not enough if the content of

6. Because the South African staff of IDASA is mostly black, and they have locally run partner offices in African countries, this characterization is only accurate in terms of the organization's origins and a few members of its current leadership. By the critical context of these references, and the comparative lack of racial labeling of the demographically similar ISS or SAIIA, it appears that civil libertarianism itself is being typed as a "white," culturally inauthentic agenda.

norm promotion is sacrificed to more material constructions of national interest. Surprisingly, South Africa shows that a developing country can be a significant source of governance development assistance. In this case, such assistance has been constructive with a modest level of resources due to the twinning and modeling from South Africa's effective democratic institutions, as well as the trilateral implementation relationship with Northern donors. Another area of unusual accomplishment has been peace promotion, where the range of South Africa's efforts has resulted in some positive results despite a predictably low yield ratio. South Africa's bilateral shortfalls reflect similar difficulties to all the countries studied, but for the case of a developing country in a "bad neighborhood," could potentially be compensated by greater outreach to like-minded global supporters, as Costa Rica seems to demonstrate. The one area in which developing country status has clearly handicapped South Africa is refugee reception, but less from absolute lack of resources than weaknesses of domestic governance. Again, Costa Rica provides some positive evidence that international support may be able to supplement national institutional impediments.

South Africa's structural preconditions for principled foreign policy are not uncommon in the middle tier of the developing world, but some of its mobilizing factors are more idiosyncratic. As a globalized, democratic, demilitarized regional power, South Africa is comparable to perhaps a dozen peers. Although South Africa's dense civil society is characteristic of many similar states, its cosmopolitan character and limited but open channels of influence on foreign policy are less common. The unique historical factors that thrust South Africa into global good citizenship were ironic results of its pervasive and persistent persecution, and the global character of the struggle to overcome it: the extraordinary leadership of Nelson Mandela, and the principled heritage of antiapartheid liberalism.

South Africa shows that a victim of abuse can become a champion of its remedy. The limitations of its principled foreign policy have come with the normalization of its dialectical construction of national interest, as material and geopolitical constraints play a more forceful role, and South Africa seeks to define its niche as a regional power. The question for the next phase is whether South Africa can leapfrog its international relations from premodern to postmodern, as it has attempted in its international economic development, from role model of recovery to postcolonial cosmopolitanism.

9

Coalitions of the Caring

Interstate Networks for Human Rights

The member countries of the Development Assistance Committee spend about $60 billion dollars each year for official development assistance. There are three principal motivations for their efforts. The first motive is fundamentally humanitarian.... The second reason ... is enlightened self-interest.... The third reason for international support for development is ... sustainable development expands the community of interests and values necessary to manage a host of global issues.
    —DAC, OECD, "Shaping the 21st Century: The Contribution
                    of Development Co-operation," 1996

Although we have seen that the individual policies of global Good Samaritans have a significant effect on global human rights conditions, that contribution is multiplied when they join together. The cumulative efforts of like-minded human rights promoters add an additional layer to the construction of the international human rights regime. The emergence of this genre of value-oriented interstate organizations also suggests the evolution of a new, specialized mechanism for global governance.

Although multipurpose, *universal* international organizations like the United Nations have come to play a central role in promoting human rights, and transnational *nongovernmental* movements usually catalyze and underpin human rights campaigns, this chapter will focus on a third sector of the human rights architecture: *purposive, interstate organizations* established specifically to promote rights, democracy, and the rule of law. Such organizations currently include regionally based organizations like the OSCE and at times the OAS; promotional coalitions such as the Community of Democracies, the Human Security Network, and IDEA; democratic governance networks including the Network of National Human Rights Institutions and the Inter-Parliamentary Union; and functional humanitarian organizations like the International Organization for Migration and the OECD Donor Action Committee. All are composed of member states, have an explicit human rights mandate, and the purposive

Table 9.1 The International Human Rights Regime

Level of Analysis	Sample Actors
IGO arenas	U.N. Human Rights Commission, International Criminal Court
Transnational action networks	Trafficking, indigenous rights
International human rights NGOs	Amnesty International, ICRC
State promoters	Canada, Costa Rica
Interstate promoter networks	**Community of democracies**
Non-state political leadership promoters	Arias Foundation, Friedrich Ebert Fund

function is primary or has become so.[1] This core of interstate value promoters adjoins a neighboring set of *value-oriented, quasi-governmental entities* that draw on the social capital of political leadership without the formal commitment of state membership in an intergovernmental body: the peace and democracy-oriented foundations of past leaders (Jimmy Carter, Oscar Arias, Olaf Palme, Pierre Trudeau); the Club of Madrid coalition of previous democratic heads of state; and the international democracy promotion wings of political parties (the German Friedrich Ebert, the U.S. National Democratic Institute). Although the range of these organizations' normative rationales is even greater than the variance of states' labeling of promotion policies as combinations of *human rights, human security, democracy, rule of law, conflict resolution,* and sometimes *good governance,* the raison d'être of these intergovernmental networks is to foster the core rights listed in the Universal Declaration of Human Rights and the International Covenant on Civil and Political Rights.

The potential contribution of such new organizations to the commonweal can be gauged against the broader panoply of roles that international organizations play in global governance. The oldest approach to international organization, the Grotian tradition culminating in world federalism, envisions the construction of a global layer of authoritative control over core activities of states (Falk 1977). Although human rights promotion networks do not aspire to global governance, it has been argued that election monitoring sets systematic international boundaries on a key component of sovereignty (Santa-Cruz 2005). Moreover, promotion networks may contribute to United Nations–sponsored human rights safety nets such as the International Criminal Court, or the "responsibility to protect" mandate for humanitarian intervention, which episodically supersedes

1. Although the OSCE was established with a regional base, its expansive membership has transcended the original Eastern European focus to include Central Asia and Canada, with further linkages to Asia and the Middle East via partnership arrangements. In terms of purposive orientation, even though the OSCE has regional security and economic components, the extensive EU architecture has come to fulfill the functional mandate so completely that the OSCE concentrates heavily and increasingly on the "human dimension." Similarly, the OECD Donor Action Committee qualifies as the purposive arm of a larger functional body, set up specifically to enhance the achievement of value-driven goals.

state sovereignty—under the dual specified conditions of massive and gross violations coupled with state persecution or negligence.

A less demanding role for global governance is when functional institutions coordinate state policies for mutual gain (Keohane 1977). Besides direct harmonization of interests, institutional collaboration may foster mutual gains in the face of evolving knowledge about social conditions, causal dynamics, and interdependence (Haas 2006). The promotion of human security aspects of human rights, linked to spillover problems such as refugees, would be an example of this dynamic. Similarly, donor coordination makes states' overseas development assistance more effective.

The intergovernmental network variant of this liberal approach points to the role of intergovernmental networks of all sorts in exchanging information, setting common standards and benchmarks, developing administrative capacity, and enhancing states' abilities to manage global flows (Slaughter 2006). Transgovernmentalism horizontally links national government officials in a way that reinforces their common understandings and organizational purpose. The network of National Human Rights Institutions (NHRI) clearly fits this model, whereas in a broader sense, interstate human rights promotion organizations that assist in the implementation of international treaty norms expand governance functionality.

Conversely, rational states may join international organizations and accords to deliberately reduce their autonomy, in areas where leaders believe that long-term national interest is served by allowing an external standard rather than shifting popular will or subsequent leadership to determine policy (Moravcsik 2000). In the area of human rights, countries bind themselves to international law. This explanation generally does not apply domestically to the global Good Samaritans who create or join intergovernmental promotion organizations, because their domestic human rights policies are usually superior to the international norm. However, participation in such networks may in a modest way lock in foreign policy practices as internal humanitarian internationalist forces wax and wane.

Beyond coordination or commitment of existing interests, membership in sectors of international society may socialize states to new sets of interests (Bull 1995). Clubs of global good citizens can shift the understanding of the common good, and build the expectation that contemporary democracies relate preferentially to each other, provide humanitarian aid and export rule of law. This should enhance lagging aspects of global Good Samaritans' policies, and inspire greater efforts by bystander states as they seek membership and reputation from such organizations. It may even inspire direct assistance to victims or nongovernmental advocates. In a more diffuse way, international organizations build new interests as they construct meanings, classifications, and norms for the stream of social problems (Barnett and Finnemore 2006).

Finally, a critical theory approach to globalization might suggest that some international organizations could serve as a source of counterhegemony to unregulated global capital and dominant powers (Cox 1992). In this case, coalitions of value promoters would operate to balance or outweigh hegemonic interests. The ability of the OSCE to operate in the interstices of Soviet domination in Eastern Europe, and the like-minded states at the ICC negotiations to overcome U.S. objections, are harbingers of this project. If and when contemporary intergovernmental human rights organizations critique corporate or superpower human rights practices, they may be laying the groundwork for an alternative, more democratic global system. On the process dimension, international organizations that encourage the participation of global civil society also help to democratize global governance.

Human rights networks perform roughly the same range of functions as individual states, with the exception of humanitarian intervention—which remains the prerogative of states and their multipurpose surrogates. The difference is that coalitions, by acting collectively, may multiply material and normative resources. The existence of a cluster of such organizations supports the potential for an implicit division of labor among them. If and when such patterns are institutionalized, they may constitute an "international regime"—a pattern of the convergence of states' expectations regarding the principles and decision-making procedures surrounding a global issue (Krasner 1993). Some analysts believe that global patterns of human rights interaction have risen to the level of an international regime (Donnelly 1984), so new coalitions would help to expand the regime's scope and mechanisms.

Thus, we will evaluate the range of global governance functions performed by intergovernmental human rights networks in accordance with the following broader criteria. First of all, these organizations can introduce new norms to the international agenda, and frame emerging problems in terms of existing norms (i.e., labeling a genocide). This is closely linked to the classic human rights NGO tactic of "naming and shaming" states that violate human rights, with the initial step of "claiming" the right. Second, by virtue of state membership, intergovernmental networks have a strong ability to diffuse existing norms into new venues, such as moving gender equity from global to regional to functional organizations. They also have a potentially privileged position to lobby existing human rights mechanisms and institutions collectively. Within their own ranks, interstate human rights groups coordinate and harmonize existing policies, and synergize financial, knowledge, and political capital. Human rights networks may become policy innovators at the global level when they help to establish new human rights mechanisms, institutions, and "best practices." Intergovernmental organizations may be a source of direct assistance to victims of human rights violations, or at-risk groups. Finally, principled promotion organizations may transform target states through capacity building, and assist with states' implementation of global norms through providing monitoring, funding, and expertise. A sample of best-case promoters of each type will be profiled below. Although all of the organizations will be assessed against each of these criteria, we will see that each makes its strongest contribution in a particular area or range of global governance functions.

THE OSCE: FROM VALUES TO IMPLEMENTATION

The Organization for Security and Cooperation in Europe (OSCE) is the most full spectrum human rights promotion organization in the current international system. Founded as a security measure in 1975, it has grown in membership from 35 to 56 states, and focused its mission heavily on value promotion, especially since the end of the Cold War. The OSCE is thus the oldest, largest, interstate promotion organization, based in the most democratic region of the world—a best case organization, and a model of the full range of possibilities.[2] Moreover, the OSCE is noted for its openness and partnership with civil society groups throughout its history. The OSCE is registered as a regional security arrangement under Chapter VIII of the U.N. Charter, and thus has a privileged partnership with that body. The OSCE's lack of formal status in international law and nonbinding character have been surprisingly irrelevant to its relative effectiveness. By 2007, the OSCE's budget had risen to 170 million euros (about $230 million). The OSCE has a total staff of around 3,500 (including 750 seconded by participating states) (http://www.osce.org).

The OSCE was set up in 1975 by 35 states as the Conference for Security and Co-operation in Europe, based on the Helsinki Accords negotiating mutual security accountability between the Soviet Union and the Western alliance. For the first time, human rights was incorporated as a "third dimension" of security. The organization operates by consensus. An initial basic commitment to human rights was expanded through a series of 1980s meetings and accords, largely at the behest of the neutral and nonaligned participants, and specific provisions were negotiated by the United Kingdom, Soviet Union, Sweden, Hungary, Austria, and (then-West) Germany. The 1989 Concluding Document "is replete with cross-references to international human rights law" (Lowe, Warbrick, and McGoldrick 1990: 924).

Principle VII of the 10 guiding principles of the Helsinki Final Act is "respect for human rights and fundamental freedoms, including the freedom of thought, conscience, religion or belief, for all without distinction as to race, sex, language or religion. They will promote and encourage the effective exercise of civil, political, economic, social, cultural and other rights and freedoms all of which derive from the inherent dignity of the human person." It further recognizes "the right of the individual to know

---

2. The OSCE is the largest *organization*, in terms of staff and budget. The Community of Democracies has the largest *membership*, with over 100 participating states.

and act upon his rights and duties in this field." The term *human dimension* is used to indicate a broader swath of activities regarding democracy, rule of law, and migration. The OSCE states that it is "a community of values." These values are explicitly framed as an international concern in the 1991 Moscow Document, which states that "the commitments undertaken in the field of the human dimension of the CSCE are matters of direct and legitimate concern to all participating States and do not belong exclusively to the internal affairs of the State concerned." In the 1992 Document on Further Development (Prague), the council affirmed that in cases of "clear, gross and uncorrected violations" of human rights, the council could modify the consensus rule to act "if necessary in the absence of the consent of the State concerned" (OSCE Human Dimension Commitments, September 19, 2005).

The main working process of the OSCE is a continuous, institutionalized process of multilateral, inclusive dialogue. The CSCE Vienna Monitoring Procedure introduced a new four-stage process for human rights by an international organization: information exchange, followed by bilateral meetings, general publicity of situations and cases to the wider membership, and finally annual human rights review conferences. For example, this is the procedure that freed Czech dissident playwright and future president Vaclav Havel. The accords specifically emphasize freedom of religion, freedom of movement, due process, and the situation of national minorities. Beyond the organization's own activities, the CSCE provided an enormous stimulus to the development of the international human rights movement by inspiring the formation of Helsinki monitoring groups in numerous countries (which later formed the core of flagship NGO Human Rights Watch). Just as the original accord had linked the stabilization of Eastern Europe's borders to Soviet acceptance of universal humanitarian standards, during the 1980s the United States linked arms control talks to Soviet compliance—in a way that ultimately reconstituted state interests (Korey 1989, Korey 1990, Thomas 2001).

The CSCE was renamed the *Organization* for Security and Cooperation in Europe in 1994, signaling the institutionalization of an ongoing commitment to a new governance model. The strengthening and expansion of the OSCE was advocated by NATO in 1990, as a complementary component of the new European architecture. In the wake of the Cold War, the creation of new states in Europe enlarged the membership of the OSCE, additional states adhered, and the organization established partnerships with a cluster of Mediterranean and later Asian states. Notably, the membership includes a number of states not incorporated in the expanded EU or NATO. The security and cooperation rationale of the OSCE shifted from management of the East-West conflict to the management of post-Soviet succession and the emergence of ethnic conflict in Europe. The 1992 Moscow Mechanism expanded the Vienna process to include missions of experts and rapporteurs to states with human dimension problems, by invitation, request of a participating state, or *even over the objections of the target state* with the support of five members (http://www.osce.org/odihr/13498.html; my emphasis). Important contentious uses of the Moscow Mechanism include monitoring attacks on civilians in Croatia and Bosnia in 1992, and investigating a destabilizing 2002 attack on the president of Turkmenistan. The 1991 Moscow Commitments also explicitly expand recognition and participation of NGOs, facilitating information exchange, country visits, and civic groups' implementation of OSCE norms. Later, the 1999 Istanbul Charter pledges "to enhance the ability of NGOs to make their full contribution to the further development of civil society and respect for human rights and fundamental freedoms." By the turn of the millennium, the organization had begun to focus on expanded global human rights concerns such as gender equity: the OSCE adopted an Action Plan to Combat Trafficking in 2003 (OSCE March 3, 2005, OSCE 2006).

Ironically, current critiques of the OSCE are a testament to its success: they contend that the human dimension has been too prominent, too intrusive, or unbalanced in its application (to Russia and Central Asia). Russia has pressed for institutional reform, greater member state control, and independence from NATO and the EU. Russia's particular demands for shifting standards for itself and its allies were not met, but a 30th anniversary reform panel did recommend greater geographic balance in staffing, a stronger three-pillar committee structure, greater transparency in election monitoring criteria, improved operational capacity, and shorter field missions (OSCE July 22, 2005, Annual Report 2006).

There are several structures within the OSCE that deal specifically with human rights: the Office of Democratic Institutions and Human Rights (ODIHR), the high commissioner on national minorities, the OSCE representative on freedom of the media, and the Office of the Special Representative for Combating Trafficking in Human Beings (which implements the Action Plan). Although the main secretariat of the OSCE is in Vienna, the ODIHR is in Warsaw and the minorities commissioner is in The Hague, reflecting hosting commitments of those member states.

The Office of Democratic Institutions was originally established in 1990, and concentrates on election monitoring and assistance, as well as human rights promotion and coordination. It includes a migration unit that promotes the rights of asylum seekers and migrant workers. The ODIHR also provides a special contact point for Roma and Sinti issues, and a broader program on tolerance and nondiscrimination. This office alone employs over 100 staff members, with a budget around 15 million euros (http://www.osce.org/odihr).

The high commissioner on national minorities, housed in The Hague, specializes in early warning and conflict prevention. The high commissioner works independently in deciding cases for intervention, but confidentially to negotiate with governments to correct problems—in the manner of the International Red Cross. Although the office gives legislative advice to states, and its policy recommendations are often implemented, there is no capacity for individual complaints regarding violations by affected groups. Nevertheless, for example, Latvia and Estonia made changes in their citizenship and language laws in accordance with OSCE high commissioner recommendations. The high commissioner has been active in most of the Balkan, Baltic, and Central Asian member states, including Russia and Turkey. A much smaller, mainly advisory office, the high commissioner operates with almost $3 million euros per year. The commissioner coordinates closely with United Nations bodies on minority protection, antidiscrimination, and genocide (http://www.osce.org.hcnm; Heintze 2000).

One stream of activities of the OSCE focuses on monitoring, reports, and education. The ODIHR and high commissioner on minorities sponsor seminars and educational campaigns on tolerance, and the ODIHR started a new database on hate crimes to better track and coordinate member state problems and policies (the Tolerance and Non-Discrimination Information System, http://tnd.odihr.pl). The same office published a manual on human rights protection in counterterrorism for public officials, to supplement training courses. In 2006, the ODIHR sponsored a conference, "Implementation and Harmonization of National Policies for Roma." The high commissioner for minorities has launched a process for truth and reconciliation in Kosovo.

Promotion of elections is also a key activity; the OSCE provides election monitoring, electoral assistance, and training. Election observations have been conducted in 30 participating states, and the organization has developed a comprehensive methodology, training materials, and civil society support. These elections have involved thousands of observers from dozens of member states.

The OSCE's budget allocates 75% to field missions, which have included negotiations of active conflicts in Georgia, Tajikistan, and Chechnya, as well as postconflict reconciliation and democratization in Bosnia, Croatia, and Kosovo. The majority of staff members for field operations are local, and most of the remainder of personnel are seconded from member states. An evaluation of these operations concludes the following: "In a nutshell, the OSCE has been fairly successful in conflict prevention, unsuccessful in conflict resolution and unevenly successful in post-conflict rehabilitation." This author classifies the Kosovo 1992, Macedonia, Estonia, Latvia, and Ukraine missions as conflict prevention, and the Bosnia, Croatia since 1996, Albania since 1997, Kosovo 1999, Macedonia 2001, and Tajikistan field operations as peace building. Prominent, less successful cases of attempts at conflict resolution include Azerbaijan, Georgia, and Chechnya (Ghebali 2005). The longest and largest mission (with 1,100 staff members), in Kosovo, included human rights capacity building for dozens of municipalities, monitoring of the justice system, antitrafficking training, creation of an ombudsperson institute, and legal education (OSCE Annual Report 2006).

The OSCE has reshaped state policy through legal reform and implementation of international legal obligations, particularly regarding minority rights and rights-respectful responses to terrorism. In response to a long-term campaign by the representative on freedom of the media on legal structures that chill free expression, seven OSCE member states have decriminalized libel, and half a dozen more have removed imprisonment for defamation. The ODIHR has fostered election law reform in 13 countries. Another example of legal reform was assisting Moldova in drafting legislation on domestic violence. Legal reform often includes promoting the involvement of civil society; a recent program involved training NGOs from the Central Asian republics to monitor detention centers (OSCE "Field Operations," OSCE Annual Report 2006).

Finally, the OSCE has provided limited direct aid to victim and advocacy groups. In the area of trafficking, a 2006 high-level conference on best practices, an annual report, and a regional intersectoral meeting in Central Asia were supplemented by direct work with NGOs to render assistance to victims. The OSCE has also funded or trained representatives of national minorities, and NGOs providing services in postconflict reconstruction.

The global Good Samaritan state members of the OSCE—Sweden, Canada, and the Netherlands—have played important catalytic and leadership roles within the organization, and each of these countries states that it sees the OSCE as a force multiplier. Some of the initial negotiations of the Helsinki Accords' incorporation of human rights standards, as well as the Vienna and Moscow supervisory mechanisms, are heavily indebted to Swedish influence. Swedish diplomat Rolf Ekéus was high commissioner on national minorities from 2001 to 2007. The Dutch proposed the initial creation of this position in 1992, and the previous high commissioner was former Dutch foreign minister Max Van der Stoel. During the Dutch chair in 2003, the Netherlands commissioned a Netherlands Human Rights Advisory Council report to guide its term, and mobilized the resources of the foreign ministry extensively to support Dutch OSCE initiatives. Dutch leadership led to the action plan on trafficking, a special session to encourage the participation of international NGOs, an initial conference on human rights and counterterror, and the beginning of organizational restructuring around strengthening relationships with other international organizations. Canada's visibility began with a Canadian initiative during the 1990 Copenhagen round to expand antidiscrimination norms to include anti-Semitism, which constituted the first international recognition of that form of discrimination by an interstate body. On an ongoing basis, Canada has contributed special funding for OSCE conflict prevention and minority protection initiatives—notably in Kosovo (Netherlands Helsinki Committee, Van Beuningen 2002).

The OSCE is above all a self-described "community of values"—a classic illustration of the power of international society to reshape state behavior through socialization. Speaking to the OSCE Parliamentary Assembly, the high commissioner on national minorities made the case for international socialization when he averred that state protection of minorities is one of the "pillars of contemporary European social and political order. For a state to be European in this sense, it is simply expected and required that it respect these standards" (Cronin 2003: 138). In one concrete illustration of the application of these standards, Yugoslavia was suspended in 1992. More broadly, the Office of the High Commissioner on National Minorities has come to be seen as a gatekeeper for entry into the EU and other European institutions, and often works in joint missions with these bodies, creating enhanced leverage (Cronin 2003). The impact on states through election monitoring, legal reform, and sometimes conflict resolution reaches deep into fundamental structures of governance. Functionalist coordination, capacity building, and implementation are also dominant functions of the OSCE. Some self-binding effect is visible from time to time; for example, when Canada changed some of its legislation regarding indigenous rights in the wake of an Indian woman's complaint about gender equity and an OSCE high commissioner on minorities recommendation. In terms of counter-hegemony, the OSCE is primarily a socializing agent within accepted parameters of world order—but it has sent a Special Representative to Guantanamo, whose report called for the United States to close the facility (OSCE Annual Report 2006: 26).

THE HUMAN SECURITY NETWORK: NORM INNOVATION

The Human Security Network is a group of like-minded countries, formed to diffuse and enact the "human security" agenda. It is the most purely promotional and least institutionalized network, with no secretariat, budget, or implementation programs. Founded by Canada and Norway in the wake of the successful land mines campaign in 1998, the network represents an attempt to direct ongoing attention to a cluster of issues that entered the international agenda with the support of temporary middle-power coalitions: the International Criminal Court, control of small arms, the protection of children in combat zones, and of course land mines.

The 13-member group includes classic promoters Austria, Canada, Chile, Costa Rica, Ireland, the Netherlands, Norway, and Switzerland—but does not include Sweden, Denmark, Finland, the major European powers, or Japan. A more positive feature of the coalition is the representation of regional transitional democracies such as Jordan, Mali, Slovenia, and Thailand. Global Good Samaritan South Africa remains an observer, for the same reasons that human security promoter Japan refuses to join: fear that the "Canadian version" of the *responsibility to protect* as a mandate for humanitarian intervention threatens state sovereignty, especially in the non-Western world. This disparity has been partially bridged by the establishment of an unofficial "Friends of Human Security" support group, which does include Japan, and Mexico. The criteria for accession to the Human Security Network were established at the 2004 meeting as ratification of the Landmines Convention, ICC, and basic U.N. human rights conventions (http://www.humansecuritynetwork.org: "Members").

Human rights and democracy are clearly included in the group's definition of human security. The first ministerial meeting in 1999 stated, "A commitment to human rights and humanitarian law is the foundation for building human security." The network has been an important venue for refining the human security concept, and bridging to new issues. The network has consistently linked human security to development and social and economic rights. In terms of issue expansion, Thailand hosted a meeting on human security and AIDS via the network, whereas Mali focused its 2004 presidency on human rights education. Norm diffusion to new venues can be seen in the adoption of four of the network's 10 elements of human security (including small arms and children in conflict) by the G-8 at the end of 1999, carried by Canada between the two bodies (http://www.humansecuritynetwork.org: "Principles," "Vision").

The main activity of the network is an annual dialogue of member states' foreign ministers. The group issues declarations, and expects its members to lobby across various diplomatic settings to achieve the principles set out in the network statements. In addition, the rotating chairs make regular representations on behalf of the network at the U.N. Security Council, Human Rights Commission/Council, General Assembly, and special conferences, as well as the OSCE and other regional bodies. The United Nations' Trust Fund for Human Security's Advisory Board of prominent promoters (chaired by Sadako Ogata) participates in some meetings of the network, as well as a looser group of like-minded nonmembers, the aforementioned Friends of Human Security (http://www.humansecuritynetwork.org).

Major humanitarian NGOs and networks have been included from the start, such as the Red Cross, Amnesty International, and the International Campaign to Ban Land Mines. The Network has also helped to inspire the exchange of research and information on human security, specifically an annual Human Security Report prepared by a Canadian research center based at Simon Fraser University. The Trust Fund for Human Security at the United Nations has no formal links to the Network, but there is informal exchange and implicit convergence on some issues. Although Canada established and sustains the network, the other promoter states are either passive members or nonmembers. The network collaborates with the U.N. Office of Civilian and Humanitarian Affairs (OCHA), the Alliance of Civilizations, and the International Trust Fund for Demining and Mine Victims Assistance (http://humansecuritynetwork.org: "Civil Society").

Although the Human Security Network limns the possibilities for concerted agenda change in global institutions, it also delineates the limits of purpose without power. It is difficult to gauge the precise magnitude of the Human Security Network's contribution; it does seem to have fostered a diplomatic safety net for the core issues of protection of civilians in armed conflict. But the group's limited membership, dearth of resources, overlapping niche, and lack of leverage have constrained the coalition's potential to address other issues, or even to implement its full mandate. The land mines and ICC coalitions comprised dozens of states, not 13, and the OSCE includes most of the members of the G-8 and U.N. Security Council—including, of course, the United States. Nonmember Japan's control of the relevant resources has narrowed the network's linkage to the U.N. Trust Fund, restricting global initiatives to Japan's developmental vision. Although the Human Security Network tried to expand rather than contest notions of national security, many states interpreted human security as a counterhegemonic challenge to their sovereignty. Interests were not reconstituted beyond the handful of founding states—network member Thailand even reverted to military rule in 2006, without losing its status in the organization. For the Human Security Network to sustain its core competence of agenda expansion and norm diffusion, it will need to broaden its horizontal membership to a wider range of middle powers, and enhance its insertion in the architecture of global governance.

"CLUB DEM": THE COMMUNITY OF DEMOCRACIES

Shortly after the Human Security Network was established, in 2000 a convening group of 10 states met in Warsaw to set up a Community of Democracies promotion network. The initiative for this organization came largely from outgoing U.S. secretary of state Madeline Albright, just as the Human Security Network had been catalyzed by Canadian foreign minister Lloyd Axworthy. The community is widely perceived as U.S. sponsored, although the United States provides no formal resources or leadership (however, the organization's Web site is hosted by the U.S. State Department). As the group has grown to over 100 members, the certification function of participation has outpaced agenda setting, monitoring, and implementation functions.

The Community of Democracy's founding and orienting Warsaw Declaration lists a dozen key civil and political rights, along with rule of law and good governance, and specifically includes "all human rights—civil, cultural, economic, political and social . . . as set forth in the Universal Declaration of Human Rights" (Community of Democracies, June 27, 2000). Current standards for membership include the following: free and fair elections, rule of law and equality before the law, multiple political parties, separation of powers, and respect for human rights—including ethnic minorities and gender equality. The 2005 Santiago Ministerial Commitment affirms that democracy and human rights "are interdependent and mutually reinforcing," and lists as the first concrete goal to "promote and protect human rights and fundamental freedoms" (Democracy Coalition Project 2005).

The core "convening group" of members was led by the United States, but included leading developing world democracies such as Chile, India, Poland, the Czech Republic, South Korea, and South Africa, and has now grown to 16 members. But the convening group does not involve any of the historic promoter states such as the Nordic states, and shows very little overlap with the Human Security Network. Alongside the inter-state structure, the community includes a nongovernmental forum that participates directly in ministerial meetings as well as in a parallel NGO setting. It meets biannually in formal session, and occasionally informally at the U.N.

The Community of Democracies distributes the diffuse prestige of belonging to the club of democracies through an annual review of states, and resulting invitation categories of member, observer, or noninvitee. Observer status is for states that fail to meet international standards but are in a transition process—and states may theoretically be downgraded from full membership to observers, as well as invited initially to observer status rather than full membership. For example, Russia and Thailand participated in the first three meetings but in 2007 were uninvited; Egypt was first downgraded from member to observer in 2002, then uninvited in 2007, whereas Afghanistan slipped from participant to observer in that year. Like the Human Security Network, the Community of Democracies has no secretariat or ongoing budget—but it has an International Advisory Committee that recommends which states to invite in what categories. The committee is composed of a dozen geographically diverse notables, such as Costa Rican Sonia Picado, chair of the Inter-American Institute of Human Rights, former ambassador to the United States, and former president of her country's National Liberation Party. The Advisory Committee is supported by a secretariat of international democracy monitoring NGOs: Germany's Bertelsmann Stiftung foundation, the Ghana Center for Democratic Development, the U.S.-based Democracy Coalition Project, and Freedom House. This assessment process developed in stages over the first five years of the organization, and in part responded to NGO criticism that criteria of democracy were too limited to formal and electoral measures, and invitations too aligned with U.S. foreign policy (Democracy Coalition Project 2006).

The community's emphasis on inclusion has led to an increase in quantity that may sacrifice quality of membership. For example, the centrist monitoring NGO Freedom House ranked 37 of the 103 signers of the Warsaw Declaration as only "partly free"—and 6 more as "not free" ("Democracy Holds a Party" 2000: 32). However, only 60 of this group were invited to attend the following Seoul meeting as members, whereas the remainder were treated as "observers." In addition to the invitation rankings, the International Advisory Committee now prepares a screening report with more in-depth information and suggestions for improvement on "countries in which the trend toward respect for democracy and human rights is in flux" (46 in 2007)—which may slightly enhance the community's reputational leverage and quality control (U.S. Department of State, "The Community of Democracies"). Strengthening the group's emerging autonomy from U.S. foreign policy, in 2007 Iraq was not invited, and Venezuela was critiqued but included.

The Community of Democracies does aspire to be a proto-lobby within global institutions, like the Human Security Network. Accordingly, it created a United Nations Democracy Caucus in 2004. In 2004, the caucus directed its members to positively consider pending resolutions on torture, religious cooperation, regional organizations and democracy promotion, and the status of women in the U.N. system; all passed. The project has also issued annual scorecards of the voting records of democracies and Community. The latest survey showed mixed success:

> The UN General Assembly's Third Committee adopted four key country resolutions despite efforts by spoiler states to end the practice of naming and shaming the worst violators, according to a new survey by the Democracy Coalition Project. The survey, released on 11th December 2006 to commemorate the 58th Anniversary of the adoption of the UN Declaration on Human Rights, analyzes the voting patterns of UN Member States at the 61st General Assembly of the United Nations. The analysis is based on a scorecard that records the voting on five country resolutions condemning human rights abuses in selected states; it also covers a sixth resolution introduced by Belarus and Uzbekistan which sought to undermine the importance of country-specific resolutions. The study showed that efforts to block UN censure of human rights violators had failed, with members of the UN Democracy Caucus voting overwhelmingly for the four country resolutions that succeeded. The scorecards also showed a poor record by leading members of the Community of Democracies, including members of its Convening Group. (Campaign for a U.N. Democracy Caucus 2005)

A program on regional organizations has helped institutional diffusion, beginning with a 2001 conference hosted by the OAS, and followed by subsequent exchanges with the OSCE (Convening Group of the Community of Democracies February 20–21, 2001). The 2002 Seoul Plan of Action emphasizes linkages with regional organizations. Regional caucuses at the 2005 Santiago conference focused on strengthening the African Peer Review Mechanism, the Inter-American Democratic Charter, and

Table 9.2 U.N. Member Votes on Human Rights Resolutions, 2005

	North Korea Resolution	Iran Resolution	Uzbekistan Resolution	Turkmenistan Resolution	Congo Resolution	Sudan Resolution*
Costa Rica	Yes	Yes	Yes	Yes	Yes	No
Canada	Yes	Yes	Yes	Yes	Yes	No
Sweden	Yes	Yes	Yes	Yes	Yes	No

* The Sudan resolution was a "no action" motion that would have *blocked* consideration of abuses in Darfur, which passed over the objections of the democratic member states.

the compatibility of Islam and democracy (Democracy Coalition Project 2005).

The community has also begun to host a small number of OSCE-style missions, such as a 2004 United States/Portuguese visit to East Timor, and a 2005 Romanian delegation to Georgia. Although there is no systematic work on capacity building or implementation, the community has pledged to set up the International Centre for Democratic Transition in Budapest that would broker experience, skills, and resources for democratization.

The Community of Democracies has played a nascent agenda-setting role that in some ways complements IDEA's implementation of the same values (see below), but somewhat rivals the Human Security Network as a norm promoter at the global level. Working within the same established normative framework as the OSCE, but with a global geographic base, the community as club is an experiment in the power of reputation in international society. More conscious coordination of club membership with projection of global governance incentives, from U.N. posts to regional mechanisms to certification for bilateral relations, could provide more universal benchmarks and enhance the leverage of human rights standards.

IDEA: IMPLEMENTATION AS PROMOTION

Although the OSCE combines norm and policy promotion, and the Human Security Network and Community of Democracies focus respectively on agenda change and certification, the International Institute for Democracy and Electoral Assistance (IDEA) concentrates almost exclusively on implementation. Founded in 1995, the 24-member body includes all of the global Good Samaritan states and other historic promoters, but not the United States. Member states are usually represented by the ministries of foreign affairs, who compose the decision-making council. IDEA recently incorporated a formal membership criterion of commitment to rule of law and human rights, and as of 2006 has the capacity to suspend members who fail to meet this standard. The intergovernmental organization is hosted and 50% funded by Sweden, and carries observer status at the United Nations. Regional offices are based in Costa Rica and South Africa, with half a dozen additional program offices throughout the world. The organization's budget is approximately 10 million euros each year, and its staff comprises around 100. It has special partnerships with the Inter-American Human Rights Institute and the OSCE, among others (http://www.idea.int).

IDEA emphasizes that its mandate is democracy, not human rights per se, and that there is no universal form of democracy. However, the organization explicitly adheres to certain core democratic values, which include respect for human rights, alongside process measures such as free and fair elections. Moreover, it states that "the rights of citizens to vote and to be elected . . . are internationally recognized human rights" (Global Declaration of Principles and Code of Conduct for International Electoral Observation, IDEA Statue 2006, 2007).

IDEA works by providing knowledge resources, policy proposals, and direct technical assistance. Its specializations are constitution building, electoral processes, political party structures, democracy assessments, and gender equity. To disseminate knowledge and expertise, the organization produces databases, handbooks and Web sites, and sponsors seminars and delegations; more than 100 publications have been produced. For example, its influential ACE database on election administration, based on UNDP, Elections Canada, and Mexico's Instituto Federal Electoral, among others, has become a key knowledge multiplier, with 20,000 CDs circulated and 900,000 hits per month (IDEA, "International IDEA: Democracy Resources Worldwide," 2006; Electoral Knowledge Network, "About ACE," 2006).

In terms of policy proposals, IDEA has worked extensively on recommendations for gender quotas, as well as conflict resolution methodologies. IDEA helped to draft a law for the regulation of political parties in Peru, and facilitated constitutional dialogues in Georgia, Bolivia, and Nepal. IDEA has attended and coordinated with the Community of Democracies, and has proposed that community delegations be composed pluralistically of joint representatives of government, opposition, and civil society. The organization is initiating a project on best practices for the use of traditional justice mechanisms in reconciliation in Africa. IDEA does not monitor elections (IDEA, "Annual Report 2005," IDEA "International IDEA: History of IDEA," 2007).

Several of the global Good Samaritan states have played especially strong roles in IDEA. Sweden has been the physical host, main funder, and first secretary-general, and the current chair of the board is Sweden's former minister for foreign affairs Lena Hjelm-Wallen. Costa Rican president Oscar Arias was one of the founders of the group, Costa Rica maintains a regional office, and Costa Rica has promoted the "Women in Parliament" study. Canada is a partner of the ACE electoral knowledge network and sponsored the publication *Democracy, Conflict, and Human Security*. The Netherlands has contributed several leading figures to IDEA's board of directors, currently Senator Jos van Gennip—a serving member of the Parliament. South Africa has hosted training seminars on constitutional reform, gender quotas, and the capacity-building BRIDGE project on election administration and governance (IDEA, "International IDEA," 2006: see separate entries under Canada, Costa Rica, Netherlands, South Africa, and Sweden; "Chief Electoral Officer of Canada Hosts Launch of the ACE Electoral Knowledge Network," CCNMatthews Newswire, Toronto, May 3, 2006, p. 1).

IDEA provides clear value added to the international human rights regime within a narrow mandate and scope of activities. It uses the strong international consensus on democracy and a highly committed membership base to influence governance through building institutions and practices. Coordinating knowledge and establishing best practices does shape local interpretations and expectations of universal norms, for example, in the area of women's participation. Indirectly, promotion of the rule of law and the autonomy of civil society protects and empowers human rights advocates and defenders. IDEA illustrates the complementary power of "functionalism plus," although this power rests on the prior achievement of norm change and multilateral accountability through more value-oriented and broad-spectrum states and organizations.

THE OECD DONOR ASSISTANCE COMMITTEE: COORDINATION AS SOCIALIZATION

The OECD Donor Assistance Committee is the body devoted to overseas humanitarian assistance, among the dozen secretariats that comprise the Organization for Economic Cooperation and Development—the club of the 30 developed northern states. Twenty-two of the OECD member states belong to the Donor Assistance Committee, and collectively they control over 85% of total overseas development assistance, as well as more than half of the votes of the IMF and World Bank. The DAC falls under the Development Co-operation Directorate of the OECD's Policy Co-ordination Division that examines cross-cutting issues such as governance, conflict, gender, and aid effectiveness. The DAC is an active committee, meeting over once a month, and is based at OECD headquarters and supported by Development Directorate staff. Working parties have been established on each of these cross-cutting issues, and the DAC Network on Governance in 2004 commissioned a study on "Integrating Human Rights into Development." This study and related meetings and exchanges attempt to systematize human rights norms related to development, review donor approaches and "best practices," and "draws together lessons ... around the 'added value' of human rights for development" (OECD, "Integrating Human Rights into Development," 2006: 4). The report has the status of a guideline, which DAC members are expected to incorporate as a benchmark in their state's aid policies. The OECD is also developing an international tool, the Metagora monitoring system, for human rights and governance assessment (OECD, "Development Co-operation Directorate: About").

The OECD norm-bridging process is embedded in a wave of transnational networking around development and human rights policy. Concomitantly, the U.N. Development Program and Office of the High Commissioner for Human Rights have established a Global Human Rights Strengthening Programme, with bilateral contributions from the Nordic states, Canada, Ireland, Germany, Switzerland, and the United Kingdom. Under the auspices of this related initiative, UNICEF has revised its programming guidelines, training, and staff, whereas the UNDP has conducted 14 human rights-based country reviews of development efforts. At the level of implementation coordination, the U.N.'s Asia-Pacific Regional Office of the High Commissioner for Human Rights has established a Practitioners Forum on Human Rights in Development, which coordinates U.N. agencies, NGOs, and state donors operating in that region. Meanwhile, the EU as a donor has created its own multi-lateral European Initiative for Democracy and Human Rights, focused on funding civil society organizations rather than state programs, which disbursed 327 million euros in 2002–2004; the European members of the OECD also participate in this program. Within the same trend, the World Bank has recently incorporated elements of the human rights agenda in its development lending policies: gender equity evaluations are now included in country analysis, and the bank has revised its policy on impact assessment and mandated participation for indigenous peoples' rights in bank-sponsored projects (OECD, "Integrating Human Rights," 2006).

The DAC Network on Governance states that it is "working to increase understanding of a human rights-based approach to development." Prior to the 2005 study, the DAC began by incorporating the 2003 Guidelines for Humanitarian Donorship, convened by Sweden and subsequently chaired by Canada, into the broader peer review process of the OECD. The first general principle of the Humanitarian Donorship code is to "respect and promote the implementation of international humanitarian law, refugee law and human rights" (Department for International Development 2006). Thus, by 2005 this standard had been applied to peer reviews of the development programs of Australia, Belgium, Germany, Norway, Sweden, and Switzerland (OECD 2004). The OECD's standard-setting report on "The 21st Century of Development Co-operation" links the attainment of measurable development goals to qualitative factors such as "capacity development for effective, democratic and accountable governance, the protection of human rights and respect for rule of law" (OECD 1996: 2). Finally, the 2005 report "Integrating Human Rights" makes the functional linkage explicit, arguing that "human rights work is seen as both an objective in its own right and as contributing to improving the quality and effectiveness of development assistance. . . . Human rights are also seen as constitutive of development" (OECD, "Integrating Human Rights," 2006: ii).

The DAC study maps five possible dimensions of human rights in development to guide assessment of various donors' programs: a fully rights-based approach, mainstreaming human rights analysis into existing interventions, sponsorship of human rights dialogues, specific human rights promotion projects, and "implicit human rights work." The study reports that most agencies' current practice falls under projects, dialogue, or mainstreaming. An illustration of the potential improvement from mainstreaming greater human rights analysis is a shift among several donors from the *rule of law* rubric to *access to justice* programs. The latter approach complements institutional capacity building like judicial training with civil society initiatives, systematically examines discrimination and structural barriers, and is more results-oriented. For example, the United Kingdom's DFID is leading a project in Bolivia to provide identification documents to undocumented citizens—usually poor and/or indigenous and/or women—who have been unable to access courts, elections, and local authorities. Similarly, simply promoting donors' use of disaggregated data on health and education has made discrimination visible in Bangladesh, which guides the flow of resources in aid interventions.

The DAC human rights report specifically examines the issue of human rights conditionality, and concludes with an emphasis on positive measures, review of best practices, and a recommendation to use conditionality only as a last resort. The models presented include the EU's Cotonou Agreement provision for structured dialogue, culminating in the option of possible aid suspension if issues are not resolved. The Netherlands' model of graduated engagement based on human rights assessment in a partner country is also discussed; aid level and modality are determined on a sliding scale based on country governance conditions. Another mode of human rights accountability the DAC suggests is the country-specific memorandum of understanding with concerned donors incorporating rule of law commitments; the DAC profiles the United Kingdom's experience with Rwanda in this regard.

The global Good Samaritan states involved in the OECD DAC all take leadership roles in promoting greater attention to human rights in overseas development assistance. Canada, Sweden, and the Netherlands are all lauded by the wider body for leading in establishing human rights policies in their bilateral aid programs, as well as currently developing "second-generation" policies to institutionalize and implement the new standards. The DAC study highlights Swedish SIDA's Kenya program as a rule of law role model, whereas Canadian CIDA is cited for its rights-based approach to child protection. DAC also highlights and encourages interagency learning, for example, from British DFID to Swedish SIDA (OECD: Canada 2002, Japan 2003, Sweden 2005, Netherlands 2006).

In terms of value added, DAC's GOVNET concludes that "what human rights offer is a coherent, normative framework which reinforces 'good programming practices' by making them non-negotiable, consistent and legitimate" (OECD, "Integrating Human Rights," 2006: v). Above and beyond this "compliance pull," the DAC's standard setting and socialization show the potential to build global governance for human rights in the following ways. At a network level, contested rights norms are being applied to areas such as health and water rights, bridging civil-political with social-economic rights standards—linked to the delivery of resources. Because development cooperation is interstate, OECD evaluations and programs increasingly hold partner country governments accountable for governance conditions, moving beyond the level of bilateral diplomatic exhortations. Good governance capacity building may directly empower victims and at-risk groups, while reshaping the social contract of state sovereignty. Although the DAC lacks any authoritative control of member or partner states, and has no institutional resources or intervention mandate like the OSCE, it is slowly reshaping global resource flows through the power of expectations and example.

"TEAM GOV": THE NETWORK OF NATIONAL HUMAN RIGHTS INSTITUTIONS

National human rights institutions have proliferated since the 1990s, at the urging of the United Nations and with the help of pioneering human rights promoter states exporting their own models. The U.N. Office of the High Commissioner for Human Rights has assisted at least 25 countries to set up a National Human Rights Institution, notably in postconflict situations or transitional democracies. Such institutions are autonomous, government-funded bodies of independent experts and representatives of social sectors with a legal mandate to monitor and advise on human rights conditions, legislation, institutions, and education within their national boundaries. Some are tasked with reporting to U.N. treaty bodies, although this function more commonly is performed by the foreign ministry. National human rights institutions are related to yet distinct from ombudsperson programs of citizen advocacy, which have also proliferated, networked, and articulated with international agencies during the same time period. For example, the 2006 International Conference of National Human Rights Institutions in Bolivia was partially sponsored by that country's ombudsman (http://www.nhri.net).

Since the turn of the millennium, the 100-plus national human rights institutions have established an international transgovernmental network to set standards, exchange resources, promote practices, and foster insertion in global institutions. Like the Human Security Network, this network is a forum without independent organizational resources, and it does not participate in implementation like IDEA or the OSCE. It does perform a certification function similar to the Community of Democracies, a coordination function like the OECD DAC, and a network-knitting enhancement of global governance.

The National Human Rights Institutions are modeled on early efforts such as the Danish Institute for Human Rights and Canada's Human Rights Commission (created in 1978 to implement that country's Human Rights Act). The 1991 Paris Principles adopted by the United Nations Human Rights Commission and General Assembly set out criteria for the independence, competence, and international status of such bodies. These principles are used to screen applications for membership in the network, because the establishment of a National Human Rights Institution occasionally appears to reflect a state's diversionary effort to derail international criticism or subvert civil society organizations, rather than a legitimate effort to improve or lock in emerging human rights policies. The members of the network in turn designate an International Coordinating Committee, consisting of 16 members—4 from each region (International Coordinating Committee of National Human Rights Institutions 2002, 2004, 2006, 2007).

The main activities of the network include information exchange, attendance at a series of conferences, and promotion of some direct exchanges between established and emerging national institutions. The network Web site and correspondence provides members with all relevant international human rights documents, updates on human rights developments in the United Nations system, information from fellow national institutions on programs and practices, bibliography, and training resources. It has also compiled U.N. treaty body recommendations relevant to national institutions, to encourage a greater role in monitoring and implementing the NHRI's mandated harmonization of national law with international human rights instruments (http://www.nhri.net).

There is a biannual International Conference on National Institutions, which issues a thematic declaration that often claims or frames new norms. For example, the 2006 Bolivia conference was devoted to migrants' rights, and declared that "NHRIs shall advocate for a human rights approach to migration." The Santa Cruz Declaration also urges NHRIs to promote the ratification of the International Convention on the Protection of the Rights of All Migrant Workers, one of the most undersubscribed U.N. human rights instruments. NHRIs are directed to participate in training of state migration authorities, to register individual complaints, and to collect accurate and disaggregated data on migration abuses and discriminatory practices. The international network has also supported the establishment of an additional layer of regional networks, which meet annually. Finally, the accredited NHRIs are official participants in the annual sessions of the United Nations Human Rights Commission/Council (Kumar 2006).

The Canadian Human Rights Commission has been notably active in funding, training, and networking newer NHRIs. Canada has a bilateral "institutional linkage project" with several million dollars of CIDA funding with India's National Human Rights Commission. Further agreements have been signed with Mexico, Indonesia, South Africa, Bolivia, and Peru. Various forms of Canadian assistance were critical to the establishment of commissions in Indonesia, Thailand, and Cambodia—including seconding Canadian officers to Indonesia's commission. Canada helped organize the regional African Conference on National Institutions in 1996, via an agreement with Cameroon (Cardenas 2003).

The transnational network anchored by the Network of National Human Rights Institutions, but including notable UNOHCHR, bilateral, and ombudsmen participation, is a nascent exercise in institution building with great potential significance. Implanting national institutions charged with implementing international standards within states is probably the single most high-yield measure possible in terms of capacity building and reshaping sovereignty, in theory. However, because states still control most of the basic operating conditions of such bodies, their autonomous influence has been thus far disappointingly limited in practice. The proliferation and iteration of multiple layers of human rights institutions, standards, conferences, and knowledge will build social capital for global governance—insufficient in the absence of accountable authority or political will, but a critical resource for meaningful change under propitious conditions.

CONCLUSION

What is the cumulative contribution of this burgeoning collection of interstate promotion networks? The congeries of regional, functional, purposive, and intergovernmental organizations are building the international human rights regime in an incremental fashion, although they do not constitute a stable, separate regime in themselves. As organization theorists characterize levels of cooperation, some of these institutions merely create a *common framework* for information exchange and monitoring (IDEA), others such as the OECD DAC promote harmonization via a *joint facility*, a few like the Network of National Human Rights Institutions aspire to a thin *common policy*, but none—except perhaps the OSCE in some minorities and electoral missions work—reach the level of a *single policy* that precedes national member objectives (Haas 2006: 101).

In terms of the humanitarian motive for interstate cooperation, the collection of value promoters spread norms vertically through layers of global governance as well as horizontally across issue areas. Although there is little evidence that they mobilize new resources, they coordinate and multiply existing finance, expertise, and occasional diplomacy. As far as enlightened self-interest in development and conflict resolution, the convergence of multiple organizations and interventions does seem to contribute to the stabilization and integration of some amenable transitional areas, such as the Balkans, although it is clearly insufficient for more starkly troubled regions. And through the creation of additional mechanisms for monitoring and promotion, interstate networks do expand the menu of policy tools for willing state promoters. Interstate promotion efforts also do appear to foster the gradual construction of a community of values and interests: through membership certifications, governance resource interdependencies, and the strengthening of the linkage of bilateral policies to global institutions.

As the current organizational composition of the interstate layer of the regime suggests, the potential for expansion should move along the same lines of global architecture. *Regional organizations* such as the African Union have announced intentions and established mechanisms to expand their human rights functions, currently extremely slow and underresourced, but potentially strengthened by modeling from peer entities and interorganizational linkages. *Humanitarian functional bodies* like the World Health Organization increasingly incorporate human rights norms and civil society participation, which should eventually assist in diffusion and mainstreaming of human rights standards. *Intergovernmental governance networks* of judicial actors have a clear normative alignment and some emerging support from the international human rights regime. Although the purely *promotional bodies* have been thus far the most limited, there is scope for enhancement of existing bodies via mechanisms such as the U.N. Democracy Caucus of the Community of Democracies. Another positive development would be the establishment of more active and organizationally autonomous principled organs.

Coalitions of the caring can help to mobilize the international human rights regime as a whole, and more commonly build preventative capacity for democratization and citizen empowerment. Through diffuse linkages to complex interdependence, functional arrangements can catalyze spillovers to rights promotion—backed by promoters' claiming, framing, and monitoring rights. Willing states do invest in institutions to lock in their long-term vision, gain international legitimacy—and level the playing field with less scrupulous powers. Such institutions, in turn, do slowly shift norms and identities throughout the global system.

10

Conclusion

"The World Needs More Canada"

We have seen that human rights foreign policy is possible, and that it matters. We have seen the power of norms to guide national interest in more constructive directions than the traditional pursuit of military dominance and economic advantage. But we can also see that the global demand for human rights constantly outstrips the supply, and that many states could do more to help. Thus, we turn to examine the lessons learned from this study about improving and expanding the network of global Good Samaritans.

LESSONS LEARNED

The record of these half-dozen states, their like-minded neighbors and friends, and the interstate coalitions they have begun to establish reinforces some overall lessons of the contemporary world order. What do we need to know about how our world works to encourage more governments to direct more attention and resources to the suffering of strangers?

Goodness Is Its Own Reward

The case for cosmopolitanism is compelling: countries that do good do well. On the whole, global Good Samaritan states are at least as prosperous, secure, and democratic as their neighbors and peers—and this follows as well as precedes the adoption of human rights foreign policies. For example, the Netherlands has thrived as an avatar of international law, surviving oil boycotts based on its principled foreign policy. Humanitarian policies rarely require pronounced trade-offs of long-term national interest, and even short-term perturbations from bilateral conditionality are usually compensated in the long run by developments such as trade diversification. The promotion of global governance yields a more predictable policy environment for all members, and collective goods in the management of global problems with spillover potential like conflict-related environmental, health, and crime crises. Moreover, the intangible resource of legitimacy gained by human rights foreign policy often delivers diffuse diplomatic rewards like improved relations with transitional regimes, enhanced credibility, expanded coalitions, and transnational migration, education, and cooperation ties that deliver real advantages in a globalized economy. Canada, for example, has increased its diplomatic capital because of its human rights promotion record.

Identity Politics Can Be Constructive

In a world riven by resurgent nationalism, reactive fundamentalisms, and constructed clashes of civilizations, modernist social science counsels universalist materialism as a bulwark against parochial chaos. But political communities are inevitably constituted and oriented by some set of values, and national versions of cosmopolitan values can serve as an alternative to both neoliberal homogenization and the defensive, competitive particularism it evokes. Canadian soldiers sacrificing their lives in Afghanistan or Swedish taxpayers bankrolling African refugees are not just trying to be better human beings—they take national pride in expressing their identity as Swedes or Canadians through these global contributions, and acting globally builds national identities as "Canadian peacekeepers" or "Swedish volunteers." The lesson of the post–Cold War world is that identities do not melt away with modernization, so that our best bet for global cooperation is to enhance and mobilize *constructive* national values, and promote national identification with positive aspects of global good citizenship, like "the Dutch way of peacekeeping."

Good Citizens Are Made, Not Born

Although some structural niches and histories are especially conducive to principled foreign policy, in every case that potential was consciously activated and guided by leaders and social forces, and reinforced by a supportive international network. Similarly, although some national values and experiences harmonize readily with human rights, foreign policy projection of those norms must be learned and mobilized. The bad news is that we cannot assume that as countries develop or democratize or Westernize they will automatically reach out to help strangers and build global governance, as demonstrated in Japan. But the silver lining of this cloud is that countries like South Africa, that barely pass the threshold of development and globalization can *choose* to move along the path to global good citizenship.

Good-Enough Good Samaritans

Like most international undertakings, the international human rights regime is a patchwork enterprise composed of many different types and levels of monitoring, information, sanctions, adjudication, and intervention. The disadvantage of this situation is an extremely porous and uneven response to violations, but the opportunity for would-be investors in this shaky start-up is that almost any contribution is welcome and needed. Although no country does everything it should, and there are synergies from coordination of different human rights policy areas, above a certain minimum threshold of credibility, we should not let the best be the enemy of the good. The Netherlands' contribution to multilateral human rights diplomacy and stellar aid policy are not negated by its troubled record on refugee reception, and South Africa's usefulness as a regional peace promoter is thankfully not impeded by an increasingly questionable U.N. voting record. Every country has blind spots and insufficiencies, and although these should be clearly critiqued and pressured, inconsistency is not a barrier to a net positive contribution. A more useful strategy is to foster bridges between areas of strength and lagging sectors; for example, pulling up Canada's lamentably low aid levels with special programs linked to its strong and innovative promotion of human security and intervention in failing states.

Different Strokes for Different Folks

Although all the modalities of human rights foreign policy form an ensemble at the global level, not all countries can or will participate fully in the range of multilateral, bilateral, aid, peace promotion, and refugee reception activities. It is important that an adequate supply of each of these forms of governance is available in the system, and this should play a role in recruitment, but some inevitable division of labor among existing global good citizens can be absorbed. For example, developing countries like Costa Rica and South Africa are not net aid providers, but can contribute surprising levels of resources via training programs and partnerships. Countries can and should specialize in projecting areas of domestic strength, like Canadian assistance in resolving cultural conflicts, and a country like Japan that faces a domestic barrier like the constitutional prohibition of military intervention that blocks traditional peacekeeping can be pushed to compensate by greater assistance in related areas, such as funding peace promotion. Meanwhile, regionalization and the growth of interstate networks in areas such as aid, peacekeeping, and democracy promotion can allow some countries to harmonize, multiply, or develop contributions in weak areas.

It Takes a (Global) Village

Although lone expressions of conscience are laudable and occasionally critical at exceptional moments in history, the bulk of social change is the result of a panoply of persistent efforts by a variety of actors, and human rights foreign policy follows this pattern. Sweden's efforts on aid and diplomacy were echoed and amplified by its Nordic neighbors, the Netherlands, and eventually the EU. Tiny Costa Rica was partially shielded from U.S. pressures by like-minded European Social Democrats, and collective solidarity by dozens of states enabled the creation of the International Criminal Court over superpower objections. Canada's cross-cutting memberships give it a diffuse alternative to junior partnership with U.S. priorities; for example, democracy promotion in Francophone Africa. The existence of U.N. standards on aid levels, OSCE mission mandates, and multilateral sanctions against pariah states has legitimized and encouraged stronger policies in these areas, even by amenable states. Global, regional, or like-minded villages socialize and support state human rights promoters, and complementary resources should be directed to this meso-level of global governance.

Laggards Lack Social Capital

It is not surprising that countries struggling with poverty and dictatorship do not mobilize around a vision of global good citizenship (although some could), but it is critically disappointing when states with ample political and material resources remain trapped in a narrow and short-sighted pursuit of national interest. These states are often global or regional hegemons with structural propensities to project conventional power to bolster the status quo, as suggested in the first chapter of this study. Nevertheless, historical experiences like the British imperial campaign against the slave trade or the U.S. founding influence on the U.N. system suggest that enlightened hegemony is an available and functional alternative. Although laggards like Japan and the contemporary United States often have cultural-historical patterns that strain cosmopolitan perspectives, the crucial shortfall is "social capital"—national and international networks and habits of trust and cooperation that militate toward identification with strangers. Hypercollectivist Japan and hyperindividualist America share the limitations of a strongly bounded identity, a thin democracy, and an instrumental view of global governance (detailed below).

Size Doesn't Matter (Much), but Equity Does

Neither Sweden nor the Netherlands nor certainly Costa Rica really meet the criteria for middle powers, or even regional powers. In some ways, the "middle power" label and literature is misleading, because it refers more to a cosmopolitan power projection strategy than a structural niche (albeit a strategy historically developed by countries that often passed through that niche). Extremely small size does create some limits in the absolute level of resources available for foreign policy, so that countries with populations below one million are simply internationally irrelevant. Nevertheless, each of the smallish countries above and several similar can "punch above their weight" because that weight is well developed and well distributed. Soft powers, even the few less-developed ones, are highly educated societies whose relatively high equity allows them to mobilize a high proportion of their citizenry and project successful social welfare programs. There is a striking association between a higher gender equity score and more successful human rights policies, even among equally formally democratic and developed countries. Japan is many times the size, much more developed, and just as formally democratic as South Africa, but its Gender Equity Index is 60, whereas South Africa's is 70 despite some serious shortfalls. There is a direct effect on human rights policy, as the case studies suggest that greater participation of women both as policy makers and as social actors catalyzes global good citizenship. But in addition, gender equity is associated with and reinforces a stronger civil society, less social hierarchy, and higher political participation—deep democracy (Young 2000).

Eternal Vigilance Is the Price of Global Citizenship

The adoption of human rights foreign policies is progressive, but not permanent. Even committed global Good Samaritans may falter as global conditions or internal coalitions change. When this occurs, leadership, vision, and international support and pressure must be renewed. The Netherlands' defection from international refugee norms was met with global and parliamentary criticism, with the cause célèbre of Ayaan Hirsi Ali reconnecting the plight of more anonymous and controversial refugees to core Dutch values of liberalism and gender equity. Although Dutch policy in this area remains contested and problematic, principled mobilization secured significant retrenchment. Further repair of this reactionary regression will require a comprehensive, responsible, and humane social policy to address the real challenges of immigration in the Netherlands. More passive setbacks, like declines in peacekeeping contributions or silences in diplomacy, are less visible—and this is why global monitoring and interstate standards are so important. Preserving progress in the face of change also requires an ongoing normative commitment by domestic promoters, to reformulate the case for cosmopolitanism against every wave of neoliberal atomization or nationalist fear, and to enhance expertise and international cooperation to design more effective policies for the challenges of globalization.

HOW THE GOOD CAN DO BETTER: BEST PRACTICES

Global Good Samaritans have made a fundamental commitment to human rights foreign policy, but the strength, breadth, and effectiveness of their efforts vary considerably. Many of the highly modern governments profiled here systematically evaluate their own performance in a variety of policy areas, especially foreign aid, or are mandated to do so by international agencies. Comprehensive and comparative human rights policy analyses are less common, but present in some cases (like the Netherlands)—and should certainly be introduced across the board. The comparative case studies and framework of this study can contribute a complementary qualitative observation of policy trends, and how they can be developed to enhance impact.

Coordinate Policy—Internally and Internationally

This mantra of public administration has particular relevance for human rights foreign policy. First of all, it is *politically* important to coordinate policy across issues and bilateral relations, even when they are functionally unconnected. Contradictions like promoting peacekeeping at the United Nations while exporting arms to dictatorships, as Sweden did for some years, do not diminish the substantive contribution of the peace promotion (as outlined above)—but certain kinds of inconsistencies do prejudice domestic political support and sometimes international credibility. Similarly, global good citizen Canada's visibly selective bilateral condemnation of pariahs opened the Liberal coalition to domestic defection on other issues, and even attack from the left on the humanitarian character of the Afghanistan intervention.

At a functional level, it is important to coordinate consensus policy among various implementation agencies. In most cases, at a minimum, ministries of trade, defense, and justice play a significant role alongside the foreign ministry in human rights foreign policy—but they often operate from different mandates, procedures, resources, and transgovernmental partnerships with foreign counterparts. In South Africa, and probably other developing countries emerging as Samaritans, the profusion of actors was so great that no one in government actually knew the total budgets or scope of the various peace and democracy promotion programs (a South African Treasury Department study to track the dispersal of resources was commissioned in 2005, a full 10 years after the initiation of human rights foreign policy).

Internationally, "donor coordination" is now conventional wisdom and takes place through the OECD DAC and country-specific donor conferences, but outside of the relatively institutionalized domain of aid, like-minded consortia and coalitions in other policy areas are often ad hoc. Even peace promotion takes place under a variety of U.N., NATO, EU, OAS, AU, subregional, "concerned group," and even unilateral rubrics, with different mandates, modalities, and connections to human rights policy and humanitarian organizations. Since the ICC coalition of the late 1990s, no interstate effort has coalesced into a U.N. voting bloc for human rights. More ongoing and identifiable international coordination, as IDEA has begun to provide for democracy promotion, would enhance policy coherence and effectiveness.

Finally, coordination of domestic and international human rights policies can be a virtuous circle—or a negative boomerang (Keck and Sikkink

1998). Canada's adoption of its Charter of Rights and Freedoms successfully inspired international rule of law promotion efforts, which in turn contributed back to Canadian jurisprudence via developments in international human rights law. On the other hand, Canada's lagging performance on aboriginal rights at home eventually undermined an initially promising record of principled international promotion of indigenous peoples.

Get to the Grass Roots

The ultimate goal of human rights policy is to protect and empower the (actual or potential) victims of abuse. Most progressive international actors now realize that direct support for at-risk populations is a minimum complement to governmental reform efforts. But it is worth emphasizing that a preferential option for civil society should be built into *all* humanitarian policy interventions. In some cases, like disaster relief, this will require working against the grain of domestic and international bureaucracies. In aid, this means microcredit and education programs for the most marginalized alongside development of infrastructure. In rule of law promotion, it means a comprehensive approach of "access to justice" rather than simple institution building. We also know that peace promotion and postconflict reconstruction that engages civilians, with some attempt to avoid reinforcing sectarian groups, is far more effective than elite pacts.

Beyond simply tilting resources toward existing civic groups, human rights promoters must be prepared to train, fund, and protect fragile and emerging civil societies—as Canada has done through its Human Rights Education Foundation, and Japan failed to do for its partners in Cambodia. In a human rights-related update of the proverb of economic empowerment that advises aid givers to "teach a man to fish," we might advise: *Give someone a right, and you protect them for a year; teach someone to protest and litigate, and you protect them for a lifetime.* This will often require coordination of capacity building with diplomatic muscle, as the Netherlands has discovered on numerous occasions when it has had to intervene to protect threatened development partner groups. Finally, global Good Samaritans must work to increase and institutionalize domestic and international civic organizations' access to national and global decision making, empowering victims and their advocates to shape the policies that seek to protect them. Funding transnational NGOs and networks, as Sweden does, or inviting them to help draft international organizations' policies, as in Costa Rica, is an excellent way to facilitate this goal.

Break Bureaucratic Barriers

The government agencies implementing human rights policy are first and foremost bureaucracies (Barnett and Finnemore 2006), and certain pathologies of bureaucratic politics have special salience for human rights policies. Because foreign ministries are almost always the lead institution, it is significant that several universal features of foreign service are widely cited as deleterious to the coherence of human rights policy. Participants from a variety of cultures and levels report that the system of two- to three-year rotations among posts often decreases the development of country knowledge and civil society relationships that are particularly critical for effective human rights interventions in transitional or fragile states. Rotations can also send inconsistent signals in a complex policy area, or foster strategic foot-dragging by target states.

Because promoters usually house human rights units in a thematic cluster, or under the Foreign Ministry's Global Institutions office, an inherent clash of interests is set up with the more numerous and usually more prestigious country desks—which are tasked to emphasize trade and strategic relationships with great powers, and to move aid money and screen for threats from the developing world. Variations include Sweden's attempt to "mainstream" human rights by explicitly assigning it to country desks alongside a reduced thematic unit, but there is little evidence that country units concentrate much attention on this nth priority in their expanding basket. At the other end of the spectrum, Canada has simply set up new units for each emerging humanitarian concern, so that the Department of Foreign Affairs and International Trade houses a thematic unit on human rights, a human rights unit attached to global institutions, a human security office, a division of humanitarian affairs, and human rights–related posts within several country desks, with related thematic units on women, children, and aboriginal affairs. This proliferation of personnel and resources does seem to increase the chance that a human rights issue will be addressed somewhere in the system, but clearly poses challenges for coherence and accountability.

Beyond the foreign ministry, there are two important areas of humanitarian policy that are affected by their bureaucratic placement. Most promoter states have autonomous foreign aid agencies; some nearly rival the diplomatic corps in size and influence. Although independent aid agencies create bureaucratic incentives for higher aid budgets, they are less conducive to principled conditionality and often more entangled with domestic clients of tied aid and recipient governments than integrated aid programs. Domestic NGO circulation into the aid bureaucracy and intergovernmental socialization regarding rights-based development can be correctives to these tendencies.

Similarly, refugee policy suffers when it is removed from international affairs, generally under justice or home ministries. In the Netherlands, deterioration in immigration policy was clearly associated with its institutional transfer from the social welfare agency to the ministry of justice; conversely, in Costa Rica foreign affairs involvement in refugee policy improved adherence to international standards and cooperation with international agencies. Refugees get a better hearing when their processing is separated from the overall flow of migration, and suffer more neglect and abuse when local authorities play a significant role, as in South Africa.

Be a "Smart Samaritan"

Public policy with principled goals must still follow the strategic logics of public administration. Smart organizations—whether firms, governments, or global institutions—are those that learn and those that institutionalize the ideas of their initiators in sustainable structures (Haas 1990). For principled human rights promoters, learning takes place on at least three levels. First, promoters need specific and comparative program evaluations (*best practices*), which are already standard but do not necessarily cover the full spectrum of promoters or efforts. The second level of evaluation is strategic, as the international community evolves better understanding of human rights policy modalities (*best instruments*), such as how to target sanctions to minimize damage to civilians, or the variety of mechanisms for transitional justice (Cortwright and Lopez 2002). Finally, global good citizens must systematize the currently random practice of venue shopping, building knowledge of *best environments* for humanitarian implementation.

Institutionalization is also multidimensional. Smart Samaritans set up space within existing institutions, like when Canadian foreign minister Lloyd Axworthy implanted a dozen experts into key mid-level posts in the Department of Foreign Affairs and International Trade to implement his human security program, knowing that these new civil servants and most of their newly titled programs would outlast his tenure. But wise promoters also establish independent boards and arms-length agencies that transcend election cycles and cross party lines, such as the Dutch Advisory Board or Canada's Rights and Democracy. Finally, cosmopolitan polities that take law seriously can institutionalize a policy by ensuring its endorsement by authoritative domestic or international legal bodies, binding future administrations.

EXPANDING THE CLUB

We can recall that the case studies presented here represent only a few outstanding members of a larger class of "honor students," which includes most of Europe and North America, the democratic leaders of Latin America, and a handful of emerging voices in Africa and Asia. What can we do to strengthen the efforts of the B and C students, and bring more aspiring Samaritans into the academy? In order to find more states that are "most likely to succeed," we must activate members of the global middle class, whose globalized moderate development and high level of democracy provide the motive and the means. And we must recruit among the strivers, newer democracies and developers who can come to see that global good citizenship builds a more democratic global system for all and consolidates their gains by stabilizing their fragile neighborhoods.

Looking for a Few Latent Democracies

Let us examine several sets of countries that have promising profiles but uneven performance, based on the rough snapshots of country capabilities and performance offered in the first chapter. A quick qualitative review shows that most of these countries share a rhetorical commitment to human rights, but are unduly passive or distracted by other policy goals. To strengthen the regime, these latent democracies need policy encouragement and further study.

The "Gentleman's B"

Our first set of developed democracies makes adequate contributions in most areas but lags in a few, and does not initiate humanitarian policies or build institutions. These privileged underachievers include Austria, France, Spain, and Australia. All are solid participants in multilateral and bilateral relations, but low on refugees and aid and mixed on peace promotion. In each case, the country shares most of the structural prerequisites and cosmopolitan value complex of the star promoters, but lacks at least one feature common to that set. For Austria, it is insufficient processing of the repressive past, whereas for Australia it is lack of reinforcing regional support networks. Australia can and should be brought into thematic promotion networks: perhaps the OSCE. In a more complex scenario, France possesses an unusual mix of domestic rights culture with an inward-looking civil society and political culture. France's Gender Equity Index of 64 is the lowest in Northern Europe, and well below the pan-European regional average. France's postcolonial relationship with Africa has also clouded its performance in both aid and peace promotion. New leadership, in the form of a foreign minister who founded Médicins Sans Frontiers, may open the possibility of "moral entrepreneurship" in France, but the larger orientation of French society must be addressed. On the other hand, Spain's placement in this set reflects an upward trend by a country that is a much more recent developer and democracy, which has moved relatively quickly to join its peers.

The Mediterranean Siesta

The leading Mediterranean members of the EU, Cyprus, Greece, Italy, and Portugal, have generally passive and reactive foreign policies. They vote with the democracies in international institutions, but make little economic or institutional contribution to those institutions. These countries give very little aid, although they have been sufficiently developed to do so for at least a generation, and aid levels still lag significantly as a *proportion* of their smaller economies. Although Italy and Cyprus do contribute to peacekeeping, all of the Mediterranean countries accept very few refugees. There is no visible commitment to international law, and they do not take responsibility for the extraterritorial abuses of their citizens (and are in the middle tier of negative influence via participation in trafficking). Greater transnational humanitarian linkage and leadership are clearly needed in these countries, along with explicit socialization bridging historic national values to cosmopolitan globalization. More parochial civil societies and lower levels of gender equity must also be addressed.

Four Tigers

Rising in the global South, there are a handful of leading democracies that are regional powers that aspire to global citizenship. Argentina and Chile have been fairly strong across the board, with Argentina especially supportive of international law and peace promotion. Chile, with the highest democracy score and Human Development Index in South America, has been a stalwart of the U.N. system, international law, and advocate of the rights of women and indigenous peoples. Brazil has been less consistent within the U.N. but is a regional peace promoter, accepting of refugees, and a moral entrepreneur on social rights issues. The most developed of the set, South Korea has also been an avid multilateralist, but not a contributor to peace promotion, refugee reception, or foreign aid—despite a Human Development Index of .912.

For these strivers, visionary leaders and strong civil societies have mobilized to process painful dictatorships through global good citizenship. Consolidation of the fundamentals of democracy and development is important to maintain their leading performance. But so is attention to their agency and vocation. On the positive side, the influence of Argentina's human rights movement clearly moved that country from populist nationalism to a cosmopolitan path. On a more cautionary note, South Korea's shortfalls correlate with an anomalously low Gender Equity Index of 56, which suggests that the low quality of its formal democracy may be holding back a greater and more multi-faceted contribution to global governance.

Least Likely Cases

Coming up from the rear, a few key countries that lack the full set of structures and resources for global good citizenship nevertheless make notable efforts. Despite a low-functioning and recent democracy along with extremely uneven development, Mexico has been an intermittent contributor to multilateral institutions and bilateral sanctions, as well as generally supportive of refugees. Regional placement and the Western hemispheric version of cosmopolitan vision clearly help to pull up Mexico's performance, but its subpar Gender Equity Index score of 61 flags the challenges for deepening democracy and improving the breadth and consistency of Mexico's efforts. The Philippines is also a regional leader and U.N. supporter, with moderate contributions to peace and refugee reception and moments of leadership on international law (such as the ICC negotiations). Although the Philippines' democracy rating of 3 and Human Development Index of .763 mark it as too poor and too internally repressive to be a foreign policy promoter, an exceptionally strong civil society (signaled by a Gender Equity Index score of 76) and cosmopolitan vocation, based on its own emergence from dictatorship, have propelled the Philippines intermittently into human rights foreign policy.

Within Africa, very low regional norms of democracy and development disqualify the vast majority of countries, and several of the few solid democracies (like Botswana) are simply too small to project. Nevertheless, medium-sized democratic Ghana has begun to make some contribution to the United Nations and peace promotion. Its low Human Development and Gender Equity indices in the .6 range are still high for its region, and importantly Ghana has been relatively secure compared to its neighbors. This suggests that stabilization and democratization of similarly situated West African countries may open the possibility of future modest contributions from that region. In North Africa, Morocco is similarly a regional leader despite globally low indices, and similarly shows the potential for greater global mobilization.

Finally, India, often referred to as "the world's largest democracy," remains a slow and partial participant in the international human rights regime. After significant activism in the nonaligned movement under Nehru, India has not been a promoter of international law or humanitarian institutions for at least a generation, with some more generalized advocacy for global equity. India has made a modest contribution to peacekeeping and refugee reception. Despite generations of elections, a strong domestic rights culture, and over a decade of rapid growth, India remains rated a "partially free" democracy and its Human Development Index is only .611, reflecting vast inequality and lagging social conditions. Regional insecurity and flagging cosmopolitan vision further impede India's potential for leadership in human rights promotion. The promise, and frustration, of India's participation is that it represents one of the world's largest non-Western civilizations—and that India did project a Gandhian foreign policy deeply tied to norms of nonviolence that could provide an alternative role model for emerging LDC Samaritans, before reverting to a more realist regional power strategy (Nayar and Paul 2003, Power 1967, Hingorani 1989).

We turn now to the issue of leadership, and why the current superpower is ill-equipped to be a global Good Samaritan. This means that the current Samaritans bear a greater burden as a collective counterhegemonic coalition, and that it is even more important to recruit greater numbers of rising democracies and even episodic or partial participants who can mobilize on particular human rights issues or provide certain kinds of collective goods. However, the sources of stagnation in the U.S. record also point the way toward the potential for change.

Limiting Factors: The United States as "Deadbeat Dad" of Global Governance

The United States' faltering presence in and intermittent blockage of the international human rights regime is perhaps the leading current obstacle to its growth and effectiveness. Declining and conditioned contributions to the United Nations, obstruction of the International Criminal Court, politicization of pariah sanctions, inadequate and poorly structured foreign aid, manipulation of humanitarian intervention, and rejection and even abuse of refugees all blot the U.S. record. Beyond the structural tendencies of hegemony outlined in the introduction, there are three strikes against American human rights policy: unilateralism, an imperial presidency, and an impoverished civic culture. As one lifelong scholar (and sometime participant) concludes, the decline of U.S. foreign policy influence across the board can be traced to the following:

> an appalling ignorance of the culture and history of other countries; an institutionalist bias toward the dominance of presidential power in foreign affairs . . . an inclination to seek a military solution to problems overseas . . . a go-it-alone attitude that downgrades working with other nations and international organizations . . . an isolationist instinct that drives some Americans back into a shell of disinterest, disregard, and even disdain for foreigners; a lack of empathy for the wrenching poverty and disease that haunts so many people in other lands; and an attitude of arrogance that is more in the spirit of the Roman Caesars than a trusted and respected world leader. (Johnson 2007: xiv–xv)

U.S. foreign policy is noted for an underlying, and recently growing, trend toward individualism. Although episodes of isolationist withdrawal alternate with expansionist intervention, both modes are characterized by an exceptionalist vision and unilateral vocation (Hartz 1955). Global participation is not seen as global citizenship, but rather as justified and necessary imposition of neoliberal values on deluded or repressed Others. American foreign policy projects a liberal democratic identity premised on increasingly limited government and even lawlessness; libertarians do not make good global citizens (Falk 2004). Even the adoption of human rights, and selective promotion during certain U.S. administrations, has been based on particularistic exceptionalism—not universal moral worth. "The United States advocates human rights for the world and state sovereignty for itself" (Mertus 2004: 9).

Meanwhile, America's thin democracy at home is not conducive to principled foreign policy making. We have seen that parliamentary democracies are generally more active global citizens, and the United States' much-vaunted checks and balances seem to stop at the water's edge, as both Congress and the judiciary play a distinctly lagging role in shaping foreign policy. This means that the institutions mandated to represent civil society and legal norms, the fountainheads of human rights, are systematically marginalized from influencing international relations in the United States. Indeed, the halcyon Carter human rights policy actually originated in and was sustained by Congress, in an era of unusual legislative influence in the aftermath of the collapse of the Nixon presidency. The U.S. judiciary thus far has been disappointingly impervious to the influence of international law, and the executive branch has numerous mechanisms to evade judicial accountability—which have been notably expanded under the Bush administration (Forsythe 2000b, Mertus 2004).

The United States is known as the heartland of civil society, but *pace* de Tocqueville (2006), the United States has the *wrong kind* of civil society to sustain global good citizenship. U.S. civil society is parochial and inward looking, with the lowest level of international travel, foreign language use, and geographic literacy of any advanced industrialized society. According to a recent survey by *National Geographic,* only 37% of young Americans (18–24) can find Iraq on a map, and 20% of young Americans think Sudan is in Asia (http://www.nationalgeographic.com/roper2006/findings.html; also see Pew Center 2007).

Human rights consciousness is not established as an ongoing referent of political culture; for example, the number of human rights courses and membership in international human rights organizations in the United States lags significantly behind peer countries. In an Amnesty International survey, 94% of American adults have no awareness of the Universal Declaration of Human Rights (Mertus 2004: 212). This means that issue campaigns must be framed narrowly to resonate with specific national experiences rather than more encompassing universal norms that can be cited in more cosmopolitan cultures. Thus, U.S. publics attend to trafficking that evokes the domestic trauma of slavery, but struggle to comprehend internationally validated health rights that many lack at home.

Moreover, when limited sectors of U.S. civil society or attentive publics do mobilize on foreign policy issues, they lack effective channels to influence foreign policy. The civic consultative mechanisms common to parliamentary democracies, like the Dutch International Relations Advisory Council, are absent—even the regularized consultations Canada's Department of Foreign Affairs conducts with NGOs are not present in the American system. NGO representatives do not circulate systematically into decision-making institutions. Congressional input is decentralized and slow for citizens and social movements, and the American pluralist modality rewards interest groups (J. Q. Wilson 1995)—not value-oriented cross-cutting coalitions. The core institutions that determine and execute U.S. foreign policy—the presidency, State Department, Pentagon, and increasingly intelligence agencies—are ideologically, institutionally, and strategically closed to civil society.

One of the comparative lessons of this inquiry is that simply critiquing U.S. hypocrisy or exhorting change in human rights promotion will not be effective until the ironic democratic deficit within the world's leading democracy is addressed. Some of the underlying blockages are more amenable to change than others. Institutional balances within a presidential democracy may shift with a cosmopolitan constitutionalist leader and emerging civic movement, though beset by domestic challenges and tainted legacies. Building Other identification in a fractured society of hyperindividualists will depend largely on cosmopolitan mobilization of bridging social forces such as immigrant groups, transnational issue networks, and universalist religious communities (Putnam 2000). One analysis sees a deep latent potential for altruism within neoliberal American culture that has been manipulated by the right and can be reclaimed by advocates of progressive causes like human rights (Graeber 2007). The Kantian cosmopolitan formula has this half right; democratization of the global system, alongside spreading democratic regimes, also depends on deepening democracy *within* thinly liberal powers. For the United States, democracy begins at home. Human rights promotion *can* be revived and enhanced despite the limitations of hegemony—when and if the United States itself becomes a deeper democracy, with greater citizen participation in foreign policy making and more input from marginalized transnationalists.

GLOBAL GOOD SAMARITANS

Every year, millions of lives are saved because some government accepted refugees, sent aid, deployed peacekeepers, sanctioned a dictator, tried a miscreant, monitored an election, trained police, or sheltered a dissident. It takes a state to sign a treaty, forbid trade, send troops, sponsor a resolution, or grant citizenship. The critical minority of global Good Samaritan states do these things because someone at a desk in Ottawa or San José, in the streets of Amsterdam, or e-mailing Stockholm from Rwanda convinced a leader it was the right thing to do. Policy makers are open to persuasion because it resonates with their cultural beliefs, because they have been schooled by a global community, because they are accountable to a domestic community, and because they accept the logic that we are all connected.

We can build a better world by nurturing every element of the international human rights regime. Global institutions, transnational civil society, and state human rights promoters are interdependent and synergistic. They can reinforce each others' efforts—and must learn from each others' visions and experiences. We must also provide and renew the normative glue that cements global governance, preaching the cosmopolitan gospels of universalism and interdependence.

Global Good Samaritans are not martyrs or messiahs. They are simply generous bystanders, who stop to help a stranger. *Go forth and do likewise...*

Bibliography

Acuña González, Guillermo, and Edith Olivares Ferreto. *La población migrante nicaragüense en Costa Rica: Realidades y respuestas.* San Jose, Costa Rica: International Development Research Center-CNUAH-Habitat-Fundación Arias, 2000.

Adams, Michael. *Fire and Ice: The U.S., Canada and the Myth of Converging Values.* Toronto: Penguin Canada, 2003.

Adebajo, Adekeye, and Christopher Landsberg. "South Africa and Nigeria as Regional Hegemons." In Mwesiga Baregu and Christopher Landsberg (eds.), *From Cape to Congo: Southern Africa's Evolving Security Challenges,* pp. 171–203. Boulder, Colo.: Lynne Rienner, 2003.

Adelman, Howard. "Canada's Counter-Terror Policy." In Alison Brysk and Gershon Shafir (eds.), *National Insecurity and Human Rights.* Berkeley: University of California Press, 2007.

Adler, Emanuel. "Seizing the Middle Ground: Constructivism in World Politics." *European Journal of International Relations* 3, no. 3 (1997): 319–363.

Adler, Emanuel, and Michael Barnett. "Governing Anarchy: A Research Agenda for the Study of Security Communities." *Ethics and International Affairs* 10 (1996): 63–98.

Adviesraad Internationale Vraagstukken (AIV). *Asylum Information and the European Union.* The Hague: Advisory Council on International Affairs, 1999a.

———. *Capital Punishment and Human Rights.* The Hague: Advisory Council on International Affairs, 1998a.

———. *Commentary on the 2001 Memorandum on Human Rights Policy.* The Hague: Advisory Council on International Affairs, 2001a.

———. *Counterterrorism in a European and International Perspective: Interim Report on the Prohibition of Torture [Advisory letter].* The Hague: Advisory Council on International Affairs, 2005a.

———. *The Draft Declaration on the Rights of Indigenous Peoples: From Deadlock to Breakthrough?* The Hague: Advisory Council on International Affairs, 2004a.

———. *A European Charter of Fundamental Rights?* The Hague: Advisory Council on International Affairs, 2000a.

———. *Failing States: A Global Responsibility.* The Hague: Advisory Council on International Affairs, 2004b.

———. *The Functioning of the United Nations Commission on Human Rights.* The Hague: Advisory Council on International Affairs, 1999b.

———. *Humanitarian Aid: Redefining the Limits.* The Hague: Advisory Council on International Affairs, 1998b.

———. *Humanitarian Intervention.* The Hague: Advisory Council on International Affairs, 2000b.

Adviesraad Internationale Vraagstukken (AIV). *A Human Rights Based Approach to Development Cooperation.* The Hague: Advisory Council on International Affairs, 2003.

———. *From Internal to External Borders: Recommendations for Developing a Common EU Asylum and Migration Policy by 2009 [Advisory letter].* The Hague: Advisory Council on International Affairs, 2004c.

———. *Migration and Development Cooperation.* The Hague: Advisory Council on International Affairs, 2005b.

———. *Reforming the United Nations: A Closer Look at the Annan Report.* The Hague: Advisory Council on International Affairs, 2005c.

———. *Registration of Communities Based on Religion or Belief.* The Hague: Advisory Council on International Affairs, 2001b.

———. *The United Nations and Human Rights.* The Hague: Advisory Council on International Affairs, 2004d.

———. *Universality of Human Rights and Cultural Diversity.* The Hague: Advisory Council on International Affairs, 1998c.

———. *Violence against Women: Legal Developments.* The Hague: Advisory Council on International Affairs, 2001c.

———. *The World Conference against Racism and the Right to Reparation.* The Hague: Advisory Council on International Affairs, 2001d.

Alden, Chris, and Garth LePere. *South Africa's Post-Apartheid Foreign Policy—From Reconciliation to Revival?* New York: Oxford University Press, 2003.

Alfredsson, Gudmundur. "A Few Practical Suggestions Concerning Human Rights and Development Co-operation." In Per Sevastik (ed.), *Legal Assistance to Developing Countries.* London: Norstedts Juridik/Kluwer Law International, 1997.

Amnesty International Canada. *Human Rights for ALL—No Exceptions: A 2006 Agenda for Canada.* Ottawa: Amnesty International, 2006.

Aning, Kwesi, Prosper Addo, Emma Birikorang, and Emmanuel Sowatey. *African Commitments to Conflict Prevention and Peacemaking: A Review of Eight NEPAD Countries.* Johannesburg, South Africa: African Human Security Initiative, 2004.

Appiah, Kwame Anthony. *Cosmopolitanism: Ethics in a World of Strangers.* New York: W. W. Norton, 2006.

Arase, David. "Japanese Policy towards Democracy and Human Rights in Asia," *Asian Survey* 33, no. 10 (October 1993): 935–952.

Arbour, Louise. "The Responsibility to Protect and the Duty to Punish: Politics and Justice in a Safer World." *Behind the Headlines* (Canadian Institute of International Affairs) 59, no. 1 (Autumn 2001).

Archibugi, Daniele. "Cosmopolitan Democracy and Its Critics: A Review." *European Journal of International Relations* 10, no. 3 (2004): 437–473.

Arendt, Hannah. *The Human Condition.* Chicago: University of Chicago Press, 1958.

Arias Foundation for Peace and Human Progress. *Report on Activities, 1997–1999.* San José, Costa Rica: Arias Foundation, 1999.

Arias Sanchez, Oscar. *Horizons of Peace: The Costa Rican Contribution to the Peace Process.* San Jose, Costa Rica: Arias Foundation: 1994.

Arredondo, Sylvia, and Fernando Naranjo (eds.). *Costa Rica Ante El Mundo.* San José, Costa Rica: AFOCOI, 2003.

Asmal, Kader, David Chidester, and Cassius Lubisi (eds.). *Legacy of Freedom: The ANC's Human Rights Tradition.* Johannesburg: Jonathan Ball Publishers, 2005.

Aso Taro. "Arc of Freedom and Prosperity: Japan's Expanding Diplomatic Horizons." Speech by Mr. Taro Aso, Minister for Foreign Affairs on the Occasion of the Japan Institute of International Affairs Seminar. November 30, 2006. http://www.mofa.go.jp/announce/fm/aso/speech0611.html.

"Assembly Derails Attempt to Postpone Immigration Law," Tico Times, August 25, 2006. http://www.ticotimes.net/Login/tt_sa_pdf.cfm?bi_id=5209.

Austen, Ian. "Canadian Court Limits Detention in Terror Cases," New York Times, February 23, 2007.

Axworthy, Lloyd. Navigating a New World. Toronto: Knopf Canada, 2003.

Baehr, P. R. "The United Nations Convention Against Torture." In Philip Everts and Guido Walraven (eds.), The Politics of Persuasion: Implementation of Foreign Policy by the Netherlands, pp. 296–309. Aldershot: Gower Publishers, 1989.

Baehr, Peter R., and Monique Castermans-Holleman. The Role of Human Rights in Foreign Policy. New York : Palgrave, 2004.

Baehr, Peter R., Monique C. Castermans-Holleman, and Fred Grünfeld. "Human Rights in the Foreign Policy of the Netherlands." Human Rights Quarterly 24, no. 4 (November 2002): 992–1010.

———. Human Rights in the Foreign Policy of the Netherlands. Antwerp: Intersentia, 2002.

Baehr, Peter R., Fried van Hoof, Liu Nanali, and Tao Zhengua (eds.). Human Rights: Chinese and Dutch Perspectives. The Hague: M. Nijhoff, 1996.

Balcombe, Andrew. "Businessman Gets 8 Years for Weapons Trading," The Times (Hague Amsterdam Rotterdam), June 9, 2006.

Barahona Montero, Manuel. "El Desarrollo Social." In Quesada Camacho, Juan Rafael et al., Costa Rica contemporánea: raíces del estado de la nación, San José, Costa Rica: Editorial de la Universidad de Costa Rica, 1999.

Barnett, Michael. Dialogues in Arab Politics: Negotiations in Regional Order. New York: Columbia University Press, 1998.

Barnett, Michael, and Martha Finnemore. "The Politics, Power and Pathologies of International Organizations." In Friedrich Kratochwil and Edward D. Mansfield (eds.), International Organization and Global Governance. New York: Pearson/Longman, 2006.

Barrantes, Lina, and Rodrigo Jiménez. Confusiones y Contradicciones en la Identidad Genérica de la Fuerzas Policiales en Centroamérica. San Jose, Costa Rica: Hivos-Fundacion Arias, 1999.

Barratt, Bethany. "Canadian Foreign Policy and International Human Rights" In Patrick James, Nelson Michaud, and Marc J. O'Reilly (eds.), Handbook of Canadian Foreign Policy, pp. 235–264. Lanham, Md.: Lexington, 2006.

Bearak, Barry. "Outbursts of Anti-Immigrant Violence Spread in Johannesburg," New York Times, May 19, 2008, A6.

Behringer, Ronald. "Middle Power Leadership on the Human Security Agenda." Cooperation and Conflict: Journal of the Nordic International Studies Association 40, no. 3, 2005: 305–342.

Berger, Thomas. Cultures of Anti-Militarism: National Security in Germany and Japan. Baltimore: Johns Hopkins University Press, 1998.

Berg-Schlosser, Dirk. "The Quality of Democracies in Europe as Measured by Current Indicators of Democratization and Good Governance." Journal of Communist Studies and Transition Politics 20, no. 1 (2004): 28–55.

Biekart, Kees, Beate Thoresen, and Fredy Ochaeta. Evaluation of the Dutch "Governance and Human Rights Programme" in Guatemala 1997–2003.

IOB—Policy and Operations Evaluation Department, Ministry of Foreign Affairs, September 2004.

Bildt, Carl. "Statement by Carl Bildt on Israel's Attacks on Gaza." Swedish Government Offices, November 8, 2006. http://www.sweden.gov.se/sb/d/7350/a/72065.

Bildt, Carl. "Sweden a Strong Shield against Injustice," Svenska Dagbladet, March 14, 2007.

Bjorkdahl, Annika. From Idea to Norm: Promoting Conflict Prevention. Lund, Sweden: Lund University, 2002.

Black, David. "Lever or Cover? South Africa, Multilateral Institutions and the Promotion of Human Rights." In Philip Nel, Ian Taylor, and Janis Van der Westhuizen (eds.), South African Multilateral Diplomacy and Global Change: The Limits of Reformism, pp. 76–89. Aldershot: Ashgate, 2001.

Bocker, Anita, and Tetty Havinga. Asylum Migration to the European Union: Patterns of Origin and Destination. Nijmegen, The Netherlands: Institute for the Sociology of Law, 1997.

Boli, John, John Meyer, Francisco Ramirez, and George Thomas. Constructing the World Polity: World Culture and International Non-Governmental Organizations. Stanford: Stanford University Press, 1999.

Bond, Patrick. Talk Left, Walk Right. Durban, South Africa: University of KwaZulu-Natal Press, 2004.

Bookmiller, Robert J. "Abdullah's Jordan: America's Anxious Ally." Alternatives 2, no. 2 (2003): 174–195.

Booth, John. Costa Rica: The Quest for Democracy. Boulder, Colo.: Westview Press, 1998.

Bosold, David, and Sascha Werthes. "Human Security and Smart Sanctions—Two Means to a Common End?" Graduate School of Media and Governance, Keio University, Japan, 2003.

Bouwhuis, Stephen. "International Human Rights at Century's End." Alternative Law Journal 25, no. 1 (2000): 9.

Boyle, Kevin, and Sigmund Simonsen. "Human Security, Human Rights and Disarmament." Disarmament Forum 3 (2004): 5–14.

Brenes, Arnoldo, and Kevin Casas (eds.). Soldiers as Businessmen: The Economic Activities of Central America's Militaries. San José, Costa Rica: Fundacíon Arias/COSUDE [Swiss Agency for Development and Cooperation], 1998.

Brenes Zy, Hárold. "Costa Rica se abstuvo de votar medida contra Israel" (Costa Rica Abstains on Vote on Israel Measure), La Nacion, April 8, 2005. http://www.nacion.com/ln_ee/2005/abril/08/pais11.html.

Brooke, James. "Japan Must Show 'Deep Remorse' For Wartime Actions, Official Says," New York Times, December 8, 2005.

Brysk, Alison. Human Rights and Private Wrongs: Constructing Global Civil Society. New York: Routledge, 2005.

———(ed.). Globalization and Human Rights. Berkeley: University of California Press, 2002.

Brysk, Alison, Craig Parsons, and Wayne Sandholtz. "After Empire: National Identity and Post-Colonial Families of Nations." European Journal of International Relations 8, no. 2 (2002): 267–305.

Bull, Hedley. The Anarchical Society: A Study of Order in World Politics. New York: Columbia University Press, 1995.

Byers, Michael. "Afghanistan: Just Where Is Canada's National Interest?" *The Globe and Mail*, September 14, 2006.

Caldwell, Christopher. "Daughter of the Enlightenment," *New York Times Magazine*, April 3, 2005, 26–31.

Campaign for a UN Democracy Caucus. "Frequently Asked Questions," 2005. http://www.democracycaucus.net/html/about02_frequ.html.

———. "UN Voting Records," 2005. http://www.democracycaucus.net/html/unvot.html.

Campbell, Leslie. "Democracy Canada: Turning Canadian Democratic Values and Experiences into International Action." *Hemisphere Focus* 12, no. 4 (2004): 1–5.

Canada. Foreign Affairs and International Trade. "Canada's International Policy Statement: A Role of Pride and Influence in the World." 2005. http://www.international.gc.ca.

Canada. Ministry of Foreign Affairs. 2007–2008 *Report on Plans and Priorities*. http://www.tbs-sct.gc.ca/rpp/0708/fait-aeci/fait-aeci01_e.asp

Canada. Standing Committee on Foreign Affairs and International Trade. Sub-Committee on Human Rights and International Development. *Conflict, Human Rights, and Democracy in Colombia: A Canadian Agenda*. Ottawa, 2002.

Canada. Standing Committee on Foreign Affairs and International Development. House of Commons. *Canada's International Policy Put to the Test in Haiti*. Ottawa, December 2006.

Caporaso, James A. "International Relations Theory and Multilateralism: The Search for Foundations." In John Ruggie (ed.), *Multilateralism Matters*. New York: Columbia University Press, 1993.

Cárdenas, Sonia. *Conflict and Compliance: State Responses to International Human Rights Pressure*. Philadelphia: University of Pennsylvania Press, 2007.

———. "Constructing Rights? Human Rights Education and the State." *International Political Science Review* 26, no. 4 (2005): 363–379.

———. "Norm Collision: Explaining the Effects of International Human Rights Pressure on State Behavior." *International Studies Review* 6 (2004): 213–231.

———. "Transgovernmental Activism: Canada's Role in Promoting National Human Rights Commissions." *Human Rights Quarterly* (August 2003): 775–790.

Casasfranco Roldán, María Virginia. *Las migraciones y los desplazamientos forzados: Análisis comparativo e integral desde un enfoque de derechos humanos*. San José, Costa Rica: Internacional Development Research Center-CNUAH-Habitat-Fundación Arias, 2001.

Centre for Humanitarian Dialogue. "HD Centre Partnerships," May 25, 2007. http://www.hdcentre.org/Partnerships.

Chan-Tiberghien, Jennifer. *Gender and Human Rights Politics in Japan*. Stanford, Calif.: Stanford University Press, 2004.

Charnovitz, Steve. "Nongovernmental Organizations and International Law." *The American Journal of International Law* 100, no. 2 (2006): 348–372.

Chikane, Frank. "Democratic Governance: A Restructured Presidency at Work." Report by the Director General and Secretary to the Cabinet, South Africa, March 2001. http://www.info.gov.za/otherdocs/2001/presidency01.pdf.

Chivers, C. J. "Dutch Soldiers Stress Restraint in Afghanistan," *The New York Times*, April 6, 2007, A1.

Cody, Edward. "China's Diplomatic Gain is Taiwan's Loss," *The Washington Post*, July 9, 2007, A09.

Community of Democracies. "Criteria for Participation and Procedures," September 12, 2000. http://www.state.gov/g/drl/26085.htm.

———. "Final Warsaw Declaration: Toward a Community of Democracies," June 27, 2000. http://www.state.gov/g/drl/rls/26811.htm

———. "Seoul Plan of Action," November 12, 2002. http://www.state.gov/g/drl/rls/15259.htm.

Community of Democracies Non-Governmental Forum, "An Appeal to Governments Gathered at the Community of Democracies Meeting." November 12, 2002. http://www.demcoalition.org/pdf/Appeal_to_governments.pdf.

[Community of Democracies] Council for a Community of Democracies. "CCD's Mission," 2006. http://www.ccd21.org/visionmission.htm.

Convening Group of the Community of Democracies. "Meeting of Regional and Multilateral Organizations on Promoting and Defending Democracy," February 20–21, 2001. http://www.demcoalition.org/pdf/final_Communique.pdf.

Cooper, Andrew F. *Tests of Global Governance: Canadian Diplomacy and United Nations World Conferences*. Tokyo: United Nations University Press, 2004.

Cooper, Andrew F., Richard A. Higgott, and Kim Richard Nossal. *Relocating Middle Powers: Australia and Canada in a Changing World Order*. Vancouver: University of British Columbia Press, 1993.

Cordero, Luis Alberto. Statement: "On the Occasion of the United Nations Conference to Review Progress Made in the Implementation of the Programme of Action to Prevent, Combat and Eradicate the Illicit Trade in Small Arms and Light Weapons in All Its Aspects," June 27, 2006. United Nations, New York. http://www.un.org/events/smallarms2006/pdf/arms060627costa_rica-eng.pdf.

Cornelissen, Scarlett. "Displaced Multilateralism? South Africa's Participation at the United Nations: Disjunctures, Continuities and Contrasts." In Donna Lee, Ian Taylor, and Paul D. Williams (eds.), *The New Multilateralism in South African Diplomacy*, pp. 26–50. New York: Palgrave, 2006.

Cortell, Andrew P., and James W. Davis, Jr. "How Do International Institutions Matter? The Domestic Impact of International Rules and Norms." *International Studies Quarterly* 40 (1996): 451–478.

Cortwright, David, and George Lopez (eds.). *Smart Sanctions: Targeting Economic Statecraft*. Lanham, Md.: Rowman & Littlefield, 2002.

Costa Rica. Ministerio de Relaciones Exteriores y Culto. *Memoria Anual, 1999–2000*.

———. *Memoria Anual, 2001–2002*.

Cox, Robert. "Multilateralism and World Order." *Review of International Studies* 18, no. 2 (1992): 161–80.

———. "Social Forces, States, and World Orders: Beyond International Relations Theory." *Millennium: Journal of International Studies* 10, no. 1 (Spring 1981): 126–155.

Cronin, Bruce. *Institutions for the Common Good: International Protection Regimes in International Society*. New York: Cambridge University Press, 2003.

Dahl, Ann-Sofie. "Sweden: Once a Moral Superpower, Always a Moral Superpower." *International Journal* 16, no. 4 (Autumn 2006): 895–908.

———. "To Be or Not to Be Neutral: Swedish Security Strategy in the Post Cold War Era." In Efraim Inbar and Gabriel Sheffer (eds.), *The National Security of Small States in a Changing World*, pp. 175–196. London: Frank Cass, 1997.

Debiel, Tobias, and Werthes, Sascha. "Human Security on Foreign Policy Agendas: Changes, Concepts and Cases." *Institute for Development and Peace Report* 80 (2006).

Defensoría de los Habitantes [Ombudsman], Costa Rica. *Annual Report, 2002* [CD].

Deiben, Diede-Jan, and Thom Dieben, "Aspects Concerning the Criminal Case against Eric O.." *Challenge: Liberty and Security*, August 1, 2005. http//www.libertysecurity.org.

Democracy Coalition Project. "Convening Council," 2006. http://www.demcoalition.org.

———. "A Community of Democracies Meetings in Santiago: Activities Related to the NGO Process," 2005. http://www.demcoalition.org/2005_html/commu_cdm05_nongo.html.

———. "Community of Democracies Meetings in Santiago," 2005. http://www.demcoalition.org/2005_html/commu_cdm05_nongo.html.

———. "Community of Democracies Meetings in Seoul: Non-Governmental Forum," 2002. http://www.demcoalition.org/2005_html/commu_cdm02_nongo.html.

———. "Community of Democracies Meetings in Warsaw," 2000. http://www.demcoalition.org/2005_html/commu_cdm00.html.

———. "From Warsaw to Seoul: Who's In, Who's Out," November 10–12, 2002. http://www.demcoalition.org/pdf/Seoul_invitation_list.pdf.

"Democracy Holds a Party." *Foreign Policy* (September/October 2002): 82–83.

Department for International Development (OECD DAC). "Good Humanitarian Donorship: Background to GHD," July 10, 2006. http://www.goodhumanitariandonorship.org/background.asp.

———. "Good Humanitarian Donorship: Activities: DAC Peer Reviews," August 3, 2006. http://www.goodhumanitariandonorship.org/dac-peer-reviews.asp#top#top.

Derghoukassian, Khatchik. "Human Security: A Brief Report on the State of the Art." *University of Miami North-South Center* 3, 2001: 1–17.

Despouy, Leandro. "El Papel de Costa Rica en el Fortalecimiento del Sistema Interamericano de Protección de los Derechos Humanos." *Revista Costarricense de Política Exterior* 1, no. 1 (May 2001).

de Tocqueville, Alexis. *Democracy in America*. Translated by George Lawrence. New York: Harper Perennial Modern Classics, 2006.

"Dispute over Immigration Throws Dutch Cabinet into a Political Bind," *New York Times*, December 14, 2006.

Dobriansky, Paula J. "Advancing Democracy." *National Interest* 77 (Summer 2004): 71–78.

Donaghy, Greg. "All God's Children: Lloyd Axworthy, Human Security and Canadian Foreign Policy, 1996–2000." *Canadian Foreign Policy* 10, no. 2 (2003): 39–58.

Connelly, Jack. "Human Rights: A New Standard of Civilization?" *International Affairs* 74, no. 1 (1998): 1–24.

———. "International Human Rights: A Regime Analysis." *International Organization* 40, no. 3 (1984): 599–642.

Dreier, David, and, Lee H. Hamilton. *Enhancing U.S. Leadership at the United Nations*. New York: Council on Foreign Relations and Freedom House, 2002.

Duffield, Mark, and Waddell, Nicholas. *Human Security and Global Danger: Exploring a Governmental Assemblage*. London: Economic and Social Research Council, 2004.

Dugger, Celia W. "Norway Gives More to Fight Ills Overseas," *New York Times*, September 30, 2007, A5.

"Dutch Parliament Approves Afghanistan Mission: Antipathy towards American Methods in Afghanistan Overcome by House Majority in the Netherlands," *Netherlands News Digest*, Febrary 3, 2006. http://www.nnd.nl.

Ebel, Roland, Raymond Taras, and James Cochran, *Political Culture and Foreign Policy in Latin America*. Albany: SUNY Press, 1991.

Eckstein, Harry. "Case-Study and Theory in Political Science." In F. I. Greenstein and N. S. Polsby (eds.), *Handbook of Political Science*, vol. 7, pp. 79–137. Reading, Mass.: Addison-Wesley, 1975.

Eguizabal, Cristina. "Latin American Foreign Policies and Human Rights." In David Forsythe (ed.), *Human Rights and Comparative Foreign Policy*. New York: United Nations University Press: 2000.

Ekéus, Rolf. "Peace and Security—Swedish Security Policy 1969–89." Sakerhetspolitiska utredningen, 2002. Fred och sakerhet-Svensk sakerhetspolitik 1969–1989. Slutbetankande av Sakerhetspolitiska utredningen, SOU (2002): 108, Stockholm: Fritzes offentliga publikationer. [Swedish, selections translated by Ted Svensson]

———, Rolf. *Practicing What We Preach: Early Action to Prevent Conflict*. Organization for Security and Cooperation in Europe: Helsingborg, August 29. Vienna, Austria: OSCE, 2002.

Electoral Knowledge Network. "About ACE: ACE Electoral Knowledge Network," 2006. http://aceproject.org/about-en/index_html.

———. "Partner Organizations—ACE Electoral Knowledge Network," 2006. http://aceproject.org/about-en/organisations/partners/default.

Elgstrom, Ole. *Images and Strategies for Autonomy*. Dordrecht, Netherlands: Kluwer Academic Press, 2000.

Elgstrom, Ole, and Magnus Jerneck. "From Adaptation to Foreign Policy Activism: Sweden as a Promoter of Peace." In Arie M. Kacowicz, Yaacov Bar-Simon-Tov, Ole Elgstrom, and Magnus Jerneck (eds.), *Stable Peace among Nations*, pp. 179–199. Lanham, Md.: Rowman and Littlefield, 2000.

European Training and Research Centre for Human Rights and Democracy. "ETC Graz: Training Material," November 28, 2006. http://www.etc-graz.at/typ03/index.php?id=703.

Everts, Philip, and Guido Walraven (eds.). *The Politics of Persuasion: Implementation of Foreign Policy by the Netherlands*. Aldershot: Gower, 1989.

Falk, Richard. "Contending Approaches to World Order." *Journal of International Affairs* 31 (Fall/Winter 1977): 171–198.

———. *The Declining World Order: America's Imperial Geopolitics*. New York: Routledge, 2004.

Farber, Henry, and Joanne Gowa. "Polities and Peace." *International Security* 20, no. 2 (1995): 123–146.

Fascell, Dante. "The Helsinki Accord: A Case Study." *Annals of the American Academy of Political and Social Science* 442 (1979): 69–76.

Fell, Mike. "Is Human Security our Main Concern in the 21st Century?" *Journal of Security Sector Management* 4, no. 3 (2006).

Finnemore, Martha. *National Interests in International Society*. Ithaca, N.Y.: Cornell University Press, 1996.

Finnemore, Martha, and Kathryn Sikkink. "International Norm Dynamics and Political Change." *International Organization* 52, no. 4 (Autumn 1998): 887–917.

Forsythe, David (ed.). *Human Rights and Comparative Foreign Policy*. Tokyo: United Nations University Press, 2000a.

———. *The United States and Human Rights: Looking Inward and Outward*. Lincoln: University of Nebraska Press, 2000b.

Fosum, John Erik. "Gidsland and Human Security." *International Journal*, 16, no. 4 (Autumn 2006): 813–828.

Freedom House. "Mission Statement." http://www.freedomhouse.org/template.cfm?page=2.

Freaks, Georg, Koenraad Van Brabant, and Marcel Scholten, *Dutch Policies and Activities Directed at Peacebuilding*. Contribution to the Joint Utstein Study of Peacebuilding. Netherlands Ministry of Foreign Affairs, German Federal Ministry for Economic Cooperation and Development, Royal Norwegian Ministry of Foreign Affairs, UK Department for International Development, 2003.

Fuioka, Mieko. "Japanese Human Rights Policy at Domestic and International Levels." *Japan Forum* 15, no. 2 (2003): 287–305.

Fu-long, William. "Costa Rica: Caught between Two Worlds." *Journal of Interamerican Studies and World Affairs* 29, no. 2 (1987): 119–154.

Gershman, Carl. "Building a Worldwide Movement for Democracy: The Role of Nongovernmental Organizations." *U.S. Foreign Policy Agenda* 8, no. 1 (2003): 28–30.

Ghebali, Victor-Yves. "The OSCE Between Crisis and Reform: Towards a New Lease on Life." Geneva: Geneva Centre for the Democratic Control of Armed Forces, 2005.

Gibney, M., L. Cornett, L., and R. Wood, R. "Political Terror Scale 1976–2006," 2007. http://www.politicalterrorscale.org/.

Glson, Julie, and Phillida Purvis. "Japan's Pursuit of Human Security." *Japan Forum* 15, no. 2 (2003).

Goldmann, Kjell. *Democracy and Foreign Policy: The Case of Sweden*. Aldershot: Gower, 1986.

———. *The Logic of Internationalism: Coercion and Accommodation*. Routledge, 1994.

Goldstein, Judith, and Robert Keohane (eds.). *Ideas and Foreign Policy: Beliefs, Institutions and Political Change*. Ithaca: Cornell University Press, 1993.

Goransson, Bo. "Reducing Poverty through Confronting Issues of Power, Democracy and Human Rights in Bilateral Development Cooperation." In *Democracy, Power and Partnership—Implications for Development Cooperation*, proceedings from a conference arranged by the Collegium for Development Studies at Uppsala University in cooperation with SIDA, May 6, 2002.

Government of Canada. "Human Rights Commission Annual Report," 2006. http://www.chrc-ccdp.ca/publications/ar_2006_ra/toc_tdm-en.asp.

———. "Independence and Internationalism: Report of the Special Joint Committee on Canada's International Relations," Ottawa, 1986.

Government of the Republic of Austria. "Human Security Network Medium Term Work Plan," Foreign Ministry, May 10, 2003. http://www.bmeia.gv.at/up-media/155_medium_term_work_plan.doc.

Government of the Republic of Slovenia. "Human Security Network," Ministry of Foreign Affairs. http://www.mzz.gov.si/en/foreign_policy/human_security_network_hsn/.

Graeber, David. "Army of Altruists: On the Alienated Right to Do Good," *Harper's Magazine*, January 2007, 1–38.

Graham, Bill. "Affirming Canadian Sovereignty in an Interdependent World." *Behind the Headlines* (Canadian Institute of International Affairs) 59, no. 1 (Autumn 2001).

"The Growing Iraqi Refugee Crisis: Trading Civil War for Small-Town Sweden." International—*Spiegel Online*, May 24, 2007. http://www.spiegel.de/international/europe/0,1518, druck-484025,00.html.

Grünfeld, Fred. "Human Rights in Chile." In Philip Everts and Guido Walraven (eds.), *The Politics of Persuasion: Implementation of Foreign Policy by the Netherlands*, pp. 269–281. Aldershot: Gower, 1989.

———. *Nederland en het Nabije Oosten: de Nederlandse rol in de internationale politiek ten aanzien van het Arabisch-Israëlisch conflict 1973–1982* [Netherlands in the Middle East]. Maastricht: Kluwer-Deventer, 1991.

Guest, Iain. *Behind the Disappearances*. Philadelphia: University of Pennsylvania Press, 1990.

Haas, Ernest B. "Why Collaborate? Issue-Linkage and International Regimes." In Friedrich Kratochwil and Edward D. Mansfield (eds.), *International Organization and Global Governance*. New York: Pearson/Longman, 2006.

———. *When Knowledge Is Power*. Berkeley: University of California Press, 1990.

Habib, Adam, and Nthakeng Selinyane. "South Africa's Foreign Policy and a Realistic Vision of an African Century." In Elizabeth Sidiropoulos (ed.), *Apartheid Past, Renaissance Future: South Africa's Foreign Policy 1994–2004*, pp. 47–60. Johannesburg: South African Institute of International Affairs, 2004.

Hamill, James. "South Africa in Africa: The Dilemmas of Multilateralism." In Donna Lee, Ian Taylor, and Paul D. Williams (eds.), *The New Multilateralism in South African Diplomacy*, pp. 118–140. New York: Palgrave, 2006.

Hamm, Brigitte. "A Human Rights Approach to Development." *Human Rights Quarterly* 23 (2001): 1005–1031.

Hampson, Fen. *Madness in the Multitude: Human Security and World Disorder*. Oxford University Press, 2002.

Hartz, Louis. *The Liberal Tradition in America: An Interpretation of American Political Thought since the Revolution*. New York: Harcourt Brace Jovanovich, 1955, 1991.

Hataley, T. S., and Kim Richard Nossal. "The Limits of the Human Security Agenda: the Case of Canada's Response to the Timor Crisis." *Global Change, Peace, and Security* 16, no. 1 (2004): 5–17.

Hawkins, Darren G. "Domestic Responses to International Pressure: Human Rights in Authoritarian Chile," *European Journal of International Relations* 3, no. 4 (1997): 403–434.

Heinrich, L. William Jr., Akiho Shibata, and Yoshihide Soeya. *United Nations Peacekeeping Operations: A Guide to Japanese Policies*. New York: United Nations University Press, 1999.

Heintze, Hans-Joachim. "Minority Issues in Western Europe and the OSCE High Commissioner on National Minorities." *International Journal on Minority and Group Rights* 7 (2000): 381–392.

Heisler, Martin O. *The Nordic Region, Changing Perspectives in International Relations*. Newbury Park: Sage Press, 1990.

Hellema, D. A. "A Special Role in the World: Fifty Years of Development Cooperation Policy." In J. A. Nekkers and P. A. M. Malcontent (eds.), *Fifty Years of Dutch Development Cooperation, 1949–1999*, pp. 323–328. The Hague: Sdu, 2000.

Henk, Dan. "Human Security: Relevance and Implications." *Parameters* (Summer 2005): 91–106.

Henrikson, Alan K. "Distance and Foreign Policy: A Political Geography Approach." *International Political Science Review* 23, no. 4 (2002): 437–466.

Herman, Joost. "The Dutch Drive for Humanitarianism." *International Journal* 16, no. 4 (Autumn 2006): 859–874.

Hey, Jeanne, and Lynn Kuzma. "Anti-U.S. Foreign Policy of Dependent States: Mexican and Costa Rican Participation in Central American Peace Plans." *Comparative Political Studies* 26 (April 1993): 30–63.

Higashizawa, Yasushi. "The Constitution of Japan and Human Rights." Japan Civil Liberties Union, November 9, 2001. http://material.ahrchk.net/charter/mainfile.php/east/3/.

Hingorani, R. C. *Nehru's foreign policy*. New Delhi: Oxford and IBH Publishing, 1989.

Hirata, Keiko. *Civil Society in Japan*. New York: Palgrave, 2002.

———. "Civil Society and Japan's Dysfunctional Democracy." *Journal of Developing Societies* 20, no. 1–2 (2004): 107–124.

Hirschman, Albert. *A Bias for Hope: Essays on Development and Latin America*. Boulder, Colo.: Westview Press, 1985.

Hodgson, Jim. "Dissonant Voices: Northern NGO and Haitian Partner Perspectives on the Future of Haiti." In Yasmine Shamsie and Andrew S. Thompson (eds.), *Haiti: Hope for a Fragile State*, pp. 99–110. Waterloo, Canada: Wilfred Laurier University Press, 2006.

Holmberg, Susan L. "Welfare Abroad: Swedish Development Assistance." In Bengt Sundelius (ed.), *The Committed Neutral: Sweden's Foreign Policy*, pp. 123–166. Boulder, Colo.: Westview, 1989.

Hook, Glenn D. *Japan's International Relations: Politics, Economics, and Security*. New York: Routledge: 2001.

Hopf, Ted. "The Promise of Constructivism in International Relations Theory." *International Security* 23, no. 1 (Summer 1998).

Hoshino, Eichi. "Human Rights and Development Aid." In Peter Van Ness (ed.), *Debating Human Rights: Critical Essays from the U.S. and Asia*. New York: Routledge: 1999.

Houghton, David Patrick. "Reinvigorating the Study of Foreign Policy Decision-Making: Toward a Constructivist Approach." *Foreign Policy Approach* 3, no. 1 (January 2007): 24–45.

Howard-Hassmann, Rhoda E. *Compassionate Canadians: Civic Leaders Discuss Human Rights*. Toronto: University of Toronto Press, 2003.

Hubert, Don. "An Idea that Works in Practice." *Security Dialogue* 35 no. 3 (2004): 351–352.

"Human Rights Now Tops the Agenda," *Toronto Star*, May 5, 2007, F5.

Human Rights Watch. "Unprotected Migrants: Zimbabweans in South Africa's Limpopo Province." *Human Rights Watch Report* 18, no. 6 (July 2006).

———. "The Netherlands—Fleeting Refuge: The Triumph of Efficiency Over Protection in Dutch Asylum Policy." *Human Rights Watch Report* 14, no. 3 (2003).

Human Security Network. "Civil Society," May 11–12, 2000. http://www.humansecuritynetwork.org/society-e.php.

———. "Events and Initiatives." http://www.humansecuritynetwork.org/events-e.php.

———. "Graz Declaration on Principles of Human Rights Education and Human Security." http://www.humansecuritynetwork.org/docs/8may2003-e.php.

Human Security Network. "The Human Security Network," October 30, 2006. http://www.humansecuritynetwork.org/network-e.php.

———. "Human Security Network Ministerial Chair's Summary," Bamako, May 27–29, 2004. http://www.humansecuritynetwork.org/docs/bamako_chair-e.php.

———. "The Human Security Network Second Ministerial Meeting." http://www.humansecuritynetwork.org/docs/Chairman_summary-e.php.

———. "Members of the Human Security Network," October 30, 2006. http://www.humansecuritynetwork.org/members-e.php.

———. "Plan of Action for the Canadian Chairmanship of the Human Security Network," 2004. http://www.humansecuritynetwork.org/docs/ottawa_plan-e.php.

———. "Principles," May 20, 1999. http://www.humansecuritynetwork.org/principles-e.php.

———. "Statements." http://www.humansecuritynetwork.org/statements-e.php.

———. "The Vision of the Human Security Network." http://www.humansecurity network.org/menu-e.php.

Hurwitz, Jon, Mark Peffley, and Mitchell A. Seligson. "Foreign Policy Belief Systems in Comparative Perspective: The United States and Costa Rica." *International Studies Quarterly* 37, no. 3 (1993): 245–270.

IDEA. "Amended IDEA Statute 2006," 2006. http://www.idea.int/about/upload/Statues_English_RevisedJan2006.pdf.

———. "IDEA Annual Report 2005," 2005. http://www.idea.int/publications/annualreport_2005/upload/IDEA%20AR2005.pdf.

———. "IDEA Mission Statement," June 15, 1999. http://www.idea.int/upload/MissionStatement.pdf.

———. "IDEA Statutes 2003," 2003. http://www.idea.int/about/upload/Statutes_English.pdf.

———. "International IDEA: Canada," December 21, 2006. http://www.idea.int/about/members/canada.cfm.

———. "International IDEA: Costa Rica," December 21, 2006. http://www.idea.int/about/members/costa_rica.cfm.

———. "International IDEA: Democracy, Conflict and Human Security." http://www.idea.int/conflict/dchs/.

———. "International IDEA: Democracy Resources Worldwide," May 18, 2006. http://www.idea.int/links/.

———. "International IDEA: Frequently Asked Questions," December 10, 2006. http://www.idea.int/about/faq/index.cfm.

———. "International IDEA: History of IDEA," March 11, 2007. http://www.idea.int/about/anniversary/history.cfm.

———. "International IDEA: International IDEA and the OAS Cooperate on Democracy in the Americas," March 2, 2007. http://www.idea.int/news/idea-oas_cooperation.cfm.

———. "International IDEA: The Netherlands," December 21, 2006. http://www.idea.int/about/members/netherlands.cfm.

———. "International IDEA: Overview," March 4, 2007. http://www.idea.int/about/index.cfm.

———. "International IDEA: Publication—Pursuing the 21st Century," November 22, 2006. http://www.idea.int/conflict/dchs/publication.cfm.

———. "International IDEA: Referendum for the First Time in Costa Rica," May 28, 2007. http://www.idea.int/americas/costarica_may07.cfm.

————. "International IDEA: South Africa," December 21, 2006. http://www. idea.int/about/members/south_africa.cfm.

————. "International IDEA: Statutes," March 7, 2007. http://www.idea.int/ about/statutes.cfm.

————. "International IDEA: Sweden," December 21, 2006. http://www.idea.int/ about/members/sweden.cfm.

————. "10 Years of Supporting Democracy Worldwide," 2005, http://www.idea. int/publications/anniversary/index.cfm.

Ignatieff, Michael "Peace, Order and Good Government: A Foreign Policy Agenda for Canada." *Human Security Bulletin* (April 2004). http://www. humansecurity.com.

Ikome, Francis, Siphamandla Zondi, and Venance Konan (eds.). *La Cote d'Ivoire: vers une transition politique pacifique, un pays unifie et un avenir prospere.* Institute for Global Dialogue Series no. 2, November. Midrand, South Africa: IGD, 2005.

Inter-American Institute of Human Rights. *Biennial Report, 2000–2002* [CD].

International Commission on Intervention and State Sovereignty. *The Responsibility to Protect.* http://www.dfait-maeci.gc.ca/iciss-cisse/report-en.asp.

International Coordinating Committee of National Human Rights Institutions. "International Conferences of National Institutions Rules of Procedure," April 2002. http://www.nhri.net/pdf/Conference%20rules-final-E.pdf.

————. "List of Accredited National Institutions," 2007. http://www.nhri.net/ 2007/List_Accredited_NIs_Nov_2007.pdf.

————. "Rules of Procedure," October 24, 2006. http://www.nhri.net/ 2007/ICCProcedureEng2006.pdf.

International Coordinating Committee, Sub-Committee on Accreditation. "Rules of Procedure," September 14, 2004. http://www.nhri.net/pdf/RP_ ICC%20_Sub-Com_%20Acc_140904_en.pdf.

International Rehabilitation Council for Torture Victims. *Country Overviews of Funding Sources of EU Based Torture Rehabilitation Centres,* May 2007.

International Security Information Service Europe. "Operation Artemis: Mission Improbable?" *European Security Review* 18 (July 2003): 171–200.

Irwin, Rosalind (ed.). *Ethics and Security in Canadian Foreign Policy.* Vancouver: University of British Columbia Press, 2001.

Isacson, Adam. *Altered States: Security and Demilitarization in Central America.* San Jose, Costa Rica: Center for International Policy-Arias Foundation, 1997.

Isopi, Alessia, and George Mavrotas. "Aid Allocation and Aid Effectiveness." United Nations University Research Paper no. 2006/07, 2006.

Japan. Ministry of Foreign Affairs. *The Trust Fund for Human Security.* March 2006.

Jepperson, Ronald, Alexander Wendt, and Peter J. Katzenstein. "Norms, Identity, and Culture in National Security." In Peter J. Katzenstein (ed.), *The Culture of National Security,* pp. 33–75. New York: Columbia University Press, 1996.

Jerneck, Magnus, Magnus Morner, Gabriel Tortella, and Sune Akerman (eds.), *Different Paths to Modernity: Nordic and Spanish Perspectives.* Lund, Sweden: Nordic Academic Press. 2005.

Jervis, Robert. *Perception and Misperception in International Politics.* Princeton, N.J.: Princeton University Press, 1976.

Jhazbhay, Iqbal. "South Africa and the Middle East: A Test of Sure-Footed Maturity and Do-Able Morality?" In Elizabeth Sidiropoulos (ed.), *Apartheid Past,*

Renaissance Future: South Africa's Foreign Policy 1994–2004, pp. 281–296. Johannesburg: South African Institute of International Affairs, 2004.

Johansen, Robert. *The National Interest and the Human Interest: An Analysis of U.S. Foreign Policy*. Princeton, N.J.: Princeton University Press, 1980.

Johnson, Loch. *Seven Sins of American Foreign Policy*. New York: Pearson Longman, 2007.

Kagan, Richard C. "Japanese International Human Rights Policy." In Harami Befu (ed.), *Japan Engaging the World*. Denver, Colo.: Center for Japanese Studies at Teikyo Loretto Heights University, 1996.

Kagan, Robert. *Paradise and Power: America and Europe in the New World Order*. London: Atlantic Books, 2003.

Kampelman, Max M. "An Alternative Route to a Global Community," *American Behavioral Scientist* 48, no. 12 (2005): 1666–1682.

Karatnycky, Adrian, and Matteo Mecacci. "A Caucus of Democracies for the UN," *International Herald Tribune*, January 1, 2005.

Katada, Saori. "New Courses in Japanese Foreign Aid Policy: More Humanitarian and More Nationalistic." In Saori N. Katada, Hanns W. Maull, and Takashi Inoguchi (eds.), *Global Governance: Germany and Japan in the International System*, pp. 179–200. Aldershot, U.K.: Ashgate, 2004.

Katzenstein, Peter J. *Cultural Norms and National Security: Police and Military in Postwar Japan*. Ithaca: Cornell University Press, 1996.

Keating, Tom. *Canada and World Order: The Multilateralist Tradition in Canadian Foreign Policy*. New York: Oxford University Press, 2002.

Keck, Margaret, and Kathryn Sikkink. *Activists beyond Borders*. Ithaca: Cornell University Press, 1998.

Kennedy, David. *The Dark Sides of Virtue: Reassessing International Humanitarianism*. Princeton, N.J.: Princeton University Press, 2004.

Keohane, Robert, and Joseph Nye. *Power and Interdependence: World Politics in Transition*. Boston: Little, Brown. 1977.

Klotz, Audie. "Norms Reconstituting Interests: Global Racial Equality and U.S. Sanctions against South Africa," *International Organization* 49, no. 3 (Summer 1995): 451–478.

Korey, William. "The CSCE and Human Rights: A New Chapter for Helsinki." *New Leader* 73, no. 10 (1990): 11–14.

———. "Helsinki in Paris: Upgrading Human Rights." *New Leader* 72, no. 11 (1989): 12–15.

Koring, Paul. "Ottawa Failed Khadr, Lawyer Says," *Globe and Mail*, February 22, 2007.

Kornegay, Francis. *Pan-African Citizenship and Identity Formation in Southern Africa: An Overview of Problems, Prospects and Possibilities*. Research Report no. 107. Johannesburg: Centre for Policy Studies, January 2006.

Kowert, Paul A. "Toward a Constructivist Theory of Foreign Policy." In Vendulka Kubalkova (ed.), *Foreign Policy in a Constructed World*, pp. 266–287. Armonk, N.Y.: M. E. Sharpe, 2001.

Krasner, Stephen. "Sovereignty, Regimes, and Human Rights." In Volker Rittberger (ed.), *Regime Theory and International Relations*. Oxford: Clarendon Press, 1993.

———. "Structural Causes and Regime Consequences: Regimes as Intervening Variables." In Friedrich Kratochwil and Edward D. Mansfield (eds.), *International Organization and Global Governance*. New York: Pearson/Longman, 2006.

Kratochwil, Friedrich, and Youssef Lapid (eds.). *The Return of Culture and Identity in International Relations Theory*. Boulder, Colo.: Lynne Rienner, 1996.

Krause, Keith. "Human Security: An Idea Whose Time Has Come?" *Security and Peace* [Sicherheit und Frieden] 1 (2005): [PAGES?].

———. "Peace, Security and Development in Post-Conflict Environments." *Security Dialogue* 36, no. 4 (2005): 447–462.

Krauss, Clifford. "Canada's Leader Is a Skinflint, Says a Former Admirer, Bono," *New York Times*, May 4, 2005a, A8.

———. "Evidence Grows that Canada Aided in Having Terrorism Suspects Interrogated in Syria," *New York Times*, September 17, 2005b, A5.

Kressler, Harry. "Sweden in the Post-9/11 World: A Conversation with Anders Mellbourn," April 19, 2004. http://globetrotter.berkeley.edu/people4/Mellbourn/mellbourn-con0.html.

Kremer, F., and A. E. Pijpers. "South Africa and European Sanctions Policy." In Philip Everts and Guido Walraven (eds.), *The Politics of Persuasion: Implementation of Foreign Policy by the Netherlands*, pp. 310–322. Aldershot: Gower, 1989.

Kubalkova, Vendulka (ed.). *Foreign Policy in a Constructed World*. Armonk, N.Y.: M. E. Sharpe, 2001.

Kuitenbrouwer, M. "A Shining Example? Development Cooperation Policy in the Netherlands and Like-Minded Countries, 1973–1985." In J. A. Nekkers and P. A. M. Malcontent (eds.), *Fifty Years of Dutch Development Cooperation, 1949–1999*, pp. 175–192. The Hague: Sdu, 2000.

Kumar, Raj. "National Human Rights Institutions and Economic, Social and Cultural Rights: Toward the Institutionalization and Developmentalization of Human Rights." *Human Rights Quarterly* 28 (2006): 755–779.

Kuper, Simon. "Why Did Denmark Jews Survive While Dutch Jews Died in the Holocaust?" *London Financial Times Weekend Magazine* (January 22, 2005).

Lamb, Guy. "Arms Control South African Style." Institute for Security Studies, occasional paper no. 62, October 1, 2002.

Lamb, Guy, and J. Paul Dunne. "Defense Industrial Participation: The South African Experience." In Jurgen Brauer and J. Paul Dunne (eds.), *Arms Trade and Economic Development*. New York: Routledge, 2004.

Lambrechts, Kato (ed.). *Crisis in Lesotho: The challenge of managing conflict in southern Africa*. African Dialogue Series no. 2. Midrand, South Africa: Foundation for Global Dialogue, March 1999.

Landau, Loren B. "Protection and Dignity in Johannesburg: Shortcomings of South Africa's Urban Refugee Policy." *Journal of Refugee Studies* 19 (2006): 308–327.

———. "The Promise of Freedom, Regional Integration, and Refugee Protection." In J. Handmaker, J. Klaaren, and L. de la Hunt (eds.), *Advancing Refugee Protection in South Africa*. Oxford: Berghan Books, 2008.

Landman, Todd. *Studying Human Rights*. New York: Routledge, 2006.

Landman, Todd, and Meghna Abraham. *Evaluation of Nine Non-governmental Human Rights Organizations*. IOB—Policy and Operations Evaluation Department, Ministry of Foreign Affairs, February 2004.

Larsson, Jan. *Raoul Wallenberg*. Stockholm: Swedish Institute, 1986.

Lee, Donna, Ian Taylor, and Paul D. Williams (eds.). *The New Multilateralism in South African Diplomacy*. New York: Palgrave: 2006.

Legro, Jeffrey. *Rethinking the World: Great Power Strategies and International Order*. Ithaca: Cornell University Press, 2005.

LePere, Garth, and B. Vickers. "Civil Society and Foreign Policy in South Africa." In Janis van der Westhuizen and Phillip Nel (eds.), *Democratising Foreign Policy? Lessons from South Africa*. Lanham, Md.: Lexington Books, 2003.

Lindberg, Staffan. *A Follow-Up and Evaluation of UN World Conferences in the 1990's—Government, Parliament, Government Agencies and Voluntary Organisations in New International Arenas: Who Has the Power over Swedish Foreign Policy in UN Issues?* Reports from the Riksdag Series, 1999. [Swedish, selections translated by Ted Svensson]

Lindh, Anna. "Challenges of Peace Operations." Speech at Folke Bernadotte Academy, May 23, 2003a.

———. Statement at the International Peace Academy Concluding Conference of the Conflict Prevention Project, June 13, 2003b.

Loconte, Joseph. "Morality for Sale," *New York Times*, April 1, 2004.

Loden, Hans. "For Safety's Sake—Ideology and Security in Swedish Active Foreign Policy 1950–1975." PhD diss., Lund University, 1999. (*För säkerhets skull: ideologi och säkerhet i svensk aktiv utrikespolitik 1950–1975*. Stockholm: Nerenius & Santérus förlag, 1999.) [Swedish selections translated by Ted Svensson.]

Lowe, A.V., Colin Warbrick, and Dominic McGoldrick. "Human Rights Developments in the Helsinki Process." *International and Comparative Law Quarterly* 39 (1990): 923–940.

Lumsdaine, David. *Moral Vision in International Politics: The Foreign Aid Regime, 1949–1989*. Princeton, N.J.: Princeton University, 1993.

Lyons, Terrence. "Post-Conflict Elections and the Process of Demilitarizing Politics: The Role of Electoral Administration." *Democratization* 11, no. 3 (2004): 36–62.

Macfarlane, Neil. "A Cheer and a Half for Axworthy-ism." *Policy Options* (January–February 2001): 56–58.

Majola, Thembi. "South Africa's Policy towards Nigeria Post-1994." In Kato Lambrechts (ed.), *Transition to Democracy in Nigeria: How Can South Africa Assist?* African Dialogue Series no. 1. Midrand, South Africa: Foundation for Global Dialogue, October 1998.

Malcontent, P. A. M. "The Shadow Minister of Foreign Affairs: Development Aid as a Political Instrument." In J. A. Nekkers and P. A. M. Malcontent (eds.), *Fifty Years of Dutch Development Cooperation, 1949–1999*, pp. 209–226. The Hague: Sdu, 2000.

Malcontent, P. A. M., and J. A. Nekkers. "Do Something and Don't Look Back." In J. A. Nekkers and P. A. M. Malcontent (eds.), *Fifty Years of Dutch Development Cooperation, 1949–1999*, pp. 11–56. The Hague: Sdu, 2000.

Malmborg, Mikael af. *Neutrality and State-Building in Sweden*. New York: Palgrave, 2001.

Mandela, Nelson. "South Africa's Future Foreign Policy." *Foreign Affairs* 72, no. 5, (1993): 87.

Masís Iverson, Daniel. "Poder Político y Sociedad." In Quesada Camacho, Juan Rafael et al., *Costa Rica contemporánea: raíces del estado de la nación*. San José, Costa Rica: Editorial de la Universidad de Costa Rica, 1999.

Maswood, S. Javed. *Japan and East Asian Regionalism*. New York: Routledge: 2001.

Matthew, Richard (ed.). *Landmines and Human Security*. Albany: SUNY Press, 2004.

Matthews, Robert O., and Cranford Pratt (eds.). *Human Rights in Canadian Foreign Policy*. Montreal: McGill-Queen's University Press, 1998.

Mbeki, Thabo. *Address to Corporate Council on Africa*, Chantilly, Virginia, April 19–22, 1997.

Mbeki, Thabo. *The African Renaissance—SABC: Gallagher Estate*. August 13, 1998. Published in *South Africa and Africa: Reflections on the African Renaissance*, Institute for Global Dialogue, Occasional Paper no. 17, October 1998. http://www.anc.org.za/ancdocs/history/mbeki/1998/tm0813.htm-12k.

McGoldrick, Dominic. "Human Rights Developments in the Helsinki Process." *The International and Comparative Law Quarterly* 39, no. 4 (1990): 923–940.

McKay, Simeon. "The Limits of Like-Mindedness." *International Journal* 16, no. 4 (Autumn 2006): 875–894.

McRae, Rob, and Don Hubert (eds.). *Human Security and the New Diplomacy*. Montreal: McGill-Queen's University Press, 2001.

Mekata, Motoko. "Building Partnerships toward a Common Goal: Experiences of the International Campaign to Ban Landmines." In Ann Florini (ed.), *The Third Force: The Rise of Transnational Civil Society*. Tokyo/Washington, D.C.: Japan Center for International Exchange/Carnegie Endowment for International Peace, 2000.

Me akopides, Costas. *Pragmatic Idealism: Canadian Foreign Policy, 1945–1995*. Montreal: McGill University Press, 1998.

Memoria de la Conferencia: Armas pequeñas y livianas en Centroamérica: Dimensiones del control y la regulación del tráfico de armas para implementar el Programa de Acción de las Naciones Unidas. San José, Costa Rica: December 3–5, 2001.

Mendes, Errol P., and Anik Lalonde-Roussy (eds.). *Bridging the Global Divide on Human Rights: A Canada-China Dialogue*. Aldershot: Ashgate, 2003.

Mertus, Julie. *Bait and Switch: Human Rights and U.S. Foreign Policy*. New York: Routledge, 2004.

Miller, Robert (ed.). *Aid as Peacemaker: Canadian Development Assistance and Third World Conflict*. Ottawa: Carleton University Press, 1992.

Mizawaki, Noboru. "The OSCE Model and the PSCBM for Human Dimension." In Ho-Won Jeong and Hideaki Shinoda (eds.), *Conflict and Human Security: A Search for New Approaches of Peace-Building*. Hiroshima, Japan: Institute for Peace Science, Hiroshima University, 2004.

Monroe, Kristen Renwick. *The Heart of Altruism: Perceptions of a Common Humanity*. Princeton, N.J.: Princeton University Press, 1996.

Moravcsik, Andrew. "The Origins of Human Rights Regimes: Democratic Delegation in Postwar Europe." *International Organization* 54 (Spring 2000): 217–252.

———. "Taking Preferences Seriously: Liberal Theory and International Politics." *International Organization* 51, no. 4 (1997): 513–554.

Morneau, Jacques. "Reflections on the Situation in Haiti and the Ongoing U.N. Mission." In Yasmine Shamsie and Andrew S. Thompson (eds.), *Haiti: Hope for a Fragile State*, 71–81. Waterloo, Canada: Wilfred Laurier University Press, 2006.

Mozaffar, Shaheen, and Andreas Schedler. "The Comparative Study of Electoral Governance—Introduction." *International Political Science Review* 23, no. 1 (2002): 5–27.

Muggah, Robert, and Keith Krause. "A True Measure of Success? The Discourse and Practice of Human Security in Haiti." *The Whitehead Journal of Diplomacy and International Relations* (2006): 129–141.

Mukae, Ryuji. "Japan's Foreign Policy and Human Rights." PhD diss., Columbia University, 1996.

Murillo, Álvaro. "CIDH declara inadmisible reclamo de Nicaragua" (CIDH Declares the Claim by Nicaragua Inadmissible), *La Nacion*, March 13, 2007.

———. "Posición en derechos humanos separa a Costa Rica de EE. UU" (Position on Human Rights Separates Costa Rica and the United States), *La Nacion*, October 31, 2005.

Naidoo, Kumi. "South African Civil Society and the Making of South African Foreign Policy." In Elizabeth Sidiropoulos (ed.), *Apartheid Past, Renaissance Future: South Africa's Foreign Policy 1994–2004*, pp. 183–198. Johannesburg: South African Institute of International Affairs, 2004.

Naidu, Sanusha. "South Africa and Africa: Mixed Messages?" In Elizabeth Sidiropoulos (ed.), *Apartheid Past, Renaissance Future: South Africa's Foreign Policy 1994–2004*, pp. 205–219. Johannesburg: South African Institute of International Affairs, 2004.

Navarro, Walter. *Nuevo Pensamiento Policial*. San José, Costa Rica: La Uruca, 2002.

Nayar, Baldev Raj, and T. V. Paul. *India in the World Order: Searching for Major-Power Status*. Cambridge: Cambridge University Press, 2003.

Neary, Ian. *The State and Politics in Japan*. London: Polity, 2002.

Neethling, Theo. "The Defense Force and Peacekeeping: Linking Policy and Capacity." In Elizabeth Sidiropoulos (ed.), *Apartheid Past, Renaissance Future: South Africa's Foreign Policy 1994–2004*, pp. 135–147. Johannesburg: South African Institute of International Affairs, 2004.

Nekkers, J. A., and P. A. M. Malcontent (eds.). *Fifty Years of Dutch Development Cooperation, 1949–1999*. The Hague: Sdu, 2000.

Nel, Philip, Ian Taylor, and Janis van der Westhuizen. "Reformist Initiatives and South African Multilateral Diplomacy: A Framework for Understanding." In Philip Nel, Ian Taylor, and Janis van der Westhuizen (eds.), *South African Multilateral Diplomacy and Global Change: The Limits of Reformism*, pp. 1–30. Aldershot: Ashgate, 2001.

Nel, Philip, and Janis van der Westhuizen (eds.). *Democratizing Foreign Policy? Lessons from South Africa*. Lanham, Md.: Lexington Books, 2004.

Nel, Philip, Jo-Ansie Van Wyck, and Kristen Johnsen, "Democracy, Participation and Foreign Policy-Making in South Africa." In Philip Nel and Janis van der Westhuizen (eds.), *Democratizing Foreign Policy? Lessons from South Africa*, pp. 39–61. Lanham, Md.: Lexington Books, 2004.

Netherlands Helsinki Committee. *Evaluation Meeting: Netherlands OSCE Chairmanship "All Things Considered, the Netherlands OSCE Chairmanship-in-Office Did Rather Well."* http://www.nhc.nl/summary-evaluationmeeting-04–03–04.htm.

Netherlands Institute for War Documentation. *Srebrenica: A "Safe" Area—Reconstruction, Background, Analysis and Consequences of the Fall of a Safe Area*, April 10, 2002. http://www.srebrenica.nl/en/a_index.htm.

"Netherlands Judicial Decisions Involving Questions on International Law: First Conviction under the Universal Jurisdiction Provisions of the UN Convention Against Torture." *Netherlands International Law Review* (2004): 439–449.

Netherlands Ministry of Defence. *Facts and Figures on Dutch Security Policy and the Armed Forces*. The Hague: Netherlands Ministry of Defense, Directorate of General Information, July 2004.

Network of National Human Rights Institutions Web site [NHRI Forum, http://www.nhri.net], http://www.demotemp360.nic.in/default.asp.

Nordborg, Gudrun, and Anita Dahlberg. "Developing Law and Gender Perspectives." In Per Sevastik (ed.), *Legal Assistance to Developing Countries*. London: Norstedts Juridik/Kluwer Law International, 1997.

Nossal, Kim. "Pinchpenny Diplomacy: The Decline of "Good International Citizenship" in Canadian Foreign Policy?" *International Journal* 54, no. 1 (Winter 1998–1999): 88–105.

Nossal, Kim Richard. "Ear Candy: Canadian Policy toward Humanitarian Intervention and Atrocity Crimes in Darfur." *International Journal* 15, no. 4 (Autumn 2005): 1017–1032.

———. *The Politics of Canadian Foreign Policy*. New York: Prentice-Hall, 1989.

———. *Rain Dancing: Sanctions in Canadian and Australian Foreign Policy*. Toronto: University of Toronto Press, 1994.

———. *Relocating Middle Powers: Canada and Australia in a Changing World Order*. Vancouver: University of British Columbia Press, 1993.

Nye, Joseph. *Soft Power: The Means to Success in World Politics*. Public Affairs, 2006.

OECD. "Aid Effectiveness: Department." http://www.oecd.org/department/0,2638,en_2649_3236398_1_1_1_1_1,00.html.

———. "Assessment Framework for Coverage of Humanitarian Action in DAC Peer Reviews," May 13, 2004. http://www.oecd.org/dataoecd/59/59/35374051.pdf.

———. "Canada (2002), DAC Peer Review," 2002. http://www.oecd.org/document/61/0,2340,en_2649_33721_2409533_1_1_1_1,00.html.

———. "Development Cooperation Report 2006," 2006. http://puck.sourceoecd.org/vl=347356/cl=34/nw=1/rpsv/dac/.

———. "DAC Members' Web Sites." http://www.oecd.org/linklist/0,2678,en_2649_33721_1797105_1_1_1_1,00.html.

———. "DAC Organizational Chart," March 2007. http://www.oecd.org/dataoecd/37/13/2348887.pdf.

———. "DAC Subsidiary Bodies," March 28, 2003. http://www.oecd.org/dataoecd/50/54/18058884.PDF.

———. "Development Aid from OECD Countries Fell 5.1% in 2006." http://www.oecd.org/document/17/0,2340,en_2649_33721_38341265_1_1_1_1,00.html.

———. "Development Assistance Committee (DAC) High Level Meeting, 2005." http://www.oecd.org/site/0,2865,en_21571361_34391787_1_1_1_1_1,00.html.

———. "The Development Assistance Committee's Mandate." http://www.oecd.org/document/62/0,2340,en_2649_33721_1918654_1_1_1_1,00.html.

———. "Development Co-operation Directorate." http://www.oecd.org/document/36/0,2340,en_2649_33721_1925604_1_1_1_1,00.html.

———. "Development Co-operation Directorate (DAC): About." http://www.oecd.org/about/0,2337,en_2649_33721_1_1_1_1_1,00.html.

———. "Donating Rights." *OECD Observer* 255 (2006): 60.

———. "Final ODA Data for 2005," 2005. http://www.oecd.org/dataoecd/52/18/37790990.pdf.

OECD. "Human Rights and Development." http://www.oecd.org/document/21/
0,2340,en_2649_34565_35901653_1_1_1_1,00.html.

————. "Integrating Human Rights into Development: Donor Approaches, Experiences and Challenges," 2006. http://puck.sourceoecd.org/vl=347356/cl=34/
nw=1/rpsv/~6669/v2006n9/s1/p11.

————. "Japan (2003), DAC Peer Review," 2003. http://www.oecd.org/document/
10/0,2340,en_2649_33721_22579914_1_1_1_1,00.htm.

————. "Making Poverty Reduction Work," September 1, 2005. http://www.oecd.
org/dataoecd/31/5/34839878.pdf.

————. "The Netherlands (2006), DAC Peer Review," 2006. http://www.oecd.
org/document/28/0,2340,en_2649_33721_37425308_1_1_1_1,00.html.

————. "Security System Reform and Governance," 2005. http://www.oecd.org/
dataoecd/8/39/31785288.pdf.

————. "Shaping the 21st Century: The Contribution of Development Cooperation," 1996. http://www.oecd.org/dataoecd/23/35/2508761.pdf.

————. "Sweden (2005), DAC Peer Review," 2005. http://www.oecd.org/
document/15/0,2340,en_2649_33721_34950223_1_1_1_1,00.html.

Ohlin, Goran. "The Organization for Economic Cooperation and Development."
International Organization 22, no. 1 (1968): 231–243.

Onishi, Norimitsu. "Japan Court Rules against Sex Slaves and Laborers," *New York
Times*, April 28, 2007, A5.

————. "Japan, Easygoing Till Now, Plans Sex Traffic Crackdown," *New York
Times*, February 16, 2005.

————. "Japan Rightists Fan Fury over North Korea Abductions," *New York Times*,
December 17, 2006.

Onuf, Nicholas. *World of Our Making: Rules and Rule in Social Theory and International Relations*. Columbia: University of South Carolina Press, 1989.

"An Opposition Gagged," *The Economist*, May 31, 2007.

Organization of American States. *31st General Assembly*. San José, Costa Rica,
June 3–5, 2001 [CD].

Orn, Torsten. "Peacekeeping—the New Challenges." *International Relations* 12,
no. 1 (1995): 1–6.

OSCE. "The Culture of Dialogue: The OSCE *Acquis* 30 Years after Helsinki," July
22, 2005. http://www.osce.org/item/15787.html.

————. "Helsinki Final Act 1975," August 1, 1975. http://www.osce.org/item/
4046.html.

————. "Office for Democratic Institutions and Human Rights: Human Dimension Mechanisms." http://www.osce.org/odihr/13483.html.

————. "Office for Democratic Institutions and Human Rights: Moscow Mechanism," March 3, 2005. http://www.osce.org/odihr/13498.html.

————. "Office for Democratic Institutions and Human Rights: The OSCE Process." http://www.osce.org/odihr/13372.html.

————. "Office for Democratic Institutions and Human Rights: Vienna Mechanism," March 3, 2005. http://www.osce.org/item/13497.html.

————. "OSCE: About—Facts and Figures." http://www.osce.org/about/19298.
html.

————. "OSCE: About—Field Operations." http://www.osce.org/about/13510.
html.

———. "OSCE: About—Partners for Co-operation." http://www.osce.org/about/19293.html.

———. "OSCE: About—The Three OSCE Dimensions." http://www.osce.org/about/18807.html.

———. "OSCE: Activities—Human Rights." http://www.osce.org/activities/13042.html.

———. "OSCE Annual Report 2006," April 23, 2007. http://www.osce.org/item/24112.html?ch=830.

———. "OSCE Feature: Helping Returnees Survive Their First Winter Back Home," March 22, 2005. http://www.osce.org/item/232.html.

———. "OSCE High Commissioner on National Minorities: Cooperation with Other Organizations." http://www.osce.org/hcnm/23618.html.

———. "OSCE High Commissioner on National Minorities: Mandate." http://www.osce.org/hcnm/13022.html.

———. "OSCE Human Dimension Commitments: Chronological Compilation," September 19, 2005. http://www.osce.org/item/16238.html?ch=441.

———. "OSCE Human Dimension Commitments: Thematic Compilation," September 19, 2005. http://www.osce.org/item/16237.html?ch=440.

———. "OSCE Mission to Moldova—Anti-trafficking in Human Beings." http://www.osce.org/moldova/13429.html.

———. "OSCE Moscow Document 1991," October 4, 1991. http://www.osce.org/item/13995.html.

———. "OSCE Permanent Council Decision No. 430: Recommendations Concerning Future Applications for Partnership," July 19, 2001. http://www.osce.org/documents/pc/2001/07/1858_en.pdf.

———. "OSCE Permanent Council Decision No. 571," December 2, 2003. http://www.osce.org.

———. "OSCE Permanent Council Decision No. 704: The Scales of Contributions for 2005–2007," November 24, 2005. http://www.osce.org/documents/pc/2005/11/17501_en.pdf.

———. "OSCE Press Release: OSCE Mission to Yugoslavia Launches Regional NGO Refugee Network," August 29, 2002. http://www.osce.org/item/6927.html.

———. "OSCE Secretariat—External Cooperation—Asian Partners for Co-operation." http://www.osce.org/ec/13069.html.

———. "OSCE Secretariat—External Cooperation—Mediterranean Partners for Co-operation." http://www.osce.org/ec/13068.html.

———. "OSCE Secretariat—External Cooperation—Summaries of Seminars with Mediterranean Partners." http://www.osce.org/ec/documents.html?lsi=true&limit=10&grp=322.

———. "Permanent Council Decision No. 780 on the Approval of the 2007 Unified Budget," February 2, 2007. http://www.osce.org/item/23164.html.

———Anti Trafficking Assistance Unit. "From Policy to Practice: Combating Trafficking in Human Beings in the OSCE Region," September 26, 2006. http://www.osce.org/item/23613.html.

Cstberg, Sonny. "Reflections on NGO Work with Democracy Aid: Cambodia," *Democracy, Power and Partnership—Implications for Development Cooperation.* Proceedings from a conference arranged by the Collegium for

Development Studies at Uppsala University in cooperation with SIDA, May 6, 2002.

Oziewicz, Estanislao. "UN Vote Paves Way for Small-Arms Treaty; US Objects, but Most Countries Back Move to Ban Weapons from Reaching War Zones," *Globe and Mail*, October 28, 2006, A22.

Oziewicz, Estanislao, and Katherine Harding. "A Struggle for Canadian Hearts and Minds," *Globe and Mail*, January 18, 2006.

Pahad, Aziz. "DRC Must Seize the Moment." *The Transition in the Democratic Republic of Congo: Problems and Prospects*. Midrand, South Africa: Institute for Global Dialogue, March 2006.

Pasqualucci, Jo M., "Sonia Picado, First Woman Judge on the Inter-American Court of Human Rights," *Human Rights Quarterly* 17, no. 4 (1995): 794–806.

Peceny, Mark. *Democracy at the Point of Bayonets*. University Park: Pennsylvania State University Press, 1999.

Persson, Sune. *Folke Bernadotte*. Stockholm: Swedish Institute, 1998.

Peters, Lilian, "War Is No Child's Play: Child Soldiers from Battlefield to Playground." *Geneva Centre for the Democratic Control of Armed Forces*. Geneva, July 2005.

Pew Research Center for the People and the Press. *Survey Reports: Public Knowledge of Current Affairs Little Changed by News and Information Revolutions What Americans Know: 1989–2007*. April 15, 2007.

Piper, Tina, and A. Wayne MacKay. "The Domestic Implementation of International Law." In Errol P. Mendes and Anik Lalonde-Roussy (eds.), *Bridging the Global Divide on Human Rights: A Canada-China Dialogue*, pp. 111–131. Aldershot: Ashgate, 2003.

Poe, S. C., C. N. Tate, and L. C. Keith. "Repression of the Human Right to Personal Integrity Revisited: A Global Cross-National Study Covering the Years 1976–1993." *International Studies Quarterly* 43 (1999): 291–313.

Pollard, Vincent Kelly. *Globalization, Democratization and Asian Leadership: Power Sharing, Foreign Policy and Society in the Philippines and Japan*. Aldershot: Ashgate, 2004.

Power, Paul (ed.). *India's Non-Alignment Policy*. Boston: Heath, 1967.

Pratt, Cranford (ed.). *Human Rights in Canadian Foreign Policy*. McGill-Queen's, 1988.

———. *Internationalism under Strain: The North-South Policies of Canada, the Netherlands, Norway, and Sweden*. University of Toronto Press, 1989.

———. *Middle Power Internationalism*. Montreal: McGill-Queen's, 1990.

Putnam, Robert. *Bowling Alone: The Collapse and Revival of American Community*. New York: Simon & Schuster, 2000.

Quesada Camacho, Juan Rafael. "Evolución a la Tica." In Quesada Camacho, Juan Rafael, et al., *Costa Rica contemporánea: raíces del estado de la nación*. San José, Costa Rica: Editorial de la Universidad de Costa Rica, 1999.

"Ranking the Rich," *Foreign Policy* (September–October 2006): 68–75.

Reddy, E. S. (ed.). *Socialism, Peace and Solidarity: Selected Speeches of Olof Palme*, New York: Vikas, 1990.

Reiding, Hilde. *The Netherlands and the Development of International Human Rights Instruments*. Antwerp: Intersentia, 2007.

Reimann, Kim. "Building Global Civil Society from the Outside In? International Development NGOs, the State, and International Norms." In Susan Pharr and Frank J. Schwartz (eds.), *The State of Civil Society in Japan*, pp. 298–315. Cambridge: Cambridge University Press, 2003.

Rhenán Segura, Jorge. "Costa Rica y Su Contexto Internacional." In Quesada Camacho, Juan Rafael et al., *Costa Rica contemporánea: raíces del estado de la nación*. San José, Costa Rica: Editorial de la Universidad de Costa Rica, 1999.

Rights and Democracy. *Annual Report 2005–2006*. Montreal: Rights and Democracy, 2006.

Risse, Thomas (ed.). *Bringing Transnational Relations Back In: Non-State Actors, Domestic Structures and International Institutions*. Cambridge: Cambridge University Press, 1995.

Risse, Thomas, Stephen Ropp, and Kathryn Sikkink (eds.). *The Power of Human Rights*. Cambridge: Cambridge University Press, 1999.

Risse-Kappen, Thomas. "Ideas Do Not Float Freely: Transnational Coalitions, Democratic Structures, and the End of the Cold War," *International Organization* 48 (1994): 185–214.

Roberson, Amanda. "Ombudsman's Office Urges Reforms to Immigration Law," *Tico Times*, July 27, 2007. http://www.ticotimes.net/Login/tt_sa_pdf.cfm?bi_id=8134.

Rodriguez, Florisabel, Silvia Castro, and Rowland Espinosa. *El sentir democrático. Estudios sobre la cultura política centroamericana*. San José: Editorial Fundacíon UNA, 1998.

Rojas, Roberto. "Los Derechos Humanos en la Política Exterior Costarricense." *Revista Costarricense de Política Exterior* 1, no. 1 (May 2001).

Rojas Aravena, Francisco. *Política exterior de la administración Arias*. UNA, 1992.

Rosenau, James. *Turbulence in World Politics: A Theory of Change and Continuity*. Princeton, N.J.: Princeton University Press, 1990.

Rozen, Laura. "Building a Better UN." *The American Prospect* (July 2004): 17–20.

Rudebeck, Lars. "On the Twofold Meaning of Democracy and Democratisation." In *Democracy, Power and Partnership-Implications for Development Cooperation*. Proceedings from a conference arranged by the Collegium for Development Studies at Uppsala University in cooperation with SIDA, May 6, 2002.

Ruggie, John Gerard. "International Regimes, Transactions, and Change: Embedded Liberalism in the Postwar Economic Order." In Stephen D. Krasner (ed.), *International Regimes*. Ithaca: Cornell University Press, 1983.

Russett, Bruce M. *Grasping the Democratic Peace: Principles for a Post-Cold War World*. Princeton, N.J.: Princeton University Press, 1993.

Rutherford, Kenneth R., Stefan Brem, and Richard A. Matthew (eds.). *Reframing the Agenda: The Impact of NGO and Middle Power Cooperation in International Security Policy*. Westport, Conn.: Praeger, 2003.

Saideman, Stephen. "Conclusion: Thinking Theoretically about Identity and Foreign Policy." In Shibley Telhami and Michael Barnett (eds.), *Identity and Foreign Policy in the Middle East*, pp. 169–200. Ithaca: Cornell University Press, 2002.

Sallot, Jeff. "PM Warns China on Economic Threats," *Globe and Mail*, February 10, 2007.

Santa-Cruz, Arturo. "Constitutional Structure, Sovereignty, and the Emergence of Norms: The Case of International Election Monitoring." *International Organization* 59 (2005): 663–693.

Scharfe, Sharon. *Complicity: Human Rights and Canadian Foreign Policy: The Case of East Timor*. Montreal: Black Rose Books, 1996.

Schoeman, Maxi, and Yolande Sadie. "Women and the Making of South Africa's Foreign Policy." In Philip Nel and Janis Van der Westhuizen (eds.), *Democratizing Foreign Policy? Lessons from South Africa*, pp. 81–95. Lanham, Md.: Lexington Books, 2004.

Sevastik, Per. "The Rule of Law and Swedish Development Assistance." In Per Sevastik (ed.), *Legal Assistance to Developing Countries*. London: Norstedts Juridik/ Kluwer Law International, 1997.

Shafir, Gershon (ed.). *The Citizenship Debates*. Minneapolis: University of Minnesota Press, 1998.

Shelton, Garth. *The South African National Defence Force (SANDF) and President Mbeki's Peace and Security Agenda: New Roles and Mission*. IGD Occasional Paper no. 42, March 2004.

SIDA (Swedish International Development Cooperation Agency). *Annual Report 2003*. 2003a.

———. Division for Democratic Governance. *Democratic Governance in International Development Cooperation—Digging Deeper*. August 2003b.

———. *Perspectives on Poverty*. October 2002.

———. *Sida-Sweden's Instrument for Development Cooperation*. 2003c.

———. SIDA Reports on Lebanon: "Continued Swedish Participation in UN Mission in Lebanon," March 8, 2007. http://www.sweden.gov.se/sb/d/ 8826/a/78413.

———. "Lebanon Explosive Ordnance Disposal," May 30, 2007. http://www. sida.se/sida/jsp/sida.jsp?d=1476&a=32261&searchWords=lebanon.

———. "Lebanon: Humanitarian Support to the Lebanon Crisis in 2006," September 12, 2006. http://www.sida.se/sida/jsp/sida.jsp?d=1236&a=25297 &searchWords=lebanon.

———. "Lebanon: Support to Children in Refugee Camp," May 30, 2007. http:// www.sida.se/?d=1476&a=32318.

———. "Lebanon: UNRWA Flash Appeal, Support to Refugees," June 13, 2007. http://www.sida.se/?d=1476&a=32489.

Sidiropoulos, Elizabeth (ed.). *Apartheid Past, Renaissance Future: South Africa's Foreign Policy 1994–2004*. Johannesburg: South African Institute of International Affairs, 2004.

Sidiropoulos, Elizabeth, and Tim Hughes. "Between Democratic Governance and Sovereignty: The Challenge of South Africa's Africa Policy." In Elizabeth Sidiropoulos (ed.), *Apartheid Past, Renaissance Future: South Africa's Foreign Policy 1994–2004*, pp. 61–84. Johannesburg: South African Institute of International Affairs, 2004.

Sikkink, Kathryn. *Mixed Signals: U.S. Human Rights Policy and Latin America*. Ithaca: Cornell University Press, 2004.

Sikorski, Radek. "Cleaning Up the UN in an Age of U.S. Hegemony." Toronto: *Commentary—C.D. Howe Institute* 212 (June 2005).

Silva, Patricio. "Human Security in an Age of Uncertainty: Reflections from Europe." In. Francisco Rojas Aravena and Moufida Goucha (eds), *Human Security, Conflict Prevention, and Peace*. Paris: UNESCO, 2001.

Simons, Marlise. "A Critic of Muslim Intolerance Faces Loss of Dutch Citizenship," *New York Times*, May 15, 2006a, A8.

———. "The Dutch Try One of Their Own over Links to Liberia," *New York Times*, May 3, 2006b, A3.

———. "8-Year Sentence for Businessman Who Smuggled Arms to Liberia," *New York Times*, June 8, 2006c, A8.

———. "Muslim's Loss of Dutch Citizenship Stirs Storm," *New York Times*, May 18, 2006d, A3.

———. "Somali in the Hague Faces a More Personal Attack," *New York Times*, May 24, 2006e, A3.

Slaughter, Anne-Marie. "Governing the Global Economy through Government Networks," in Friedrich Kratochwil and Edward D. Mansfield (eds.), *International Organization and Global Governance*. New York: Pearson/Longman, 2006.

———. *A New World Order*. Princeton, N.J.: Princeton University Press, 2004.

Smith, Steve. "Foreign Policy Is What States Make of It." In V. Kubalkova (ed.), *Foreign Policy in a Constructed World*. Armonk: M. E. Sharpe, 2001.

Snyder, Richard C., H. W. Bruck, Burton Sapin, Valerie M. Hudson, Derek M. Chollet, and James M. Goldgeier. *Foreign Policy Decision-Making (Revisited)*. London: Palgrave Macmillan, 2002.

Soderbergh, Bengt. "Democracy and Poverty: Are They Interlinked?" *Choices* 9, no. 3 (2000): 25.

Soto Harrison, Fernando. *Los nuevos horizontes del derecho internacional*. Heredia, Costa Rica: Escuela de Relaciones Internacionales, Universidad Nacional, 1998.

Spence, Jack. "South Africa's Foreign Policy: Vision and Reality." In Elizabeth Sidiropoulos (ed.), *Apartheid Past, Renaissance Future: South Africa's Foreign Policy 1994–2004*, pp. 35–48. Johannesburg: South African Institute of International Affairs, 2004.

Stairs, Denis. "Myths, Morals and Reality in Canadian Foreign Policy." *International Journal* 58, no. 2 (Spring 2003).

Stenelo, Lars-Goran. *The International Critic*. Westview, 1984.

Stromvik, Maria. "To Act as a Union: Explaining the Development of the EU's Collective Foreign Policy." PhD diss., Lund University, 2005.

Sugita, Rene. "Challenges for Implementing ADB's Resettlement Policy in Cambodia: The Case of Highway One." *Watershed* 11, no. 1 (July–October): 2005.

Sundelius, Bengt (ed.). *The Committed Neutral—Swedish Foreign Policy*. Boulder, Colo.: Westview Press, 1989.

Sweden. Government Bill 2002/03: 122. *Shared Responsibility: Sweden's Policy for Global Development*. Stockholm: Government Printing Office, 2003.

Sweden. Government Communication 2003/04: 114. *Strategic Export Controls in 2003—Military Equipment and Dual-Use Goods*. Stockholm: Government Printing Office, 2004.

Sweden. Government Communication 2005/06: 204. *Sweden's Policy for Global Development*. Stockholm: Government Printing Office, 2006.

"Sweden Grants Fewer Requests for Asylum," *New York Times*, July 25, 2004.

Sweden. Ministry for Foreign Affairs. Department for Migration and Asylum Policy. *Sweden in 2000—A Country of Migration: Past, Present, and Future*. 2001.

———. Government Communication 2003/04:20. *Human Rights in Swedish Foreign Policy*, Stockholm. October 30, 2003. http://www.sweden.gov.se/content/1/c6/03/29/06/b7544a96.pdf

Sweden. Psychological Defense Board. *Opinion 2003*. http://www.psycdef.se.
"Sweden to Support Burundi Peace-Keeping Mission," *Nordic Business Report*, March 15, 2004.
Ministry of Foreign Affairs. Press Release, March 11, 2004. http://www. utrikes.regeringen.se/sb/d/713/a/16637; jsessionid=azO_ocLYZfSc
Sweden's Government Reports on Sudan:
"Conference on Sudan," June 21, 2007.
http://www.sweden.gov.se/sb/d/ 9227/a/84656.
"Humanitarian Support...," June 12, 2006.
http://www.sida.se/sida/jsp/sida.jsp?d=1236&a=24329&searchWords =sudan%20humanitarian%20support
"New Strategy for Swedish Support," June 15, 2007.
http://www.sweden.gov.se/sb/d/9227/a/84264
"Sweden to Contribute SEK 10 million...," March 7, 2007.
http://www.sweden.gov.se/sb/d/8826/a/78238
"Swedish Troops to Sudan," October 4, 2007.
http://www.sweden.gov.se/sb/d/9659/a/89596.
Swedish Institute. *Sweden and the United Nations*. New York: Carnegie Endowment for International Peace, 1956; update posted on Swedish Institute website 12/8/2004 as http://www.sweden.se/templates/PrinterFriendlyFactSheet. asp?id=4173.
Swedish NGO Foundation for Human Rights. *Biennial Report 2001–2002*. Stockholm: Swedish NGO Foundation, 2002.
———. *Human Rights Newsletter*.
Swedish Parliament. *Sweden's New Policy for Global Development*. Stockholm: Government Printing Office, 2004.
Swidler, Ann. "Culture in Action: Symbols and Strategies," *American Sociological Review* 51, no. 2 (1986).
Takashi, Inoguchi, and Purnendra Jain. *Japanese Foreign Policy Today*. Houndmills, U.K.: Palgrave, 2000.
Tan, Kok-Chor. *Justice without Borders: Cosmopolitanism, Nationalism, and Patriotism*. Cambridge: Cambridge University Press, 2004.
Thomas, Daniel C. *The Helsinki Effect: International Norms, Human Rights, and the Demise of Communism*. Princeton, N.J.: Princeton University Press, 2001.
Thomsen, Robert, and Nikola Hynek. "Keeping the Peace and National Unity: Canada's National and International Identity Nexus," *International Journal* 16, no. 4 (Autumn 2006): 845–858.
Thompson, Andrew S. "In Defence of Principles: NGOs, Human Rights and the Supreme Court of Canada, 1985–1992." PhD diss., University of Waterloo, 2005.
TOL Editor. "No Longer Passive Bystanders." *Transitions Online* (February 2003).
Towse, Raymond J. "Canada in a Global Context," *Europa* (2005).
Tucker, Michael J., Raymond B. Blake, P. E. Bryden (eds.). *Canada and the New World Order*. Toronto: Irwin, 2000.
UNAIDS (Joint United Nations Programme on HIV/AIDS). "Sweden Standing Up for HIV Prevention," June 2006. http://www.unaids.org/en/Knowledge-Centre/Resources/FeatureStories/archive/2006/20060510-sweden.asp.
United Nations Economic and Social Council, Commission on Human Rights. *Report on the Fifty-Ninth Session* (March 17–April 24, 2003). E/2003/23,E/ CN.4/2003/135.

United Nations General Assembly. "Declaration on the Right and Responsibility of Individuals, Groups, and Organs of Society to Promote and Protect Universally Recognized Human Rights and Fundamental Freedoms," November 2, 2005. http://www.un.org/ga/60/third/draftproplist.htm.

UNHCR (United Nations High Commission on Refugees) [ACNUR y los Refugiados.] "Consejo Económico y Social [ECOSOC] de las Naciones Unidas elige por aclamación a Costa Rica nuevo miembro del Comité Ejecutivo del ACNUR," 2007. http://www.acnur.org/index.php?id_pag=6357.

UNHCR (United Nations High Commission on Refugees). *Diagnóstico sobre el grado de integración local de los Refugiados en Costa Rica (2002)*. ACNUR-UCR, 2003.

United Nations Human Rights Council. "Council Concludes Discussion on Report of Working Group on Draft Convention against Enforced Disappearance," June 27, 2006. http://www.unhchr.ch/huricane/huricane.nsf/0/AA7BE0CD6D6FF531C125719A006F8FFB?opendocument;http://www.ohchr.org/english/countries/ratification/16.htm.

United Nations Office at Geneva. "ECOSOC Adopts Texts on Palestinian Women and Violence against Girls from Report of Commission on Status of Women," July 24, 2007a. http://www.unog.ch/unog/website/news_media.nsf/(httpNewsByYear_en)/DEDDDBCF310336EAC1257322004B9D3E?OpenDocument.

———. "ECOSOC Adopts Texts on Palestinian People, Independence for Colonial Countries and Social Development," July 26, 2007b. http://www.unog.ch/unog/website/news_media.nsf/(httpNewsByYear_en)/E19EE2DFC3D93AA3C125732400490C99?OpenDocument.

———. "Human Rights Council Concludes High-Level Segment," June 22, 2006. http://www.unog.ch/unog/website/news_media.nsf/(httpNewsByYear_en)/9EE40EA7F396E9D4C12571950058CBA3?OpenDocument.

U.S. Committee for Refugees. *World Refugee Survey 2003 Country Report*. http://www.refugees.org/world/countryrpt/europe/2003/sweden.cfm.

U.S. Department of State. "The Community of Democracies." http://www.state.gov/g/drl/c10790.htm.

———. "Community of Democracies Foreign Ministers Meeting at the UN." http://www.state.gov/g/drl/36454.htm.

———. "2000 Warsaw Ministerial." http://www.state.gov/g/drl/c10710.htm.

———. "2002 Seoul Ministerial." http://www.state.gov/g/drl/c10711.htm.

———. "2005 Santiago Ministerial." http://www.state.gov/g/drl/c10712.htm.

Valpy, Michael. "The Myth of Canada as Global Peacekeeper," *Globe and Mail*, February 28, 2007.

Van Baarda, Th. A., and D. E. M. Verweij (eds.). *Military Ethics: The Dutch Approach*. Leiden, The Netherlands: Brill Academic Publishers, 2006.

Van Beuningen, Frank. "A Contribution to the Agenda for the Dutch Chairmanship of the OSCE: A Recapitulation of Findings of the Advisory Council on International Affairs." *Helsinki Monitor* 4 (2002).

van den Berg, Esther. *The Influence of Domestic NGOs on Dutch Human Rights Policy*. Antwerp: Intersentia, 2001.

Van Galen, J. Jansen. "A Testing Ground for Dutch Development Cooperation Policy: Suriname 1975–1982." In J. A. Nekkers and P. A. M. Malcontent (eds.), *Fifty Years of Dutch Development Cooperation, 1949–1999*, pp. 227–251. The Hague: Sdu, 2000.

Van Krieken, Peter J., and David McKay (eds.). *The Hague: Legal Capital of the World*. New York: Cambridge University Press, 2005.

Vargas Garcia, Bernadina. "La gestión del Ministerio de Relaciones Exteriores y Culto en Materia de Derechos Humanos: Alcances y limitaciones (1987–1998)." Master's Thesis, Universidad Nacional de Costa Rica, Heredia, 2001.

Ventura, Manuel. "Costa Rica and the Inter-American Court of Human Rights." *Human Rights Law Journal* 4, no. 3 (1983): 273–281.

Vizcaino, Irene. "Libertad de prensa disminuyó en el país" (Freedom of Press Went Down in the Country), *La Nacion*, September 27, 2005. http://www.nacion.com/ln_ee/2005/septiembre/27/pais12.html.

Voorhoeve, J. J. C. *Peace, Profits and Principles: A Study of Dutch Foreign Policy.* Boston: Martin Nijhoff, 1979.

Walker, R. B. J. *Inside/Outside: International Relations as Political Theory.* Cambridge: Cambridge University Press, 1993.

Walker, Stephen G. *Role Theory and Foreign Policy Analysis.* Durham, N.C.: Duke University Press, 1987.

Waltz, Kenneth. *Theory of International Politics.* Reading, Mass.: Addison-Wesley, 1979.

Wannenberg, Gail. "From Pariah to Pioneer: The Foreign Policy of the South African Police Service." In Elizabeth Sidiropoulos (ed.), *Apartheid Past, Renaissance Future: South Africa's Foreign Policy 1994–2004*, pp. 149–167. Johannesburg: South African Institute of International Affairs, 2004.

Wapner, Paul. *Environmental Activism and World Civic Politics.* Albany: SUNY Press, 1996.

Waschuk, Roman, "The New Multilateralism." In Rob McRae and Don Hubert (eds.), *Human Security and the New Diplomacy*, pp. 213–222. Montreal: McGill-Queen's University Press, 2001.

Watanabe, Chisaki. "Japan PM Vows Assertive Foreign Policy," Associated Press, January 4, 2007. http://www.boston.com/news/world/asia/articles/2007/01/04/japan_pm_vows_assertive_foreign_policy/

Weinert, Matthew. "Globalizing Democracy or Democratizing Globalism?" *Human Rights and Human Welfare* 5 (2005): 17–30.

Weldes, Jutta. "Constructing National Interests." *European Journal of International Relations* 2 (1996): 275–318.

Wels, Cornelis Boudewin. *Aloofness and Neutrality: Studies on Dutch Foreign Relations.* Utrecht: H and S, 1982.

Wendt, Alexander. "Anarchy Is What States Make of It." *International Organization* 46 (1992): 391–425.

———. *A Social Theory of International Politics.* Cambridge: Cambridge University Press, 1999.

Wheeler, Tom. "Multilateral Diplomacy: South Africa's Achievements." In Elizabeth Sidiropoulos (ed.), *Apartheid Past, Renaissance Future: South Africa's Foreign Policy 1994–2004*, pp. 85–103. Johannesburg: South African Institute of International Affairs, 2004.

Whelan, Susan. "Advancing Human Security: The Role of Technology and Politics." Halifax and Pugwash, Nova Scotia, Canada, July 14–22, 2003.

Whittington, Les. "Public Backs Canada Playing a Leading Role in Darfur," *Toronto Star*, May 21, 2007.

Whyte, Elayne. "El Valor de la Diversidad: Antecendentes y reflexiones con ocasión de la Conferencia Mundial contra el racismo, la discriminación racial, la xenofobia y las formas conexas de intolerancia." *Revista Costarricense de Política Exterior* 2, no. 1 (May 2002).

Williams, Paul D. "Pragmatic Multilateralism? South Africa and Peace Operations." In Donna Lee, Ian Taylor, and Paul D. Williams (eds.), *The New Multilateralism in South African Diplomacy*, 182–204. New York: Palgrave, 2006.

Wilson, Bruce. *Costa Rica: Politics, Economics, and Democracy*. Boulder, Colo.: Lynne Rienner, 1998.

Wilson, James Q. *Political Organizations*. Princeton, N.J.: Princeton University Press, 1995.

Wines, Michael. "Once World Cause, South Africa Lowers Voice on Human Rights," *New York Times*, March 24, 2007.

Yashar, Deborah. *Demanding Democracy: Reform and Reaction in Costa Rica and Guatemala, 1890–1950*. Stanford: Stanford University Press, 1997.

Yee, Albert S. "The Causal Effects of Ideas on Policies." *International Organization* 50 (1996): 69–108.

Yokota, Yozo, and Chiyuki Aoi. "Japan's Foreign Policy towards Human Rights: Uncertain Changes." In David Forsythe (ed.), *Human Rights and Comparative Foreign Policy*. New York: United Nations University Press, 2000.

York, Geoffrey. "Canada 'Harping on Human Rights,'" *Globe and Mail*, May 2, 2007.

Young, Iris Marion. *Inclusion and Democracy*. Oxford: Oxford University Press, 2000.

Zárate, Rubí, Rodrigo Jiménez, and Lina Barrantes. *Manual hacia el nuevo policía*. San José, Costa Rica: Fundación Arias, 1999.

Zwaan, Karin. *UNHCR and the European Asylum Law*. Center for Migration Law, Radboud University Nijmegen, 2005.

Zwamborn, Marcel, Hilde Hey, and Mirjam van Reisen. *Human Rights Policy Versus Practice—An Evaluation of the Implementation of the Human Rights Policy of the Netherlands in Its Relations with China, Indonesia, Iran, Mexico and Rwanda in the Period 1999–2004*. Ministry of Foreign Affairs/IOB Working Documents, April 2006.

Interviews

N.B. Affiliations listed are those relevant to the subject of the interview and are current at the time of the interview, unless otherwise indicated. Some titles and affiliations are translated from their original language.

Canada

The Honorable Lloyd Axworthy, Foreign Minister 1996–2000: University of San Diego, February 11, 2005.

Leonard Beaulne, Director of Inter-American Relations, Foreign Affairs: Ottawa, July 21, 2005.

Elissa Golberg, Deputy Director of Humanitarian Affairs, Foreign Affairs: Ottawa, July 21, 2005.

Michael Gort, Canadian International Development Agency: Gatineau, July 28, 2005.

Paul Heinbecker, Canadian Ambassador to the United Nations 2000–2004: Ottawa, July 24, 2005; Waterloo, May 18, 2007.

Don Hubert, Director of the Human Security Division, former Coordinator of Humanitarian Affairs, former Deputy to the Chair of the Kimberley Process, Department of Foreign Affairs and International Trade: Ottawa, July 27, 2005.

Heidi Hulan, former Deputy Director of International Commission on Intervention and State Sovereignty, Department of Foreign Affairs and International Trade: Ottawa, July 26, 2005.

Robert Lawson, Human Security, Department of Foreign Affairs and International Trade: Ottawa, July 20, 2005.

Professor Peter Leuprecht, Director of International Studies, University of Quebec at Montreal: Montreal, January 18, 2006.

Tim Martin, Director of Peace-Building, Foreign Affairs: Ottawa, July 26, 2005.

Henri-Paul Normandin, Director of Human Rights, Foreign Affairs: Ottawa, July 25, 2005.

John Packer, OSCE, CIDA Regional Institution Capacity-Building: Ottawa, July 27, 2005.

Senator Landon Pearson: Ottawa, July 27, 2005.

Marcus Pistor, Gerald Schmitz, Parliamentary Research Unit: Ottawa, July 25, 2005.

Gareth Pratt, Democratic Governance, CIDA: Gatineau, July 29, 2005.

Evelyn Puxley, Director, International Crime and Terrorism Division, Foreign Affairs Canada: Ottawa, July 29, 2005.

Edward Ratushny, Canadian Bar Association, University of Ottawa Law School: Ottawa, July 29, 2005.

Jean-Louis Roy, President, Rights and Democracy: Montreal, August 2, 2005.

Rob Shropshire, Daniel Roy, Canadian Human Rights Foundation [now Equitas]: Montreal, August 2, 2005.

Susan Steffen, Canadian International Development Agency: Gatineau, July 27, 2005.

Joseph Stern, Former Chair, Refugee Assessment Board: Ottawa, July 22, 2005.

Costa Rica

Anonymous, Deputy for Refugee Assessment, Department of Migration: San José, June 4, 2003.

Arnoldo Brenes, Advisor to the Minister, Ministry of International Relations: San José, June 2, 2003.

Rodrigo Carreras, former Vice-Minister of Foreign Relations 1986–90, Ambassador to Israel; current Ambassador to Nicaragua: San José, June 9, 2003.

Carlos Cordero, Multilateral Affairs, Ministry of International Relations: San José, June 2, 2003.

Luis Alberto Cordero, Director, Arias Foundation: San José, June 5, 2003.

Nestor Mourelo, Professor of Human Rights, National University of Costa Rica: San José, June 5, 2003.

Hugo Alfonso Muñoz, Law Professor, University of Costa Rica; former Minister of Justice: San José, June 4, 2003.

Adriana Murrillo, Department of Human Rights, Ministry of International Relations: San José, June 2, 2003.

Walter Navarro, Chief of Police and Public Security: San José, June 10, 2003.

Sonia Picado, Judge on Inter-American Human Rights Court, 1988–1994; Director of Inter-American Human Rights Institute, 1984–1994; U.S. Ambassador, 1994–1998: San José, June 3, 2003.

Andrés Ramírez, United Nations High Commission on Refugees: San José, June 9, 2003.

Gabriela Rodríguez Pizarro, Special Rapporteur on Human Rights of Migrants, United Nations: San José, June 6, 2003.

Katlya Rodríguez, Director of Special Protection, Ombudsman's Office: San José, June 4, 2003.

Victor Rodríguez, Inter-American Human Rights Institute: San José, June 10, 2003.

Luis Guillermo Solís, Arias Foundation 1991–94, Director of Foreign Relations 1996–1998, Chair of Partido Liberación Nacional 2000–2003: San José, June 6, 2003.

Fernando Soto Harrison, Ambassador to the United Nations 1945–1946; U.S. Ambassador 1982–1985; O.A.S. Ambassador 1982–1985: San José, June 5, 2003.

Gioconda Ubeda, Director of Juridical Affairs, Ministry of International Relations: San José, June 3, 2003.

Carlos Walker Uribe, Arias Foundation 1995–2002: San José, June 3, 2003.

Japan

Kazutoshi Aikawa, Director, United Nations Policy Division, Ministry of Foreign Affairs: Tokyo, April 20, 2006.

Ayumi Goto, Mekong Watch: Tokyo, April 7, 2006.

Sonoko Kawakami, Amnesty International: Tokyo, April 4, 2006.

Akiko Komori, Program Officer (Human Security), Japan International Cooperation Agency: Tokyo, April 26, 2006.

Professor Kinhide Mushakogi, International Movement Against Discrimination and Racism (IMADR): Tokyo, April 17, 2006.

Mikiko Otani, Attorney-At-Law: Tokyo, April 21, 2006.

Professor Yasunobu Sato, Graduate Program in Human Security, The University of Tokyo: Tokyo, April 26, 2006.

Tosnihiro Shimizu, Secretary General, Japan International Volunteer Center: Tokyo, April 17, 2006.

Sorg He Suk, The Association of Korean Human Rights in Japan: Tokyo, April 10, 2006.

Masako Suzuki, Attorney-at-Law, Refugee Legal Association: Tokyo, April 25, 2006.

Yoriko Suzuki, Principal Deputy Director, Human Rights and Humanitarian Affairs, Ministry of Foreign Affairs: Tokyo, April 18, 2006.

Kiyotaka Takahashi, Research and Policy Manager, Japan International Volunteer Center: Tokyo, April 17, 2006.

Ambassador Yukio Takasu, Human Security, Ministry of Foreign Affairs: Tokyo, April 20, 2006.

Hasebe Takatoshi, Program Officer for Afghanistan, Japan International Volunteer Center: Tokyo, April 17, 2006.

Hiroshi Takayama, Korean Human Rights: Tokyo, April 19, 2006.

Shogo Watanabe, Attorney at Law, Izumibashi Law Office, Association for Burmese Refugees: Tokyo, April 25, 2006.

Jun Yamada, Global Issues Policy Division, Ministry of Foreign Affairs: Tokyo, April 18, 2006.

Tamura Yoko, Program Officer for Palestine and Iraq, Japan International Volunteer Center: Tokyo, April 17, 2006.

Netherlands

Professor Peter Baehr, Utrecht University, Leiden University, Advisory Council of International Affairs—Human Rights: Amsterdam, June 22, 2006.

Professor Ineke Boerefijn, Netherlands Institute for Human Rights (SIM): Utrecht, July 4, 2006.

Professor Cees Flinterman, Director of SIMS, Netherlands' representative to the United Nations—United Nations Sub-Commission on Prevention of Discrimination and Protection of Minorities (1987–1991), Vice-Chairperson of the 49th session of the United Nations Commission on Human Rights (1993), 49th and 50th sessions of the UN Commission on Human Rights (1993 and 1994) and World Conference on Human Rights (1993): Utrecht, July 4, 2006.

Professor Fred Grünfeld, Maastricht University and Utrecht University: Maastricht, June 28, 2006.

Professor Menno Kamminga, former Legal Adviser and Representative at the United Nations of Amnesty International (1978–1986), International Executive Committee of Amnesty International (1994–1999): Maastricht, June 28, 2006.

Ambassador Piet de Klerk, Human Rights Ambassador of the Netherlands: The Hague, June 29, 2006.

Professor Richard Lawson, Netherlands Commission of Jurists: University of Leiden, July 6, 2006.

Professor Peter Malcontent, SIM, Secretary of the Association of Human Rights Institutes (AHRI): Utrecht, July 4, 2006.

Tiemo Oostenbrink, Secretary of Advisory Board on International Affairs—Human Rights, Foreign Ministry: The Hague, June 21, 2006.

Marike Radstaake, Humanist Committee on Human Rights (HOM): Utrecht, June 27, 2006.

Professor Nico Schrijver, Netherlands Foreign Ministry: Advisory Councils on International Law, Development, and Human Rights: Leiden, July 6, 2006.

Marijke Stegeman, Evaluation Unit, Dutch Foreign Ministry: The Hague, June 29, 2006.

Birgitte Tazelaar, Foreign Ministry Human Rights Desk: The Hague, June 29, 2006.

University of Nijmegen Immigration Program: Professor Anita Bocker, Roel Fernhout (Ombudsman 1999–2005), Karina Fransen: Nijmegen, June 30, 2006.

Theo Van Boven, former Director of the U.N. Human Rights Center, United Nations' Special Rapporteur on Torture: Maastricht, June 28, 2006.

Lars van Troost, Amnesty International Netherlands: Amsterdam, July 10, 2006.

Professor Desiree Verweij, Military Ethics Program, National Defense Academy: Amsterdam, July 5, 2006.

South Africa

The Honorable Kadar Asmal, Parliamentary Arms Export Committee, Minister of Water 1994–1999, Minister of Education 1999–2005, Drafting Committee for the 1994 South African Constitution: Capetown, October 27, 2006.

Centre for Civil Society, Professors Patrick Bond, David Black, and Baruti Amisi: University of Kwa-Zulu Natal, October 30, 2006.

Patrick Craven, COSATU (Confederation of South African Trade Unions): Johannesburg, November 6, 2006.

Paul Graham, IDASA (Institute for Democracy in South Africa): Pretoria, November 19, 2006.

Professor Adam Habib, Director, Human Science Research Council: Johannesburg, November 17, 2006.

Cheryl Hendricks, Institute for Security Studies: Pretoria, November 1, 2006.

The Honorable Fatima Hujaij, MP, Parliamentary International Relations Committee: Capetown, October 25, 2006.

Iqbal Jhazyby, ANC (African National Congress) International Relations Committee: Pretoria, November 18, 2006.

Dr. Francis Kornegay, Center for Political Studies: Johannesburg, November 17, 2006.

Guy Lamb, Institute for Security Studies: Pretoria, November 1, 2006.

Loren Landau, Center for the Study of Forced Migration, University of Witswaterand: Johannesburg, November 3, 2006.

Garth LePere, Institute for Global Dialogue: Midrand, November 19, 2006.

Noria Mashumba, Centre for Conflict Resolution: Capetown, October 23, 2006.

Pitso Mutwedi, Luvuyo Ndimeni, Nelelo Kwepile, Clementine Nkhumishe, Department of Foreign Affairs—Human Rights: Pretoria, November 20, 2006.

Mandla Rametsi, COSATU (Council of South African Trade Unions): Johannesburg, November 6, 2006.

Professor Elizabeth Siridopolous, Director, South African Institute for International Affairs: Johannesburg, November 6, 2006.

Professor Janis van der Westhuizen, University of Stellenbosch, October 26, 2006.

Professor Jo-Ansie van Wyck, UNISA (National University of South Africa), Governance Exchange with Sudan: Pretoria, November 18, 2006.

Sweden

Anonymous. Former Foreign Ministry Official: Lund, July 20, 2004.

Nils Eliasson, Refugee and Migration Division, Foreign Ministry of Sweden: Stockholm, June 7, 2004.

Lisa Fredriksson, Lennart Nordstrom, Per Sevastik, Division of Democratic Governance, Swedish International Development and Cooperation Agency: Stockholm, June 8, 2004.

Anita Klum, Swedish NGO Foundation for Human Rights: Stockholm, June 7, 2004.

Ambassador Anders Liden, Swedish Ambassador to the United Nations: New York, September 9, 2004.

Anders Mellbourn, President, Swedish Institute for International Affairs: Lund, July 13, 2004.

Anders Ronquist, Human Rights Division, Foreign Ministry of Sweden: Stockholm, June 7, 2004.

Ambassador Ulla Strom, Ambassador for Human Rights, Foreign Ministry of Sweden: Stockholm, June 11, 2004.

Index